THE BOOK OF PRAYER AND MEDITATION

THE BOOK OF PRAYER AND MEDITATION

VENERABLE LOUIS
of GRANADA, OP

TAN Books
Gastonia, North Carolina

Imprinted at Rouen, by George L'oiselet in 1584.

Transliteration completed at Hulbert, by Sean McAlister in 2023.

Cover design by Jordan Avery

ISBN: 978-1-5051-3361-5
Kindle ISBN: 978-1-5051-3454-4
ePUB ISBN: 978-1-5051-3453-7

Published in the United States by
TAN Books
PO Box 269
Gastonia, NC 28053
www.TANBooks.com

Printed in India

CONTENTS

Second Chapter: Of the Five Parts of Prayer

Third Chapter: Advices for Meditation

Fourth Chapter: Of Six Points That Are to Be Meditated Upon in the Holy Passion of Our Savior Jesus Christ

THE FIRST SEVEN MEDITATIONS FOR THE SEVEN DAYS OF THE WEEK, IN THE MORNINGS

Monday Morning

Tuesday Morning

Wednesday Morning

Thursday Morning

THE SEVEN MEDITATIONS FOR THE SAME SEVEN DAYS AT NIGHT

Monday Night

Tuesday Night

Wednesday Night

Thursday Night

Friday Night

Saturday Night

Sunday Night

THE TRANSLITERATOR'S NOTE TO THE READER

THIS transliteration of the Venerable's most profound work is intended to provide the reader with the precise text of the original 1584 translation, simply transliterated into a form more readable to us, in order to maintain the exact prosa oratio with which the Venerable wrote. To this end, it was discerned necessary to leave intact the exact wording, prose, and even punctuation with which the Venerable and the original translator wrote. Some words remain herein which have fallen from use in our modern tongue, or whose meanings have changed through the centuries. These words must be discovered and discerned by the reader in order to attain to the full meaning of these meditations. I recommend the help of the Blessed Mother, through the intercession of Venerable Louis of Granada, Venerable Fulton Sheen, Venerable Matt Talbot, Saint Padre Pio, and your Guardian Angel, when seeking to discern these words.

It is also noteworthy that the Venerable recommends those new unto the service of Almighty God begin with the night meditations first, before proceeding to the morning meditations. Therefore, he refers to the second half of this book as the first part. I would also note that the advices and writings of the Venerable regarding prayer, and the Passion, which are found herein, are most necessary for the proper exercise of these meditations.

Many Saints spoke highly of Venerable Louis of Granada's writings, including St. Vincent de Paul, St. Louise de Marillac, St. Francis de Sales, St. Charles Borromeo, and St. Teresa of Avila. St. Rose of Lima said this was her favorite book and while protecting herself from the devil with this book, the devil became enraged and took it from her.[11]

We must consider why the devil himself would have taken such a particular interest in this book, and why it so quickly seems to have fallen into obscurity. More importantly, we must consider why Almighty God might have allowed this book to remain (nearly) hidden through the centuries, until now.

Our given time runs short now. Edify your soul. Steel your soul with these daily meditations. Steel your soul against the world, the flesh, and the devils. Steel your soul now, against the False Prophet, and the coming of Antichrist. Time runneth short.

Sit nomen Domini ✠ *benedictum in saecula.*
Esto Vir. Esto Sanctus.
Be here now.
S.M.M.

"It is granted to few to recognize the True Church amid the darkness of so many schisms and heresies. And to fewer still so to love the Truth which they have seen as to fly to its embrace."
-St. Robert Bellarmine

"Ask, and it shall be given you: seek, and you shall find: knock, and it shall be opened to you."
-Our Blessed Lord (Matt. 7.7.)

Transliteration completed at Hulbert, by Sean McAlister.
Anno Domini. M. M. XXIII.

[1] Found in the introduction of "A Sinner's Guide" by Venerable Louis of Granada. Introduction taken largely from the work of Fr. Alvaro Huerga, O.P., Regent of Studies, Convent of the Holy Cross, Granada, Spain.

For the Glory of God and the Triumph of the Immaculate Heart of Mary.

THE TRANSLATOR'S DEDICATORY EPISTLE[1]

THE holy scriptures affirm in divers places, that the nearer we approach towards the coming of the Antichrist, and the end of the world, the more perilous will the times be for all Christians.[2] And the peril hereof ariseth chiefly of the great envy and malice of Satan, who fearing the end of the world, knowing that then his tyrannous kingdom therein will have an end also therewith, extendeth the uttermost of his rage against all faithful Christians, and assaulteth them daily more and more with divers wily temptations and terrible persecutions, to procure them thereby to follow his most wicked rebellious example: that is, to break God's holy commandments, to contemn his divine ordinances, to neglect his service, and honor, and by pride and rebellion to lose the image of God, and embrace the image of Satan, and so to be utterly unapt to attain unto those everlasting heavenly mansions of felicity, and glory, for which man was created.

Wherefore to the intent that all Christians might be more circumspect, and strengthened, to resist faithfully against all Satan's

1 To the right honorable, and worshipful, of the four principal houses of Couerte in London, professing the study of the Common Laws of our Realm, Richard Hopkins wishethe due consideration of the holy Mysteries of the Christian Religion.

2 See Dan. 9:11–12; Matt. 24; Mark 13; Luke 21; 2 Thess. 2; 1 Tim. 4; 1 Tim. 4; 2 Tim. 3; 2 Ptr. 2–3; Jude 18; Apoc. 12:12–13.

wily deceitful temptations in this our dangerous age, approaching so near towards the coming of Antichrist, and the end of the world (as by many conjectural signs it seemeth), a holy Angel hath forewarned us hereof very precisely in the revelations of St. John, thundering out these words with a great voice: *Woe be to the land, and sea, because the Devil is descended unto you, having a great rage, for that he knoweth he hath but a short time.*[3] And this great rage of his is the more to be feared in this our corrupt age, for that we read also in Saint John's revelations, that the Devil shall be let loose towards the end of the world for a final time.[4] In other ages and times of our holy Christian forefathers, the devils exceeding great malice and mighty power hath been much restrained, and bound, through the great virtue of the Cross, and Passion of our Savior Jesus Christ, communicated then very plentifully unto the Christian people generally by their devout frequenting of the holy Sacraments of the Catholic Church, (which be holy vessels of grace) whereby our Christian forefathers have been greatly strengthened to resist faithfully against the most horrible temptations of Schism, Heresy, Infidelity, and Atheism, and to live generally very holy and austere Christian lives in the fear and service of almighty God, and in due reverent obedience to the Catholic Church. But now whereas in this our ungracious age such a number of horrible Sects, and Heresies, and such a general corruption with pride, disobedience, lying, detraction, gluttony, incontinence, infidelity, Atheism, and all kind of dissolute wickedness do abound and reign more and more in all parts of Christendom, woe be therefore to the Land, and sea (as the holy Angel hath forewarned us) because the Devil is now descended, and let loose towards the end of the world for a final time, having a great rage, for that he Knoweth he hath but a short time to continue his tyrannous kingdom in this world.

And the very cause of this so extraordinary letting loose of the devil now more and more towards the coming of Antichrist in the end of the world, Saint Paul seemeth to explain in this sense: that

[3] Apoc. 12:12.
[4] See Apoc. 20:3.

for so much as the wicked will not receive the true doctrine of the Catholic Church with charity, humility, obedience, and thankfulness, to the end they may be saved, therefore Almighty God letteth loose the devil now among them, by permitting him to sow in their proud inconstant willful minds many erroneous opinions, and Heresies, that they may believe in lying.[5]

And certainly, if we will advisedly consider the wily proceedings of the devil in sowing so manifold Sects and Heresies in this ungracious age, and the final end whereunto he directeth them, we may evidently perceive, that it is to cause all Christians now towards the coming of Antichrist to be first dissolute in their lives, and after doubtful in their faith, and then to contemn all the holy Sacraments, and other Mysteries of the Christian Religion, and afterwards having by degrees removed away out of their Churches all holy memories of our Savior Christ, and of his blessed Mother, Apostles, Martyrs, and other of his glorious Saints, and also out of their minds all fear of God, and of his dreadful judgements, then they be easily induced by him shortly after to become hard hearted, and unsensible to conceive any spiritual things, and also at the last to become Atheists, without any conscience, Religion, or belief that there is a God. And so Antichrist finding his way so open and ready prepared for him, may then come freely when he will, and cause himself to be received as a Messiah, and adored as God, finding the Christian people generally without any devotion and zeal to the service and honor of our Savior Jesus Christ, and without any belief that there is a God.

Now among all the wily deceitful devises of Satan for overthrowing of the Christian Religion, and so to prepare the way for Antichrist's coming, there is none (in my simple judgement) of greater force, and consequence, than his so earnest endeavor to procure all Christians utterly to contemn and forget all the holy Mysteries of the Christian faith. Which if he could possibly compass (as he laboreth very earnestly therein by divers crafty means in this our corrupt age) then undoubtedly all the whole Christian Religion, and even

5 See 2 Thess. 2:10–11.

our Savior Christ himself, and his blessed Mother, and all his holy Apostles, and Martyrs, and other of his glorious Saints would consequently in a short time after be generally contemned, neglected, and forgotten throughout all Christian countries.

And to write here freely my mind as I think, it would seem very marvelous unto me, (if I were not fully persuaded that the devil is now more and more let loose (as Saint John in his revelations hath forewarned us he should be for a short time towards the end of the world) how the devil could prevail so farforth among Christians, as to induce a whole new late Sect of Heretics that be called Puritans (professing in gay words to be more pure, more sincere, and better professors of Christ's gospel, than any other Christians either be, or have been in any age since the Apostle's time) to write of late so unchristianly by common consent even in English printed books, against observing in the Church the most ancient yearly solemn holy Feasts of Christmass, Easter, and Pentecost, and against all special meditations at any one solemn time of the year more than at others, either of Christ's nativity, or Resurrection, or of the Coming of the Holy Ghost, or of the hour of our death: because (say they) these meditations should be used continually every day in the year, and ought not to be appointed by the governors of the Church to be used at any one special time more than at others.[6] Whereby every godly Christian reader may easily perceive, how the devil being now let loose laboreth very busily by these counterfeit pure gospellers under a wily deceitful colure of advancing continual meditation and memory of the holy Mysteries of the Christian Religion every day in the year, to have no manner of meditation or memory of them among Christians any day at all: that so by their subtle wicked doctrine a ready open way may be prepared in all Christian men's Churches, and minds, for Antichrist's coming.

But O the wonderful providence and care of our Savior Christ to preserve a continual knowledge, memory, and reverence, of his

---

6 In the puritans reply against D. Whitgifte, 120–122, 162; in R. Brownes book of reformation.

holy Mysteries among all faithful Christians in his Catholic Church, as hath very manifestly appeared in all ages since Christ's Ascension until this our corrupt age. And surely it is a matter worthy of great and devout admiration for any good Christian to consider, how the Apostles, and the ancient holy Catholic Bishops their successors being by our Savior Christ's own promise assuredly inspired, assisted, and directed by the Holy Ghost from time to time in government of the Catholic Church in all truth,[7] have with such divine wisdom disposed the whole year into so many several holy Festival days, as that thereby have been represented, and preached unto all Christian people in all Christian Churches throughout Christendom a continual solemn instruction, memory, and reverence of the holy Mysteries of the Christian Religion. In so much as the common Christian people by those holy Festival days alone (albeit they wanted not also divers other holy instructions therein in Confessions, and Sermons), were in all ages sufficiently instructed in the holy Mysteries of their Christian belief: I mean, they were thereby made to understand so much of them, as (having withal a due religious respect to preserve a continual humble reverence in them to the dignity of such high holy Mysteries) was fully convenient for their weak capacities, and for the comforting and strengthening of their faith, and as they were bound of necessity to know.

As for example, by the ancient institution of the holy feasts of Advent: of our savior Christ's Nativity, and Circumcision: of his Adoration by the three Kings: and of the holy solemnity of Lent, at which time the Catholic Church teacheth all Christian people to imitate so near as they can our Savior's fasting of forty days in the desert, and representeth then also with sorrowful mourning penance, and compassion, all the whole order and history of our Savior Christ's most bitter Passion, and death, for the redemption of all mankind: And afterwards the Church solemnizeth with great Joy the holy Feasts of our Savior's Resurrection from death to life: of his Ascension into heaven: and of the Coming of the Holy Ghost.

7 See Matt. 28:20; John 14:16; John 16:13; 1 Tim. 3:15.

And then follow also the holy Feasts of the blessed Trinity, and of the most holy Sacrament, commonly called Corpus Christi day: And the holy Feasts of the blessed Mother of our Savior: And of Saint John the Baptist his precursor: And then the holy Feasts of Saint Peter, Saint Paul, and of other of our Savior's holy Apostles, and most famous Martyrs, and Confessors: And also the holy Feasts of Saint Michael the Archangel, and of all the glorious Saints in heaven: And with all a solemn day of devout memory, and general prayers, and almsdeeds, for all faithful Christian Souls departed out of this transitory life, and as yet remaining in the fire of Purgatory, to make satisfaction there for all pains due and prescribed for their sins in the merciful just balance of the divine Majesty. All which holy Festival days being so divinely and orderly disposed into so many several parts of the year, and adorned with the holy reverent Ceremonies appointed to be used in all Christian Churches throughout all Christendom, with great solemnity and reverence upon those Holy days, have yearly from time to time in every age since the Ascension of our Savior Christ into heaven very lively and continually preached, represented, and explained unto the common simple Christian people all the holy Mysteries of the Christian Religion, which they had professed at their Baptism, and were taught in the Apostles' Creed to believe. And the reverent solemnity in every year of these holy Festival days induced them unto a continual memory, admiration, love, and reverence of those holy Mysteries, and greatly strengthened their faith in them, and caused them to have a wonderful fervent piety, devotion, and zeal towards the honor and service of Almighty God, whereby they lived very virtuous lives like the children of light, (as the holy scripture termeth them,)[8] and died generally as holy faithful Christians in the obedience, love, and favor of his divine Majesty.

But alas these golden times be past, and ended, and the devil being let lose now more and more towards the coming of Antichrist, and the end of the world, we find by pulpable experience, that since the time that such a free licentious liberty hath been permitted unto

8 See Luke 16:8; John 12:36; Eph. 5:8; 1 Thess. 5:5.

every leud babbling Minister to rail against all the holy ancient divine ordinances, used and allowed generally so many ages in all Christian Churches, and to term them in blasphemous manner Antichristian inventions, and to preach openly in pulpits, and publish in printed books whatsoever new heretical opinions the enemy of mankind suggesteth into their fantastical heads, the faith of Christians is thereby generally become so weak, and inconstant, and in very many or most persons so wholly undermined, and utterly overthrown, and their hope is so transformed into presumption, and their charity is waxen so cold, and so little piety, love, devotion, reverence, and zeal remain in them towards the service of Almighty God, and so much Pride, gluttony, incontinence, lying, detraction, disobedience, with most horrible contention, Schism, Heresy, Infidelity, Atheism, and all kind of iniquity do generally abound more and more throughout Christendom, that we have good cause to fear, least that terrible time approacheth now very near at hand, which our Savior forewarned us in the gospel, to wit: that at his coming to judge he should hardly find faith in the earth.[9]

Wherefore we have now very great need of extraordinary spiritual help to strengthen our weak minds, to withstand so many deceitful temptations of the enemy of mankind in this so corrupt and dangerous age. And for this purpose I have translated out of the Spanish tongue divers books of a very holy and famous learned religious father, called Lewis de Granada, whose devout manner of writing hath (in my simple judgement) a singular rare grace to pierce the hard heart of a dissolute sinner, and to move and dispose his mind to the abhorring of sin, to the contempt of the world, and to the fear, love, and service of almighty God. And I understand that his books have wrought wonderful much good, not only in Spain, and Portugal, but also in Italy, France, and Germany. And I think there be few countries in Christendom but have his Spanish works translated into their tongues. And it is now about fourteen years ago, since the time that Master Doctor Harding (a man for his great virtue,

9 See Luke 18:8.

learning, wisdom, Zeal, and sincerity in writing against Heresies, of very godly and famous memory) persuaded me earnestly to translate some of those Spanish books into our English tongue: affirming, that more spiritual profit would undoubtedly ensue thereby to the gaining of Christian souls in our country from Schism, and Heresy, and from all sin, and iniquity, than by books that treat of controversies in Religion: which (as experience hath now plainly tried) do nothing so well dispose the common peoples minds to the fear, love, and service of almighty God, as books treating of devotion, and how to lead a virtuous life do. The due consideration whereof hath so provoked, or rather pricked me in conscience, that I have resolved to publish (God willing) in print all my translations, in case I shall perceive that such as be godly, wise, and learned, shall like of them. And first (as it were for an assay) I have here printed his devout Meditations of the principal holy Mysteries of the Christian Religion, which book I find greatly commended by divers godly learned men.

It may be, that some readers of this book being not greatly acquainted with the holy exercise of a spiritual life, will imagine that the Author dealeth to austerely in some of these meditations: as namely in his Meditation of sins: of the hour of death: of our dreadful account at the terrible day of Judgement: and of the most horrible pains of hell. And perhaps some politique wise men will say, that for so much as the common people in our country have been for the most part of our corrupt age altogether accustomed with hearing and reading of divers other contrary new erroneous doctrines, tending directly to a careless dissolute life, they be therefore now waxen so carnal and negligent of the salvation of their souls, that these Meditations be to full of threatening, and terror, for such nice and loose consciences. For answer to this objection, it is to be noted, that the Author being (as I am informed) not only a great learned and religious devout old father, but also of great wisdom, gravity, judgement, discretion, and of long experience, as well in preaching, and hearing of Confessions, as in divers governments in his religious order, and perceiving very evidently that far more Christion souls be lost in this our corrupt age with overmuch presumptuous confidence, and security of their salvation, than with overmuch fear of losing the same, hath therefore framed his manner of writing in these meditations chiefly against the infinite number of presumptuous and careless dissolute Christians, that presume most certainly, and assuredly to be saved, and yet do live very dissolutely all their whole life time, without all care of keeping God's Commandments, and without all fear of their account at the dreadful day of judgement, notwithstanding that our Savior Christ himself who shall be then our Judge, hath by plain and express words forewarned us in the gospel of saint Matthew, that *If we will enter into the Kingdom of heaven, we must Keep his commandments:*[10] which every Christian may be able to keep, being assisted, strengthened, and holpen therein with the grace of God, which is never denied to any that prayeth duly for it:[11] and also that we must at the day of judgement give an account of every idle word.[12]

And verily, if we peruse diligently the holy Scriptures, we shall find that not only Enoch in the law of Nature,[13] and afterwards all the Prophets, but also Saint John Baptist, and our Savior Christ himself used the same manner of preaching that this religious godly father doth here. And they thought it to be the very best and readiest way for conversion of sinners from their sinful dissolute lives, to show plainly unto them the damnable state they live in, and to put them in mind of the severe justice of almighty God at the terrible day of judgement against all such as endeavor not to keep his commandments. And Saint Peter protesteth (as it appeareth in the Acts of the Apostles) that our Savior Christ commanded likewise him, and the rest of the Apostles, to preach and testify this point especially, that Christ is appointed to be the Judge both of the quick, and the dead.[14] And therefore in another place he requireth all Christians to

---

10 See Matt. 19:17.

11 See 1 Cor. 3:9; 15:10; 2 Cor. 12:9; Phil. 2:13.

12 See Matt. 12:36; 2 Cor. 5:10.

13 See Jude 14–15.

14 See Acts 10:42.

live in fear during the time of their conversation upon the earth.[15] And Saint Paul maketh also the like solemn protestation of the terrible day of judgement, and what a straight account every one of us must make at that dreadful time, and exhorted the Corinthians with the knowledge and consideration thereof to persuade all men to live in the fear of God.[16] And disputing also before the President Felix of the Christian religion, and namely of the dreadful day of Judgement, he uttered such wonderful terrible things thereof, that as the holy scripture mentioneth, he made the very President himself (though he were an infidel) even to tremble and quake for fear, with the only hearing of them.[17] And Saint John likewise in his Revelations affirmeth, that he saw an Angel preaching the everlasting gospel unto all Nations, tribes, tongues, and people, (meaning thereby, that he preached as well to the good, as to the wicked, without any exception therein of the faithful Christians,) saying: *Fear our Lord, and give honor unto him, because the hour of his judgement is come.*[18] And I am persuaded that all godly wise and grave men will easily agree in this opinion with me, that this manner of preaching of the terror of the day of Judgement, and of the most horrible pains of hell, is much more needful now in this our corrupt age in England, and Scotland, than in Italy, Spain, or other Catholic countries, since so great numbers of them are infected with so many heretical licentious doctrines, that have caused them to put quite away out of their minds all fear of God, and of his terrible judgements, and to presume most certainly and assuredly to be saved by their only faith, and so are generally become utterly careless of endeavoring to work their salvation with fear, and trembling,[19] and do live as carnally, and dissolutely, both to the flesh, and the world, as any barbarous Pagans, and Atheists: In so much as all godly ancient wise men do greatly lament to see by experience the terrible prophesy of David to be generally verified

---

15 See 1 Ptr. 1:17.
16 See 2 Cor. 5:10–11.
17 See Acts 24:25.
18 Apoc. 14:7.
19 See Phil. 2:12; 1 Cor. 4:4; 2 Ptr. 1:10.

at this day throughout our Realm: which is, that the judgements of almighty God be taken quite away from the face of the ungodly.[20] And if these and such like godly Meditations and Considerations of the terrible threatenings and judgements of almighty God against the wicked, be not a fit remedy for their conversion from their careless dissolute lives, what other remedy then can possibly be devised for them?

Howbeit I have very great hope, that with the grace of God these godly Meditations will work much good effect for the conversion of many of them. For undoubtedly that man is very willful, and obstinate in his wickedness, that reading advisedly all these godly Meditations is not moved inwardly in his heart in some part of them to the fear, love, and service of almighty God, and to the abhorring of all sin, and amendment of his life. And such readers as shall be inwardly moved and called thereunto by almighty God, I conjure them in his holy name, and in regard of their own salvation, not to make sad the Holy Ghost, in hardening their hearts, and resisting ungratefully and willfully against his divine inspirations, when it shall please his infinite goodness, and mercy, with such singular love to knock and call at the door of their hearts, but in any wise to open it out of hand, and receive him most humbly into their hearts, with such loving hearty entertainment, submission, thankfulness, service, and honor, as duty requireth they should do unto their most high sovereign lord, and Creator, that hath such a special loving care of their salvation.[21]

Now this book of Meditations, and whatsoever else I have translated, and shall God willing hereafter publish in print, I do most humbly offer unto the service of almighty God for the benefit of our country. And for so much as I am very wary and assured that this book containeth not any thing whereby I may justly incur any penalty prescribed by any laws of our Realm, I am the bolder humbly to recommend it by this my dedicatory Epistle unto your Honors, and

20 See Ps. 9:26.

21 Eph. 4:30; Ps. 94:8; Heb. 4:7; Acts 7:51; Rom. 10:21; 1 Cor. 2:16; Matt. 23:37; Apoc. 3:20; Ps. 80:11.

worships: partly for that I have spent some part of my time in the study of our Common Laws in the Middle Temple among you, and am very much bound unto divers of you: But chiefly for that I know right well the great capacity and dexterity of your spirits, the gravity of your judgements, and your wisdoms, experiences, authority, and example, to be of such principal estimation, and worthy respect in our Realm, that in case ye do zealously employ your endeavors to the due reverent consideration of the holy Mysteries of the Christian Religion, (as I doubt not but very many among you do,) your holy example will generally allure a great number throughout our whole Realm from all contentious disputing, and jarring about these late new controversies in Religion, to embrace firmly and zealously the ancient Catholic belief, and to imitate the virtuous lives of our holy Christian forefathers, who had much more abundance of the grace and light of the Gospel of our Savior Christ, than we have in this our ungracious corrupt age, as very manifestly appeareth by their so manifold good Christian fruits left by them unto us, to the glory of our Savior Christ, and of his dear spouse the Catholic Church, and to the continual great admiration, confusion, envy, and despite, of Lucifer, and of all his rebellious wicked spirits, and of all Jews, Turks, Heretics, and other Infidels his adherents.

And (requesting here humbly pardon, and license, to treat in a familiar manner with the younger sort) I desire your Honors and worships continually to remember what great inclination ye have unto virtue more than others of obscure parentage, and base estate, in regard of your nobleness, and magnanimity, which ever inviteth you to imitate the noble virtuous steps of your noble Christian ancestors, and to set upon high and noble virtuous enterprises, and to do all your works nobly, and excellently, that ye take in hand. As also to consider, that a virtuous life is the greatest and most noble ornament of nobility. And that for this end chiefly almighty God bestoweth upon noble personages here in earth, principality, rule, government, and honor, that they should give virtuous and godly example unto all others that be under their rule, and government. And by experience we find that ordinarily no bishop or other preacher is able with such facility to plant virtue among the common people, and cause them sincerely to love, honor, and embrace it, as Noblemen, gentlemen, Magistrates, and Governors are able to do, in case they themselves do give good apparent example of virtue, religion, and devotion, and be zealous also in procuring all others to do the like. And therefore I beseech you to determine with an honorable constant resolution to employ your time in the most noble exercises of virtue, and to fear, love, serve, and honor almighty God, who is your most noble, high, sovereign Lord, and Creator: and not to suffer either your study or practice of the laws, or other your worldly offices, and affairs to be so great an impediment unto your spiritual exercises, but that you may have ever one window open towards the heavenly Jerusalem, as Daniel had in his chamber in Babylon, praying there three times in the day towards the earthly Jerusalem.[22] And in case your worldly impediments be over great, then wisdom requireth that for salvation of your souls you do cast them away from you. And imitate herein the worldly foresight of wise Merchants when they be in danger of drowning in a stormy tempest upon the sea, who use at such times for salvation of their lives to cast into the sea their rich merchandise, and all their troublesome encumbrances, thereby to cause their ship to sail more safely. And I do also humbly beseech all good Christian readers that shall like well of these spiritual exercises to remember me in their devout prayers, that I prove not like unto those foolish carpenters that made Noes ark, who made it to save others from drowning in the general flood, and yet were drowned themselves.

Thus with all due humble submission of myself, and my travails herein to your honors, and worships, I humbly crave pardon for passing here somewhat the bounds of my profession, and treating as a divine of spiritual matters, according as since my departure from the Middle Temple by some study, and reading of divers spiritual books, and continual conversation these fifteen years with many virtuous and Learned Catholic Priests in these parts I have been instructed.

22 See Dan. 6:10.

And I most humbly beseech almighty God that these Godly Meditations may work so good effect in all your minds, as I have often times very earnestly requested of his divine Majesty. From Paris, upon the holy festival day of Pentecost. In the year of our Lord. 1582.

AN ADVERTISEMENT BY THE TRANSLATOR TO THE LEARNED READER

FORSOMUCH as the Author of this book hath published at divers times several editions thereof in the Spanish tongue, and in the later editions hath from time to time very much and often corrected, altered, and augmented the same, not only in manifold words, and sentences, but also in divers chapters, otherwise than in the former editions, that were printed either in Toledo, Salamanca, Lisbon, Antwerp, or in any other place before the year of our Lord. 1567. I think it very convenient to give notice of it to the Reader: and withal that in my Translation I do follow the edition in the Spanish tongue, printed at Antwerp by Christopher Plantine, in the year of our Lord. 1572. For I perceive that the French Translation differeth in divers places from this best corrected edition of Plantins: and so do likewise all the Translations that I have seen in the Italian tongue, printed in divers years at Rome, Naples, and Venice, by Michael Tramezzino, Horatio Salviani, Jovanni Baptista Guerra, and Gabriel Jolito: until that now of late all the Authors works have been newly Translated into the Italian tongue, and printed at Venice, by Georgio Angelicri, in the year of our Lord. 1581.

AN EXHORTATION MADE BY THE BISHOP OF CUENCA[1]

IT is the doctrine of the holy fathers, that there be three things very necessary and of inestimable importance to the just man to preserve him in his Justice: to wit, Prayer, Reading and doing of good works. In these three things ought the just man to exercise himself every day, and divide his time so discreetly, and so like a good Christian, that he be ever found occupied in some of them. Prayer illuminateth, purgeth, comforteth, rejoiceth, obtaineth fervor, causeth all travail to seem sweet, and light, breedeth devotion, engendereth confidence, (in case our own spirit does not reprove us:) Prayer bannisheth away sloth, frayeth the enemy, and overcometh temptation. And therefore a certain wise man said: *Non te pigeat orare, si vis a vitiis liberari.* Be not slack to pray, if thou wilt be delivered from vices.

Prayer is very necessary towards the obtaining of the grace of God, without which the spiritual life will utterly decay, and perish. And therefore prayer is preferred before reading. Tertullian speaking of prayer saith: That thing is always to be used, which is always good: And he addeth furthermore, and saith: If prayer be necessary

1 An exhortation to the Christian Reader, made by the Right Reverend Father in God, Bernard de Fresneda, Bishop of Cuenca, one of the privy Council of Estate to the mighty King Philip of Spain, etc. And his Ghostly Father, to read this book with good attention, and with a desire to profit, and proceed forwards in godliness.

in all places, and at all times, then is continency necessary also unto prayer: for so much as prayer proceedeth of continency wherefore if thy continency hath cause to be ashamed, then shall thy prayer likewise be ashamed. The spirit carryeth our prayer unto God: and if the spirit find itself faulty, then our prayer ascendeth with shame unto him. Again, Cassiodorus saith, that perseverance in prayer availeth much to obtain firmness of heart. By means of continual prayer the devils and their deceitful snares are overcome, and by the same the just man weakeneth their forces, and vexations. By means of prayer he maketh them become weak, cowardly, and easy to be conquered: and by the same he maketh himself also become strong, and a conqueror over them. If thou pray with perseverance thou shalt obtain sweetness, and withal a more fervent desire to pray. And then do we pray in truth, when we have none other thing in our mind, but do apply all our intention unto heavenly things and have our heart wholly enflamed with the fire of the Holy Ghost.

1. There be three effects of prayer. The first effect is common unto all works done in charity: which is, to be meritorious. And for this effect actual attention is not of necessity required in prayer, but it is sufficient to have an habitual attention, as in all other meritorious acts.

2. The second effect, is proper unto prayer alone, which is to obtain of almighty God the thing we desire. And for this effect it is sufficient also to have the first intention, which is the thing that God respecteth in our works. For if this first intention fail, we shall not obtain the thing we require: because almighty God will not hear his prayer, that seeketh not the thing he asketh of him in such sort as he ought, and for such end as he ought.

3. The third effect of prayer, is a spiritual refection of the soul. And for this effect it is necessarily required to have an attention in prayer: and not only such an attention as is attent to the material words, or as the second attention, that market the

sense and meaning of the words, but much more that attention, that market and is attent to the end of prayer, which is almighty God, and unto the thing for which we pray.[2]

The reading of holy books containing fruitful and profitable matters, not only lighteneth our ignorance, but it also dischargeth our duty in well spending our time therein: it correcteth our faults, teacheth good and holy manners, discovereth vices, exhorteth unto virtues, stirreth up fervor, causeth a fear of God, recollecteth the mind, recreateth and comforteth the heavy, sorrowful, and discomforted soul. Undoubtedly it procureth great profit and fruit to read books of holy matters: of such matters I mean, as do recollect the soul that is distracted, and wandering abroad among so many divers and sundry things. Reading teacheth and sheweth us the way how to lead a good life: Examples do induce and provoke us to imitate and follow the same: And prayer obtaineth us grace to accomplish it fully, and perfectly. Reading (say the holy fathers) is good: Prayer unto God is better: but the doing of good works for God's sake is above all. Out of holy reading the good devout persons do gather how to meditate upon God: And out of godly meditation proceedeth an earnest affection and a very prompt and ready elevation of the spirit unto God, out of which issueth that inward prayer, that pierceth the heavens, passeth above the highest places, and hath a desire to unit itself unto almighty God, in whom are all good things that may be desired.

But because our weakness is not able to continue and persevere always in prayer, and reading, it is therefore very profitable, yea and necessary to work also, and to do some thing that is good, and profitable: which cannot choose but so it will be, in case prayer go before the work: and yet shall be much better, if prayer do accompany it: but best of all if the work do also end in prayer, and then is the work most perfect. To do some kind of work with our own hands, besides that it is very profitable and wholesome for the body, it helpeth our spirit also, our neighbor is thereby edified, and our senses are comforted,

2 See St. Thomas Aquinas, *Summa Theologica*, II-II, q. 83, a. 13.

and refreshed. And in case thou find thyself slothful, heavy, and unwilling to work, and labor with thy hands, yet persevere therein, and thou shalt overcome it. O that we might once come to have such a perseverance, and constancy, as the Saints had, who prayed without intermission. And yet notwithstanding their continence in prayer, good Lord, it is marvelous to consider, how studious and continual they were in reading, how fervent and laborious in bodily exercises, and in doing of good works: insomuch as no kind of labors, pains, nor trials, could ever overcome them. Now what other thing is the life of the Saints unto us, but only a holy reading, which we ought to imitate without ceasing. That man that shall enforce himself to take pains and labors for God's sake, shall obtain the greater grace of his divine goodness, and shall out of hand feel the profit and commodity of his travail. An evil custom is overcome by a good: the which good custom if it be converted as it were into nature, it waxeth so strong, that it turneth the things that were hard, and difficult, and causeth them to become easy, and light. And all this (as Saint Paul saith) cometh to the just man by means of continual prayer. And therefore he saith, *Sine intermissione orate*: pray ye without intermission.[3] Saint Paul knew right well, that whilst we walk here in this life, we are compassed all about with enemies, temptations, tribulations, and with infinite deceitful ginnes, with wars without, and fears within,[4] and therefore he adviseth us to pray without intermission. For whereas almighty God permiteth so many vexations and troubles to come for the sins of the world, his intent thereby is to stir up his elect, and to awake them, that they should lift up their spirit unto heavenly things. For he that prayeth not, fighteth not, and he that fighteth not manfully, and maketh resistance, is forthwith overcome, and looseth his crown, and reward.[5] And if thou demand of me who is able to pray and fight continually: I say, that everyone can do it, that in truth and humility of heart calleth upon almighty God for succour, and putteth

3 1 Thess. 5:17.
4 2 Cor. 7:5.
5 See 2 Tim. 2.

his full trust in him in very deed. For (as the prophet David saith) Our Lord is mighty unto them, that call upon him, if so be they call upon him in truth.[6] And if thou canst not pray continually with thy mouth, yet pray with thy spirit, and with a godly intention. For it is a very continual sacrifice unto almighty God in the soul of our heart to have a desire to do good works, and to serve him with all our hearts. And truly that man doth always pray, that doth always good works. And whosoever is heartily sorry for his offences he that committed, and fighteth, mourneth, and longeth for the good things that are to come, prayeth always, and saith with the prophet David. O Lord before thee is all my desire, and my mourning is not hid from thee.[7]

These three points now good Christian Reader, which serve (as we have declared) to preserve the righteous man in his righteousness, are so well taught, and so wonderfully set forth in these notable books of the Reverend religious Learned Father, F. Lewis de Granada, that he must needs be very hard hearted, who reading them with attention, devotion, and with a Christian desire to take profit by them, doth not marvelously enrich himself with these three treasures: to wit, with prayer, reading, and doing of good works. Wherefore whosoever is desirous to profit in these three things, hath here very Catholic, sound, and profitable doctrine, and in all points agreeable with the universal doctrine of the holy ancient Fathers, and of the divine Scriptures. In these singular devout holy books he shall not find any thing that may either offend him, or bring him into any error, or scruple. Here shall he find many things that may edify, delight, teach, and provoke him to the love of God, and withal to the abhorring of sin, and contempt of the world. From receiving which fruits no man is here excluded: forsomuch as the Author hath with a rare wisdom in such wise tempered doctrine, and accommodated himself unto all states, and conditions of the persons, that neither the very high and learned have any cause to leave it, as over base for them: nor the very low and unlearned to refuse it, as over high for their capacities. For

6 See Ps. 144:18.
7 Ps. 37:10.

here is made a convenient provision of competent meats both for the one sort, and for the other. And because the Author understood right well how far the mouths of men nowadays are out of taste, and how much they are more affectionate unto the fleshpots of Egypt, than to the bread of Angels, I mean hereby, rather to the reading of profane books, by reason of the pleasant style wherewith they think they are written, than to the books of spiritual doctrine, which are commonly written with more simplicity, he hath therefore dressed this meat in such wise, and hath written this doctrine in such a sweet and pleasant style, that it may provoke an appetite unto this book, even in such persons as do otherwise loathe good and wholesome food: besides, that the very matters themselves are exceedingly well chosen, and of great profit. And because it were the part of rude and rustical persons to give thanks to the bees that make the honeycombs, and not unto almighty God who created the flowers from whence the bees gather the honey, which they work in their hives: I exhort all persons to give thanks to the devout and Learned Author of these works, for these so sweet and savory honeycombs which he hath here given us, in such sort that they omit not to proceed further, and to give thanks to almighty God also, who hath sent the flowers, wherewith this honey is made. And withal I make humble request unto all men, that I may be partaker of the prayers they shall make by means of the good disposition, which (I trust) with the grace of God the reading of these holy and excellent devout works shall cause in all godly and devout Christian Readers.

Bernard de Fresneda
Bishop of Cuenca.

THE EPISTLE OF THE AUTHOR[1]

I CANNOT find any other place, whither I may better direct this my small present then to your Reverend hands. For (setting apart divers and sundry reasons of great importance, that bind me so to do) certainly the wonderful change of life, which your Reverences have made, and the holy example which you have given to the world in this our corrupt age, are sufficient causes to move all such as do any thing desire the glory of Christ, to serve you in this your spiritual journey, that have in such wise amplified his glory.[2] I might well speak of this matter more largely in this place, and surely without lying, or flattery, and to speak herein, were not to employ the time in the praises of men, but in the praise of almighty God. Forsomuch as it is manifest, that this your wonderful change of life, hath not proceeded of flesh, and blood, but of the right hand of the highest. But because it behooveth all men of our cote, and profession, to be free not only from all flattery, but also even from all suspicion of the same: I will therefore content myself at this present, only with giving thanks to our lord for this notable virtuous act of yours: and I will confess, that we have seen that wonder in our days, which the holy ancient father St. Jerome declareth to have chanced in his time. He writeth it in a certain Epistle to Ruffinus in these words.

---

1 To the very reverend and right honorable personages: Don Antonio De Cordova: and Father Lorenco De Figueroa.

2 Note reader, that these to whom the author directeth this book are two noble personages, of the most noble and ancient houses of Spain: which have forsaken all their worldly possessions, and entered into religion.

> Bonosus thy friend and mine, is now gone up by that mystical ladder, which the Patriarch Jacob saw: and according to the mystery of Moses he hath now sacrificed the brazen serpent in the desert. Where at this present he soweth with tears, that hereafter he may reap with joy. Let the truth of this worthy act put to silence all the lying wonders which the Greeks and Latins have written in their histories. Behold here a young man brought up in our company, and instructed in all good arts, and learning, who had no want neither of lands, nor riches, nor honor, nor dignity, among his equals, who forsaking his mother, and his sisters, and above all, his most dearly beloved brother, went to live in an Island, which is very solitary, and fearful, and environed with divers seas, there to dwell like a new inhabitor of paradise. And being alone in this place (howbeit not alone, forsomuch as he is in the company of Christ,) he seeth now the glory of almighty God, which the Apostles themselves never saw, but when they were alone in the mount.

Thus far be St. Jeromes words. This holy example of Bonosus is truly a thing wherein almighty God is to be praised, as in a singular work of his grace. And surely no less is he to be praised in your Reverend and most honorable personages, who having much more to forsake in the world, than Bonosus had, and being now in the very flowers of your youth, have forsaken the world, and all the vain pomp, and pride thereof: and withal your great lands, and possessions, the dignity of your high noble estates, and the hope of so great honorable promotions, that were due unto your nobility and virtue, and to the renowned deserts of your very ancient and most noble families. And all this you have done to embrace even the poverty, nakedness, and obedience of Christ. You have not done like that young man in the gospel, who remembering how great possessions he had, refused to follow the way of perfection, which our Savior Christ taught him.[3] But ye have done like that wise and prudent merchant, who after he

3 See Matt. 19.

had found the precious pearl, sold all he had in the world to buy the same.[4] And if unto this wonderful change of yours, we join also the notable virtuous change of life which the most noble and renowned Duke of Gandia hath made in our days,[5] and the marvelous changes of sundry other right honorable personages which might here be rehearsed, it will very evidently appear, that there is more sweetness in the way of Christ, than the world thinketh there is: sithence even those, that have had so long and so great experience both of the one kind of life, and of the other, do very heartily and willingly renounce all that ever the world giveth and promiseth unto them, for the least crumb that falleth from Christ's table: saying with the spouse in the Canticles. *If a man give all his substance for charity, he will contemn it as nothing.*[6]

Forsomuch therefore, as very reason would, that every one should serve them, that serve our most merciful and loving lord, it seemeth unto me, that it is my bounden duty also, to do you some service in this your spiritual journey, at the least with this little volume: which treateth of prayer and meditation, and that the holy and devout exercises of your Reverences may be holpen somewhat by the same: the which (I trust in our lord) shall be always furthered, and proceed prosperously, both with it, and without it. And although this be a debt which I owe unto you: yet do I for this debt crave of you a grace, and this is, that your Reverences will most humbly beseech our lord, that it may please him of his infinite mercy, and goodness, to grant his favor and assistance to this book: that the profit of them that shall read it, may be answerable to the pains of him that made it, and to the good heart wherewith he offereth it unto them.

4 See Matt. 13.

5 This Duke of Gandia forsook his great Dukedom in Spain, and became a religious man of the holy Society of Jesus: commonly called Jesuits.

6 Cant. 8:7.

THE PROLOGUE AND ARGUMENT OF THIS BOOK

PRAYER (to define it properly) is a petition we make unto almighty God, for such things as are appertaining to our salvation. Howbeit prayer is also taken in another more large sense: to wit, for every lifting up of our heart unto God. And according to this definition, both Meditation, and Contemplation, and every other good thought may be also called prayer. And in this sense we do now use this word, because the principal matter of this book, is of Meditation, and Consideration of things appertaining to Almighty God, and of the principal mysteries of the Catholic faith.

The very thing that moved me to treat of this matter, was for that I understood that one of the principal causes of all the evils that be in the world, is the want of consideration: According as the Prophet Jeremias signified, when he said. *All the earth is destroyed with desolation, because there is none that thinketh with attention upon the things appertaining unto God.*[1] Whereby it appeareth, that the very cause of our evils is not so much the want of faith, as the want of due consideration of the mysteries of our faith. For truly if there were no want in this behalf, the mysteries of our faith be of so great virtue, and efficacy, that if the very least mystery of them were considered with attention, and devotion, even the same would be a great bridle, and redress of our life. For who would ever go about to commit any sin, if

1 See Jer. 12:11.

he considered that almighty God died for sin? And that he punisheth sin, with perpetual banishment out of the kingdom of heaven, and with everlasting pains, and torments in the horrible fire of hell?

Whereby ye may see, that although the mysteries of our faith be of very great force to incline our hearts unto goodness: yet because there be very many Christians that have no due consideration of the things they believe, therefore they work not such effect in their hearts, as such mysteries being well weighed, considered, were able to work. For like as the physicians affirm, that if we will have a medicine to help a sick man, it is necessary it be first wrought and digested in the stomach with natural heat, (because otherwise it shall not be any profit to him at all:) even so also, if we will have the mysteries of our faith to be profitable and healthful unto our souls it is requisite they be first wrought and digested in our hearts, with the heat of devotion, and meditation: because otherwise they shall profit us very little. And for want hereof, we see that many Christians, which are very whole and sound in matters of faith, be yet in their lives very licentious, and dissolute. And the reason is, because they do not consider, and weigh the holy mysteries which they believe: and so they keep their faith, as it were fast locked in a corner of a chest, or as a sword in the scabbard, or as a medicine in the apothecaries shop, and use not the benefit thereof for such purposes as it serveth. They believe generally, and as it were in a fardel, or gross sum, all such things as the Catholic Church believeth. They believe that there shall be a judgement, that there shall be pains for the wicked, and glory for the good: but how many Christians shall ye find, that do consider after what sort this judgement, these pains, and this glory shall be, with other the like circumstances?

Now this is the cause, why the holy Scripture so earnestly commendeth unto us the continual consideration, and meditation of the law of God, and of the mysteries thereof: which is indeed the study of true wisdom. Consider I pray you, how instantly Moses that great prophet, and friend of God commendeth this unto us: saying: *Print these my words in your hearts, and carry them bound as it were for a sign in your hands, and teach them to your children, that they may think upon them. When thou shalt be sitting in thy house, or traveling in the way, when thou shalt lie down to sleep, or rise up in the morning, think and meditate upon them, and write them on the thresholds, and gates of thy house, that thou mayst always have them before thine eyes.*[2] With what more effectual words could he commend unto us the continual meditation, and consideration of heavenly things, than with these? And no less doth Salomon commend the same holy exercise unto us in his Proverbs: where he exhorteth us, to carry the law of God always as it were a chain of gold about our necks, and at night to go to bed with it, and in the morning so soon as we awake, to begin immediately to exercise ourselves in the same.[3] Blessed is that man, that is so occupied. And so doth Ecclesiasticus term him, when he saith: *Blessed is the man, that dwelleth in the house of wisdom, and meditateth upon the law and the commandments of God, and exerciseth himself in justice, and reasoneth of holy things by his understanding. Blessed is he that considereth her ways in his heart, and understandeth her secrets. He shall look in at her windows, and hearken at her doors. He shall abide beside her house, and fasten a stake in her walls. He shall pitch his tent beside her.*[4]

Now what other thing may we infer of all this, but that the holy Ghost intended by all these metaphors to express unto us the continual exercise, and consideration, wherewith the just man is always occupied, in searching the works, and wonders of almighty God. And for this very cause, among the praises of the just man, this is put for one of the most principal: that his exercise is to meditate upon the law of our lord day, and night:[5] and that he is always conversant in the secrecy of parables:[6] giving us hereby to understand, that all his trade and conversation must be in searching, and meditating upon the secrets, and wonderful works of almighty God. And even for this very cause also, were those mystical beasts of Ezechiel represented

2 See Deut. 6:6–9.
3 See Prov. 1:3.
4 See Ecclus. 14:22–25.
5 See Ps. 1.
6 See Ecclus. 39.

unto us with so many eyes: to signify unto us, that the just man standeth in greater need of the continual consideration, and fight of spiritual things, than of a number of other exercises.[7]

By this therefore we see plainly, what great need we have of this holy exercise: and consequently how blindly and foully they are deceived, that either despise or make little accompt of the holy exercise of prayer, and meditation: not considering that this is openly to gainsay, and contemn that thing, which the holy Ghost hath with so great instancy commended unto us. I wish that such persons would read those five books of consideration, which St. Bernard wrote unto Eugenius the Pope. And there shall they perceive, of how great importance this holy exercise is, towards the obtaining of all virtues.

Now for this cause many Catholic and religious persons, understanding what great and inestimable fruit ensueth of this godly meditation, have gone about to exercise themselves ordinarily therein, and have appointed every day certain special times and hours for the same. Howbeit of ten times they wax cold, and give over this holy exercise, by reason of two difficulties they find in it. The one is the want of matter, and of considerations, wherein they may occupy their cogitation at that time. And the other is the want of service, and devotion, which is very requisite to accompany this holy exercise, in case we mind to have any fruit and commodity thereby. Instead whereof they find many times great dryness of heart, and withal a great combat of divers and sundry thoughts. For remedy of which two inconveniences, I have ordained this present book, which is divided into two principal parts.

The first part, for remedy of the first inconvenience, treateth of the matter of prayer, or meditation: wherein are contained fourteen meditations, serving for all the seven days of the week, both in the mornings, and evenings. And these meditations do contain the principal places and mysteries of our faith, and especially the consideration of those mysteries, that are of most force, and power, to bridle our hearts, and to incline them to the love, and fear of God, and to

7 See Ezech. 1.

the abhorring of sin. In like manner there are set out the five parts of this exercise, which be, Preparation: reading: meditation: thanksgiving: and petition: which is done to this end, that a man may have great variety of matters, wherein to occupy his heart, wherewith to procure and stir up the taste of devotion, and withal wherewith to illuminate and instruct his understanding with divers considerations, and instructions: Besides this, there is also treated therein, of six kinds of things that are to be considered in every one of the points of the Passion of our Savior: that both they, and all the rest, may minister unto us more plentiful matter for meditation. These three things are set forth in the first part of this work, for remedy of the first inconvenience.

The second part, for remedy of the second inconvenience, treateth of those things, that do help us unto devotion, and likewise of those, that do hinder us from the same. It treateth also of the most common temptations, that are wont to molest devout persons. Moreover, there are given certain advices to be a direction unto us that we err not in this way. These four articles are set out in the second part of this book.

After these I have added the third part, in which is treated of the virtue of prayer, and of her two companions, Fasting and Almsdeeds: to the intent, that when a man seeth that in all the book there is treated of prayer, and of the pains he ought to take for the same: he may understand, how well his labor is employed, which is bestowed in obtaining of a thing of so great and wonderful profit.

Peradventure the Christian reader will be offended with the length of the meditations, which we have here set forth for the seven days of the week. Howbeit for this I have many answers. The first is, considering that in these meditations is treated of the principal places and mysteries of our faith, (the consideration whereof is of so great importance, for the due ordering and reforming of our life) it behooveth me therefore to enlarge my style (in these matters especially) by reason of the great fruit, and commodity, that may ensue unto us by the same. For in this book our meaning is not only to give matter of meditation, but much more to shew the end of meditation, which is fear of God, and amendment of our life. For the procuring whereof, one of the things that most helpeth us, is the profound and long consideration of the mysteries, that are treated in these meditations. For certainly these fourteen meditations, be as it were so many Sermons, in which is laid as it were a certain battery to man's heart, to cause it to yield, (so much as is possible,) and to surrender itself up into the hands of his rightful and true sovereign Lord.

This was the chiefest cause that moved me to make the meditations so long. Besides this, I see not why the guest that is invited, should complain that the table is too full furnished with many dishes, sith we bind him not (as by way of constraint) to make an end of them all, but only among so many sundry things to make his choice of that, which serveth best for his purpose. Moreover, (that there might be the less occasion of complaint) I have put the sum of each meditation at the beginning thereof, to the intent that such as mind not to pass any further, might there have such things briefly abridged, as be necessary for the time, they intend to bestow in this holy exercise.

✝

THE FIRST PART, WHICH TREATETH OF THE MATTER OF CONSIDERATION

The First Chapter

WHEREIN IS TREATED OF THE GREAT PROFIT, AND NECESSITY OF CONSIDERATION

FOR so much as in the exercise of consideration, it can not be, but that some labor and pains must needs be taken, as well by reason of the employing and occupying of the time, which it requireth of us every day: As also in regard of the quieting, and close recollecting of the heart, (which is a thing very requisite for the same,) I think it therefore very necessary before all other things to declare here what great fruits, and commodities, do ensue of this exercise; to the intent that the heart of man, which without great promises and allurements is not moved to take great pains, may by this mean be the more moved, and provoked, to the love of this holy exercise and to bestow greater pains, and labor therein.

Now the greatest commendation we can give to this virtue is this, that it is a great helper and furtherer of all other virtues. I mean not in supplying the proper office of them, but in helping them in their exercise. In so much that like as devotion is a general stirrer and provoker unto all virtues (as St. Thomas affirmeth:)[1] And as the hearing of a Sermon, (if it be heard with such attention and devotion, as it ought to be) is also an exercise that moveth us, not to any one

1 See St. Thomas Aquinas, *Summa Theologica*, II-II, q. 82, a. 1.

virtue alone, but to all virtues, (for so much as each good instruction is directed to this end:) even so likewise is Consideration a great help and furtherance not only to any one virtue alone, but unto all kind of virtues. For there is no more difference between a Sermon, and Consideration, then is between the reading of a lesson, and the repetition of the same reading, or between the meat that is set before us in a dish, and the same meat when it is digested, and concocted in the stomach. Now this is one of the greatest, and most assured praises we can give to this virtue. For by this means it putteth not away the labors of other virtues, but rather maketh provision how to help and further them in their labors, yea and stirreth and provoketh them thereunto. This is the thing, which by the grace of God we intend now to prove very manifestly in this place.

For the better understanding whereof, it is to be known that among virtues some be common both to the Christian, and to the pagan philosopher: (as those four that be called Cardinal virtues, To wit, PRUDENCE, JUSTICE, FORTITUDE, AND TEMPERANCE. Of which virtues the philosophers understood, and wrote very much.) Other virtues there be, that are proper and peculiar unto a Christian only, in that he is a Christian: whereof the pagan philosophers neither knew, nor wrote any thing at all: or if they did, it was surely very little. These are principally those three most noble virtues called *Theological virtues:* To wit. FAITH, HOPE, AND CHARITY. Which have for their object almighty God himself: and their proper office is, to dispose and direct a man towards him. These Theological virtues have the empire, and sovereignty over all other inferior virtues, and therefore they move and provoke them to do their operations, whensoever the same is expedient for their service. After these, there follow other very principal, and excellent virtues, (which be very near of affinity unto them.) As the virtue called Religion: whose object is the service and honor of God: The virtue called Devotion: which is the act and exercise of the same religion: and the office of it is to make us very prompt, and ready, to do all such things as appertain unto his service. The fear of God, which refraineth, and bridleth us from sin.

Humility which is also after a sort (as Saint Thomas saith) the root and foundation of all virtues.[2] And penance, which is the gate of our salvation, whereunto appertaineth the sorrow and grief for our life past, and withal a firm purpose, and determination, to amend our life in time to come. Of all these virtues the pagan philosophers understood very little, or nothing at all, notwithstanding that these be the virtues that have the sovereignty, and principality, over all others, yea they be the roots and fountains of all our weal. First, because (for the most part) they be spiritual virtues, that have the accomplishment of their perfection in the inward part of our soul, (where all the beauty of the daughter of the king standeth:)[3] And secondly, because all these virtues (faith excepted) be affective virtues, and consequently they be unto us great motions, and provocations, to do good works. Wherein the providence of the grace of God wonderfully appeareth. For like as nature hath provided for us natural affections, and desires, that should be as it were certain spurs to provoke us to do all such things as are requisite for our natural life: even so likewise hath the grace of God provided for us other supernatural affections, that might be also spurs and provocations unto us, to do all such things as are behooveful for our spiritual life. And such be these virtues before mentioned: to wit, LOVE, SORROW, FEAR, HOPE, with the rest, without which virtues the spiritual life were like a barge without ores, or like a ship without sails. Forsomuch as without these virtues we should not have any thing to move and provoke us to do good works. And yet hereof we have greater need in this life, than in the other. For (considering that the way of virtue is so sharp, and full of difficulty) what should become of us, if we had not these spurs and provocations of love, of fear, and of hope, to spur and prick us forwards to labor and travail in the same? For this cause therefore are these virtues so much commended. For besides that they are such principal virtues, (as we have declared,) they be also very great provocations, and motions, to move us to do good works.

---

2 See St. Thomas, II-II, q. 161, a. 5, ad 2.

3 See Ps. 44:14.

This foundation being now laid, I say that the greatest praise we give to the virtue of consideration, is that the same is a great minister and helper unto all these virtues, as well of the one sort, as of the other, according as we will now declare. Where also it shall appear, that the commendation we give to this virtue, is not so much in respect of the virtue itself, as for the service, and commodity, it bringeth to other virtues.

§. I. How Consideration Helpeth Faith.

Now therefore to take our first beginning of faith: it is manifest that faith is the first beginning, and foundation of all the Christian life. For faith maketh us to believe, that almighty God is our creator, our governor, our redeemer, our sanctifier, our glorifier, to be short, our beginning, and our last end.[4] Faith is that which teacheth us, that there is another life after this, and that there shall be a general judgement of all our works: and that we shall receive either everlasting glory for the good, or else everlasting pain for the evil. And it is clear, that the faith and belief men have in these things bridleth their hearts, and cause them to stand in awe, and to live in the fear of God. For if faith were not among us as a mean to bridle and direct us herein, what (trow ye) would become of the life of man? And therefore the Prophet said: *That the just man liveth by faith*:[5] not that faith alone is sufficient to give us life: but because faith (by means of the representation and consideration of those things that it teacheth us) provoketh us to refrain from sin, and wickedness, and to follow virtue, and goodness. And this is the cause why the Apostle willeth us to take faith as a shield against all the fiery darts of the enemy.[6] For certainly, there is no better shield against the darts of sin, than to call those things to mind, that faith hath revealed unto us against the same.

---

4 See Heb. 11:6.

5 Hab. 2:4; Rom. 1:17; Gal. 3:11; Heb. 10:38.

6 See Eph. 6:16.

Wherefore that this faith may work this effect in us, it is very requisite that we do some times ponder and consider in our minds with good attention and devotion such things as our faith teacheth us. For if we do not so, it seemeth that our faith shall be unto us, as it were a letter closed up, and sealed: in which although there come notable important news of very great sorrow, or joy: yet it moveth us not at all, neither to the one, nor to the other, no more than if we had received no letter at all. And the reason is, because we have not opened the letter, nor considered what things are contained in it. Now what thing could be said more aptly, or more to the purpose, touching the faith of the wicked and dissolute Christians? For surely there can not be things of great terror, and joy, than those are, which our faith declareth unto us. But the wicked Christians because they do never open this letter, to see what things be contained in it, (I mean hereby, because they do never think and meditate upon these mysteries of our Christian faith, or if they think upon them, they pass them over very lightly, and in great haste,) they cause not in them this manner of motion, and alteration, to wit, of joy, or of fear. Wherefore it behooveth us some times to open this letter of our faith, I mean, the mysteries thereof, and to read the same very leisurely, and to consider with good attention, what things are taught us in the same: the which is done by means of the exercise of consideration. For it is consideration that openeth that which is locked, and unfoldeth that which is folded together, and maketh that clear unto us, which is otherwise dark, and obscure. And so by illuminating our understanding with the greatness of the mysteries of our faith, it inclineth our will, (so farforth as appertaineth to the office of consideration) to conform our life to the same. This office of consideration almighty God figured very notably in the law, when among the conditions that were required in the clean beast, he assigned this for one, that the beast should chew the cud, to wit, the meat that it had eaten before.[7] Now it is certain, that it was little to the purpose, whether the beast were clean, or unclean, and surely almighty God

7 See Lev. 11; Deut. 14.

made little accompt of that: But his meaning was, to represent unto us in that clean beast, that be spiritually clean, (to wit, of the just and righteous persons) that are not content only to care such things, as appertain unto almighty God, in believing them by faith, but after they have eaten them, they do also chew them by means of consideration, in searching and pondering the mysteries which they believe. And after they have understood the meaning and excellency of them that distribute and divide this meat unto all the spiritual members of the soul, for the sustentation, and repairing of the same.

Insomuch that if we mark this matter well, we shall find, that it fareth in this case, as in the seed of a tree, which although it do virtually contain within it the substance of the tree, yet hath it need of the virtue and influence of heaven, and of the benefit and moisture of the earth, to cause the virtue that is inclosed in the seed, to some forth to light, and to grow up by little, and little, and wax a tree. Even so in like manner we say, that although faith be the first seed, and original of all our weal, yet must it needs be holpen with this benefit of consideration, that by the same, and by means of charity, the green and fruitful tree of good life (which is virtually contained therein) may grow, and come to light.

§. II. How Consideration Helpeth Hope.

Consideration helpeth also no less the virtue of hope. This hope is an affection of our will that hath his motive and root in the understanding.[8] As the Apostle signifieth plainly unto us, saying: *All things that are written, are written for our instruction: that through patience, and consolation, which the Scriptures give unto us, we may have hope and affiance in almighty God.*[9] For undoubtedly the holy scripture is the fountain, from whence the just man gathereth the water of comfort, wherewith he strengtheneth himself, to put his hope and trust in God. For first of all he seeth in the holy Scriptures the greatness

[8] See St. Thomas Aquinas, *Summa Theologica*, II-II, q. 17, a. 7; q. 18, a. 1.
[9] Rom. 15:4.

of the works and merits of our Savior Jesus Christ, which are the principal stay and foundation of our hope. There he seeth likewise in a thousand places the greatness of the goodness, sweetness, and majesty of almighty God lively expressed, and set out to the eye, and withal the merciful loving providence he hath over them that be his: the gentleness, and benignity, wherewith he receiveth them that come unto him: and the faithful promises and pledges he hath given unto them, whereby they are very well assured, that he will never forsake them, that repose their hope and trust in him.

There he seeth, that there is no one thing more often repeated in the Psalms, more commonly promised in the Prophets, more evidently declared in the histories from the beginning of the world, than the loving favors, graces, and benefits, that our Lord continually bestoweth upon such as be his servants: and how he hath most mercifully holpen and defended them in all their calamities, and distresses. How he helped Abraham in all his journeys: Jacob in his dangers: Joseph in his banishment: David in his persecutions: Job in his adversities: Tobias in his blindness: Judith in her enterprise: Hester in her petition: The noble Machabees in their battles, and triumphs: and to be short, as many as with humble and religious hearts committed themselves unto him. These and other the like examples do strengthen and encourage our heart in labors, and adversities, and cause it to hope, and trust assuredly in God. Now what doth consideration work in all this? Forsooth, it taketh this medicine into her hands, and applieth it to the weak and diseased member, that hath need of it. I mean hereby, that consideration bringeth all these things into our remembrance, and representeth them to our heart: it searcheth and weigheth the greatness of these loving pledges and mercies of almighty God, and with them animateth, and encourageth the afflicted person, that he be not dismayed, but rather fortifieth him with a strong hope, and induceth him also to put his trust in that most merciful and loving Lord, who never failed any one man, that had recourse unto him with all his heart. By this therefore thou seest Christian reader, how consideration is the minister and servant of hope, and how it serveth her, and representeth unto her all such things as may strengthen, and encourage her. But that man that considereth not any of these things, and hath no eyes to see any part of them, wherewith can he possibly strengthen, and fortify this virtue of hope in himself, that it may be profitable unto him in his labors, and adversities?

§. III. How Consideration Helpeth Charity.

After Hope, followeth Charity, whose due praises can not be uttered in few words. For Charity is the most excellent virtue of all virtues, as well Theological, as Cardinal.[10]

Charity is the life and soul of them all: and charity is also the accomplishment of all the law. For as the Apostle saith: *He that loveth (that is, he that is in perfect charity) hath fulfilled the law.*[11] This is the virtue that maketh the yoke of God Sweet, and his burden light.[12] This is the measure whereby the portion of glory that shall be given unto us in the life to come must be measured. This is that virtue that is liking and acceptable unto almighty God, and for whose sake all such things are very acceptable unto him, as be indeed acceptable unto him. For truly without charity neither faith, nor prophecy, nor martyrdom be of any value in the sight of God.[13] To conclude, Charity is the fountain and original of all other virtues, by reason of the preeminency and sovereignty it hath to command them, and to make them to do their offices. As the same Apostle confirmeth, saying: *Charity is patient, and benign: Charity is not envious, it doth no hurt to any man, it is not proud, nor ambitious, neither doth it seek her own commodity: Charity is not angry, it thinketh no evil, it rejoiceth not at wickedness, and it is very glad of the truth: Charity suffereth all things, it believeth all things, trusteth all things, and beareth all things.*[14]

10 See 1 Cor. 13:13.
11 See Rom. 13:10.
12 See Matt. 11:30.
13 See 1 Cor. 13:2–3.
14 1 Cor. 13:4–7.

Now although it be true, that all virtues and good works do help us towards the obtaining of this most excellent and precious jewel: yet of all others consideration helpeth us most specially. For certain it is, that our will is a blind power, that can not step one foot, unless the understanding do go before, and illuminate, and teach it, what thing it ought to desire, and withal how much it ought to will and desire the same. It is also certain (as Aristotle saith) that each good thing is amiable in itself, and that every thing doth naturally love his own proper weal. And therefore that our will may be inclined to love almighty God, it is requisite that the understanding do go before it, to examine, and try, and so consequently to declare unto the will, how amiable almighty God is, both in respect of himself: (to wit, in regard of his divine perfections,) as also in respect of us, (to wit, in regard of his wonderful love and mercies shewed towards us,) that is: the understanding must weigh the greatness and excellence of his bounty, and goodness, of his benignity, of his mercy, of his beauty, of his sweetness, of his meekness, of his liberality, of his nobleness, and of all other his perfections, which are innumerable. Besides this, the understanding hath to consider, how loving and merciful almighty God hath been towards us: how much he hath loved us: how much he hath done and suffered for our sakes, even from the manger until his very death upon the cross: how many great blessings and benefits he hath prepared for us for the time to come: how many he doth presently bestow upon us: from how many great evils and miseries he hath delivered us: with how great patience he hath suffered us: and how gently and lovingly he hath dealt with us: with all his other benefits, which be also innumerable. And thus by considering, and pondering very much in the consideration of these things, our heart shall by little and little be enkindled, and inflamed in the love of such a merciful and bountiful loving Lord.[15] For if the very wild and savage beasts do love their well willers, and benefactors, and if gifts (as it is commonly said) do break the hard and stony rocks, and if that a man that findeth benefits, findeth withal (as the Philosopher

15 See St. Thomas Aquinas, *Summa Theologica*, I-II, q. 27, a. 2; II-II, q. 82, a. 3.

saith) *Chains whereby to take and bind men's hearts*: what heart is there then so stony hard, or savage, that considering the passing bountiful goodness and greatness of all these inestimable benefits, is not enkindled and inflamed in the love of our most loving and merciful Lord, that hath bestowed them upon us?

Add also hereunto, that when a man considereth these things attentively with himself, and endeavoreth with the grace of God to do so much as he is able to do for his part, almighty God will then also do that, that appertaineth unto him: that is, almighty God will move him, that moveth himself, and help him, that helpeth himself, by helping our consideration with the light of the holy Ghost, and with the gift of understanding: the which the more it penetrateth and understandeth all these reasons that induce us to the love of God, the more doth it enkindle, and inflame us in the same love of him. For like as that everlasting light and word of the father is not a barren word, but a fruitful word, which together with the father produceth the holy Ghost, which is a love consubstantial: even so doth this light and word of God work in our hearts, by enkindling, and inspiring this love of God in them.

This may yet be confirmed and declared more plainly by another reason. For it is manifest, that although this virtue of charity do grow and increase (as we have said) with the acts of all other virtues, being done in the state of grace: yet doth it chiefly increase with her own proper acts, when such acts be vehement, according as St. Thomas affirmeth.[16] For like as by writing well, and with an earnest care, and diligence, a man attaineth to be a good writer: by painting, a painter: and by the exercise of singing, a musician: even so likewise by loving, he may become a lover. I mean hereby, that like as the use of writing well, causeth a man to be a good writer, and of painting well, a good painter and even so likewise the use, exercise, and continuance of loving much almighty God, maketh a man at length to become a great lover of God. For albeit this heavenly hability, and virtue be the gift of God, and a thing which he

---

[16] See St. Thomas, II-II, q. 24, a. 6.

infuseth, powereth, and worketh in our souls, yet nevertheless he worketh this by this mean: I mean hereby, that as well the virtues infused into our souls by almighty God, as the virtues acquisite (to wit, the virtues that be obtained by our own labor, and industry,) do both of them grow and increase with the exercise of their own acts, although in a different manner. Whereupon we may infer thus much, that the more a man shall multiply the acts of the love of God, and the more he shall exercise himself in this virtue of charity, and the longer he shall endure and persevere in this work of love, the more shall this heavenly gift of charity be rooted and fortified in him. But now how can this be done without the exercise of consideration? How can the will be occupied in loving of almighty God, unless the understanding be exercised in blowing, enkindling, and discovering unto it the causes of the love of God? For like as when two horses draw in a chariot, the one can not go forwards without the other: even so these two powers (to wit the will, and understanding) be in such sort linked together, that ordinarily the one can not go forwards without the other: (at the least the will can not move without the understanding.) Thou seest now good Christian reader how inwardly and entirely the exercise of consideration is annexed to the love of God. Forsomuch as a man can never (or very hardly) set himself to love, unless he do also consider, or have before considered such things as may move him unto this love. And it is very needful for us to use some exercise of consideration, not only for the increasing of this virtue of charity, but also for the preservation of the same: that is to say, consideration is necessary, not only that charity may increase, but also that it may not fail, and decrease, among so many contradictions, and stumbling blocks, as it hath in this frail and miserable life. We see that a fish being out of the water dieth forthwith: and a drop of water being out of the sea is quickly dried up: and the fire being out of his natural region is incontinently consumed, unless there be some care and diligence used to feed and maintain it, by putting often times wood unto it wherewith to preserve it. Now the very like need hath the fire of charity also to preserve it in this life, where it is as it were a stranger, and pilgrim. And the wood wherewith it must be preserved, is the consideration of the benefits of almighty God, and of his perfections. For each one of these things being well considered, is as it were a fagot, or firebrand, that enkindleth and inflameth this fire of the love of God in our hearts. Wherefore it behooveth us to nourish and maintain this fire of charity often times with the wood of consideration, that this divine flame may never fail in us. According as almighty God hath signified in the law, when he said: *Upon my Altar* (which is the heart of the just man) *there shall be always fire.*[17] And therefore let good diligence and care be taken every day in the morning, to maintain this fire of charity with wood, (to wit, with the Consideration of all these things,) that by this mean it may be always preserved. And so it is said in the Psalm: *Through my meditation there is enkindled a fire*: to wit, the fire of charity.[18]

This necessity of Consideration may be proved by an other reason also. For we see by experience in all habilities, and graces, both such as are natural, as those also that are acquisite, (I mean, gotten by our own travail, and industry,) that like as they increase by use, and exercise, even so are they also forgotten, if we leave to exercise them. And this we see plainly verified even in such things as be very natural, and customably used. For what thing is more usual than the tongue, and language, which a man in enured, and acquainted withal even from his mother's paps, and yet may it be forgotten in time, if it be not used, and exercised. But what speak I of the tongue, seeing it happeneth sometimes, that when a man hath lyen sick in his bed, but only four or five months, he can scarcely afterwards frame himself to go again when he riseth, notwithstanding that going is a thing so natural, and so customably used. Now if the habilities which be so natural, and so much exercised, do so much decay when they be not used: what will the supernatural habilities do, which are but as it were certain props and stays adjoined unto us,

17 Lev. 6:12.
18 Ps. 38:4.

to supply the defects of nature? And if charity with all other virtues infused be in like manner to be reckoned in this accompt, in what case then shall we be, if we do but very seldom or never exercise ourselves in them? For if that thing that is even natural will be lost for want of exercise, how much more will that be lost that is supernatural? And if that thing may be lost that is fastriveted even in our very bowels, what shall that do, that is but as it were only fastened unto us with little pins?

Again, if it be true, that all amity, and friendship, is both preserved, and increased by means of familiarity, and communication: and by the want thereof is utterly quenched, and lost, (according as Aristotle affirmeth:) what shall then become of those persons, that have no manner of communication with almighty God at all? And what can we hope of them, not so much as think, consider, or treat of any heavenly matter? Thou seest then (dear Christian brother) of how great importance the exercise of consideration, and communication with almighty God is unto us, for the preservation of this virtue of charity.

§. IV. How Consideration Helpeth Devotion, and All Other Virtues Affective.

And Consideration is no less behooveful to be had for all such virtues, as are called affective: that is, appertaining to the affection, whereof we have made mention before. Among which virtues, one of the most principal is devotion: which is a certain heavenly hability and gift, that inclineth our will to desire all such things with great affection, and earnestness, as appertain to the service of almighty God: which is one of the things, that man hath most need of, in this state of nature corrupted.[19] For we see by experience, that men do sin, not so much for want of understanding, as for want of will: I mean hereby: that they sin not so much for want of knowledge what is good, as for that they are unwilling to do the thing they know to be

[19] See St. Thomas Aquinas, *Summa Theologica*, II-II, q. 82, a. 1.

good. And this unwillingness proceedeth not of the nature of virtue, (which of itself is most sweet, delectable, and very agreeable to the nature of man,) but of the corruption of man.

Now considering that this defect of our will is the very chief and principal impediment we have to hinder us from virtue, and goodness: our principal care must be, to seek a remedy for the curing of this defect. For which purpose, one of the things that helpeth us most, is devotion. For devotion is none other thing, but a heavenly refreshing, and a blast, or inspiration of the holy Ghost, that breaketh and maketh his way through all these difficulties, shaketh of this heaviness, cureth this loathsomeness of our will, and causeth us to have a taste and savor in that thing, that was otherwise unsavory, and thereby maketh us very prompt, agile, and quick, unto all goodness. And this wonderful effect of devotion the servants of God do daily try and perceive by experience in themselves, at what time they have some great and singular devotion. For then they find themselves more willing and lusty unto all labor, and pains, than they be at other times. And then it seemeth, that the youth of their souls rejoiceth, and is renewed:[20] and then they try by experience in themselves the truth of those words of the prophet, where he saith: *They that trust in our lord, shall change their strength: they shall take wings, as it were of an Eagle: they shall run, and not be weary: they shall go, and not be faint.*[21]

Devotion hath also an other property, which is, to be as it were a certain fountain, and perpetual spring of good and holy desires. For which cause in the holy scriptures it is commonly called an ointment, which is compounded of many sundry sorts of odoriferous spices, and thereby yieldeth out from it many sweet odors:[22] Now the very like operation hath devotion also, for the time it endureth in our hearts: for so much as it wholly spreadeth itself abroad into a thousand sundry kinds of holy purposes, and desires, the which the more they

20 See Ps. 102.
21 Is. 40:31.
22 See Cant. 1; 4.

increase, and are dilated, the more doth the stenches of our appetite decrease, and diminish: which are the evil desires, that proceed from the same. For like as the evil savour in a sick man's chamber, is not so much perceived, when there is a little frankincense, or some other odoriferous thing burnt therein: even so the savour of our evil desires is not so much perceived, so long as the most sweet savour of this precious ointment continueth within us. And forsomuch as it is certain, that all the corruption of our life cometh of the corruption, and stench of our appetite, and of the evil desires that proceed from the same, it shall be our part therefore to use great diligence in procuring this heavenly ointment of devotion, which is of very great force, and efficacy, to diminish and consume this pestilent corruption.

And in like manner, as consideration serveth in all the premises, even so doth it also serve and further all the other virtues before mentioned: which are, the fear of God, the sorrow for our sins, the contempt of ourselves, (wherein consisteth the virtue of humility,) and thanks giving unto almighty God for his benefits. For (as we have said before) there can be no good affection in the will, unless it proceed of some consideration of the understanding.[23] For how can a man have sorrow and contrition for his sins, but by considering the filthiness, and multitude of them? The loss we receive by them? The hatred almighty God conceiveth against them? And withal, how polluted the soul remaineth by reason of them? Again, how can a man stir up his heart unto the fear of God, but by considering the highness of his majesty, the greatness of his justice, the profoundness of his judgements, the multitude of his own sins, with other the like things? How can a man humble and despise himself with all his heart, unless he consider the great number of his own frailties, infirmities, falls, and miseries? For if humility be (as St. Bernard saith) the contempt of ourselves, which proceedeth of the knowledge of ourselves, it is manifest that the deeper a man shall wade by means of consideration into this knowledge of himself, and the more he shall dig into this dunghill, the better and more

[23] See St Thomas, *Summa*, II-II, q. 82, a. 3.

truly shall he understand, what he is of himself, and the more shall he contemn, and humble himself. Now to speak of thanks giving unto almighty God for his manifold inestimable benefits, out of which do proceed those songs, and praises of God (which is a principal part of true religion) from whence (I say) doth this rendering of thanks proceed, but from the profound Consideration of the same benefits? For the more a man shall by means of Consideration penetrate, and understand the greatness, and excellency of God's benefits, the more is he provoked to praise, and give thanks unto almighty God with all his heart for the same. I do here also pass over the contempt of the world, and the hatred of sin, with other the like virtuous affections, which next after grace, do proceed of this exercise of Consideration, which is the spur and provoker of them all, and the oil wherewith the lamps of all these virtues, and good affections, and of other the like graces, are still nourished, and maintained.

§. V. How Prayer Joined with Consideration Helpeth All the Virtuous Affections.

Prayer likewise when it is joined with consideration (as ordinarily it is wont to be) helpeth no less than Consideration itself: yea sometimes it helpeth much more. For consideration commonly is not occupied any further but only about enkindling of some one of these virtuous affections: but prayer (when it is attent, and devout, and is withal accompanied with spirit, and fervency of the mind,) is wont to stir up all these virtues aforesaid. For when the soul presenteth herself before almighty God with an earnest great desire to appease his wrath, and to desire him of mercy, then there is no stone so hard, but that it is moved hereunto. I mean hereby, that there is no holy affection, but that it is then wholly exercised and employed to this purpose. And it fareth in this case as it doth with a mother, that is desirous to still her child, or as it doth with a good and loving wife, that hath a desire to pacify her husband, when she perceiveth him to be angry: In which cases, they are wont to omit no means they can devise, that may anywise further the matter. Forsomuch as in prayer the religious soul accuseth herself before almighty God: there with the publican she is confounded, and ashamed for her sins, and offences: there she purposeth an amendment of life: there she humbleth herself, and trembleth before the supreme divine majesty.[24] There she believeth: there she hopeth: there she loveth: there she adoreth: there she praiseth: there she giveth thanks for all benefits: and there she offereth sacrifice unto almighty God, both for herself, and for all her neighbors. All these things be performed in a devout prayer. And because the habits of virtues do increase with the exercise of their acts, hereof it proceedeth, that the soul by means of this exercise of prayer remaineth very much beautified, and perfited in these virtues. As *St. Lourentius Justinianus* affirmeth in these words. *In the exercise of prayer the soul is cleansed from sin: Charity is nourished: Faith is illuminated: Hope is strengthened: the spirit is comforted: the bowels are mollified: the heart is quieted: truth is discovered: temptation is overcome: heaviness is put to flight: the senses are revived: the strength that was weakened is repaired: lukewarmness is abandoned: the rustiness of vices is consumed: and in this exercise the lively sparkles of heavenly desires do rise up, and shew themselves, among which burneth the flame of the love of God.*

By this we understand, that prayer is a most convenient exercise for that man, that mindeth to reform his manners, and life, and to change himself into an other man. As our Savior hath plainly signified unto us in the mystery of his glorious transfiguration, whereof St. Luke writeth thus: *that as he was praying in the mount, he suddenly transfigured himself in such wise, that his face shined very bright like the son, and his garments became white like snow.*[25]

Our Savior could right well have transfigured himself at other times, than at prayer, if it had pleased him: But he would of very purpose be transfigured whiles he was at prayer: to signify unto us in the

24 See Luke 18.

25 See Matt. 17:2; Luke 9:29.

transfiguration of his body, what virtue prayer hath to transfigure our souls: that is: to make them to lose the customs of the old man, and to clothe them with the new man, which is created after the image of God. There it is, where the understanding is illuminated with the beams of the true sun of justice, and where the garments, and ornaments of the soul are renewed, and become whiter than snow. This is the very thing, that almighty God signified to holy Job, when he said.

What? Is it by thy wisdom, that the hawk pruneth, and changeth her feathers, when she beateth her wings against the south?[26] Certainly it is a thing greatly to be wondered at, that this bird knoweth how to cast of her old feathers, and how to feather herself with new. And that for this purpose, she seeketh the hot air of the south, that with the heat thereof her pores may be opened, and with her moving the old feathers fall off, and so give place to the new, that begin to spring out. But how much more wonderful is it, to see a soul unclothe herself of Adam, and to put on Christ, to change the conditions of the old man, and to adorn herself with the conditions of the new man? Now this change that is so wonderful is then wrought, when the devout soul turneth herself to the south, and there beateth her wings in the air. And what is it to turn herself to the south, but to lift up her spirit to the consideration of the eternal light, and to the beams of the true sun of justice? And what is it to beat her wings in the air, but to be there sighing and panting with heavenly affections, and desires, calling upon almighty God, with great anguish of mind, and desiring most humbly his favor and grace? For then bloweth the air of the south, that is the heavenly refreshing of the holy Ghost, who with his temperate heat, and sweet moving, strengtheneth, and helpeth us to cast of all the old feathers of the old Adam, that they may give place to the new feathers of virtues, and holy desires, which there do begin to grow, and bud out. And this is that thing, that Ecclesiasticus signified by other words, he said, *They that fear our lord will prepare their hearts, and sanctify their souls before him.*[27] The which

---

[26] Job 39:26.
[27] Ecclus. 2:20.

is principally done in the exercise of devout prayer. For there it is, where the soul presenteth herself most familiarly before almighty God, (as St. Bernard saith.) And there it is, where by approaching near unto the everlasting light, she seeth more clearly her own defects, and so bewaileth, and accuseth them, and seeketh remedy for them, desiring our lord of his grace, and fully purposing an amendment on her part, and thus by little and little she sanctifieth and amendeth her life. Thou seest now good Christian reader, what a great help this exercise of consideration is, towards the obtaining of those most high, and excellent virtues, which are (as we have said) peculiar to a Christian man.

§. VI. How Consideration Helpeth towards the Obtaining of the Four Cardinal Virtues, Which Be: Prudence: Justice: Fortitude: and Temperance.

Moreover consideration helpeth also (after a sort) towards the obtaining of the other four virtues, called Cardinal virtues: which be PRUDENCE, JUSTICE, FORTITUDE, AND TEMPERANCE: as Saint Bernard plainly affirmeth in his book of consideration, by these words: *First of all, consideration purifieth and cleanseth the very fountain, from whence it proceedeth: which is the soul. Besides that, it governeth our natural passions, it directeth our works, it correcteth our faults, it frameth our manners, it beautifieth and directeth our life: to be short, it giveth knowledge to a man of things both divine, and human. It is consideration that distinguisheth things confounded, it recollecteth those that be scattered abroad, it searcheth secrets, it seeketh for truths, and trieth and examineth such things, as are in deed but apparent, and counterfeit. It is consideration that disposeth for the time to come, and thinketh of the time past, providing for the one, and bewailing the other, that so nothing may remain without correction, and due chastisement. It is consideration that in the midst of prosperity forseeth adversity, and therefore is not dismayed when it cometh: for that it hath prevented the same before hand with consideration. Of which two things, the one appertaineth to Prudence, and the other to Fortitude. It is consideration that sitteth down as a judge, to give sentence between pleasure, and necessity, and appointeth to every of them their bounds, and limits: giving to necessity, that which is sufficient, and taking from pleasure that which is superfluous, and in so doing it maketh and formeth the virtue of temperance, whereunto this office appertaineth.* Thus far be the words of Saint Bernard: whereby thou mayst perceive, how great, and general a help consideration is towards the obtaining of these virtues.

§. VII. How Consideration Helpeth to Resist Vices.

And consideration doth not only help to obtain virtues, but also to resist the vices, that be contrary unto them. For what kind of temptation is there, against which a man doth not fight with the weapons of prayer and consideration? For although it be most necessary to use other weapons for this purpose, as fasting, taking of discipline, (by scourging ourselves,) alms deeds, austerity, and affliction of body, and to eschew the occasions of evils, with other like things: yet at a sodain, what other weapon can be devised more ready, and as it were ever at hand, than prayer, and consideration? With what other weapons doth the just man fight, and overcome in these battles, than with them? If he be assaulted with the cogitation of carnal pleasure, and delight, he hideth himself wholly in the holes of the rock: that is, in the precious wounds of our Savior Christ crucified. If he be assaulted with anger, and desire of revenge, he thinketh upon the wonderful patience, and meekness of our Savior Christ, and upon those sweet words he spake, when he desired pardon on the Cross for those very persons, that crucified him. If he be enticed with gluttony, and delicious fare, if he be allured with the desire to lie in a soft bed, and to lead a delicate and wanton life, he lifteth up his eyes, and considereth the bitter gall, and vinegar, which that fountain of life, our sweet Savior Christ, drank upon the cross, and also the hard bed of the cross, whereupon he died, and the painful and austere troublesome life which he led for our sakes. When he beginneth to be puffed up with pride, he considereth the greatness of our Savior Christ's humility. When he is moved with covetousness, he considereth the extremity of the poverty of our Savior Christ. When sleep and slothfulness maketh him to become heavy, and dull, he considereth the painful watchings, and travails, that our savior endured for us in his prayers. When he is wearied with the troublesome labors and pains of this present life, he considereth the greatness of the heavenly treasures, and glorious delights, which he shall receive in the life to come. When he is tempted with the fickle pleasures, and delights, of this miserable world, he considereth the everlastingness, and bitterness of the horrible pains, and torments of hell fire? When he is molested, and wearied, with the exercises of penance he thinketh upon the virtuous examples, of the Martyrs, of the Apostles, of the Prophets, and of the ancient holy religious Monks: and with the consideration of that which is past, he causeth all that he doth presently, to seem little unto him. And when it so happeneth, that with all these defensives he can not well sustain the weight of his burden, he addeth then unto the diligence of consideration the voice of prayer, calling, and crying with great anguish of mind upon almighty God, who (be you well assured) will never forsake them that call upon him, but promiseth that he will give ear unto them: and hath given us very manifest, and sundry examples, that he never forsaked them, that called upon him with all their hearts. This is that, which the prophet David affirmeth in a thousand places he did, when he saw himself compassed about with the snares of his enemies, and with tribulations, and afflictions, saying *I presented my prayer before him, and I imparted unto him my tribulation.*[28]

[28] Ps. 141:3.

§. VIII. How Consideration Helpeth Us to Achieve and Accomplish All Works of Virtue, That Be Austere and Full of Hardness, and Difficulty.

And consideration helpeth us not only in overcoming the temptation of vices: but also in every virtuous work, that is hard, and full of difficulty unto us. For when taking of discipline: (which is whipping our rebellious flesh for our sins,) the wearing of haircloth: the going barefoot: the fasting with bread, and water: the rising to prayer at midnight: and the labors, troubles, and persecutions of this life be irksome unto us, if then we intend (like faithful servants of God) to persevere, and go forward with our good beginning, unto what other haven we do resort, but to prayer, and consideration? For there do we humbly beseech our Lord to grant us fortitude and grace, that we fall not under our burthen, and there do we lift up our eyes, and consider a thousand kinds of examples, and remedies, that may encourage us to persevere in our good purposes? Thou seest now devout Christian reader, what a great help, and succor, we have in this virtue of consideration, towards the service, and use, of all other virtues.

§. IX. How Consideration Excludeth Not Other Particular Helps unto Virtue.

Howbeit let no man for all this imagine, that hereby is excluded the particular labor, and study, that is to be used about every one of the other virtues, for that consideration is so great a help to obtain them. Forsomuch as general helps do not exclude the particular helps that be required in every thing. And the general helps required towards the obtaining of all virtues, are not only consideration, but also fasting, silence, prayer, hearing of Sermons, going to Confession, receiving of the blessed Sacrament of the altar, and devotion, with other the like virtues, which be general helps and provocations unto all virtues. But besides these general helps, that do give light to the understanding, and move the will to goodness, it is very requisite also to use the proper exercises of the same virtues, whereby to root, and make the habits of them more perfect by use, and to cause a man to have a more promptness, and facility, in the exercise of good works. For otherwise, like as the sword that never cometh out of the scabbard, is commonly very hard to be drawn out, at the time that a man hath need to occupy it: even so whosoever doth never exercise himself in the acts of virtues, shall never be prompt, or quick in doing them, when he shall have need to use them.

And although charity be the greatest, and most general help we have unto all virtues, yet consideration is, as it were, the general instrument of charity, whereby to attain unto all goodness, as we have here declared. And therefore like as the soul is the first beginning of all the works of man, and yet it useth natural heat as a general instrument unto all such things as it doth: even so is charity the beginning of all our good works, and yet charity useth consideration, and devotion, as general instruments to bring them to pass. So that it is no derogation to charity, to give this preeminence unto these virtues: forsomuch as this preeminence belongeth unto charity, as to the mistress, and principal agent, but to consideration, and devotion, as to her instruments, and helpers.

§. X. How the Exercises of Prayer, Consideration, and Meditation, etc. Appertain Not Only to the Religious Persons, and Priests, (Though Principally unto Them,) but unto the Laity Also.

But peradventure thou wilt say, that these exercises of prayer, consideration, and meditation do appertain only unto religious persons, and priests, and not to the laity. True it is I grant, that these exercises do principally appertain unto religious persons, and priests, by reason of their state, and profession of life: but yet nevertheless, the laity are not utterly excused of using some kind of exercise of prayer (though not in so high a degree, and perfection,) if they mind continually to preserve themselves, and to live in the fear of God, without committing any deadly sin. For even the laity also are bound to have Faith, Hope, Charity, Humility, the fear of God, contrition, devotion, and an hatred against sin. How seeing all these virtues be for the most part virtues affective, (as we have already declared,) which affections must necessarily proceed of some consideration of the understanding, if this consideration be not exercised, how shall these virtues be preserved? How shall a man help himself by faith, if he do not sometimes consider such things, as his faith telleth him? How shall he be enkindled in charity, and strengthened in hope, how shall he bridle himself with the fear of God, how shall he be moved to devotion, to sorrow for his sins, and to the contempt of himself (wherein consisteth the virtue of humility, which appertaineth unto all kinds of persons) if he do not consider those things, wherewith these affections are wont to be enkindled, according as we have before declared? Neither ought a man to pass over these things in the exercise of consideration with to much speed, and in post haste. For among the miseries of man's heart, one of the greatest is, that it is so sensible to understand the things of the world, and so unsensible to understand the things appertaining unto almighty God. Insomuch that unto the one, it is, as it were a very dry reed, and to the other, as it were green wood that can not be set on fire, and enkindled, but with very great labor, and travail. And therefore we must not in our exercise of consideration pass over these things in such haste, but stay, and pause for a time in them, more or less, according as the holy Ghost shall instruct us, and according also, as the business and occupations of every man in his state, and vocation of life shall give him leave. And it is not a matter of mere necessity to have certain times appointed every day for consideration.

Unto these things ye may add furthermore, the dangers of the world, with all the great difficulties men have to preserve themselves without deadly sin, in a body of evil disposed, and in a world so dangerous, and among so many enemies, as we have continually assaulting us on every side. And therefore (if for that thou art not a religious person) thy state of life do not bind thee unto so much exercise of prayer, and meditation: yet the greatness of the danger wherein thou livest in the world, must needs bind thee to use some exercise therein. The state of a religious person (I confess) is greater than thine, but thy danger of falling into deadly sin, is also greater than his. For the religious person is protected, and guarded, by his superior, by enclosure within his monastery, by observance of his rules, by obedience, by prayers, by fastings, by saying daily divine service, by the austerity of his order, by good company, and religious conversation, and by all other spiritual exercises, and virtuous labors of the holy monastical life; insomuch as even the very walls of their monasteries be a great defense, and safeguard unto them, to keep them from the occasions and dangers of deadly sin: But the lay person living, practicing, and dealing daily and hourly in the throng, and press of the world, (besides that he is destitute, and unprovided, of all these great helps, and safeguards) he is compassed about also on all sides, with dragons, and scorpions, and treadeth always upon serpents, and basilisks: I mean, the dangerous conversation with wicked persons, and the continual occasions, and temptations, of falling into deadly sin, both at home, and abroad, within himself, and without himself, both at doors, and at windows, and hath a thousand several devilish engines, and snares, laid to entrap him at all times, both day, and night. Among all which dangers, and temptations, for him to keep his heart pure, and his eyes chaste, and his body clean, in the midst of the raging fires of youth, of naughty company, of lewd conversation, and among so many evil examples of this wicked world, (where there is scarcely heard one word of God, but rather jesting and scoffing at all such, as be given to virtue, and godliness) it is one of the greatest wonders, that almighty God worketh in the world. Wherefore if the religious person ought to be always armed, because he is by his profession a man of war: even so must the lay man be armed also in his manner, (although not in so high a degree:) not because the perfection of his state of life doth bind him so much thereunto, but by reason of the great peril and danger he liveth in. For as well do they go armed, that have enemies, as those that be soldiers, and men of war. The soldiers go armed by reason of the bond, and duty of their profession, and the others go armed by reason of their necessity. Among which spiritual weapons, we do not only put prayer, consideration, and meditation: but also fasting, silence, hearing of Sermons, reading of devout books, frequenting the Sacraments, and avoiding the occasions of sins, with all other austere usage of the body. All which things be as it were a certain brine, and pickle, to keep and preserve this corruptible, and evil inclined flesh of ours, that it breed not worms, and stench in it. For undoubtedly, since the corruption of original sin, it is the greatest and hardest matter of the world, for men to keep themselves any long time without deadly sin, living in such a corrupt and dissolute wicked world as this is. For if those very persons, that do use all these spiritual helps, and exercises, are all that notwithstanding much molested with the fear, and danger of falling into deadly sin: what shall become of those, that do never use any of all these spiritual exercises scarcely in all their life? And if the holy king David, and many other saints (that lived with so great wariness, and virtuous discipline, and went armed with so many kinds of spiritual weapons) did notwithstanding take such great falls, at what time the occasions of sin were ministered unto them, what shall become of them (trow ye) that make none accompt at all, of any of these spiritual exercises.

§. XI. An Answer to an Objection, That Some Slothful Christians Do Make Against the Holy Exercise of Prayer, Meditation, and Consideration, Saying: That They Are Bound to No More, but to Keep and Observe the Commandments of God, and of His Catholic Church.

But thou wilt say, I am not bound to keep any more than the Commandments of almighty God, and of his Catholic Church. True it is, I grant. But yet to keep well this wall, we have need of a forewall, or bulwark: and to keep this vessel, we have need of a cupboard to keep it in: and to raise up this building, we have need of a scaffold, and other engines to raise it up withal. I mean hereby, that to keep the law of God, we have need of many things to strengthen, and encourage our hearts, for the keeping, and observation of the same law. For if the nature of man were in such good plight, as it was before sin, then were it a very easy matter to fulfil our duty herein: but now alas having so many lettes, and contradictions, we have need to have ever two cares, the one how to keep the law of God, and the other how to strengthen our heart, that it may overcome the impediments, and contraditions, that do hinder us from fulfilling the laws, and commandments of God. When the children of Israel returned from the captivity of Babylon, they went about to build Jerusalem again, and they intended to do nothing else, but only to build: but because the borders round about them sought to hinder them in their building, their labor and travail was thereby doubled. So that they were constrained to appoint the one part of the people to attend to the building, and the other to fight, and drive away their enemies from the wall.[29] Now in our case, whereas there be so many enemies, that do daily and hourly seek to hinder us in this spiritual building of virtues: the devils on the one side, with a thousand subtle snares,

[29] See 2 Esd. 4.

and deceits: the world on the other side, with a thousand kinds of scandalous offences, and evil examples: and the flesh in the middle, with divers and sundry kinds of appetites, which be so fiery, and so contrary unto the law of God, (for God requireth chastity, and the flesh longeth after sensuality: God requireth humility, and the flesh seeketh after vanity: God would have austerity of life, and the flesh hunteth after delights, and pleasures:) if now there be no spiritual weapons exercised to drive away these enemies, if there be no medicines used to cure this corrupted flesh, how shall a man keep chastity among so many dangers, charity, among so many scandalous offences: peace, among so many contradictions: simplicity, among so many malicious deceits: cleanness of life, in a body so filthy: and humility, in a world so much given unto pompous pride, and vain glory. Now to cure this flesh, and to make resistance against these enemies, that do hinder us in this building of virtues, we have need of other virtues. Some to carry the burthen, and some others to help us to carry the same. For the virtue of chastity fulfilleth the burthen of the commandment: which saith: *Thou shalt not commit fornication*: but fasting, prayer, avoiding of occasions of sin, taking of discipline, by whipping our rebellious flesh and other the like holy exercises, do help to mortify the flesh, that it may be the better able to bear this burthen. All which virtues, although they be not always of precept, and bound duty: yet are they often times of very necessity, and bounden duty to be exercised, whensoever the danger we be in is so great, that it requireth the exercise of them, for the keeping and fulfilling of the commandments.

But among these virtues, and defensives (that do help us to observe the commandments) one of the most principal is prayer. For prayer is a principal mean to obtain grace, which is the thing that is of chiefest force, to sustain the burthen of the law of God. And therefore Ecclesiasticus saith. *He that keepeth the law, multiplieth prayer.*[30] For whereas he seeth by experience, that none can keep the law of God (by the observation whereof everlasting glory is

30 Ecclus. 35:1.

obtained)[31] without the grace of God, he helpeth himself by prayer to obtain grace, by means whereof he may be able to keep the law of God. The law commandeth us to be chaste. But besides this, the holy Ghost addeth, and saith by the wise man. *Understanding that none could be chaste unless thou (O Lord didst give him grace for the same, and it was a great grace to know of whose gift this was) I went unto our Lord, and I demanded of him this grace with all my heart.*[32] Whereby thou mayst see (according as we declared in the beginning) that the wall hath need of a forewall, or bulwark, and the vessel hath need of a cupboard to keep it in, and some virtues have need of other virtues to defend, and guard one another.

Now if this be true that thou art bound to keep the law of God, and not to commit any deadly sin, it is good reason, that thou do seek out all such means, as may help thee to keep the same law, and to preserve thee without deadly sin. The which means although generally they be but of counsel, yet sometimes they may be of precept, when the necessity of exercising them (as we have said) is so great, that without the use of those means, the very commandments themselves cannot be kept, and fulfilled, as all the learned divines do affirm. Howbeit every Christian that hath an earnest desire of his salvation ought not to expect, and delay the seeking for these remedies, until the very last, and extreme danger, when the knife is already at his throat: but he ought to make good provision, and to furnish himself before hand, by means of these foresaid spiritual exercises, that he may live more safe, and secure, from the peril of breaking God's commandments.

Again I confess, that these means (as we have said) do appertain to the religious, and to the lay people, after a divers sort: and that prayer, and consideration itself, which is one of these means, must be used of then in divers degrees. For the religious person must exercise the same, as a thing appertaining to his office, and duty of his profession, (because he walketh towards perfection:) but the lay person must exercise it as a mean, whereby he may the better fulfill his

31 See Matt. 19.

32 Wis. 8:21; see 1 Cor. 15:10; 2 Cor. 12:9; Phil. 2:13; 4:13.

bounden duty of keeping the commandments of almighty God. And therefore the lay person must take so much of this medicine, (to wit of prayer, meditation, etc.,) as may suffice to cure his disease: and so much must he take of these means, as may suffice to obtain his end. It is sufficient for the lay person to withdraw himself sometimes, for to enter, and take an inward view within himself, and then by means of these, or any other spiritual exercises, and prayers, to attend unto the repairing of his conscience, and to the reformation of his life: for considering that this is the greatest of all our business, it is requisite that this be not the last of our cares.

§. XII. Of the Matter of Consideration.

Having now spoken both of the profit, and necessity of consideration, and our hearts being now well affected herewith towards this virtue: let us begin to treat of the matter of consideration, which consisteth of certain godly, and devout considerations, which are of greatest force, to induce us to the love and fear of God, to the abhorring of sin, and contempt of the world. For which purpose, there be no considerations better, nor of greater force and efficacy, than those that are taken out of the principal articles, and mysteries of our faith: as the bitter passion and death of our Savior: the remembrance of the terrible day of judgement: of the horrible torments of hell: of the glory of heaven: of the benefits of almighty God: of our sins: and of our life, and death: For every one of these points being well weighed, and considered, be able to provoke our hearts very much to all the effects above mentioned. These very points St. Bonaventure hath treated in a book, that he entitled, FASCICULARIUS, and hath divided them into the seven days of the week. And thus he did, that a man might have every day new food for his soul, and new provocations unto virtue, and so avoid the tediousness, that he should otherwise have in thinking always upon one same matter. And for this cause it seemed good unto me, to follow the same division, which this renowned, and blessed holy father hath made, who of all others hath treated most largely of these matters. And if there by any, that shall not well like of this division, but will follow some other, he is at free liberty so to do, and hath also examples to follow therein. For it importeth not much, what order and division he follow in the same. And surely, that is the best order to be used in these matters, that each man findeth to be best for himself, and wherein he taketh most profit and commodity.

Moreover, I thought it expedient, considering that the food and sustenance of our soul is the word of God, and the consideration of heavenly matters, (for therewith is our soul sustained in the spiritual life, which consisteth in the love, and fear of God,) that like as we give ordinarily to our body his refection twice every day, to preserve it from fainting in this life: even so we should also give to our soul her ordinary refection twice every day, that she fail not in her life. Howbeit this is not a thing of bounded duty, nor of precept: but only of wholesome council: especially considering, that the Saints have used this exercise more often times. For we read, that the prophet Daniel withdrew himself to this exercise, three times in the day.[33] And the prophet David also used to praise God seven times in the day.[34] After whose virtuous example, our holy mother the Catholic Church, hath instituted the seven Canonical hours of daily service. And for this cause have we here assigned two kinds of meditations: The one for the morning, which treateth of the most bitter passion of our redeemer: and the other for the evening, or night, which treateth of the other points and matters here before mentioned.

But if any man shall have such want of time, or of devotion, that he can not withdraw himself unto this exercise twice in the day: let him yet find the means to withdraw himself thereunto at the least once in the day. And that he may not lose the fruit of all these meditations following, he may exercise himself one week in the one sort: and another week in the other sort. And in so doing he may taste, and take profit of all these godly instructions, which we have here set forth unto him.

---

33 See Dan. 6.

34 See Ps. 118.

The Second Chapter

OF THE FIVE PARTS OF PRAYER

HERE I must advertise the devout Christian reader, that he must not spend all the whole time of this exercise in meditation only: For before meditation there may go two other parts of prayer, which be preparation, and reading: and after the same, there may follow other two, which be thanksgiving, and petition. For the first thing that we must do herein, is to prepare our hearts unto this exercise: and then it shall do well to read those points, that we intend to meditate upon. And after the reading, we have to meditate upon such things, as we have read: the which being done, we may then make an end with some devout giving of thanks unto almighty God for all his benefits: and with a petition, or demand of a such things, as we shall think are necessary both for our own souls, and for the souls of our neighbors. Of which five parts, we mind God willing to treat hereafter more at large in their proper place. This division, and order may be followed by them, that are as yet but young beginners, and novices in this trade.

As for those that have had greater exercise, they stand not in so great need of these introductions, and rules.

And it is to be noted, that the meditations that are here appointed to be used at night, are first of all abridged into a brief sum: wherein I have set out in order the principal points, that are to be considered in every one of them: (and afterwards I have added thereunto a more large and ample declaration of all the same points.) And this summary abridgement I made, to the intent, that after they have been read over divers times, they may be the better understood, and meditated upon. True it is, that of the meditations upon the holy passion, I have not made the like abridgement at the beginning of them, as I have done of the others: because I judge, that the text of the holy Evangelists, which I have there set before, may suffice for that purpose.

And it is not needful for us at every time we go to meditation, to consider all the principal points, that are there particularly noted: but it shall suffice to take two, or three of them, more, or less, according as the devotion, and time, that every one hath shall require. For certainly there is more profit taken by one mystery or point well thought upon, and duly considered: than by many that are slightly passed over in haste. Howbeit I thought good, to note diverse and sundry points, to the intent that among so great variety of considerations, every one might make his choice of such things, as might best serve his devotion.

Of Five Parts That May Be Exercised in Prayer.

These be the meditations (good Christian reader) wherein thou mayest exercise thyself in the seven days of the week, and in so doing thou shalt not want matter whereupon to meditate. But here it is to be noted, that (as we have already said) there be two things that may go before meditation, and other two that may follow after it. So that in all there be five parts which may concur in this exercise: to wit, preparation: reading: meditation: thanks-giving: and petition.

For before we enter into prayer it is very requisite that we do first prepare our heart unto this holy exercise: following therein the manner and custom of musicians, who use to temper and tune their lute, viall, or other instrument, before they play upon it. And therefore Ecclesiasticus saith: *Before prayer prepare thy soul, and be not as a man that tempteth God.*[1] To tempt God, is to desire that he should work a miracle in such things, as may be done by other ordinary means.

---

1 Ecclus. 18:23.

Seeing therefore that the preparation of the heart is such a principal mean to obtain devotion, he that goeth about to obtain it without this mean, sheweth himself to have a desire that almighty God should work a miracle therein: the which (as Ecclesiasticus saith) is as it were a tempting of God.

After preparation it followeth that a man do read that matter which he hath to meditate upon that day, according to the division of the days of the week, which we have made heretofore. And this manner of reading is undoubtedly very necessary for such as are but novices and young beginners in this exercise, until such time as a man do know what he ought to meditate upon. But afterwards, when by the use and practice of certain days he is well instructed therein, then this reading shall not be so needful, but that he may forthwith proceed unto Meditation.

After meditation there may follow out of hand a devout giving of thanks to almighty God for all such benefits as we have received, the which ought evermore to accompany all our prayers, according as the Apostle exhorteth us, saying: *Occupy yourselves very earnestly in prayer: watching therein with thanks-giving.*[2] For as St. Augustine saith: What thing is there that we can better conceive in our hearts, better pronounce with our mouths, and better write with our pens, than this short sentence, *Deo Gratias*: Thanks be unto God? Nothing can be said more briefly: nothing can be heard more sweetly, or understood more joyfully, or done more fruitfully.

The last part is Petition, which is properly called prayer: wherein we desire of almighty God all such things as are behooveful as well for the salvation of ourselves, as of our neighbors, and of all the whole Catholic Church.

These five parts may be exercised in prayer: and among other profits, and commodities, that are wont to come thereby, this is one, that these points being duly exercised do minister unto a man great plenty of matter whereupon to meditate: setting before him all these diversities of meats, that in case he list not to eat of one, he may yet

2 Col. 4:2.

eat of an other: and that when he hath made an end of meditation in one matter, he may forthwith enter into an other, and so find variety of matter wherein to continue his meditation.

I know right well, that neither all these parts nor this order is always necessary for all persons. Howbeit this manner may serve very well for all such as are but novices and young beginners in this exercise, that so they may have some order and direction whereby to direct themselves at the beginning. For certain it is, that some things be necessary in the beginning to teach an art, which afterwards when they be once known are but superfluous. And therefore of any thing that shall be here treated I will not that any man should think that I intend to make the same a perpetual law, or general rule. For mine intent is not in these instructions to make any law, but only to shew an introduction for the direction of such persons as are but novices and beginners in this way. In which course after that they shall be once entered by following this introduction, then the very use and experience they shall have in this exercise, and much more the holy Ghost will teach them each thing that they have to do herein. The which being once said in this place, I desire it may be understood in all the rest of this book.

I. Of Preparation, Which Is a Thing Very Requisite to Be Used before Prayer, and Meditation.

Now it shall be requisite for us to treat particularly of every one of these five parts aforesaid, and first of Preparation, which ought to go before the others.

We said even now that it was needful to use some preparation of our mind before we enter into prayer. This preparation may be made divers manners of ways. For a man may dispose himself unto prayer by calling to mind his sins, and offences, and namely such sins as he hath committed that present day, and he may accuse himself of them, and desire of our Lord pardon for them, according to the saying of the Wise man. *The just man at the beginning is an accuser of himself.*[3]

This manner of Preparation seemeth to be as it were the pulling off of our hose and shoes to enter into the holy land,[4] and as it were the washing of our garments to go to receive almighty God, when he cometh to treat with men, and to teach them his holy law.[5] This manner of preparation we are taught to use even by nature itself. For we see it is a common manner, that when we go to request any benefit of any friend of ours whom we have offended, we do first desire of him pardon, and forgiveness, before we demand any other thing of him. This may be done some times with the heart only, and some times by saying the general confession, *Confiteor Deo, etc.* or the psalm: *Miserere mei Deus*:[6] or some other like prayers. Wherein good heed must be taken, that these prayers be not said in post haste, but with as great quietness, attention, feeling, and repentance of heart as we can.

Howbeit a man ought not to stay over long in this consideration of his sins, (as some persons do, that both begin and end herewith, yea and pass all their whole life therein.) For albeit this consideration of our sins be always good (and at the beginning very necessary) yet it is meet that it be taken with such moderation, as that it occupy not that time which should be bestowed about other better matters. Neither is it needful in this exercise for a man to consider very particularly his sins, and namely such as the remembrance whereof may move him to some evil cogitations: But it is sufficient to make as it were a bundle of them all, and to drown them in the bottomless Sea of the infinite goodness and mercy of almighty God, with good hope to receive pardon and remedy of them from the same.

We may also prepare ourselves unto prayer, by considering the majesty and greatness of that Lord unto whom we go to speak in prayer. For this consideration will teach us, with what great reverence,

3 Prov. 18:17.
4 See Ex. 3.
5 See Ex. 19.
6 Ps. 50.

and humility, and with how great attention it behooveth such a miserable creature as man is, to speak unto a lord of so great majesty as almighty God is, concerning a matter of so great importance as is his own salvation. But that thou mayest understand somewhat of the majesty of almighty God, thou must consider, that the heavens, the earth, and all that is created, is no more before the majesty of almighty God, than a little emite, or (as the Wiseman saith) a grain of weight in the balance.[7] Now if all creatures be no more than an emite before him, what shalt thou then seem to be before him, that art so small a part of the whole?

This consideration of the majesty and greatness of almighty God is as it were a profound reverence, that the soul maketh within itself before the throne of that supreme majesty, at what time she entereth into his palace to speak with him. With this manner of humility and reverence the Son of God taught us to pray, when making his prayer he cast himself prostrate upon the ground:[8] giving us thereby to understand, how humble and lowly a man ought to be, and how much he ought to consider of his own baseness, and vileness, whensoever he goeth about to speak unto almighty God. With this spirit and humble reverence a man may repeat those words of the holy Patriarch, where he saith: *I will speak to my Lord, although I be but dust, and ashes.*[9]

But above all this, it shall help us very much in this preparation to consider well what we go about to do, when we settle ourselves to prayer. For if we do well consider it, we go to pray for none other purpose, but to receive the spirit of almighty God, and the influences of his grace, and the joy of charity, and devotion, wherewith we see how the souls of just persons are replenished at the end of their long and devout prayers. Now this being so, thou mayest perceive hereby, with how great humility, and reverence, and with how great attention, and devotion, thou oughtest to come, when thou dost open the

---

7 See Wis. 11.

8 See Matt. 26:39.

9 Gen. 18:27.

mouth of thy soul to receive almighty God. Consider with what great fervent devotion the holy Apostles were inflamed, at what time they expected and looked for the coming of the holy Ghost, and by that mayest thou understand, how thou oughtest to prepare thyself when thou goest about to look for and receive the same holy Ghost, albeit it be not in such plentiful and abundant wise as the Apostles was.[10] Hereby thou seest, how close shut thou oughtest to have the gates of thy understanding and will at the time of prayer from all the cares and thoughts of the world: and how open they ought then to be unto almighty God alone, in that case he come to enter therein, he return not back again, finding the gates shut against him, or the lodging taken up and pestered with other guests.

Now with this preparation and spirit mayest thou present thyself in prayer before the face of our Lord, as that sick man of the dropsy did, who stood before him expecting from his merciful hand to be restored unto his health:[11] or as that leprous person did, who kneeled down at his feet, and said humbly unto him. *O Lord if thou wilt thou canst make me clean.*[12] Consider that in like manner as a little hungry dog standeth before his master's table, fawning very earnestly upon him with his eyes, and all his whole body, looking ever for some little piece of bread to come from his table, and after the same sort oughtest thou to present thyself before the rich table of the Lord of heaven, confessing thyself to be unworthy of the whole abundance of his mercies, and desiring him most humbly to bestow some little portion thereof upon thee for thy relief. With this lowly spirit mayest thou say the psalm: *Ad te levavi oculos meos qui habitas in caelis, etc.*[13] The which albeit it be but short, yet it is very fit and convenient to stir up and enkindle this foresaid affection, in preparing thyself unto prayer.

This manner of preparation or the other thou mayest (gentle reader) use at thy liberty: but the first seemeth to be more convenient

10 See Acts 1–2.
11 See Luke 14.
12 Matt. 8:2; Mark 1:40.
13 Ps. 122.

for the night, when a man ought to examine his conscience, and desire pardon and forgiveness of almighty God, of all such defects, and offences, as he hath offended him in that day. And the second manner of preparation is most fit for the morning, when he riseth before the day break, to desire then of almighty God the assistance and succor of his grace, whereby he may the better bestow that day in his service.

But because to know how to pray as a man ought, is a very special gift of almighty God, and a work of the holy Ghost, therefore desire him most humbly both in the one preparation, and the other, to instruct thee how to do thy duty herein, and to give thee grace that thou mayest speak unto him in thy prayer with such attention, and devotion, with such recollection and closeness of mind, and with such fear, and reverence, as is behooveful to be used before so great a majesty: and withal desire him, that thou mayest in such wise persevere, and spend that little time in this exercise of prayer, that thou mayest in the end arise from the same with new force, and strength, to do all such things as appertain to his service.

It is thought also to be a good manner of preparation to say some vocal prayers before meditation: of which sort there be many in divers books of devotion, and namely in the meditations of St. Augustine, and in the Psalter of David, where there be some very devout Psalms that will help very much to enkindle and stir up devotion. For it is the property of devout sentences (being said with an earnest mind and attention) to wound the heart, and to lift it up unto almighty God: the which devout sentences are so much the more behooveful and necessary for us, by how much we find our spirit to be more cold, and distracted.

And these same prayers do serve much better for this purpose when they be in mitre, as are many Hymns of the Saints, and the Proses, and Versicles. Forsomuch as (I know not how it is, that) the words of God used in this kind of style, and harmony, do bring with them a greater sweetness, and delight to our souls. And therefore we find in the works of St. Bonaventure (who was a very devout holy man) many of these Hymns. The like we find in the works of St. Bernard, and in divers and sundry other of the holy fathers. Likewise there is great commendation given by many learned men (and surely not without good cause) to those three devout Hymns that Jeronimo de Vida made to the three persons in Trinity, which being learned by heart, and said devoutly, be as it were a most sweet Manna to sweeten the taste of our soul at the beginning of prayer, and to dispose it to take a delight in spiritual and divine matters.

Here I think it necessary to declare with what intention a man ought to come unto prayer. For he must not go thereunto chiefly for his own consolation, and delight, (as some that be great lovers of themselves use to do,) but only to fulfil herein the will of almighty God, and to desire of him his grace, and to dispose himself for the obtaining of the same. And herewith he must submit himself in such wise into the hands of almighty God, that he must be as ready and content to be without consolations in his prayer as to have them, remitting himself humbly into his hands, to dispose of him, and of all things belonging unto him, as he shall think good, acknowledging on the one side, that he deserveth not any thing of him, and believing on the other, that although it be so in very deed, yet our Lord of his infinite goodness and mercy will do whatsoever shall be most convenient and behooveful for his salvation. And therefore a man ought to content himself alike, whether the consolations be great, or little, and to take in good part whatsoever usage our Lord shall shew unto him, accounting himself utterly unworthy of all those things that he bestoweth upon him, and being ready to fulfil all such things as he shall command him, not in respect of the benefits he hopeth to receive, but in respect of them he hath already received, and in consideration of his bounden duty unto almighty God. But we see that many persons do quite contrary to this rule, and be like herein unto young shrewd boys, who unless they be dandled, and coerced, will not do the thing that they are commanded.

I think it also requisite here to advertise, that when a man mindeth to use the exercise of prayer in the morning, he do go to bed with this care over night: and like as those that intend to bake the next day, do use to lay the leaven over night, even so must a man with a godly carefulness prevent and recommend over night unto our Lord that thing which he intendeth to meditate the next day following. And in the morning so soon as he awaketh, he ought forthwith to occupy his heart with this holy thought, before any other do enter therein. For at that time the disposition of our heart is such, that whatsoever thought doth first enter into us, it seizeth and taketh possession of our heart in such wise, that we shall very hardly afterwards put it away from us.

And forsomuch as the prayer of many persons is very acceptable unto our Lord, therefore thou shalt do well to consider in thy prayer both in the morning, and evening, what a number of God's servants both men, and women, as well in Monasteries, as without, be at that time watching, and persevering before the presence of almighty God, shedding many devout tears, yea and perhaps also disciplining and whipping themselves, and shedding great abundance of blood for the love of God: with which persons thou oughtest humbly to join thyself, that the presence and sweet remembrance of them may be unto thee a provocation of devotion, and an example of perseverance in thy prayer, and also that whensoever thou shalt find thyself cold and negligent in this exercise of prayer, and that some thoughts come into thy mind moving thee to end the same, thou mayest be ashamed, and reprehend thyself, by the example of so many good and virtuous persons, which with so good attention and carefulness do persevere so long time in this exercise of prayer without ceasing, offering their bodies and souls unto almighty God in sacrifice.

II. Of Reading.

After Preparation followeth Reading: the which ought to be done, not lightly, as passed over in haste, but with very great deliberation, and attention: applying thereunto not only thy understanding, to conceive such things as thou readest, but much more thy will, to taste those things that thou understandest. And when thou comest to any devout place, thou shalt do well to stay and pause somewhat longer thereupon, and to make there as it were a station, in thinking upon that matter which thou hast read, and in making some short prayer upon it, according as St. Bernard counseleth us, saying: It is requisite often times to gather and procure a little spirit and devotion out of the matters that we read, and to break of the course of our reading with some kind of prayer, by means whereof we may lift up our heart unto almighty God, and talk with him, according as the sense and matter of such things as we read do require.

Here must I advertise, that the reading be not very long, least it occupy the greatest part of the time, that ought otherwise to be bestowed upon other more principal and necessary exercises. For as St. Augustine saith: It is very good both to read, and to pray, if we can do both the one, and the other: but in case we cannot perform them both, then prayer is better then reading. But because in prayer there is some times labor, and in reading a facility, therefore our miserable heart doth often times refuse the labor of prayer, and runneth to the delight of reading, as the same holy father complaining of himself saith that some times he hath so done.

True it is I grant, that like as when there wanteth wheaten bread, men do eat bread of rye, or of oats, because they would not be altogether fasting: even so when thy heart is in such wise distracted, that it can not enter into prayer, then mayest thou stay somewhat the longer in reading, or join meditation and reading together, by reading one place, and meditating upon it, and then an other, and an other, after the like sort. For by this mean when the understanding is once bound unto the words of the reading, it cannot so easily wander abroad into divers imaginations, and thoughts, as when it goeth freely, and at liberty. And yet better it were to wrestle all that time with Almighty God, as the Patriarch Jacob did, that in the end when the wrestling is done, he may give us his blessing, or grant unto us the devotion which we seek for, or some other greater grace, which he never denyeth unto them that do faithfully labor and strive for the love of him.[14]

---

14 See Gen. 32.

III. Of Meditation.

After Reading it followeth that we do meditate upon the place that we have read. Concerning which point it is to be known, that this meditation is sometimes upon things that may be figured with the imagination as are all the points of the life and passion of our Savior Christ. And some times again this meditation is upon things that do rather appertain to the understanding, than to the imagination: as when we think upon the benefits of almighty God, or upon his goodness, and mercy, or upon any other of his perfections. This manner of meditation is called INTELLECTUAL: and the other IMAGINARY: and we use both the one manner and the other in these exercises, according as the matter of the things doth require.

And therefore when the mystery whereupon we intend to meditate is of the life and passion of our Savior Christ, or of any other thing that may be figured with the imagination: as of the last day of Judgement, or of hell, or of Paradise, we must then figure and represent every one of these matters in our imagination, in such wise as it is, or in such wise as it passed, and make accompt, that even there in the very same place where we are, all the same passeth in our presence. And this manner of meditating serveth to this end, that by means of such a representation of these things, the consideration and feeling of them may be the more lively in us. Some there be, that imagine that every one of these things whereupon they meditate passeth within their own heart: for sithence our heart is able to contain within it the form of cities, and kingdoms, it is no great matter for it to contain also within it the representation and form of these mysteries. And this manner of meditating is commonly a great help also to keep in the mind more closely recollected, by causing it to attend to her work, after the manner of bees, which work their honey-combs within their own hives. Either of these two ways we may use in this kind of imaginary meditation. For in case we go with our cogitation to Jerusalem, to meditate the things that passed there each thing in his own proper place, it is a thing that doth commonly weaken and hurt the head.

And for this very cause likewise a man must not fix his imagination overmuch upon the things whereupon he meditateth. For besides that it wearieth the head, a man may also fall into some deceit by reason of this vehement apprehension, in persuading himself that he seeth the things really in very deed, which he imagineth with such vehemency, and force.

IV. Of Thanksgiving.

These three parts being ended, there may follow immediately a thanks-giving unto almighty God for the benefits we have received. And that we may not interrupt the course of our devotion with divers affections, and matters, a man may continue this part with the former, taking occasion of such things as he hath meditated upon, to give thanks unto our Lord for the benefit he hath done unto him in that meditation: and with this benefit to join also all other benefits, and to give him most humble and hearty thanks for them all. As for example, when we have ended our meditation upon any point of the passion, we may then forthwith give most humble thanks to our Lord for the benefit of our redemption: and especially for that it pleased him to redeem us with so great pains, and torments. And even then also let us give him most humble thanks for all his other benefits. In like manner, when we have meditated upon our sins, we may give him thanks for that he hath expected us so long time, and called us to do penance. And when we have meditated upon the miseries of this life, we may give him thanks for that he hath delivered us from a great number of them. And when we have meditated upon the departing out of this world, we may give him thanks for that he hath given us life, and granted unto us so long a time to do penance. And when we have meditated upon the glory of paradise, we may give him thanks for that he hath created us to be partakers of so great a felicity. And so likewise may we proceed in all the rest. And afterwards (according as we have declared) a man must join with this benefit all other benefits: as the benefits of creation, conservation, redemption, vocation, and glorification: of the which benefits we have treated heretofore in the meditation for Saturday at night. And then for these and other infinite benefits, as well public, as secret, we must give him as many humble and hearty thanks as we can, and call upon all creatures both of heaven and earth to help us herein. And with this spirit we may some times say that Canticle: *Benedicite omnia opera Domini Domino*:[15] or else the Psalm: *Benedic anima mea Domino, et omnia quae intra me sunt, etc.*[16]

V. Of Petition.

Now it remaineth that we do treat of the last part of all, which is petition: which containeth in it two parts: in the one part, we make petition unto almighty God for our neighbors: and in the other, for ourselves.

The first part may be continued with thanks giving, desiring that all creatures may serve and praise our Lord, who is so worthy to be praised, and served, for that he is so merciful and bountiful unto all his creatures. And with this affection and desire of the glory of almighty God, let him pray first and principally for all the universal world, that all nations and people may know and serve so mighty a Lord. Then for all the Catholic Church, and for all the governors in the same. As for example, we must pray for the Pope, and for all the Cardinals, Archbishops, Bishops, and for all other inferior Prelates, Pastors, and Curates: that they may be careful of their duty in directing all the faithful in the knowledge and service of their Creator.

Likewise let him pray for all the members of the Catholic Church: For the just persons, that it may please almighty God to continue them in their virtuous life: For sinners, that it may please him to pardon them: And for the souls departed out of this world, that it may please him to deliver them out of the grievous pains of Purgatory, and bring them to rest of life everlasting. Let him pray also for his parents, and for his godfathers, and godmothers, and for

---

15 Dan. 3:57–88, 56.

16 Ps. 102.

his ghostly father, and for all his kinsfolk, friends, and benefactors, and for all that be in tribulation, and captivity, and for all prisoners, and sick persons, unto whom he may (without any distraction or intermission of his prayer) do the works of mercy, in recommending them unto almighty God who created them, and referring the necessities of all persons into those hands, which were stretched upon the cross for them all.

After this, he may desire such things for himself, as he perceiveth himself to stand in need of, according to the particular necessities and miseries that he feeleth in his soul, and especially when he desireth help and remedy of almighty God against such vices, and passions, as do most trouble and molest him, and to grant him such virtues as be most needful for him. This kind of petition (among other commodities) hath this withal, that it reneweth daily in the soul good purposes, and desires of virtues, and moveth it to be the more earnest in doing that thing, which he hath so often times and so heartly desired, and it maketh him to be the more ashamed of himself when he doth it not, by calling to mind with how great desire and instancy he hath desired our Lord to grant him grace to do it. And of this mind is St. Chrysostom, where he saith thus: *Such as pray earnestly in very deed will not suffer their heart to commit any thing that is unseemly for such an exercise, but have ever their eye upon almighty God, with whom a little before they talked, and were conversant. And so by that cogitation they put away from them all the suggestions of the devil, when they think and consider what a heinous matter it were, that he who had a little before talked with almighty God, and desired of him chastity, and holiness, with all other virtues, should immediately run to his enemies side, and open the gate of his soul to receive in filthy and dishonest delights, and suffer the devil to place himself in that heart, where a little before the holy Ghost made his abode.*

But it is very much to be lamented, that there be some persons that think to excuse themselves, by saying, that they know not what thing to desire of almighty God. Surely, this is no sufficient excuse. For what beast is so insensible, but that he knoweth some manner of way how to signify the need he standeth in? What sick man is there, that can not say, here it grieveth me? Consider therefore (O man) thyself. Consider (I say) with what vices and passions thou art most troubled, and molested: If with covetousness, if with anger, if with detraction, if with vain glory, if with stubbornness of thine own will, if with looseness of tongue, if with lightness of heart, if with the love of honor, estimation, and delights, if with inconstancy in such good purposes as thou intendest, if with self love, or any other the like passions, and pestilences of the mind, and discover all these wounds plainly, one by one, unto that heavenly physician, that he may heal and cure them with the ointment of his grace.

After that thou hast demanded remedy against thy vices, desire him then to grant thee all such virtues as be most behooveful for thy salvation. And because this is a principal part of this exercise of prayer, wherein often times is spent all the time thereof, with very great taste, and profit, I think it good to note here unto the devout reader those principal virtues which be as it were the pillars of the spiritual life, that thou mayest always long and sigh for them, and always desire them very instantly of our Lord in thy prayer.

§. I. Of the Most Necessary Virtues, That Are to Be Demanded In Petition.

First thou must desire of our Lord these four virtues, which be as it were the foundation of all the spiritual life: the which virtues we must always have before our eyes, because they be always necessary in all the steps of our life.

These virtues be a comely composition of the inward and outward man: discretion, and attention in all such things as we shall either do, or say, that every thing may be directed according to the judgement and order of reason: and withal to bridle our tongue, and to take a due accompt of it: and to use rigor, and austerity in the government of our person. Now among these virtues we have put the comely composition of the inward and outward man in the first place: because it is the beginning, that disposeth unto all the others.

The composition of the inward man consisteth in having almighty God present in his heart: And the composition of the outward man consisteth in doing all things in such sort, as is seemly for one that is always in the presence of almighty God, and that hath him always before his eyes, as the judge and witness of his whole life.

After these do follow other four virtues, wherein consisteth the sum of perfection, which virtues be in such wise annexed and linked the one to the other, that the one can not be had without the other. These virtues be perfect obedience: Mortification of our own proper will: Fortitude to overcome all manner of difficulty, and labor: and to have a hatred and contempt of ourselves. For it is manifest that the sum of all Christian doctrine is a perfect obedience and conformity unto the will of almighty God, as well in all such things as he commandeth, counseleth, and inspireth, as in all that he ordaineth, and disposeth, concerning us. This obedience can not be kept unless we have a knife in our hand, to cut away all the inordinate appetites of our sensuality, and will, which do withstand the will of almighty God. But this stroke no man is able to give, unless he have great fortitude of mind to fight with himself, and to make mortal war against his own inclinations, and appetites. And this kind of war none other shall ever make, but he that hath for the love of God attained to have a true and holy abhorring and contempt of himself. For look where abhorring is, there doth easily follow evil entreating and contempt of the thing that is abhorred: but where is nothing but love, there doth a man very unwillingly take the whip in his hand, to deal roughly with that thing which he loveth. Whereby it appeareth, that no one of these virtues is able to move one step, without the help and succor of the others.

After these do follow immediately other four very high and noble virtues, which be, Humility both inward, and outward: Poverty both of spirit, and of body: Patience in all adversities, and tribulations: Pureness of intention in good works, doing all things that we shall do all only for the love of God, without mixture of any commodity, or respect, either temporal, or spiritual.

After these do follow other four virtues: which are the beginning and end of all perfection: to wit: a most firm faith of such things, as almighty God saith, and promiseth: and an assured hope in him, as in our true and loving father in all the necessities and tribulations that shall happen unto us: a love of almighty God, which must always burn in our hearts: and jointly with this love, to have a fear and reverence of his great majesty, and justice, which must evermore accompany all our works.

And with all this aforesaid we must join perseverance and continuance in the exercise of all these virtues, the which causeth a man in a small time to attain to the top of perfection. In these foresaid virtues doth the sum of all perfection principally consist: and therefore all our study, and diligence, must be employed in seeking them by all means possible, and especially by prayer, which is the principal mean, whereby all goodness is obtained.

Here I think good to give this advice, that when a man shall demand of almighty God any of these virtues, he stay himself therein for a time, and make as it were a station in every one of them, in considering briefly the principal motives that may most induce us to the love and exercise of such a virtue. As for example. When we shall desire of almighty God the virtue of charity, which is the love of God, we may say in this wise: Grant me grace O Lord I beseech thee, that I may love thee with all my heart, and with all my soul, for that thou art an infinite goodness, and excellency, that deserveth to be loved with infinite love: and besides this, for that thou art my only benefactor, my father, my creator, my last end, and the spouse of my soul, unto whom all love is due. In the like manner when thou shalt desire the virtue of hope, thou mayest say in this wise: Give me grace also O Lord I beseech thee, that in all the necessities and tribulations that shall happen unto me in this life, I may trust in thee, seeing thy mercy is infinite, and thy promises true, and the merits of thy only begotten son be of infinite value, which do speak and make intercession for me. After this sort mayest thou desire the fear of God, and humility, with other virtues. The form of which petitions

I think not meet to note here particularly in writing. For like as it is said, that that meat doth more profit the sick man, which he himself eateth and cheweth with his teeth, than that which is given unto him in drink: even so is that prayer wont to be more profitable which is framed by him that prayeth with such words as the holy Ghost teacheth him, than that prayer which is made and compounded with other folks words, which often times be said and passed very lightly over, without any manner of attention, or affection.

This last part which is petition (besides that it is very easy to be done) is also very profitable. For (as we said before) it is not only an exercise of prayer, but also of all virtues, and as it were a reading and conference of them all: wherein a man reneweth all his good purposes, and desires, and recordeth in his memory the principal points and articles of the law of God, which is the continual exercise of the just man: of whom it is said, that he meditateth upon the law of our Lord both day, and night.[17]

These five parts aforesaid may be used in the exercise of prayer: albeit (as we have said) they be not all necessary to be used at all times. For some times all the time of prayer is spent in meditation alone, or in petition. Nevertheless I thought good to specify here all these parts of prayer, that no man might leave of this holy exercise for want of matter, and also that at such time as devotion faileth, (which is no just cause why we should relent and withdraw ourselves from good exercises) a man might have matter whereupon to occupy himself during that time, doing on his part so much as lieth in him, which is the thing that almighty God requireth principally of us.

Here is diligently to be noted, that among all these five parts of prayer, the best is, when the soul talketh with almighty God, as it doth in petition. For in reading, or meditation, the understanding discourseth with little labor wheresoever it thinketh good. But when we talk unto almighty God, then the understanding mounteth up on high, and after it followeth also the will, and then hath a man commonly on his part greater devotion, and attention, and greater fear,

17 See Ps. 1:2.

and reverence of the majesty of almighty God, with whom he speaketh, and withal an humble, and fervent desire of the thing which he demandeth of him. And this moving, and lifting up of the spirit, with all these acts of virtues accompanying it, do leave the soul in a more noble state, and better edified, than any other discourse whatsoever it be, as every man may perceive by experience in himself. For it is evident, that in the discourse of meditation there is none other thing but only a godly inquisition and consideration of spiritual things, the which as it is an act of the understanding, so is it of little profit, or commodity: but in the devout prayer there is made a concurrence and general assembly in a manner of all virtues, and with there wings the soul lifteth itself up on high, and attaineth to be joined and united with almighty God.

And although this spiritual communication and conference with almighty God be the best point of all the exercises of prayer, yet among all the communications with him, the best and most profitable is the communication of love, at such time as we be actually loving of almighty God, and praising him, and desiring him with great instancy, and most earnest desires, to grant us that we may love him. For sithence Charity is the greatest of all virtues, there is nothing more acceptable unto almighty God, nor more pleasant and profitable to a man, than the use, practice, and exercise of this so excellent a virtue.

This the holy fathers do call the exercise of aspiring unto the love of God. And to this end were meditation and prayer, and all other good exercises ordained. And therefore it is given for a general rule unto all such as do pray, that they labor and endeavor so much as lieth in them to lift up their spirit unto this divine communication, which is to speak and treat with almighty God himself, and especially concerning his love, and the exercises of aspiring unto him. And for this cause it shall do well to leave this petition of the love of God until the end of all the exercise of prayer, and so to reserve the best wine for the end of this banquet, to the intent that when a man is come to the end of his journey, he may stay himself herein so long as he listeth. Howbeit it shall not be amiss both to begin and end with this petition of the love of God, whensoever the holy Ghost shall open him a way, and direct him unto the same.

Moreover, I think it meet here to give this advertisement, that in all such things as we shall demand, we do allege always in our behalf the merits of Jesus Christ our only and true Savior: who (as the Apostle saith) *Is our justice, wisdom, sanctification, and redemption.*[18] Upon his merits we ought principally to stay our confidence. And his merits we ought to present before the divine majesty, reckoning them, and offering them one by one unto the heavenly father, and taking (as St. Bernard saith) out of that treasure all such things as are necessary for us. For this is that Lord, that hath sanctified and offered himself in sacrifice, to the intent that we might be holy in deed. Wherefore *If God be for us, who shall be against us?* If God justify us, who shall condemn us? This is he (saith St. Peter) of whom all the Prophets bear witness: that by him is obtained pardon and remission of sins. So that in the virtue and name of this Lord we ought to take a good heart and courage with us, when we go to make our prayers to almighty God, and have this confidence, that whatsoever we shall duly demand by him shall be granted unto us. For the principal condition that our petition must have that it may be effectual before almighty God, is (as St. James saith) to make the same with faith, and confidence.[19] And this confidence must not be grounded principally upon our own selves, nor upon our own works, and merits, but upon the works and merits of our Savior Jesus Christ, and jointly therewith upon the infinite goodness and mercy of almighty God, which can never be overcome with any kind of sin, or iniquity: and besides this, our confidence must be also grounded upon the truth of the words and promises of almighty God, who hath promised in all the holy scriptures never to fail that man that with all his heart shall convert himself unto him, and call upon him, and repose his trust and confidence in him. And albeit he that prayeth hath been until that

[18] 1 Cor. 1:30.
[19] See Jas. 1:6.

time never so great and heinous a sinner, yet let him not therefore be dismayed: for (as St. Jerome saith) our sins past do not condemn us, if we take no delight in them. Whereby it appeareth, that they be deceived, that in considering their own defects, and weaknesses, do mistrust that almighty God will not hear them: and they do not consider that the principal foundations of this confidence are the merits of our Savior Christ, and the mercy of almighty God, and the truth of his holy word, which (as the Prophet saith) is a shield unto them that put their trust in him.[20]

---

20 See 2 Kgs. 22:31.

The Third Chapter

CERTAIN ADVICES TO BE OBSERVED IN THESE FIVE PARTS ABOVE NAMED. AND ESPECIALLY IN MEDITATION

HAVING now spoken of the principal parts of prayer, I think it convenient to give certain advices, and instructions, which ought to be observed in them all, and especially in meditation, whereof we mind to treat principally in this place.

§. I. The First Advice: That in Our Meditation We Must Not for the Observing of Our Ordinary Course Put away from Us Any Other Good Thought, or Consideration, Wherein We Find More Devotion.

The first advice is (concerning the matter of meditation) that although it be well done for a man to observe these special points of meditation, according as they be here before divided by the days of the week, for to exercise himself in them: yet if in the midst of his way there be offered unto him any other consideration, wherein he findeth more sweetness, or profit, he ought not to put the same away from him to fulfil his ordinary task. For it standeth not with reason, that we should extinguish the light which the holy Ghost hath begun to give us in any good thought, for to occupy ourselves in an other thought, wherein perhaps the same light shall not be given unto us. And besides this, sith the principal end of these meditations is to obtain some devotion, and feeling of divine things, it were against reason, when we have already obtained the same with some good consideration, that we should go about to seek for it by an other way. Howbeit although this be very true (speaking ordinarily,) yet may not a man therefore take herein so great liberty, as upon every occasion that is offered unto him, to be moved forthwith very lightly to forego that thing out of his hands, which he hath as it were in possession, for some other thing which he is desirous to have: unless it be at such a time, as he perceiveth a more certain profit in the one, than in the other.

§. II. The Second Advice: That in Our Meditation We Must Eschew the Superfluous Speculation of Our Understanding, and Commit This Business to the Exercise of the Affections of Our Will.

The second advice is, that he labor to eschew in this exercise the superfluous speculation of the understanding and endeavor to use this matter rather with affections, and feelings of the will, than with discourses and speculations of the understanding.

It is therefore to be noted, that the understanding on the one side helpeth, and on the other side it may hinder the operation of the will: to wit, the love, and feeling of divine things. For as it is necessary that the understanding do go before the will to guide it, and give it knowledge what it ought to love: so when the speculation of the understanding is overmuch, then it hindereth this operation of the will: forsomuch as it suffereth it not to have place and time to work. And therefore like as it is said of the poison which is put into treacle, that if it be little it is wholesome, and necessary, but if it be overmuch it is hurtful: even so likewise may we say after a sort in this exercise, that the seeking to know God with simplicity helpeth the will the more to love him, but the seeking to know him with overmuch speculation hindereth the will, and causeth the operation thereof for that time to be the more feeble, and weak. And the reason hereof is, for that the virtue and power of our soul being finite and straited within certain bounds, and limits, the more it employeth her virtue and force on the one part, the less remaineth to be employed on the other: even like the fountain that runneth through two pipes, the more water that it dischargeth by the one pipe, the less it hath to yield through the other. And after the like sort doth the soul principally by the operation of the understanding, by the which (for that it is so noble and so excellent a power) the soul employeth and poureth out all her whole force in such wise, that in a manner she worketh nothing at all by her other powers, at such time as the understanding is very attent and earnestly occupied in the vehement speculation of any matter. And therefore we find by experience, that a man may with more facility preserve the affection of devotion in any exercise of the body wherein he laboreth with his hands, than when he hath his understanding busily occupied and attent in the speculation of any matter. For the understanding and the will be as it were two balances of our soul, the which are disposed in such sort, that the ascending of the one is the descending of the other, and so contrariwise. So that if the speculation do increase overmuch, then the affection thereby decreaseth: and if contrariwise the affection do increase, then the speculation forthwith decreaseth. And this is the cause why the Patriarch Jacob was made lame of one of his feet at what time he received benediction:[1] for whereas our soul hath two feet wherewith to go unto almighty God, which be the understanding, and the will, it is requisite that the one foot be weakened, to wit, the understanding in his speculation, if the will which is the other foot shall enjoy almighty God in the rest and quietness of contemplation. And so it is seen by experience, that in case at such time as the soul is enjoining of almighty God, it do but turn a-side to

1 See Gen. 32.

seek to understand or search some point or matter appertaining unto God, it loseth forthwith at the very same instant the devotion which it had, and that sovereign good thing vanisheth then away from him which before he enjoyed. And therefore not without good cause doth the bridegroom advise the spouse in the Canticles, saying: *Turn away thine eyes from me, for they have made me to fly.*[2] Wherefore I counsel a man in this exercise of meditation to occupy his understanding in speculation with as little curiosity as is possible, and to content himself with a simple sight and knowledge of divine things, to the intent that the virtue of his soul recollecting all her forces together, may employ herself by this affective part, (I mean, by the affections of the will) in loving and reverencing the chiefest goodness: to wit, almighty God.

Whereby it appeareth, that those men take not the right course herein, that in prayer do meditate in such wise upon divine mysteries, as if they should study to preach them: the which disorderly manner is rather to cause the Spirit to wander more abroad than to recollect it: and rather to go out of himself, than to keep within himself. And hereof it cometh, that when they have made an end of their exercise of prayer, they remain as dry, and without any joice of devotion, and as easily moved to follow every kind of lightness, and vanity of the world, as they were before their exercise. For (to speak the very truth) they have not prayed, but rather talked and studied, which is a thing far differing from prayer. Such persons ought to consider, that in this exercise of prayer and meditation we rather come to hear, than to speak. For (as the Prophet saith) *Such as come to our Lord's feet shall receive his doctrine:*[3] as he received it, that said: *I will hearken, what our Lord speaketh within me.*[4] Wherefore I conclude, that all this business of meditation consisteth in speaking little, and in loving much, and in giving place to the will, that it may join itself with all his forces unto almighty God. And we must not spur forwards these two powers of the soul a-like, nor walk in this way with equal paces: but a

2 Cant. 6:4.
3 Deut. 33:3.
4 Ps. 84:9.

special dexterity is requisite to be used to stir up the will, and to quiet the understanding, that it hinder not with his curious discourses the operations of love. And thou must make accompt that in this exercise thou goest in a chariot drawn with two horses, whereof the one is very forward, and quick, and the other very slow, and dull: and that thou must bear the bridles in thy hand with such dexterity, that the one thou must hasten forward, and hold the other back, that so they may go together the one by the other.

And if thou desire to have an other more lively example, make accompt that the understanding must behave itself towards the will, as the nurse doth towards the child which she nurseth, who after that she hath chewed the meat, she then putteth it into the child's mouth, that the child may taste and feed thereupon. For otherwise if the nurse should both chew the meat, and also eat it up herself, leaving the child without any meat, it is certain that she should do great injury to the child, in suffering it to die for hunger, by eating up that meat which was given unto her for the child. Now in this wise must the understanding behave itself towards the will in the exercise of prayer: for it appertaineth to the understanding to chew the spiritual matters, as the nurse cheweth the meat for the child, but the understanding must not retain the same spiritual matters for itself alone, but after that it hath once chewed them, it must offer them to the will, to the intent that the will may taste and feed thereupon, and be the more enkindled and confirmed in virtue, and goodness, with the taste and feeling of those spiritual matters.

The victuals that do enter in by the gates of a city ought to pay only a tribute, and import: but in case the porter should take up all the victuals for himself alone, and suffer none to come to the market, it is certain that the inhabitants of the city would die for hunger. Now in like manner, if the understanding which is as it were the first gate of our soul, (whereby the spiritual sustenance entereth unto it) do take up all that should pass by it for itself alone, in what case shall the will then be, but even very hungry, and dry, and in great necessity of all virtue, and goodness?

The hunting hound if he be good, will not eat the hare that he hath taken, but keepeth it faithfully until his master's coming: and in like manner ought our understanding to do, when it hath found out any high and secret truths: forsomuch as it must not retain all for itself alone, but reason would that it should assign them over to the will, that she as the mistress in this behalf may serve herself with them. And for this respect divers devout and simple persons are truly very happy, who as they know little, so when they come unto almighty God, they are little hindered with the discourses of their understanding, and therefore in their prayers and meditations they find their wills more tender, and more pliant, and better prepared unto every godly affection.

Now if thou desire to know how thou shouldest behave thyself herein, among many other ways that may serve in this case, thou mayest use this: In every good thing that thou shalt think upon either in prayer, or out of prayer, be careful to go out of hand therewith unto almighty God, as the young child doth, who with every thing that he findeth goeth out of hand to his mother, and tattleth with her of it. And so in like manner when in thy prayer or at other times thou findest any spiritual jewel, thou must lift up thine heart to almighty God, either to love him, or to adore him, or to reverence him, or to praise him for the same, according as the matter requireth: and thereby also to take occasion to humble thyself before him, and to desire of him his grace. It shall be a great help also hereunto to have the spirit of true humility, which causeth a man to appear before almighty God very poor, and naked, and to prostrate himself before that most high sovereign majesty, and to be more careful to desire him of his mercy for the curing of the great miseries which he knoweth in himself, than to search the profoundness of his high mysteries to understand them. And by so doing he cometh to be in the presence of almighty God, as a malefactor that is condemned to death would be when he should enter into the king's palace to ask him pardon: who would go with such a great and deep impression of his misery, that he would scarcely have either eyes to see, or heart to think upon any other thing but only upon his own present danger.

§. III. The Third Advice: Which Prescribeth Also Bounds and Limits to the Will, That It Be Neither Too Excessive, nor Too Vehement in Her Exercise.

The former advice teacheth us how we ought to quiet our understanding, and commit all this business to our will: but this present advice prescribeth also bounds, and limits to the will, that it be neither too excessive, nor to vehement in her exercise. Wherefore ye must understand, that the devotion which we seek to obtain, is not a thing that may be gotten with force of arms (as some persons think,) who lay on great lode of enforced sighings, and sobbings, imagining thereby to procure tears, and compassion, when they think upon the passion of our Savior. For such force doth commonly cause the heart to become more dry, and more unable to receive our Lord's visitation, according as the holy father Cassianus affirmeth. Moreover it doth commonly prejudice and hurt the health of the body, yea and some times leaveth the soul so astonied, and aghast, by reason of the little taste she hath there received, that she is loath to return again to this exercise, as to a thing which she hath tried by experience to have been very painful and irksome unto her. And therefore if our Lord shall send us tears or other the like feelings in our prayer, we ought humbly to accept them, and to give him thanks for them. But for a man to wring them out as it were with force of arms, it is no wisdom. He must content himself with doing sincerely what lieth in him: that is, he must suppose himself to be present at such grievous torments as our Savior hath suffered, beholding with a sincere and quiet eye, as well such pains as he hath suffered, as also the love and charity, that moved him to suffer them. And when he hath thus done, let him not vex nor trouble himself any further, though our Lord send him not tears and compunction of heart.

And he that can not thus do, but shall perceive himself to be overmuch troubled in his exercise, let him not strive to pass forwards, but let him humble himself before almighty God with inward quietness, and simplicity, and desire him of his grace, that he may be able to proceed in his prayer and meditation without such great trouble and danger unto him. And in case it shall please our Lord to grant him this quietness of mind, he shall feel a more inward hearty devotion thereby, than he was wont to feel with the disquietness of his mind, and it shall endure much longer. After this sort may a man continue in prayer and meditation a long time together, without feeling any heaviness, or grief: but that man can not so do, that shall meditate after the other enforced manner before specified.

And for this cause we must take diligent heed, that if at any time there do arise in the soul very fervent motions of sensible devotion, or excessive sobbings, and sighings, we suffer not ourselves to be carried away with them, but we must temper them with great moderation, and dissemble them as much as we can, and withal endeavor to keep and continue that consideration and thought within us, which caused those fervent motions: I mean hereby, that we must remove away from us those storms and alterations of the flesh: to wit, these vehement sobbings, and sighings, and enjoy in our soul with quietness the light, and devotion, which almighty God hath sent unto us. And after this sort we shall continue in our exercise a longer time, and our consolation shall take deeper root inwardly in our souls, and shall not give any outward shew thereof with weeping, sobbing, and other external signs, which can hardly be avoided without great pain, in case a man do once accustom himself very much unto such sensible motions, and fervors, which the stronger and mightier they shew outwardly, the more do they quench the light inwardly, and be an impediment unto us that we can not proceed forward in our prayer, and meditation.

True it is, that at the first beginning of novices in spiritual exercises such fervors can very hardly be eschewed. For then the great wonder that a man hath of the newness and profoundness of divine things, maketh him to enter into so great an admiration, and astonishment, that he can not refrain himself from this fervency. But after that with the use of daily meditation of divine things the newness of them ceaseth, then is his heart quieted, and although he love almighty

God with greater vehemency, yet hath he not such sensible fervor and disquietness in his love. And so we see, that the new wine, and the pot of water when it beginneth first to try the unwonted heat of the fire, it boileth so forcibly, that it bubbleth up, and runneth over the brim: but after that it hath boiled a certain space, it ceaseth then much better, and is much hotter, and yet with less noise, and vehemency. That man which was lame from his mother's womb, whom St. Peter healed, (as it is declared in the acts of the Apostles,) so soon as he perceived himself to be whole and perfectly cured of his former lameness, the holy Scripture saith, that he walked, and leaped, and praised almighty God.[5] This man was not content only to go, but as one that had been so long time as it were bound hands and feet, and finding by experience his new liberty, he then stretched forth his limbs to the uttermost he could, and leaped, and skipped with great joy, and admiration. Howbeit it is to be thought, that afterwards he would walk more quietly, and not leap and skip all his life time: but as then the great joy he had of his new and unaccustomed health would not suffer him to be in quiet.

§. IV. The Fourth Advice: Which Followeth of the Foresaid Advices: And Here It Is Declared What Manner of Attention We Ought to Have in Our Exercise of Prayer and Meditation.

Of all these advices aforesaid we may gather what manner of attention we ought to have in prayer. For in this exercise it is chiefly expedient for us to have our heart, not heavy, nor dull, but lively, attent, and lifted up on high. In figure whereof we read that the Angel said to the Prophet Ezechiel, that he should arise, and stand upon his feet, when the Angel would talk with him, and declare unto him the divine mysteries.[6] In like manner we read, that those two Cherubins which Salomon placed at the two sides of the Ark of the testament,

5 See Acts 3:8.
6 See Ezech. 2:1.

stood with their wings lifted up on high, and stretched abroad, as if they would fly, to signify what a great attention and lifting up of the spirit a man ought to have at such time as he presenteth himself before almighty God, to speak and stand before him.[7]

But it is necessary on the one side to be in prayer with such an attention, and close recollection of the mind, even so on the other side it behooveth that this attention be qualified with temperance, and moderation, that it be neither prejudicial to our health, nor any impediment to devotion. For some there be, that do weary their heads with overmuch violence, whiles they labor to be attent unto those things, that they meditate upon. And others again there be, that to avoid this inconvenience, are in their meditation very slack, and negligent, and very easy to be carried away with every wind. Now to eschew these two extremities, it is expedient that we use such a mean, that we do neither with overmuch attention weary our head, nor with carelessness, or negligence suffer our thoughts to go wandering whither so ever they will. So that like as we use commonly to say unto him that rideth upon a kicking flinging horse, that he must take good heed how he holdeth the reins of his bridle, and keep a mean therein, that is, he must hold them neither too hard, nor too slack, that the horse neither turn backward, nor run to headlong forward: even so must we endeavor that our attention may proceed in our prayers with moderation, and not with violence, and with a temperate carefulness, and diligence, and not with excessive labor, and travail. Of both these points we be advertised in the holy Scripture. For of the one Salomon saith: Who so squeezeth overmuch the paps to get out milk, shall wring out blood.[8] And of the other point the Prophet Isaias saith: Rejoice with her all ye that mourn for her, that ye may suck, and be satisfied with the breasts of her consolation.[9]

Howbeit in case we fail of the mean, and do lean unto any of these two extremities, it is less hurt to lean unto overmuch attention,

---

7 See 3 Kgs. 6.
8 See Prov. 30:33.
9 Is. 66:10–11.

than unto carelessness, and neglecting of our attention. For a man is provoked to carelessness and negligence by his own corrupt and evil inclined nature: but he is not so provoked unto attention. And therefore like as a house that is built upon the side of a hill should not loose much in the building, if at such time as it can not be built by line and level just upright, the building thereof do more bend rather upward, than downward: even so shall not our attention take any prejudice, if at what time it cannot continue in our prayers in such a mediocrity as we desire, it do rather decline to that extremity wherein is least danger, which is (as we have said) rather to overmuch attention, than to carelessness, and negligence.

This advice is of so great importance, that for want hereof we have seen that certain persons have passed over many years with taking little profit by their prayers, for that they have been careless, dull, and as it were neither hot nor cold therein. And others contrariwise have fallen into great sickness, and have hurt their heads with overmuch heat, and vehemency, which they have used in their meditations. But especially we must be well wary, that at the beginning of meditation we do not trouble and weary our head with overmuch attention. For by so doing we shall want force and strength to pass forwards therein: as it commonly happeneth to the traveler, when he maketh to great haste in his going at the beginning of his journey.

§. V. The Fifth Advice: That We Must Not Be Dismayed, nor Give Over Our Exercise of Prayer, and Meditation, at Such Time as We Want Devotion Therein.

But among all these advices the principal is, that he that prayeth be not dismayed, nor give over his exercise, when he feeleth not forthwith such sweetness of devotion, as he desireth: as some persons use to do, who are very much deceived herein. Wherefore it is to be noted, that in very deed the heart of man is very like unto a troubled water, which can not suddenly be cleared again, be the diligence never so great that is bestowed about it, but it must have time, and space, to be cleared, and settled by little, and little. And in such case undoubtedly is our heart, which as it is wont to be troubled with the daily intermeddling and dealing in worldly affairs, so after that it is once troubled, it can not forthwith be settled and quieted in so short a space again, but it must needs have convenient space and time for the same. And therefore Ecclesiastes saith very well: *That the end of prayer is better than the beginning*:[10] because at the beginning of prayer the heart is troubled, and disquieted, but in the end it is more settled, and quieted, and better disposed unto this holy exercise.

Wherefore like as he that will enkindle a fire in green wood, must have patience, and expect until the wood be dried by little, and little, and besides all this, it is requisite, that he continue for a time in blowing and enkindling it, and do shed also some tears with the smoke, if he will enjoy the fire according to his desire: even so it behooveth us often times to labor and persevere in the beginning of prayer, in case we will in the end enjoy the sweet and clear fire of devotion, and of the love of God.

Now for this cause it is requisite for him that prayeth, to expect the coming of our Lord with longanimity, and perseverance. For it is very convenient, as well in respect of the glory of his high divine majesty, and baseness of our condition, as also for the greatness and importance of the affairs we have in hand, that we do often times attend and watch at the gates of his sacred palace. *Blessed is the man* (saith the everlasting wisdom) *that heareth my words, and watcheth daily at my gates, and tarrieth at the porch of my house, for who so shall find me, shall find life, and he shall receive salvation of our Lord.*[11] And the Prophet Jeremias saith, *It is good to expect the salvation of our Lord God with silence.*[12]

The proud man and he that mistrusteth the promises of almighty God hath neither patience nor humility to expect our Lord's coming:

---

10 Eccles. 7:9.
11 Prov. 8:34–35.
12 Lam. 3:26.

but the humble man saith (with the Prophet:) I expected again, and again for our Lord, and he heard my prayer.[13] If the fisher or hunter have not patience to expect for the game that he seeketh, what profit shall he get by his travail? Now in this our fishing and hunting in prayer, being of so great importance as it is, we may account a long time well bestowed, that is employed in watching and expecting for so rich and so happy a treasure, as is almighty God.

Of that courageous and constant woman which Salomon describeth in his Proverbs (among other notable things) he saith thus: *That she did as the merchants ship, that brought his bread from far countries.*[14] Whereby he giveth us to understand, that when we shall not find this bread of life forthwith according to our desire, we must then travail and sail so long time, as shall be necessary until we find it. If thou shalt persevere in calling, (saith our Savior) assure thyself that at the length thou shalt have answer.[15] For it happeneth often times that that thing which is denied in the beginning of prayer, is granted at the end of prayer with great increase.

I have understood for a certain truth of a religious father that persevered for the space of three years in these good exercises, using daily to bestow in prayer and meditation after matins two or three hours, and could get none other fruit thereby but dryness of heart, until such time as our Lord considering the affliction of his soul, poured upon him the bountifulness of his goodness with such an abundant benediction of graces, that he was very well recompensed for all the barrenness of the other years past. And the like is proved daily by experience in many other devout persons. Happy therefore are those souls, that persevere in prayer after this sort: for undoubtedly the greater their perseverance is, the greater abundance shall they have of his grace. One of the principal things that those persons must have that do dispose themselves to receive great gifts and favors of almighty God is longanimity and patience of heart, to expect faithfully so long time

---

13 See Ps. 39:2.

14 Prov. 31:14.

15 See Matt. 7; Mark 11; Luke 11.

for them as almighty God would they should expect: and in the mean season to comfort themselves with that hope of the Prophet, which saith: If he shall delay his coming, I will not fail to tarry for him, for he will surely come, and will not stay over long.[16]

Now when thou hast after this sort expected a certain time for our Lord's coming, in case our Lord shall then come unto thee, give him most hearty thanks for his coming: and if it seem unto thee that he cometh not, humble thyself then before him, and acknowledge that thou art not worthy to receive that thing which he giveth not unto thee: and let this content thee for that time, that thou hast made a sacrifice of thyself, denied thine own will, crucified thy appetite, strived with the devil, and with thyself, and done at the least what thou couldest for thine own part. And in case thou have not adored our Lord with sensible adoration according to thy desire, it is sufficient that thou hast adored him in spirit, and in truth, according as his will is to be adored.[17] And trust me assuredly in this point, that this is the most dangerous passage of all this navigation, and the place where true devout persons are proved, and tried: and that if thou escape well out of this danger, thou shalt have prosperous success in all the rest.

To conclude, if all this notwithstanding it seem unto thee, that it were but time lost to persevere in prayer, and to trouble and weary they head without any profit, in such a case I accompt it not any inconvenience, if when thou hast done what lieth in thee, thou take then some devout book, and change for that time thy prayer into reading: Howbeit with this condition, that thy reading be not passed over with too great haste, or speed, but leisurely, and with great attention and consideration unto such things as thou dost read, and intermingle now and then in places convenient prayer with reading, which is a thing both very profitable, and very easily to be done by all kind of persons, be they never so rude, and newly entered into this way.

---

16 See Hab. 2:3.

17 See John 4:23.

§. VI. The Sixth Advice: That We Must Endeavor to Have a Long and Profound Prayer, and Great Abundance of Devotion.

An other advice there is not much differing from this aforesaid, nor of less necessity than it: which is, that the servant of God do not content himself with every little taste he findeth in his prayer, as some persons use to do, who when they shed a few tears, or feel a little tenderness of heart, persuade themselves forthwith that they have then accomplished and performed their exercise. But surely this is not enough for the obtaining of that thing, which we here seek to have. For like as a little dew, or sprinkling of water is not sufficient to cause the earth to bring forth fruit, (which doth no more but only allay the dust, and wet the uppermost part of the ground) but it is needful also to have so great abundance of water, that it may enter into the innermost part of the earth, and there soak and water through the same: even so if we will have our soul to bring forth the fruits of virtues, and good works, it is not sufficient to have that little dew and sprinkling of devotion, which at the turning of the head is dried up with the least blast of wind or heat of sun that cometh, (with the which the soul maketh some outward appearance that it is devout, but in very deed it is not so within,) but it is also requisite to have a long profound prayer, and great devotion, which after the manner of a great shower of rain may descend and sink down into the bottom of the heart, and there cause it to be so well watered and washed therewith, that neither sun, nor wind, I mean hereby, that neither any business, nor cares of the world may be able to dry it up, nor make any alteration therein. According hereunto we read of the blessed holy religious woman St. Clare, that she rose some times from prayer, and meditation, so wholly absorbed in contemplation upon almighty God, that she could not (but with very great difficulty) frame her heart to deal in such business as she was enforced to attend unto by reason of her office. This kind of devotion is not like unto that, which is carried away with the wind, and dried up with every air: but it is like unto that devotion, whereof it is written in the Canticles, *That many waters shall not be able to quench the fire of charity, neither shall the great rivers overflow it.*[18]

And therefore we are counseled (and that for very good cause) to take as long a time for this holy exercise of prayer and meditation as we may. And surely it is better to have one long time for the same, than two short times. For if the time of prayer be short, all is spent in settling the imagination, and in quieting the heart: and then so soon as we have quieted the same, we rise up forthwith from our exercise at the very time when we should begin it. So that we are like unto the Miner, which in searching for gold giveth over digging at the very time when he findeth the vane thereof, and so loseth his former travail, when he should presently enjoy the fruit of his labor. For undoubtedly the fruit and profit of a long and profound prayer is wont some times to be so great, that a man hath thereby store enough to spend many days together, and to go with Elias to the mount of almighty God, with the virtue and force of the food and sustenance which he hath there received.[19]

But to descend more particularly in limiting this time, I am of opinion, that whatsoever is less than one hour and a half, or two hours, is too short a time for prayer, and meditation. For often times there is spent more than half an hour in tempering and tuning our instrument, (to with, our heart,) and in quieting our imagination, and so all the rest of this time is little enough for the enjoying of the fruit of prayer. True it is I grant, that when we go to this exercise after some other holy exercises, as for example, after matins, or after that we have heard or said Mass, or after some devout reading, or vocal prayers, our heart is then better disposed unto this exercise. For then this heavenly fire of devotion is enkindled with less difficulty in our heart, which by reason of the former holy exercise is very apt (like dry wood) to take fire much more quickly therein. Likewise early in the morning before day the time of our prayer and meditation may

18 Cant. 8:7.
19 See 3 Kgs. 19.

be the shorter: because then our heart is much better disposed for this exercise, as hereafter shall be declared. Howbeit in case it be so, that a man by reason of his manifold business, and affairs, have but little time to bestow in prayer, and meditation, yet let him not omit to offer up his mite with the poor widow in the temple.[20] For (if he fail not of his duty herein through his own negligence) almighty God who provideth for all creatures according to their nature, and necessity, will provide for him also according unto his necessity.

§. VII. The Seventh Advice: That We Must Not Receive the Visitations of Our Lord in Vain.

Agreeable unto this foresaid advice we will give an other very like unto it: which is, that when our soul is visited either in prayer, or out of prayer, with any special visitation of our Lord, we suffer it not to pass away in vain, but take the commodity and benefit of that occasion, that is offered unto us. For certain it is, that with this wind a man shall sail more in one hour, than without it in many days. For as St. Peter took more abundance of fish at that one draught when our Savior commanded him to cast in his net, than he had done in all the whole night before:[21] even so doth it happen unto us often times in this heavenly fishing, in case we know how to help ourselves by taking benefit of the opportunities, and occasions, that be offered unto us therein. And therefore for good cause are we advised by Ecclesiasticus, saying: Omit not to enjoy the good day that God sendeth thee, and suffer not the least part of his good gift to pass away without taking benefit thereof.[22]

Opportunity is of great force, and helpeth much in all things, and more in this exercise of prayer than in any other. For herein it seemeth, as it were, that the Angel descendeth to move the water of

20 See Mark 12; Luke 21.
21 See Luke 5:4–6; John 21:6.
22 See Ecclus. 14:14.

the fishpond, and to give it virtue to heal.[23] Or else to speak more plainly to this purpose, it is as it were the descending of almighty God to draw at the plough with a man, and to help him in his labor: whose help is more profitable, and available, than all the industry and diligence in the world. The mariner when he seeth that the time serveth him well to get out of the haven, forthwith he draweth up his anchors, and hoiseth up his sail, and stayeth not any longer, for fear of loosing that good opportunity, which the time offereth unto him. The like ought all spiritual persons to do when they receive any visitations from our Lord in their prayer, and meditation: and their diligence should be so much the greater, by how much this exercise of meditation is greater, and this divine blast more necessary for prayer, than that for navigation.

And so we read that the blessed holy religious father St. Francis did, of whom St. Bonaventure writeth, that he had such a special care of this point, that in case our Lord did visit him with any special visitation while he was traveling by the way, he caused his companions to go before, and he stayed alone behind, until he had made an end of chewing and digesting that sweet morsel, that was there sent unto him from heaven. Whosoever they be that do not well observe this point, are wont commonly to be chastised with this punishment, that they find not almighty God when they seek him, because he found not them when he sought for them.

These be the principal advices, that are to be observed in the exercise of mediation and in every of the other parts that do accompany the same, in case we mind fully to accomplish this business, and not to leave it in the mid way. Now it shall do well that we make haste to proceed forwards to treat of the rest, and so to bring this first part to an end, which perhaps hath been longer, than is requisite.

---

23 See John 5.

The Fourth Chapter

OF SIX POINTS THAT ARE TO BE MEDITATED UPON IN THE HOLY PASSION OF OUR SAVIOR JESUS CHRIST

FORSOMUCH as the most holy Passion of our Savior Jesus Christ is the principal matter of meditation, it is meet that sithence we have hitherto treated of meditation in general, we do now treat particularly how we ought to meditate upon the holy passion of our Savior Christ: to the intent that we may know, how to behave ourselves in this matter.

But here we must first presuppose, that among all the devotions in the world, there is none more secure, none more profitable, or more universal for all kind of persons, than the remembrance of the holy passion of our Savior Christ. Albertus Magnus saith, *That it is more profitable for a man to meditate every day a little upon the holy passion of our Savior Christ, than to fast with bread and water all the Fridays in the year and to discipline and scourge himself until he shed blood, and to say all the whole Psalter from one end thereof to an other.* At the least wise this is very certain, that this holy exercise is a passing great help to direct the soul in all virtue, and goodness. For considering that our Savior Christ is (as he himself saith) *The way, the truth, and the life,*[1] there is none other exercise more fit and convenient to direct us to go unto God, to know God, and to enjoy God, than to fix always our eyes upon our Savior Christ. For though Christ be unto us the way, the truth, and the life, in all things wheresoever we consider him, yet is he most especially so unto us, when we behold him upon the Cross. And therefore St. Bernard said very devoutly: *Well may I (O Lord) compass about heaven, and earth, yet shall I not find thee but upon the cross. There thou liest, there thou sleepest at noon day.*

But leaving now this matter for an other place, I will only treat at this present after what sort we ought to behave ourselves when we meditate upon the holy passion of our Savior Christ. For there be some simple persons, that seek nothing else in this holy exercise, but only to shed a few tears, in taking compassion upon the bitter pains and sorrows of our Savior, and so do stay themselves in this point alone, without passing any further. And albeit this taking compassion of our Savior's pains be very good, and necessary, (forsomuch as it is the foundation of all the rest, as hereafter shall be declared) yet this is not the only fruit that may be gathered of this holy tree, but there be others far greater than this: forsomuch as out of the meditation of the holy passion doth all the profit of the spiritual life proceed.

Wherefore we must understand, that there be six things (among many others) that may be considered in the holy Passion of our Savior: To wit, The greatness of his pains: The grievousness of our sins: The excellency of the benefit: The magnificency of the goodness of almighty God: The multitude of the virtues of our Savior Christ, which do very brightly shine in his holy passion: And the conveniency of this mean, whereby almighty God vouchsafed to work our redemption. These six points ought we to consider for six effects, wherein consisteth all the profit of the spiritual life. For we must consider the greatness of the pains of our Savior Christ, that we may take compassion of them. We must consider the greatness of our own sins, that we may abhor them. We must consider the greatness of the benefit of his passion, that we may give him thanks for it.

---

1 John 14:6.

We must consider the excellency of the goodness of almighty God, which in this holy passion of our Savior is discovered unto us, that we may very heartly love the same passing great goodness. We must consider the multitude of the virtues of our Savior Christ, which do likewise shine very brightly in his passion, that we may be provoked thereby to imitate them. And we must consider the conveniency of the mystery of his holy passion, that we may be brought thereby in admiration of the wisdom of almighty God, and be the more confirmed in the faith of this holy mystery. Of these six points we intend now to great, and of each one of them in his due place, and order.

§. I. Of the Passing Great Pains, and Torments, Which Our Savior Jesus Christ Suffered in His Most Bitter Passion.

First, we must consider the passing great pains of our Savior Christ, to provoke ourselves by that consideration to take compassion of them, as reason it is that the members should take compassion of their head. Wherefore it is to be noted, that the pains which our Savior suffered in his bitter passion, were (as the holy fathers say) the greatest that ever were suffered in this world.[2] This shall appear manifestly to be true, if we do consider five principal causes, from whence the passing greatness of these pains proceeded.

The first cause was, the passing greatness of his charity, which made him desirous to redeem mankind most abundantly, and to satisfy most perfectly for the injuries, and offences, committed against the divine majesty. And because the greater pains he should suffer, the more perfectly he should accomplish both the one, and the other, (and he wanted not the forces of grace to bear as great a burthen as he would,) therefore he would that his pains should be passing great, that so likewise the satisfaction which he should make for our debt, and the work of our redemption might be also passing great.

2 See St. Thomas Aquinas, *Summa Theologica*, III, q. 46, a. 6.

The second cause (which followeth hereof) was, that he suffered his pains without any manner of ease, or consolation. For (according to the reason before mentioned) he shut up from himself all the gates, whereby any manner of consolation might come unto him, either from heaven, or from earth: insomuch that he was content to be forsaken not only of his disciples, and friends, but also of his own father, yea, and of himself also: to the intent that so being destitute of all company, he might be burning in the furnace of his most grievous pains, and torments, without all manner of refreshing of any ease, or consolation whatsoever, that by any means might come unto him. And therefore he said in the Psalm: I am become as a man destitute of all help, I am left among the dead, notwithstanding that I alone am he that among the dead by right am free from sin, and from death.[3] And in an other Psalm he saith: I am plunged in the bottom of waters, and of mire, and I find no place where to stay my feet.[4] This is that forsaking, which our Savior signified upon the cross, when he said: *My God, My God, why hast thou forsaken me.*[5] For at that time his holy humanity was forsaken in the midst of the furious stream of his pains, and torments, and was left destitute of all things that might either withstand or mitigate the force and vehemency of them. This was figured in the law, by those two beasts, that were offered for the sins of the people, of the which the one was killed, and offered up in sacrifice, and the other departed away, and was sent into the wilderness, leaving her companion alone in the torments.[6] The like was done in this heavenly sacrifice, where God and man was offered for the sins of the world, and the one of the two natures, to wit, the humanity, was sacrificed, and did suffer: but the other nature, to wit, the divinity, departed away, leaving her sister and companion all alone to suffer the torments. For albeit that (as concerning the bond of union) the divine nature never forsook the human nature which it had once taken, yet as touching the consolation and ease of

3 See Ps. 87.
4 See Ps. 68.
5 Matt. 27:46; Ps. 21:2.
6 See Lev. 16.

the pains, and torments, (in the inferior part) it did wholly forsake the same. And therefore we see, that the Martyrs when they went to suffer death, shewed themselves very courageous, merry, and joyful, (as we read of St. Agnes, St. Agatha, St. Laurence, and of many others:) but our Savior being the very fountain of grace, and of strength (through whose virtue the Martyrs had such force, and courage, to be able to do that which they did,) trembled, and sweated even very drops of blood, when he went to suffer pains and torments for us. For in the martyrs the virtue of charity which redounded into the inferior forces of the soul caused them to have very great courage, and joy: But in our Savior Christ both these and all other influences were by special miracle suspended, that so he might drink the cup of his most bitter pains, pure, and without mixture of any manner of ease, or consolation.

The third cause of his so grievous pains, was the tenderness of his complexion. For whereas his holy body was formed miraculously by the holy Ghost, and the things that are done by miracle be more perfect than those that be done by nature, (as St. Chrysostom declareth, speaking of the water, which was turned into wine at the marriage,) it followeth that our Savior's body was the most best complexioned, and most tender of all bodies that ever were, or shall be: insomuch as a holy father saith: *That if there had been no external violence done unto our Savior's body, it would have endured a very great number of years, by reason of the perfection, and tenderness of the composition thereof.*[7]

And not only the composition of his body, but also the matter thereof was very tender: forsomuch as the matter of it was wholly most pure virgins flesh, taken of the most pure and virginal bowels of our blessed Lady, without any other kind of mixture. And for this cause (as St. Bonaventure saith) his body was the more tender, and of a more perfect sense in feeling.

The fourth cause of his so grievous pains, was the very kind of death which he suffered, with all the circumstances that happened in all the continuance of his passion: forsomuch as each one of them (if

7 St. John Chrysostom, *On St. John*, 2.

they be well considered) was a kind of martyrdom by itself. And that thou mayst more clearly perceive the same, begin even from the first entry of his passion until the end of it, and thou shalt find among others twelve most grievous pains, which our Savior there suffered: the which I will rehearse here very briefly, notwithstanding that in every one of them there is very much to be said, and considered.

The first was, the agony in the garden, and that wonderful bloody sweat, which trickled down throughout all the parts of his body unto the earth, which was the most new and most strangest thing of all that ever hath happened in the world.

The second was, to be sold for so base a price of his own Apostle, and disciple, unto so cruel enemies.

The third was, to be so often times carried through the common streets bound, and manacled, as if he had been a very thief.

The fourth was, the punishment with whipping, and scourging, which besides that the lashes were very cruelly laid on him, and very many in number, it is not a punishment for a man of any credit, or honesty, but for bondslaves, vagabonds, and men of most vile and base condition.

The fifth was, that most cruel invention of the crown of thorns, wherein were joined together both most grievous shame, and dishonor, and withal most grievous pain, and torment.

The sixth was, those so manifold blasphemies, and sundry kinds of most villainous mockeries, injuries, and reproaches, which were joined with the torments: as to spit so often times in his face, as though he had been a blasphemer: to give him buffets, and blows, as if he had been a vagabond: to apparel him some times in white garments, and some times in red, as if he had been a fool: to hoodwink his eyes, and to jest at him, saying, *Areed, who hath smitten thee*,[8] as if he had been a very dissard: to clothe him with a purple garment, to set a reed in his hand, to kneel on one knee before him, to smite him on the head with a reed, as if he had been a counterfeit king: and besides all this, to proclaim him through the common streets as

8 Matt. 26:68.

a malefactor. Who ever saw so many kinds of reproachful injuries heaped together upon one man?

The seventh was, that wonderful contempt, and despite, which was done unto him (being the son of almighty God,) when they compared him with Barrabas, and made less accompt of him, than of Barrabas. Insomuch as that Lord by whom all things were created, and in whom all things do live, and are preserved, was accompted more unprofitable, and more unworthy to live, than Barrabas an infamous malefactor.

The eighth was, in that they enforced him to carry upon his shoulders, (which were all rent, and bruised,) the very same instrument of the cross, whereupon he should suffer death. The tormentors themselves (which are commonly the ministers of cruelty) do use to hide the eyes of them that are to be beheaded, that they may not see the instrument, that shall bereave them of their life: but here they do not only not use this kind of humanity towards our Savior, but they lay the same instrument of his death even upon his own shoulders, to the intent that his heart might first suffer the torment of the cross inwardly, before that his body should prove it outwardly.

The ninth was, the very martyrdom of the cross: which is a most cruel kind of torment: for it is not a speedy kind of death, (as to be hanged, or beheaded) but very long, and lingering: and the wounds be in the most sensible parts of the body: to wit, in the feet, and hands, which are most full of veins, and sinews, which be the instruments of the feeling. Moreover, his pains were increased with the poise and weight of his own body, which always tended and swayed downward: and so it ever rented, and enlarged his wounds, and augmented the grief of his torments continually: and this caused his martyrdom to become so extremely grievous, that although he had no deadly wound, yet by reason of the passing greatness of his pains, his most holy soul departed out of his most precious body.

The tenth was, that whereas our Savior was thus tormented upon the cross, and there became a very Sea of pains, and torments, yea, whereas he was in such a doleful case, that if we should see a very dog in the street so pitifully tormented it were able to break our hearts, yet all this notwithstanding his cruel enemies were so far of from taking any pity of compassion upon him, that even at that very time, they mocked, and scoffed at him, and wagged their heads, saying: *Fie on thee, that destroyest the temple of God, and within three days buildest it again.*[9]

The eleventh was, to have his most innocent mother present before his eyes at all these martyrdoms, knowing so well as he did, what a passing great grief it was unto her most innocent heart.

The twelfth was such a cruelty, as the like was never seen: to wit, that whereas his most holy body was all void of blood, and all the fountains of his veins emptied, and his bowels dried up, by reason of the great abundance of blood which he had shed, when he requested a little water, they did not only not grant it unto him, but in steed thereof they gave him to drink Easell, and Gall.

Now what thing could be more cruelly done than this? True it is, that that rich covetous man, which was tormented in hell had a drop of water denied him when he required it, but yet he had no gall given unto him.[10] But here they do not only deny the son of almighty God the thing that he desired, but besides that, they increase his most grievous pains with an other new kind of torment.

Every one of these points being considered severally by itself, will minister sufficient matter of very great grief and sorrow to any good Christian heart. And therefore whosoever is desirous to have an earnest and inward compassion of the pains of our Savior, let him go through every one of them, and make a station at each of them: and (be he never so hard hearted,) it is not almost possible, but that in some one or other of them he shall find very vehement motions to provoke him unto grief, and compassion.

Howbeit, the pains of our Savior Christ are not thus ended: there be yet others without all comparison far greater than these, to wit, the pains of his blessed soul. For all these pains above-named, do for

---

9 Matt. 27:40.

10 See Luke 16.

the most part appertain to the pains of the cross, wherein his body suffered outwardly: but besides this visible Cross, there was yet an other invisible cross, wherein his most holy soul was crucified within his body, having also four arms, and four nails, (which were four dolorous considerations) and these were a far greater torment unto him, than the very outward cross. For first of all, there were represented unto him all the sins of the world that were present, past, and to come, (for all which he suffered) and that so distinctly, as if they had been the sins but of one man alone. Now to him that bare such a passing great love and zeal unto the honor of his father, what an unspeakable grief was it, to behold such an infinite number of abominations, and offences, committed against so high a majesty? For it is certain, that the sins of one man alone were able to torment him more, than all the torments of the cross. The which being so, what a passing great grief would the sins of all men, and of all worlds cause unto him? Surely, there is no understanding able to comprehend the passing greatness of this grief.

Secondly, there was also represented unto him the ungratitude and damnation of many men, and especially of many wicked Christians, which would never acknowledge this singular benefit, nor endeavor to profit and help themselves with this so great and so costly a remedy, as he there prepared for them. This was also a far greater torment unto him, than the torment of the cross. For it is a greater pain unto a laborer to be denied his day wages, and the fruit of his labor, than the very labor itself, albeit it were very great. And for this cause our Savior complained by his Prophet Isaias of this injury unto his father, saying: *I said: In vain have I travailed: In vain, and without cause have I wasted my strength.*[11] And he complained of this ingratitude not only to his father, but also even unto men themselves by St. Bernard, saying: *O man, consider what cruel torments I suffer for thy sake. There is no pain that tormenteth me so extremely as thy ingratitude doth: I call unto thee that do suffer death for thee: Behold the pains that do torment me: Behold the nails that do pierce through my*

[11] Is. 49:4.

hands, and feet: Behold the shameful reproaches, and despites, wherewith they dishonor me. And although the pain which I suffer outwardly be so passing great, yet is the pain far greater which I suffer inwardly, when I see thee so ungrateful and unkind towards me for the same.

In like manner there was represented unto him the horrible sin of that miserable people of Jewry, and the terrible punishment that was prepared for them within a short time after, which undoubtedly was a greater grief, and torment unto him, that the cup of his bitter passion. For if the Prophet Jeremias signified, that the sin which the Jews committed in going about to kill him, grieved him much more than his own very death, what a grief would it be to our Savior, who had without all comparison far greater charity, and grace, than the Prophet Jeremias.

There were moreover represented unto him the griefs, and doleful sword of sorrow, which pierced the heart of his blessed mother,[12] when she saw him suffer between two thieves upon a cross, the which undoubtedly was so great a grief and pain unto him, as the love was great which he bare unto her, which love was inestimable: forsomuch as next unto the love of God, he loved her most of all creatures.

Now these four considerations and griefs were as it were four arms of an other inward cross, wherewith his blessed soul was likewise crucified within his holy body. So that our Savior suffered that day the pains and torments of two crosses, the one visible, and the other invisible. Upon the one cross his body suffered outwardly, and upon the other his soul suffered much more inwardly. Now how passing great the grief was, which proceeded of these four considerations, there is no understanding able to comprehend it: and yet we may conjecture somewhat thereof, by that outward shew of his bloody sweat in the garden.

Whosoever then shall attentively consider all these causes, shall clearly see how passing great the pains and torments of our Savior were, which is the intent of this first manner of meditating upon his most bitter passion. Howbeit, this must not be the final end of this

12 See Luke 2:35.

exercise, but rather it must be used as a mean to come to other ends: to wit, to understand hereby what a passing great love he bare unto thee, that would suffer so much for thee: and what a great benefit he did unto thee, in buying thee with so dear a price: and how much thou art bound to do for him, who hath done, and suffered so much for thee: and above all this, how greatly thou oughtest to abhor thy sins, and be grieved with them, sith they were the cause of his so long and painful martyrdom. Now for these four ends, (whereof we will intreat in the chapters following) serveth this manner of contemplation. Whereby it appeareth, that this first manner of meditating (by way of taking compassion of the bitter pains of our Savior) is as it were a mean, or a ladder, unto all the others. And for this very cause St. Bonaventure made great accompt of this manner of meditation upon the passion: because it is sensibly seen, that this manner of meditation openeth the way unto all the other manners of meditating upon the same.

And the same holy father saith, that for this purpose it shall be a great help also for us to take some discipline, which may cause some smart, and do no hurt to the body, that so by feeling of that so little pain of whipping, and scourging ourselves, we may the better lift up our spirit, to consider somewhat of the passing great pains, and torments, which the most tender body of our sweet Savior suffered for our sakes.

§. II. How in the Passion of Our Savior Christ, Appeareth Very Manifestly What a Grievous Thing Sin Is, in the Sight of Almighty God.

The second point that we have to consider in the passion of our Savior, is the grievousness of our sins, whereby to move our hearts to be sorrowful for them, and to abhor them. Wherefore we must understand, that (as all the holy learned fathers do affirm,) our sins were the very cause why the son of almighty God suffered such grievous pains, torments, and cruel death, as he suffered in this world.[13] For it is certain, that if there had been no sin to be the mean and occasion of his suffering, it had not been needful for him to have suffered as he did. It is not agreed among the learned divines, whether the son of God should have been incarnate, in case man had not sinned, (for some do affirm it, and some do deny it,)[14] but this is holden for a most certain truth, that in case man had not sinned, the son of God should not have died. Whereby it appeareth, that our sins were the very cause that moved him to suffer all these miseries, and that our sins were they that threw him into this prison, and that our sins were they that nailed him upon the cross.

And think not, because they were not thy sins alone which were the cause hereof, that thou art therefore worthy of the less punishment: for according to the laws of justice, he deserveth no less punishment that killeth an innocent being accompanied with many in committing the fact, than if he alone had killed him. So that by this rule thou seest, what great reason thou hast to move thee to abhor thy sins, and to be earnestly sorry for them, by calling to mind, that they were the tormentors which in very deed crucified the son of almighty God, and caused him to suffer so great pains, and torments. This is a greater cause to move a man to abhor sin, and to be sorry for the same, than all other losses and miseries that ensue of sin, yea although we should reckon among our losses the deprivation of the everlasting glory and felicity which is lost by a deadly sin, and the everlasting horrible pains which be purchased by the same.

Now according unto this doctrine, when thou shalt be occupied in meditating upon the holy passion, and shalt see how the enemies do apprehend our Savior, and how they accuse him, and buffet him, and how they spit upon him, and whip him, etc. think for certain, that thou art in very deed in company with them, and that thou hast joined with them in this conspiracy against our Savior. So that thou mayst truly say, that thy sins do accuse him, that thy

13 See St. Thomas Aquinas, *Summa Theologica*, III, q. 1, a. 2; q. 46, aa. 1–2.

14 See St. Thomas, III, q. 1, a. 3.

dissolute behavior bindeth him, that thy anger and malice whipeth him, that thy presumption and rashness buffeteth him, that thy pride crowneth him with thorns, that thy fond braveries and vanities do cloth him with purple, that thy pleasures, and delights give him to drink gall, and vinegar, and to be short, that thy disobedience naileth his hands and feet upon the cross. Forsomuch as the pains which thou deservest by these thy sins, he vouchsafed of his infinite charity to suffer for thee. For it is certain, that the tormentors should never have had power to torment him as they did, in case thy sins had not given them force and strength to do the same.

This is one very profitable way of meditating upon the holy passion for all kind of persons: but it is much more requisite for such as do but newly begin to enter into the service of almighty God, and do endeavor to cleanse the sins of their former dissolute life with the holy exercises of Penance.

§. III. Of the Passing Great Benefit of Our Redemption.

Thirdly we ought to consider in the holy passion the greatness of the benefit which our Savior hath done unto us, in redeeming us by this mean. And although there be infinite things to be said in this matter, yet at this present I will do no more, but only note briefly three principal points, which are to be considered in this most excellent benefit of our Redemption. First, what our Savior hath bestowed upon us by the same redemption. Secondly, what mean he used in giving it unto us. And thirdly, with what passing great love he gave it unto us.

How passing great that is, which our Savior hath bestowed upon us by this benefit of our redemption, there is no tongue able to express. Howbeit we may conceive somewhat thereof by two ways. The first way, is by considering all the evils and miseries whereinto mankind incurred through the sin of the first man Adam: for all these miseries were sufficiently remedied by our Savior Jesus Christ, who bestowed upon us all such benefits as were contrary unto these miseries: forsomuch as it is evident, that he was given unto us to be a universal repairer of all the evils and miseries of the world. Now he that were able to reckon how many the miseries are, whereinto the world hath fallen by the sin of the first man Adam, might also understand, how many the benefits are, that came unto us by the second Adam, (to wit, by our Savior Christ,) which benefits be undoubtedly innumerable.

The second way, is by considering not all the miseries which our first father Adam brought unto us, but all the benefits which came unto us by our Savior Christ: Forsomuch as we are made partakers of all those benefits, by means of communicating his spirit unto us. For all such as are made partakers of the spirit of Christ, are made partakers also of the virtues and merits of Christ. Wherefore the Apostle saith, that all such as have received the Sacrament of Baptism have put on Christ.[15] Giving us thereby to understand, that they all are made partakers of Christ, and are adorned with his virtues, and merits, and that so being clothed with this livery they seem in the sight of the heavenly father to be such after a sort (in their degree,) as his own very son seemeth before him. And therefore for good cause doth Ecclesiasticus allege this wonderful title of the son of God in his prayer: saying: have mercy O Lord upon thy people Israel, whom thou hast made equal and like to thy first begotten son.[16] What dignity, what glory can be greater than this? Now according hereunto he that could reckon how many the virtues, and merits of our Savior Christ have been, might likewise understand how many the benefits have been that are come unto us by him: Forsomuch as we are made partakers of them all by the mean of his passion.

To conclude, by him is given unto us remission of our sins, grace, glory, liberty, peace, salvation, redemption, sanctification, justice, satisfaction, sacraments, merits, doctrine, and all other things, which he had, and were behooveful for our salvation. And by reason of this his so bountiful communicating, he is called in the holy Scriptures,

---

15 See Gal. 3:27.

16 See Ecclus. 36:14.

the father, the bridegroom, and the universal head of the Catholic Church: because whatsoever the father hath, appertaineth to his children, and whatsoever the bridegroom hath, he imparteth to his spouse, and whatsoever the head hath, the members are made partakers of the same.

These are the benefits which our Savior Christ hath bestowed upon us. But by what mean hath he given them unto us? It is evident that by the mean of his holy incarnation, and passion, whereby he made himself partaker of all our debts, and miseries: and so by taking upon him all our miseries, he made us partakers of all his benefits. This taking upon him all our miseries is undoubtedly a far greater thing, than to make us partakers of all his benefits. For certainly it is a more wonderful thing in God to suffer miseries, than to bestow benefits: because as there is nothing more proper and convenient to his infinite goodness, than to bestow benefits, so is there nothing more strange and further from that infinite felicity, than to suffer miseries. Whereby it appeareth, that we are much more bound unto him for the pains and torments which he hath suffered for us, than for the great benefits which he hath given unto us: I mean hereby, that we are much more bound unto him for the manner whereby he hath remedied our miseries, than for the very remedy itself.

But how passing great was the love wherewith our Savior bestowed all this upon us? This is without all comparison far greater, than all the rest. For certainly the desire which our Savior had to suffer pains for us, was far greater, than the very pains which he suffered: and much more pains would he have suffered, in case it had been needful for us. Three hours he continued suffering pains and torments upon the cross for our sins: But what is this in comparison of that, which the greatness of his charity could have vouchsafed to do for us? Verily, if it had been needful for us, that he should there have suffered pains and torments until the day of judgement, the love was so passing great which he bare unto us, that he would undoubtedly have done it. So that albeit he suffered much for us, yet was the love which he bare unto us far greater, than the pains which he suffered for us. And therefore if we be greatly bound unto him for the great pains which he suffered for us, much more are we bound unto him for that which he desired to suffer for us. This consideration is very profitable to provoke us to give most humble thanks unto him, who hath bestowed so great benefits upon us: and withal to love him, who hath loved us much more, than by his benefits he hath shewed unto us. Other infinite things there be to be said concerning this matter, but now they shall remain for an other place, and somewhat I have specified already in the meditation of the benefits of almighty God.

§. IV. Of the Wonderful Great Goodness of Almighty God, Which Appeareth Very Evidently in the Holy Passion of Our Savior Christ.

Fourthly, we ought to consider the passing great goodness, and mercy of almighty God, which shineth more evidently and brightly in the holy passion of our Savior, than in any other of his works. Wherefore thou hast deeply to consider therein four things: which are to be considered in all the whole history of the holy passion, and in every part thereof. The first is, who suffereth: The second is, what pains he suffereth: The third is, for whom he suffereth: The fourth is, for what cause he suffereth. Now if thou wilt stay thyself awhile in every one of these points, and consider first the highness, and excellency of him that suffereth, which is almighty God: and in such wise stay in this consideration, that thou art astonied at this so high, and so wonderful a thing: and afterwards comest to descend from thence unto the consideration of the baseness, and vileness of the most grievous pains, and reproachful injuries, which he was content to suffer: and that not for Angels, or Archangels, but even for men, which are most vile, and abominable creatures, and in their works like unto the devils themselves: if (as I say) in each one of these points thou make as it were a station, and do compare the one point with the other, undoubtedly thou shalt be greatly amazed, and astonied, to consider how much so great and excellent a majesty would abase himself, to redeem so vile, and so base a creature: and then mayst thou cry out with the Prophet, and say: O Lord I have heard thy words, and was afraid, I have considered they works, and was astonied.[17]

But if after all this, thou do consider the cause of his so great abasing, and comest to understand that it was not for any manner of commodity towards himself, nor yet provoked by any desert of ours, but was only moved thereunto with the bowels of his tender mercy and love towards us, by the which he vouchsafed to visit us from on high:[18] this point being well and duly considered, will lift up thy mind into such a great admiration and love of him, that thou wilt be astonied as Moses was in the Mount, when he saw the figure of this mystery, and began to proclaim with a loud voice the unspeakable great mercy of almighty God which was there revealed unto him.[19] This was that great languishing and faintness of spirit, which the spouse felt in the Canticles, when she said: *Stay me up with flowers, and comfort me with apples, for I languish with love.*[20] Upon which words St. Bernard saith: *The amorous soul seeth here king Salomon with the crown which his mother crowned him withal: She seeth the only son of almighty God carrying a cross upon his shoulders: She seeth the Lord of majesty whipped and spitted upon: She seeth the author of life and of glory thrust through with nails, pierced with a spear, and many despiteful reproaches and contempts done unto him: And finally, she seeth him bestow his most holy life for his friends: She seeth all this, and in seeing it she is pierced through with a knife of love, and therefore she saith: stay me up with flowers, and comfort me with apples, for I languish with love.*

---

17 Hab. 3:2.

18 See Luke 1:78.

19 See Ex. 3.

20 Cant. 2:5.

§. V. Of the Excellent Virtues, That Do Shine Very Brightly in the Holy Passion of Our Savior Christ.

The fifth point that we have to consider in the holy passion of our Savior is the great number of virtues that do shine very clearly in it: the which consideration serveth to encourage us to endeavor ourselves to imitate some part of that which is there represented unto us. This is one of the highest manners of meditating that is upon the holy Passion. For it is manifest, that all the perfection of a Christian life consisteth in the imitation and following of the virtues of our Savior Christ. Whereunto the Apostle St. Peter exhorteth us, saying: *Christ suffered for us, leaving unto you an example, that you should follow his foot-steps, who when he was evil spoken of, did not speak evil again: and when he was tormented, did not threaten them, but delivered himself unto him that did most unjustly condemn him.*[21]

And albeit that all virtues shined so brightly and in such excellent wise in all the life of our Savior Christ, yet did they much more perfectly shine in his holy passion. And therefore in his passion principally it behooveth us to behold the beauty and excellency of his virtues: the which do much more evidently shine there among his pains, and torments, than do the flowers among the thorns.

Consider therefore first of all that so profound humility, wherewith the most high and only begotten son of almighty God vouchsafed to be contemned, and less esteemed than Barrabas, and to be crucified upon a cross between two thieves as though he had been a Captain and ringleader of malefactors.

Consider his so wonderful patience in the midst of so many reproachful injuries, and torments: and withal his so passing great magnanimity, in that he offered himself so willingly into the hands of his enemies, and to suffer the greatest pains, and conflicts, that ever were suffered in this world.

21 1 Ptr. 2:21, 23.

Consider that so constant perseverance, which he had from the beginning to the end, yea even to suffer death upon the cross, and to descend into hell, and to finish the work of our salvation.

Consider his most fervent charity, which passeth all understanding, by the which only he was moved to offer himself in sacrifice for the sins of the world, and to suffer death, that he might give life not only unto his friends, but also to his enemies, yea even to those very persons that shed his most precious blood.

Consider his most abundant mercy, which extended itself so far forth, as to take upon him all the miseries and debts of the world, and to make satisfaction for them, as if they had been peculiarly his own debts.

Consider that so perfect obedience which he used towards his father, whom he obeyed unto death, yea even to the death of the cross: where finally bowing down his head, he offered up unto him his most holy soul, giving us thereby to understand, that the work of his obedience was then perfectly fulfilled.

Consider that so passing great meekness which he shewed in all the process of his passion, suffering himself to be carried like a sheep to the butchery, and like a most meek lamb, that holdeth his peace when he is sheared.

Consider his so wonderful silence amongst so many false accusations, and lying witnesses, which was so great, that it was able to bring the very Judge himself that condemned him in a great admiration of him.

Now if thou be desirous to see a most perfect pattern of the contempt of the world, and of all the honors, riches, pleasures, and delights that be therein, behold our Savior upon the cross so dishonored, tormented, and naked, that he had none other, bed to lie upon, but only a cross: none other pillow to rest his head upon, but only a crown of thorns: none other delicates to feed upon, but only gall, and vinegar: none other persons to comfort him, but only those cruel scoffing ministers which wagged their heads at him, and said: Fie on thee, that destroyest the temple of God, and in three days buildest it up again: etc.[22] I conclude therefore, that the Evangelical poverty, abstinence, and austerity of life, with all other virtues do no where shine more evidently than in the cross.

But among all these virtues, humility and patience do shew themselves most notably in the bitter passion of our Savior. For patience (as the holy fathers affirm) as the wedding garment wherewith the son of almighty God clothed himself when he came to be affianced with the Catholic Church, and to be married with her. By which Metaphor they give us to understand, that albeit our Savior Christ shined most brightly with the garment of all virtues, when he came to celebrate matrimony with the Catholic Church upon the bed of the cross, yet did he most principally shine there with the robe of patience. For by means of the act of this virtue, which is to suffer, he drank the bitter cup of his passion: by the value, and merit whereof the Catholic Church was redeemed, beautified, and espoused by our Savior Christ.

Now in these and other the like virtues we ought to fix our eyes when we meditate upon the holy passion of our Savior: to the intent that we may be thereby provoked to imitate somewhat of that, which was there done, not only for our redemption, but also for our example. For the greatest glory that a Christian can attain unto in this world, is to have a semblance and likeness unto our Savior Christ: Howbeit not such a likeness as proud Lucifer desired to have,[23] but such a likeness of life as our Savior Christ himself commanded us to have, when he said: I have given you an example, that as I have done, so should ye do likewise.[24]

§. VI. Of the Conveniency of the Mystery of Our Redemption.

The sixth point that we have to contemplate upon in the holy passion, is the conveniency of the mystery of our Redemption: to wit, how convenient a mean this was which almighty God chose whereby

22 Mark 15:29.
23 See Is. 14:14.
24 John 13:15.

to work the salvation of man, and to heal and cure him of his miseries.[25] This manner of contemplation serveth to illuminate the understanding, to confirm it more firmly in the faith of this mystery, and to lift up the heart of man into a great admiration of the goodness, and wisdom of almighty God, who chose so wonderful and convenient a mean to heal our miseries, and to relieve our necessities.

This is so copious and so plentiful a matter to meditate upon, that certainly if a man should continue thinking upon it until the end of the world he should always find new reasons of the conveniency of this holy mystery, and new causes to induce him to lift up his spirt more and more in admiration of the high wisdom and providence of almighty God herein. But because this volume would be to great in case I should treat of this matter at large: I will therefore at this present only shew the order and foundation of this consideration, to the intent that the devout and religious soul may hereby have a way opened unto her to prosecute all the rest.

Wherefore it is to be noted, that if we will see what proportion and conveniency a mean hath with his end, it is necessary to make a comparison between the same mean, and the end, and the greater helps that the mean hath towards the attaining of the end, the more proper and convenient is the mean for the same end. As for example: If we will examine whether a medicine be convenient for a disease, we must consider the accidents of the disease, and the properties and virtues of the medicine: and when we have seen what proportion there is between the one, and the other, we may then judge whether the medicine be convenient for the same disease or not. And even in like manner is it in this case: for whereas it is evident unto us, that the passion and blood of our Savior Jesus Christ is a general medicine for all the miseries and necessities of man, if we will try the conveniency of this medicine, we must make a long comparison between the medicine, and the disease: and in case we be able to search and examine well both the one, and the other, we shall certainly find, that this medicine is so fit and convenient for the curing of this disease, and of all

25 See St. Thomas Aquinas, *Summa Theologica*, III, q. 46, aa. 3–4.

the branches, and accidents of the same, as if the medicine had been only instituted for the curing of each defect in the disease: the which undoubtedly is a matter able to bring a man that should consider of it attentively into a great astonishment, and admiration. If thou be not fully persuaded herein, tell me then I pray thee, what satisfaction could be offered more sufficient for payment of the common debts of mankind, than the most precious blood which the son of almighty God shed for us upon the Cross? To cure also the wounds of our pride, covetousness, ingratitude, pleasures, delights, and the love of ourselves, with all other evils which proceed thereof, what thing could be more convenient, than God upon a Cross? Likewise to give us knowledge of the goodness, and mercy of almighty God, to enkindle us more in the love of him, to strengthen more our confidence, and to awake more our forgetfulness, and unthankfulness, what thing could be more convenient, than God upon a Cross? Moreover, to enrich a man with merits, to exalt him unto greater honor, to enkindle his spirit in devotion, to comfort him in his tribulations, to succor him in his temptations, to help him in his labors, to encourage him unto great enterprises, and finally to give a perfect example of all virtues, what thing could be more convenient, than Jesus Christ upon the cross? And to comprehend all in one word, if the Evangelical life be well considered, it is nothing else, but only a continual cross: and so consequently, what thing could be more convenient to direct a kind of life which is altogether a cross, than an other cross?

And if thou be yet desirous to understand this conveniency more evidently, consider attentively what thing a Christian life is, (for the leading of a Christian life is the end of all the travails and pains of our Savior Christ,) and the same consideration will declare very plainly unto thee, what conveniency there is between this mean, and this end. A Christian life (taking it in his full perfection) is not such a kind of life as the Christians use to live at this day in the world: but such a life as our Savior Christ lived, and such a life as his disciples lived, whose pains, labors, and miseries were so great, that one of them saith thus of them: We are become a spectacle unto God, unto

Angels, and unto men.[26] For truly so great are our pains, and miseries, and in such wise are we reviled and persecuted of the world, that (as though we were wild beasts baited at a stake) we are specially looked upon, not only of men, and of Angels, but also of almighty God himself. And afterwards he saith thus: Until this present hour we do sustain hunger, thirst, nakedness, and blows, and have not so much as a den wherein to hide ourselves. We go from place to place, and we gain the bread that we eat with our own hands. They curse us, and we bless them: They persecute us, and we suffer them: They blaspheme us, and we pray for them: To conclude, in such wise are we turmoiled and contemned of the world, as if we were the very dust, and dirt, that they tread underneath their feet:[27] And as though we were most wicked, and abominable men, the world is fully persuaded, that nothing can be more acceptable unto almighty God, than to procure our death, and condemnation.

This is (my dear brother) a Christian life. This very Christian life did the Prophets live, and so did also the Martyrs, the Confessors, and those blessed holy Monks that lived in the primitive Church in the wilderness. To be short, this Christian life did all the Saints live. And this Christian life the Apostle describeth very plainly in his Epistle to the Hebrews in these words: The saints were mocked, scourged, apprehended, imprisoned, stoned, sawed in pieces, tempted, and put to death with the sword: They went in this world appareled in sheep and goats' skins, very poor, needy, and afflicted, of whom the world was not worthy: They live in wilderness, and in solitary places, apart from the company of men, and had none other habitation, but the dens and clefts of the earth.[28] This is indeed the perfection of the Christian life, which the gospel teacheth us, and which our Savior Christ came to bring into the world. This Christian life if it be well considered is a continual cross, and death of the whole man, to the intent that after he is thus mortified and annihilated he may be able, and disposed to be

26 See 1 Cor. 4:9.
27 See 1 Cor. 4:11–13.
28 See Heb. 11.

transformed into God. For like as there can not be generation without corruption, (forsomuch as that thing which is must perish, to the end that that may be made which is not,) even so this spiritual regeneration and transformation of man into God can not be made, unless the old man do first die, that so by death and corruption of the old man he may be transformed into God. Whereupon it plainly ensueth, that all the Evangelical life is nothing else (as we have said) but death, and a cross. And therefore what thing can be more convenient to direct such a kind of life as is altogether a continual cross, than an other cross: And if there be nothing more apt to and convenient to engender a fire, than an other fire, and if every thing be most apt to engender a thing like unto itself, what thing can be more proportionable and convenient to engender a cross, than an other cross? Undoubtedly so it is: and therefore there is nothing of greater force to encourage and strengthen at this day all holy Catholic men, and women, to suffer pains, unjustice, wrongs, poverty, subjection, discipline, hunger, thirst, cold, nakedness, and to be short, all the troubles, calamities, afflictions, persecutions, imprisonment, torments, and miseries of this world, and all the austerity of the Evangelical life, than to fix their eyes upon the cross. Out of this school of the cross came the Martyrs. In this school learned also the Apostles. And this school hath likewise taught and strengthened the virgins, the Confessors, the holy Monks, and to conclude, all the Saints, to live a holy austere kind of life. And it was the cross that hath accompanied and comforted them in all their labors, troubles, pains, afflictions, and persecutions.

Now when the devout soul findeth so many kinds of fruits in this tree of life for all times, and for all necessities, she can not but wonder at the high wisdom of that sovereign master, that hath found out such an excellent mean for our remedy: and she is also provoked thereby to acknowledge the unspeakable goodness of so merciful a father, who being able to have holpen and remedied man with his only will, chose rather to put himself to so great pains, and dishonors, to the intent that man might be more honored and more holpen by this mean, than by any other.

These be the six principal ways to meditate upon the holy passion: and the order that may commonly be used in meditating upon them, is to begin at the first, to wit, to consider the most grievous pains which our Savior suffered for us, (the which consideration is as it were the very foundation of all the others) and from that consideration we may go forwards immediately unto all the rest, according as the very course of meditation will open unto us the way, and especially the grace of the holy Ghost, who is the principal teacher of these exercises. For as we have declared before, when we have considered the passing great pains which our Savior suffered for us, we may then immediately proceed forwards, and consider the greatness of our sins, and which caused him to suffer so many grievous pains, and torments: and withal the passing greatness of this benefit of our redemption, in that almighty God would vouchsafe for the love of us to suffer such extreme pains: And we may likewise consider the highness of the goodness, and mercy of almighty God, who for the great love he bare unto us abased himself so far forth, as to suffer so many reproachful contempts, villainies, and miseries: And above all this we may consider how great examples of virtues our Savior Christ hath given unto us herein: to wit of patience, obedience, charity, humility, meekness, constancy, and of all other virtues, whereof we have hitherto treated.

Howbeit, although it be a very convenient order of meditating upon this holy mystery to pass orderly by degrees through all these foresaid considerations, and so to proceed in order from one consideration to an other, even to the last: yet is it not needful for a man (so often as he meditateth upon this holy mystery) to go in this precise manner through them all, (for many times he shall not have sufficient time for the same,) but let him content himself in his meditation with that consideration, wherein he shall find most spiritual taste, and liking: Forsomuch as in these exercises we must have respect not to the great quantity of the matter that is meditated upon, but to the great devotion wherewith it is done.

✝

HERE FOLLOW THE FIRST SEVEN MEDITATIONS FOR THE SEVEN DAYS OF THE WEEK, IN THE MORNINGS

MONDAY MORNING

THIS day, when thou hast made the sign of the cross, with such preparation as shall hereafter be declared in the fourth chapter, thou hast to meditate upon our Savior Christ's washing of his Apostles' feet: and upon the institution of the most blessed Sacrament of the Altar.

The Text of the Holy Evangelists.

When the hour of supper was come, our savior Christ sat down at the table, and his twelve Apostles with him. And he said unto them. I have had a great desire to eat this Passover with you before my passion.[1] And as they were eating, he said: Verily I say unto you, that one of you shall betray me. And they were exceeding sorrowful, and began every one of them to say unto him. Is it I, Lord? And he answered, and said. He that dippeth his hand with me in the dish, he shall betray me. The son of man goeth his way, as it is written of him. But woe be to that man, by whom the son of man is betrayed. It had been good for that man, if he had never been born. Then Judas that betrayed him, answered, and said: Is it I, master? And he said unto him: Thou hast said.[2]

When supper was done, he arose up from the table, and put of his garments: and taking a towel, he girded himself with it. After that, he poured water into a basin, and began to wash his disciples'

1 Luke 22:14–15.
2 Matt. 26:21–25.

feet, and to wipe them with the towel, wherewith he was girded. Then he came to Simon Peter. Who said to him: Lord, doest thou wash my feet? Jesus answered, and said unto him: What I do, thou knowest not now: but thou shalt know it hereafter. Peter said unto him. Thou shalt never wash my feet. Jesus answered him. If I wash thee not, thou shalt have no part with me. Simon Peter said unto him. Lord, not only my feet, but my hands, and head also. Jesus said unto him. He that is washed, needeth not to wash saving only his feet: but he is clean everywhit. And ye are clean, but not all. For he knew who should betray him. And therefore he said: ye are not all clean. So after he had washed their feet, and had taken his garments, and was set down again, he said unto them. Know ye, what I have done to you? Ye call me master, and Lord. And ye say well. For so I am indeed. If I then being your Lord, and master, have washed your feet, ye ought also to wash one another's feet. For I have given you an example, that ye should do, even as I have done to you.[3]

After our Savior had thus washed their feet, he took bread, and when he had blessed, he brake, and gave to his disciples, saying. Take, and eat: this is my body. He took the Cup likewise, and when he had blessed it, he gave it them, saying: Drink ye all of this. For this is my blood of the new testament, which shall be shed for many for the remission of sins. So often as ye shall do this thing, do it in remembrance of me.[4]

Meditations upon These Points of the Text.

§. I. Of Our Savior's Washing of His Apostles' Feet: and of the Institution of the Most Blessed Sacrament of the Altar.

Contemplate now (O my soul) in this supper upon thy sweet and mild Jesus: And behold this wonderful example of inestimable humility, which he here sheweth unto thee, in rising from the table,

---

3 John 13:4–15.

4 See Matt. 26:26–28.

and washing his disciples' feet? O good Jesus, what is this that thou dost? O sweet Jesus, what meaneth this so great abasing of thy divine majesty? O my soul, what wouldst thou have thought, if thou hadst been there present, and hadst seen even almighty God himself, kneeling before the feet of men, yea before the feet of Judas? O Cruel Judas, why doth not this so great humility mollify thy stony heart? How is it, that it causeth not even thy very bowels to burst, and rive in sunder, considering this so great and wonderful meekness? Is it possible thou traitor, that thou hast conspired to betray this most meek, and gentle lamb? Is it possible that thou shouldest not feel some remorse of conscience, in beholding this example? O ye white and beautiful hands, how could ye vouchsafe to touch such loathsome, and abominable feet? O most pure and clean hands, why disdained ye not, to wash those very feet, that were all to be dirted in foul ways, whiles they travailed to shed your blood? Behold here O ye blessed spirits, what your creator doth? Come ye, and behold even from the heavens, and ye shall see even the almighty himself kneeling before the feet of men, and tell me, if ever he used the like kind of courtesy with you? O Lord, I have heard thy words, and I was afraid: I have considered thy works, and was wholly amazed.[5] O ye blessed Apostles, why quake and tremble ye not, at the wonderful sight of this so great humility? Peter what doest thou? What? Wilt thou condescend, that this Lord of majesty shall wash thy feet?

Saint Peter when he beheld our savior kneeling before him, wondered exceedingly, yea he was altogether astonied thereat, and began to say in this wise? What meaneth this O Lord! What? Wilt thou wash my feet. Art not thou the son of the living God? Art not thou the creator of the world? The beauty of the heavens? The paradise of the angels? The redeemer of men? The brightness of the glory of the father? The fountain of the wisdom of God, which dwellest in the highest? And wilt thou (all this notwithstanding) wash my feet? What? Wilt thou (being a Lord of so great majesty, and glory, take such a vile and base office upon thee? Wilt thou (I say) thus abase thyself, that hast laid the foundation of the earth, and beautified

5 Hab. 3:2.

the same with so many wonders, that hast enclosed the wide world within thy hand, that movest the heavens, rulest the earth, dividest the waters, ordainest the times, disposest the causes, beautifiest the angels, directeth men, and governest all things with thy wisdom, Is it seemly that thou shouldest wash my feet? Mine I say, who am but a mortal man, a little clod of earth, and ashes, a vessel of corruption, a creature full freight with vanity, and ignorance, full of infinite miseries, and (which exceedeth all misery) full of sins, and yet all this notwithstanding, wilt thou o Lord wash my feet? What? Wilt thou being the Lord of all things, abase thyself under me, that am inferior to them all? Verily the highness of thy majesty, and the profundity of my miseries, do as it were enforce me, that I can not consent to such a deed. Leave therefore O my Lord:) leave (I pray thee) this base office for thy servants: lay down the towel, and put on thy apparel again, and sit in thy seat, and wash not my feet. Beware, that the heavens be not ashamed of it, when they shall see how by this ceremony, thou doest set them beneath the earth. For by doing this servile office, those very hands into whose power the father hath committed the heavens, and all other things, should be abased under the feet of men. Take heed that all natural creatures be not very much grieved, or rather in great disdain, to see themselves thus subjected under any other feet, than thine. Take heed also least the daughter of king Saul despise thee not, when she shall see thee girded about with this towel, after the manner of a servant, and say, that she will not take him for her spouse, and much less for her God, whom she seeth to attend upon so base, and vile an office.[6]

Such words, or the like spake Saint Peter, as a man that had not as yet any taste or feeling of things appertaining unto almighty God: and as one that understood not what great glory lay hidden in this work, which shewed to the eye so base, and vile. But our savior who knew it right well, and was withal desirous to leave unto us for a memory at that time, such a wonderful example of humility, satisfied the simplicity of his disciple, and went forward afterwards in the

6 See 2 Kgs. 6.

good work he had begun. Here we have to note with all diligence, what a great and earnest care our savior had to make us humble, in that being now at the gate, and entry into his most grievous, and bitter passion, wherein he knew he should give us such great and wonderful examples of humility, as might suffice to astonish both heaven, and earth, he thought all that not enough, but would furthermore add this notable example also besides all the rest, whereby this virtue of humility might the better be commended unto us. O wonderful virtue! How great must thy riches be, seeing thou art thus commended to us! How can thy treasures be but notoriously known, seeing thou art by so many ways set out unto us! O humility, that art preached, and taught in all the whole life of our Savior Christ, sung, and praised by the mouth of his own most blessed mother![7] O most beautiful flower among virtues! O divine adamant, that drawest unto thee even the creator of all things! Whosoever he be that banisheth thee away, shall be banished away from almighty God, yea though he be in the highest place of heaven: And whosoever he be, that embraceth thee, shall be embraced of almighty God, yea although he be even the greatest sinner in the world. Great are thy graces, and marvelous are thy effects. Thou pleasest men: thou contentest the angels: thou confoundest the devils, and bindest the hands of the creator. Thou art the foundation of virtues, the death of vices, the glass of virgins, and the habitation of the most blessed trinity. Who so gathereth without thee, disperseth: who so buildeth, and not upon thee, pulleth down: And who so heapeth virtues together without thee, the dust carrieth them quite away before the face of the wind. Without thee the virgin is shut out of the gates of heaven, and with thee even the public sinner is received at the feet of Christ.[8] Embrace this virtue of humility, O ye virgins, that hereby your virginity may be available unto you. Ye that be religious persons, see that you seek earnestly also for this virtue, for without it your religion is but vain, and to no purpose. And ye of the laity, seek no less for this virtue,

7 See Luke 1.
8 See Matt. 25; Luke 7.

than the religious do, that by the same ye may be delivered from the snares of this sinful world.

This being done, consider also how after our savior had washed their feet, he wiped them clean with that sacred towel wherewith he was girded: And lift up the eyes of thy soul somewhat higher, and there shalt thou see represented the mystery of our redemption. Consider how that fair towel received into it all the filth, and uncleanness of those feet, which were altogether very foul and filthy. And as the feet were made clean, and fair, so the towel contrariwise (after he had wiped their feet with it) was wholly bespotted, and defiled. Now what is more filthy, than a man conceived in sin? And what is more clean, and beautiful, than our Savior Christ conceived of the holy Ghost. *My well beloved is white, and well colored (saith the spouse,) and chosen out among thousands.*[9] This most sweet, and loving Lord then, that was so fair, and so clean, was content to receive into himself all the spots and filthiness of our souls, to wit, the pains which our sins deserved: and that he might leave our souls clean and free from them, he himself remained (as ye see him upon the cross,) all bespotted and defiled with the same. Insomuch that the very angels were as it were astonied (and surely not without good cause) to see their Lord, and creator, so berayed with this so strange foulness. And therefore they demanded by the prophet Isaias, saying, *Wherefore doest thou (O Lord) wear garments dyed with the color of blood, all bespotted, and berayed like unto them, that stamp grapes in the winepress?*[10] Now if this blood, and these foul spots be of others, (to wit, of our sins,) tell me o king of glory, were it not more meet that men themselves should suffer according to their own deserts, than that thou O most innocent Lord, shouldest be thus defiled, and tormented for their sakes? Had it not been more decent that this filthiness should have remained upon his own dunghill, and not upon thee, the mirror of all beauty? What a wonderful piety, and compassion was it, that moved thee to have such a fervent desire of the cleanness of my soul, that thou

9 Cant. 5:10.
10 See Is. 63:2.

wouldst with so great charge, and loss of thine own beauty, bestow it upon me? What man alive would take a fine towel wrought with gold, and wipe therewith a foul sluttish dish, especially such a dish, as were greatly broken, and rent in many places? Blessed art thou (o my most merciful, and loving Lord.) All the angels praise thee (O God) for evermore. For that it hath pleased thee to become as it were an outcast of the world, taking upon thee all our filthiness, and miseries, (which are the pains due unto us for our sins,) to deliver us quite, and make us free from them.

After this, consider those words, wherewith our savior made an end of this history: saying: *I have given you an example, that ye should do, even as I have done to you.*[11] Which words are to be referred not only to this matter, and example of humility, but even also to all the other works, and life of our savior Christ. Forsomuch as his whole life is a most perfect pattern of all virtues, especially of that virtue which in this place is represented unto us, to wit of, humility, as the blessed martyr Saint Ciprian declareth more at large in these words. It was chiefly (saith he) a work of great patience, and humility, that so high and excellent a majesty would vouchsafe to come down from heaven unto the earth, and clothe himself with our clay: and that he would dissemble the glory of his immortality, and become mortal, to the end, that being himself innocent, and faultless, he might be punished for such as were guilty. The Lord would be baptized of his servant: He that came to pardon sins, would be washed with the water of sinners: He that feedeth all creatures, fasted forty days in the wilderness, and in the end suffered hunger: which he did to this end, that all such as had a hungry appetite after God's word, and longed after his grace, might be satisfied and furnished with the same. He fought with the devil that tempted him, and contenting himself with the victory, offered his enemy no further harm, but by word only. His disciples he never despised, as a Lord doth his servants: but entertained them with great charity, and benevolence: yea he used them lovingly as brethren. Neither is it to be marveled at, that he thus

[11] John 13:15.

behaved himself towards his disciples, being as they were obedient: seeing he could suffer that arrant traitor Judas so patiently, and bear with him even until the end, and suffer him being his enemy to eat together with him at his own table, and knowing full well whereabout he went, would never discover him, but was content to receive a kiss of him, even of him (I say) that had sold him with such a traitorous peace.

Moreover, with what great patience did he bear with the Jews until that present hour? How painfully did he labor to move those unbelieving hearts with his preaching, to embrace the faith? What great travail took he to alure those ungrateful men unto him with good works? How meekly answered he to such as contraried him in his speech? With what clemency bare he with the proud? With what a wonderful humility yielded he to the furious rage of his enemies, and persecutors? How travailed he even until the very hour of his most bitter passion to recover them, that had been the murderers of the Prophets, and heinous rebels against almighty God. In like manner at the very hour of his passion (before they came to the shedding of his most precious blood, and to put him to a most cruel death,) how great were the opprobrious injuries they offered unto him? How patiently gave he them the hearing thereof? How great were the mocks and taunts he suffered? How patiently did he bear the vile spitting of those infernal mouths, that had himself not long before with the spittle of his own mouth restored a blind man to his perfect sight? How suffered he their whippings, whose servants are wont in his name with mighty power to whip the very devils? How was he crowned with thorns, that crowneth his martyrs with everlasting garlands? How was he smitten on the face with the palms of men's hands, that giveth the palm of victory unto such as be conquerors? How was he spoiled of his earthly garments, that appareleth the Saints with the garments of immortality? How was he proffered most bitter gall, that giveth us the bread of heaven? How was he offered vinegar to drink, that giveth us the cup of salvation? He that was so innocent, he that was so just, or rather very innocence, and justice itself, was accompted among thieves: the everlasting truth was accused with false witness: the judge of the whole world was condemned by wicked men: and the word of god received the sentence of death with silence? Consider moreover, at what time the Savior of our world was nailed upon the cross, and at the very hour of his death, when the stars were obscured, the elements troubled, when the earth quaked, when the light was darkened, when the sun turned away his eyes, and would not suffer his beams to shine upon the earth, least haply it might see such a great cruelty: Consider (I say) how even at this time our Savior did not so much as once open his mouth, or move himself: how he would not at the very last hour, and point of death, discover the glory of his majesty, but suffered continually that extreme, and violent conflict, even until the end, intending thereby to leave unto us an example of perfect patience.

Yea, moreover and all this, if those cruel bloody ministers, that crucified, and tormented his most blessed body, would have converted, and been penitent, he was ready to receive them to his grace, and favor, even at this very last instant: neither would he have shut up the gates of his Church from any man. Now therefore, what thing in the world can possibly be of greater benignity, and patience, than the blood of Christ, that giveth life, even unto them, that shed the same blood? But such, and so great is the patience of our sweet Savior Christ, which if it had not been such, and of so great power, the Church had not had Saint Paul in it at this day. Hitherto be the words of Saint Cyprian.

§. II. Of the Most Blessed Sacrament of the Altar: and of the Causes Wherefore It Was Instituted.

One of the principal causes of the coming of our Savior into this world, was to enkindle the hearts of men in the love of almighty God. For so said he by saint Luke: *I am come to put fire in the earth, and what would I else, but that it should burn?*[12] This fire did our savior

12 Luke 12:49.

put in the earth, when he bestowed upon men such, and so many wonderful benefits, when he wrought so great works of love among them, whereby he might steal away their hearts from them, and wholly inflame them in this fire of love. Now albeit that all the works of his most holy life do serve to this end: yet of all other, those do most effectually serve for this purpose, which he did in the end of his life: According as Saint John the Evangelist signifieth, saying. *His friends that he had in the world, he loved them especially in the end.*[13] For at that time as he bestowed greater benefits upon them, and discovered unto them greatest pledges and tokens of his love. Among which singular pledges, one of the most principal was the institution of the most blessed Sacrament of the Altar: the which thing shall appear very plainly unto him, that will consider with good attention the causes of the institution of the same. But in this behalf, I beseech thee (o most merciful Lord) that thou wilt vouchsafe to open our eyes, and grant us light, that we may see what causes they were, that moved thy loving heart to institute for us this so wonderful a Sacrament, and to leave it unto us.

Now that we may understand somewhat of this divine mystery, it is to be presupposed (good Christian reader) that no tongue created is able to express the passing great love, that our savior Christ beareth towards the Catholic Church his spouse, and consequently unto every soul, that is in the state of grace: Forsomuch as every such soul is also his spouse. For this cause, one of the things that the Apostle Saint Paul requested, and desired, was that almighty God would reveal unto us the greatness of his love:[14] which undoubtedly is so great, that it far passeth all the wisdom, and knowledge created: yea though it were even that wonderful knowledge of the angels.

Wherefore this our most sweet Bridegroom, when he minded to depart out of this life, and to absent himself from the Catholic Church his dear spouse: (to the intent, that this his absence might not be any occasion unto her to forget him) he left unto her for a remembrance,

---

13 See John 13:1.

14 See Eph. 3.

this most blessed Sacrament, wherein he himself would remain. For he could not bear, that between him and her there should be any less pledge to provoke her to be mindful of him, then even himself. And therefore he pronounced at that time those sweet words. *So often as ye shall do this thing, do it in the remembrance of me*:[15] that is, do it, that ye may be always mindful, how much I am willing to do for you, and how much I go now to do, and suffer for your salvation.

Moreover, this most sweet and loving bridegroom intended in this his long absence, to leave some company to his spouse, that she might not remain solitary, and comfortless. And therefore he left her the company of this most holy Sacrament, where even the bridegroom himself is really present, which is in very deed the best, and most delightful company, that he could possibly provide her.

At that time also, our savior would go to suffer death for his spouse, and to redeem and enrich her with the price of his own most precious blood: and to the intent that she might whensoever she would enjoy this most precious, and divine treasure, he left her the keys thereof in this most blessed Sacrament. For as Saint Chrysostom saith. *So often as we come to receive this most blessed Sacrament, we must make accompt, that we come to lay our mouths to Christ's very side, to drink of his most precious blood, and to be partakers of this sovereign, and divine mystery*. Consider therefore in what a dangerous case those men are, that for a little slothfulness do abstain to come unto this royal banquet, and to enjoy such a great, and most inestimable divine treasure. These be those unfortunate sluggards, of whom the wiseman speaketh, saying. *The sluggard hideth his hand in his bosom, and suffereth himself rather to die for hunger, than he will lift it up to his mouth*.[16] Now what greater slothfulness can there be imagined in a man, than this is, that because he will not abide to take so little labor, as he should bestow in preparing himself for the receiving of this most holy Sacrament, he will rather want the benefit of so great, and

15 See Luke 22:19; 1 Cor. 11:25.

16 See Prov. 19:24; 26:15.

inestimable divine treasure, which is of greater value, than all that ever almighty God hath created.

This heavenly bridegroom desired also to be loved of his spouse with a passing great love, and therefore he ordained this divine mystical morsel, consecrated with such words, that whosoever receiveth it worthily, is forthwith touched, and stricken with this love. O wonderful mystery, worthy to be engraved even in the innermost part of our hearts! Tell me (o thou ungrateful man) if a prince should bear such a great affection and love towards a seely wench, that were his bondslave, that he could find in his heart to take her for his spouse, and make her queen, and lady, of all he is Lord of, how great would we say, that the love of that prince had been, that would do such a deed? And if peradventure after marriage solemnized, this slave should shew herself coldly affected towards the prince her husband, and he understanding the same, would as a man forlorn, go to seek with all diligence for some precious morsel, and give it her to eat, whereby to win her love unto him, how passing great would we say that the love of that prince were, that should be thus affected towards her? Now therefore (O king of glory) what meaneth this, that thou (for the entire love thou bearest unto me) hast vouchsafed not only to take my soul to be thy spouse, (being as she was the very bondslave of thine enemy the devil,) but seeing her also, all this notwithstanding very coldly affected towards thee, hast ordained for her this mystical and divine morsel, which thou hast transformed with such words, that it hath virtue in it, to transform such souls into thee, as shall feed thereon, and make them to burn with lively flames of love? There is no one thing that declareth the affection of love more evidently, than when a man hath a desire to be beloved. Considering therefore that thou hast been so greatly desirous of our love, that thou hast sought it with such strange inventions, who shall from henceforth stand in doubt of thy love? Certain I am (o my most loving and merciful Lord) that if I love thee, thou also lovest me: And certain I am also, that I need not to seek any inventions to allure thy heart to love me, as thou hast sought to allure my heart to love thee.

That most sweet bridegroom would also be absent from his spouse, and yet because love cannot abide to be absent from the beloved, he would depart in such wise, that he might not altogether depart from her, and he would so go away, that he might also remain with her. Wherefore considering that it was not expedient for our Savior to tarry here still, and the spouse might not as then go from hence with him, he devised a mean, that although he went his way, and his spouse remained still behind, yet should then never be separated, and set a sonder. For this cause therefore he instituted this divine Sacrament, that by means thereof, the souls might be united, and incorporated spiritually with Christ, and that with such a strong bond of love, that of them two there should be made one thing. For like as of meat, and of him that eateth the meat, there is made one same thing: even so likewise after a certain manner, is there made of the soul, and of Christ: saving that (as St. Augustine saith) Christ is not changed into our souls, but our souls be changed into him: not by nature, but by love, conformity, and likeness of life.

Moreover, our Savior's will and pleasure was to assure his spouse, and to give her a pledge of that blessed inheritance of eternal glory, that she being fortified with the hope of this felicity, might pass cheerfully through all the troubles, adversities, afflictions, and persecutions of this life. For truly there is no one thing, that causeth us so much to despise all things, that are to be had in this life, as an assured hope of that blessedness, and felicity, we shall enjoy in the life to come. According as our Savior signified unto us in those words, he spake to his disciples, before his passion: *If ye loved me (said he) ye would be right glad of my departure, because I go to the father.*[17] As though he had said, it is a great felicity to go to the father: For although the way to go to him, be through whips, thorns, nails, crosses, and all other tribulations, and martyrdoms of this life: Yet all that notwithstanding, it is a thing of inestimable gain, and comfort, to go unto him. Wherefore, to the intent that his spouse might have a very firm and assured hope of this felicity, he left her here in

17 John 14:28.

pledge of this inestimable divine treasure, which is of as great value, as all that is there hoped for: that she should not mistrust, but that almighty God will give himself unto her in glory, where she shall live wholly in spirit, seeing he denieth not himself unto her in this vale of tears, where she liveth in flesh.

Our Savior purposed also at the hour of his death, to make his testament, and to leave unto his spouse some notable legacy to be as a relief, and comfort for her at all times. And so he left her this most blessed Sacrament, (wherein Christ himself is truly present,) which was the most precious, and most profitable bequest, that he could possibly leave unto her. Elias, when he would depart away from the earth, left his cloak to his disciple Elizeus, as one that had none other riches, whereof to make him his heir.[18] But our most sweet loving Savior, and master, when he would ascend into heaven, left here unto us the cloak of his sacred body, in this most holy Sacrament, appointing us here to be his heirs (as by the right of children) of this so great, and inestimable divine treasure. With that mantle Elizeus passed the waters of the flood Jourdan, and was neither drowned, nor wetshod: and with the virtue, and grace of this most blessed Sacrament, the faithful do pass the waters of the vanities, and tribulations of this life, without sin, and without danger.

To conclude, our Savior intended to leave unto our souls sufficient provision, and food, wherewith they might live: forsomuch as the soul hath no less need of her proper sustenance, to maintain her in the spiritual life, than the body hath of his proper food, for maintenance of the corporal life. If thou think otherwise, tell me (I pray thee,) why hath the body need of his ordinary meat every day? Undoubtedly the cause is, for that the natural heat continually wasteth, and consumeth the substance of our bodies, and therefore it is needful, that that be restored again with daily sustenance, which is consumed with daily heat. For otherwise the natural strength of man would very soon be at an end, and his powers would quickly decay. O that it pleased almighty God, that men might by this understand

[18] See 4 Kgs. 2.

the great necessity they have of this divine Sacrament! O that they could by this conceive the great wisdom, and mercy of him, that hath instituted and ordained the same for our behoof! Is it not a thing well known, that we have within these bowels of ours, a certain pestilent heat, that came unto us by the occasion of sin, which consumeth all the goodness, that is in man? This is that, which inclineth us to the love of the world, of our flesh, of all vices, of all sensual pleasures, and delights: and so by these means seperateth us from almighty God, maketh us to relent and wax cold in the love of him, and causeth us to become very dull, slothful, and heavy to all good works, and very quick and lively to work all wickedness. If then we have this continual waster and consumer so rooted within us, were it not good reason (trow ye) that there should be some restorative provided, to restore that always again, which is always wasting, and consuming? If we have a continual consumer, and have not withal a continual repairer, what may be looked for of us, but a continual decaying, and within short time after, a most certain and undoubted ruin? For proof hereof, it shall suffice to consider the course of the Christian people: by comparing the great fervency, and zeal in religion, of the Christians in the primitive Church, with the little, or rather no zeal of the Christians in our corrupt age. For in the primitive Church, when the Christians did eat continually of this divine meat, they lived therewith a very spiritual life, and had thereby force, and strength, not only to observe God's laws, and commandments, but also even to die, and suffer martyrdom for God's sake. But now alas, in this our corrupt age, the Christians for the most part are found to be very weak and feeble in their faith, and very dissolute and licentious in their lives, because they eat not of this divine food, and therefore in the end they perish, and die for hunger. As the prophet signified, when he said. *Therefore was my people carried away into captivity, because they had no knowledge of God, and there nobles perished for hunger, and the multitude of them died for thirst.*[19] For this cause therefore hath that wise physician our Savior Christ (who had also

19 Is. 5:13.

felt the pulses of our weakness) ordained this most holy and divine Sacrament, and for this purpose hath he instituted the same in form of meat, that the very form wherein he instituted it, might declare unto us the effect it worketh, and withal the great necessity our souls have of the same.

Consider then now, if there may be found in the whole world, any greater shew of love, than that almighty God himself should leave unto us his own very flesh, and blood, for our sustenance, and relief. We may read in many histories, that some mothers being constrained with intolerable hunger, have embrewed their hands in the flesh and blood of their own little children, to sustain themselves with feeding upon them, and that for the great desire they had to live, they have bereaved their own very natural children of their lives, thereby to preserve their own life.[20] This have we read often times. But who hath ever read, that any mother hath fed her child, that was ready to perish, and die for hunger, with her own very flesh? Or that she cut of one of her own arms, to give her child to eat, and that she would be cruel upon herself, to shew herself pitiful towards her child? Certainly there was never mother living yet in the earth, that ever hath done such a deed. But our most loving and sweet savior Christ, far passing any mother in love, perceiving thee to be ready to perish, and die for hunger, and seeing withal, that there was none other better mean to maintain thy life, than to give thee his own very flesh to eat, cometh down from heaven, and yieldeth himself here to the cruel butchers, and tormentors to be put to death, that thou mightiest preserve and sustain thy life, with this divine meat, and this he doth, not at one time only, but his blessed will is, that it shall be done continually, and therefore he ordaineth this most blessed Sacrament, that thou mightest hereby understand an other degree of greater love: which is, that as he giveth thee always the same meat, to wit, his own very body in this most blessed Sacrament, so is he ready always to pay the same price, and redemption, if it were necessary for thee.

---

20 See 4 Kgs. 6:28–29.

Besides all this, thou must consider, that this most holy reformer of the world, intended to restore man unto his ancient dignity, and to raise him up again so much by grace, as he had fallen by sin. And therefore as his fall was from a life that he had of God, (which life our first father Adam before his fall had enjoyed,) to the life of beasts (wherein after his fall he remained:) even so contrariwise, his will was, that he should be raised up again from the life of beasts, in which he remained, to the life of God, which (through sin) he had lost: and so for this end hath our savior Christ ordained the communion of this most holy, and divine Sacrament, by means whereof, man attaineth to be partaker of God, and to live the life of God: as our savior himself signifieth in those most high words, which he said: *He that eateth my flesh, and drinketh my blood, dwelleth in me, and I in him,*[21] And like as by the dwelling of my father in me, the life that I live is altogether conformable to the life of my father (which is the life of God:) even so he in whom I shall dwell by means of this divine Sacrament, shall live as I do live, and so shall he not now live the life of a man, but even the life of God. For this is that most high divine Sacrament, wherein God is received corporally: not that he is changed into men, but men are changed into him by love, and conformity of will: forsomuch as this divine meat worketh the same operation in him, that doth worthily receive it, that is wrought and represented in it, when it is consecrated. For like as by the virtue of the words of consecration, that which was bread, in converted into the substance of Christ: even so by virtue of this holy communion, he that was man, is by a marvelous manner transformed spiritually into God. So that like as that divine bread is one thing, and appeareth as an other, and was one thing before consecration, and is an other thing afterwards: even so he that eateth the same, is one thing before the receiving, and an other thing afterwards: and he appeareth one thing outwardly, but in very deed is an other thing, (and that far more high and excellent) inwardly: forsomuch as he hath the being and substance of man, and withal the spirit of God. Now then, what glory can be greater than this? What

---

[21] John 6:57.

gift more precious? What benefit of more value? What greater shew of love? Let all the works of nature keep silence. Let all the works of grace give place. For this is a singular grace above all graces. O most wonderful Sacrament, what shall I say of thee? With what words shall I commend thee? Thou art the life of our souls: the medicine of our wounds: the comfort of our troubles: the memory of Jesus Christ: the testimony of his love: the most precious legacy of his testament: the companion of our peregrination: the consolation of our banishment: the burning coal to enkindle the fire of the love of God in us: the mean whereby to receive grace: the pledge of everlasting felicity: and the treasure of the Christian life. By means of this divine meat, the soul is united unto her spouse: by this, the understanding is illuminated: the memory quickened: the will enamored: the inward taste delighted: the devotion increased: the bowels mollified, the fountain of tears opened: the passions of the mind quieted: the good motions awakened: our weakness fortified: and by mean of this divine meat, we receive strength and loftiness, to ascend up even to the hill of almighty God. What tongue is able fully to express the excellency of this most blessed Sacrament? Who can give worthy thanks for so great a benefit? Who will not be altogether resolved into tears, when he seeth almighty God united unto him? Assuredly, the more we go about to consider the excellency, and virtues, of this divine sovereign mystery, the more do we want words to express it: and the more doth our understanding fail us therein. Now what pleasure? What sweetness? What delightful favors of good life doth the soul of the just man feel at that time, when he receiveth this divine Sacrament? There is none other found hard at that time, but only sweet songs of the inward man, vehement bursting out of holy desires, yielding of thanks, and uttering most sweet words, all tending to the praise of our sweet Savior Christ her beloved. There the devout soul through the virtue of this most holy and reverent Sacrament, is altogether inwardly renewed, and replenished with joy. There she is recreated with devotion: fed with peace: fortified in faith: confirmed in hope: and tied fast with bonds, and knots of charity, unto her most sweet savior, and redeemer: Whereby she waxeth daily more fervent in love: more strong in resisting temptation: more prompt, and ready, to sustain labor, and travail: more careful, and diligent, to do good works: and more desirous to frequent this most holy mystery.

Such are thy gifts (O sweet Jesus:) such are the works, and delights of thy love, which thou art wont to communicare unto thy friends, by means of this divine Sacrament. And this thou doest, to the end that we being filled with these so great, and mighty delights, should despise all other vain, and deceitful delights. Now therefore (O most mellifluous love) open the eyes of thy faithful Catholic people, open them, I beseech thee, O most divine light, that with the bright beams of lively faith they may know thee, and dilate their hearts, that they may receive thee into them: that being instructed by thee, they may seek thee by thee, and repose and rest themselves in thee, and finally by means of this most blessed Sacrament be united with thee, as members with their head, and as branches with their vine, that so they may live through thy virtue, and enjoy the influences of thy grace, for ever, and ever, world without end. Amen.

The meditation being ended, there follow immediately thanks giving, and petition, as hath been before declared.

TUESDAY MORNING

The Text of the Holy Evangelists.

WHEN supper was done, Christ went with his disciples into a garden, which is called Gethsemane. And he said unto them. Sit ye here, whilst I go, and pray yonder. And he took with him Peter, and the two sons of Zebedee. And he began to be in a great fear, and heaviness. And he said unto them. My soul is heavy even unto death. Tarie ye here, and watch with me. So he went a little further from them, where he cast himself down prostrate on the earth, and fell on his face, and prayed, saying. O my Father, if it be possible, let this cup pass from me: nevertheless, not as I will, but as thou wilt. This done, he came to his Disciples, and found them asleep. And he said to Peter: What? Could ye not watch with me one hour? Watch, and pray, that ye enter not into temptation. The spirit is ready, but the flesh is weak. Again he went away the second time, and made the same prayer: saying. O my Father, if this cup cannot pass away from me, but that I must needs drink it, thy will be done. And he came a second time, and found his Disciples asleep: for their eyes were heavy. So he left them, and went away again, and prayed the third time, saying the same words. And there appeared an angel to him from heaven, comforting him. And being in an agony, he prayed more at length. And his sweat was like drops of blood, trickling down to the ground. Then he came to his Disciples, and said unto them. Sleep from hence forth, and take your rest. Behold the hour is at hand, and the son of man shall be delivered into the hands of sinners. Arise, let us go, behold he is at hand, that shall betray me. And whiles he yet spake, lo, Judas one of the twelve came, and with him a great multitude, with swords, and staves, and torches, and lanterns, being sent from the high priests, and elders of the people. Now he that betrayed him, had given them a token: saying: whomsoever I shall kiss, that is he, lay hands on him. And forthwith he came to Jesus, and said: Hail master, and kissed him. Then Jesus said unto him. Friend, wherefore art thou come? And Simon Peter drew out his sword, and stroke a servant of the high priest, and cut off his right ear. This servant was called Malcus. Then Jesus said unto Peter: put up thy sword into the scabbard. The cup that my Father hath given me, wilt thou not, that I drink it? And he touched the ear, and forthwith made it whole. At that time Jesus said to the high priests, and to the officers of the temple, and to the elders, that came unto him. Ye be come out, as it were, against a thief, with swords, and staves. I sat daily among you, teaching in the temple, and ye laid no hands on me. But this is your hour, and the power of darkness. Then the soldiers, and the captain, and the officers of the Jews, took Jesus, and bound him, and led him away to Annas first, (for he was father in law to Caiphas,) who was the high priest for that year. Then all the Disciples forsook him, and fled.[1]

Meditations upon These Points of the Text.

§. I. Of the Prayer of Our Savior in the Garden: and of His Apprehension.

What doest thou O my soul? What thinkest thou? It is no time now to sleep: Come with me I pray thee into the garden of Gethsemane, and there shalt thou hear, and see great mysteries. There shalt thou see joy stroken with sadness: fortitude waxen afraid: strength discomfited: majesty and omnipotence confounded: greatness, and

1 See Matt. 26:36–56; Mark 14:32–50; Luke 22:39–54; John 18:1–13.

mightiness, very narrowly straightened: and glory itself obscured, and darkened.

Consider now first, how after that supper (which was so full of mystery) was ended, our Savior went with his disciples unto the mount Olivet to make his prayer, before he would enter into the combat of his passion: to give us thereby to understand, that in all troubles, and temptations of this life, we must always have recourse unto prayer, as it were to an holy anchor, by virtue whereof, the burden of tribulation shall either be taken quite away from us: or else we shall have strength given us, to be able to bear it: which is a far greater grace. For (as St. Gregory saith) our Lord doth us a greater benefit, when he giveth us force, and strength, to be able to sustain troubles, and temptations, than when he taketh the same troubles and temptations away from us.

Our Savior took with him (to accompany him in this way) three of his best beloved Disciples: to wit: St. Peter: St. James, and St. John: which three a little before, had been witness of his glorious transfiguration. And this he did, that the very same persons might see, what a far different shape he took now upon him for the love of men, from that glorious shape, wherein he had shewed himself unto them at his transfiguration. And because they should understand, that the inward troubles, and agony of his soul, were no less than those that began to be discovered outwardly, he spake unto them those sorrowful words. *My soul is heavy even unto death: tarry me here, and watch with me.*[2] That very God, and true man, that man that far excelleth both our human nature, and all things created, whose dealing, and conference, was with the very brest of the high Deity itself, with whom only he communicated his secrets, is now fallen into so great sorrow, and heaviness, that he is contented to give part of his pains unto his creatures, and to require of them their company saying: *tarry me here, and watch with me.* O treasure of heaven! O perfect felicity! Who hath brought thee O Lord unto such a harrow straight? Who hath driven thee to seek at other men's gates? Who

[2] Matt. 26:38.

hath caused thee to become a beggar, even of thine own creatures? Who hath done all this, but only the very great love thou hast to make them rich.

Tell me O most sweet and merciful redeemer? Wherefore art thou now so much afraid of death, which before thou didst so much desire: seeing the fulfilling of the desire, is a cause rather of joy, than of fear? Verily the Martyrs had neither the fortitude, nor yet the grace, that thou hast. They had only a little portion, which thou (being the fountain of grace) didst impart unto them: and yet they with that only small quantity of grace, entered very cheerfully into the combat of their martyrdoms, and achieved the victory. And art thou (O Lord) being the giver of strength, and grace, sad, and fearful now, even before the battle begins? Assuredly (O Lord) this thy fear is not thine, but mine: as likewise the strength, and fortitude of thy Martyrs, was not theirs, but thine. The fear that thou hast, cometh of that, thou hast of us, and the strength and fortitude that the martyrs had, came of that, they had received of thee. The weakness of my human nature is discovered in that God was afraid: and the strength of thy godhead is shewed in the fortitude of man. So that this fear is mine, and that fortitude is thine. And therefore thy reproach is mine, and my praise is thine.

There was taken a rib bone out of the side of our forefather Adam to form a woman thereof: and in steed of the bone, that was taken away, there was put weak and feeble flesh.[3] Now what else is signified hereby, but that the everlasting father took from thee, being our second Adam, the force and strength of grace, to place the same in thy spouse the Catholic Church: and took from her the feeble flesh, and weakness, to place it in thee? By means whereof thy spouse remained strong, and thou weak: the strong, by reason of thy strength: and thou weak, by reason of her weakness. Thou hast herein (O heavenly Lord) bestowed a double benefit upon us, in that thou hast vouchsafed, not only to clothe us with thee, but even also to clothe thyself with us. For these two so singular benefits the angels praise thee for

3 See Gen. 2.

evermore, for that thou hast been no niggard in communicating thy benefits unto us, nor yet disdained to take upon thee our miseries. Now when I consider these things (O Lord,) what else should I do, but seeing myself, as it were loden with thy mercies, glory in thee, and seeing thee to be likewise replenished with my miseries for my sake, take compassion upon thee? For the one I will rejoice, and be glad: and for the other I will sorrow, and lament. And so with joy and lamentation together, I will sing and bewail the mystery of thy most dolorous passion: and I will study continually in that book of Ezechiel contents whereof are songs, and lamentations.[4]

When our savior had spoken these words he departed from his disciples a stone's cast, where lying prostrate upon the ground, he began his prayer with very great reverence: saying, *O father, if it be possible, let this cup pass from me, howbeit not as I will, but as thou wilt.*[5] And after he had made this prayer three times, at the third time he was in such a great agony, that he began to sweat even drops of blood, which ran down all along his sacred body, and trickled down to the ground.[6]

Consider now attentively, in what a dolorous case our savior was, and how there were then represented unto him all the cruel pains and torments he had to suffer, even as though they had been then presently in doing before his eyes: all which he apprehended after a most perfect manner in his most excellent imagination, each one in such sort, as they were prepared for his body, which was certainly more tender, and delicate, than ever any other body was in the whole world. He set also at that time before his eyes all the sins of the world, for which he should suffer: and withal the great unthankfulness and ingratitude of so many souls, as (he knew) would never acknowledge this his singular benefit, nor further and help themselves with this most precious, and so costly remedy. These things being profoundly weighed, and considered by our savior at this time,

4 See Ezech. 2.

5 Matt. 26:39.

6 See Luke 22.

his soul was vexed in such sort, and his senses, and most tender flesh, were so wonderfully troubled, that all the forces, and elements of his body were distempered, and his blessed flesh opened on every side, and gave place to the blood, that it might pass and distill through all parts of his body in very great abundance, and stream down to the ground. Now if the flesh suffered such grievous pains, with the only remembrance, and imagination, of that which as then was to come, in what a doleful case then, trow ye, was his soul, that suffered those pains even directly in itself.

In other men we see, when they are disquieted with any sudden, and great anguish, the blood useth commonly to have recourse unto the heart, leaving the other members of the body cold and destitute of their strength, to comfort the most principal member. But our sweet Savior Christ contrariwise, (because he would suffer without any manner of comfort, thereby to make our redemption more abundant,) such was his passing love towards us, that he would not admit so much, as that little relief, and comfort of nature.

Behold our sweet savior now in this dolorous agony, and consider not only the painful anguishes, and griefs of his soul, but also the form of his sacred, and reverent countenance.

The sweat is wont to have his most chief, and principal recourse to the forehead, and to the face. If then the blood issued out through all the body of our Savior, in such sort, that it trickled down to the very earth: in what plight then was that goodly clear forehead think you, that giveth light to the very light itself? And how was that face berayed, which is so reverenced of the heavens, being as it was all in drops, and covered over with a bloody sweat. If such as be kind, and loving, are wont when they come to visit their friends, being sick, and in danger of death, to behold their countenance advisedly, and to mark the color, and other accidents, that proceed of the disease, tell me o my soul, that beholdest the face of our sweet savior, what thinkest thou, when thou beholdest in the same such wonderful, strange, and deadly signs? What painful fits, and dolorous griefs, are those like to be hereafter, if in the very beginning of the disease he suffer such a great agony? In what dolorous pangs is he like to be, when he shall feel those most grievous pains, and cruel torments themselves, if in the only thinking of them, he sweateth even drops of blood? If thou be not moved to take compassion of our sweet savior, seeing him in this doleful case for thy sake: If now when he sweateth drops of blood throughout all his body, thou canst not shed any tears from thine eyes, think verily with thyself, that thou hast a very hard and stony heart: and if thou canst not weep for want of love towards him, yet at the least weep for the multitude of thy sins: forsomuch as they were the very cause of this his agony, and grief. Now the tormentors do not whip him: neither do the soldiers crown him with thorns: It is not now the nails, nor the thorns, that do cause the blood to gush out of his body at this time: but it is thy very sins, and offences. Those are the thorns that do prick him: those are the tormentors that do torment him: those are the heavy burden, that cause him to sweat this so strange, and wonderful bloody sweat. O my sweet savior, and redeemer, how dearly hast thou bought my salvation, and redemption! O my true Adam, that art come out of paradise for my sins, and laborest here in earth with thy bloody sweat, to get the bread that I must feed upon.

Consider also in this place, on the one side, the great agony, and watching of our Savior Christ, and on the other, the sound and deep sleeping of his disciples, and thou shalt see here represented a great mystery. For truly there is nothing more to be lamented in the world, than to see how careless and negligent men be in their lives, and how little accompt they make of a matter of so great importance, as is their own salvation. What thing is more to be bewailed, than to see men so careless in such weighty affairs? Now if thou wilt understand both the one, and the other, consider in this matter, the doings of our savior, and withal the doings of his disciples. See how our savior applying his mind earnestly to this business of our redemption, is in such a great care, and agony therewith, that it maketh him to sweat even drops of blood: and see on the other side, how his disciples do lie along on the ground, and are so heavy asleep that neither their master's rebuking of them, nor their ill favored and hard lodging on the bare ground, nor yet the obscure and dark dewy night, are able to awake them out of their heavy and drowsy sleep. Note also of what importance the salvation of mankind is, sith it is able to make him to sweat drops of blood, by whose power the heavens are sustained. And consider on the other side, how little accompt men themselves make of their own salvation, sith at such time as almighty God himself is so careful, and watchful for them, they are in a deep heavy sleep, and utterly careless thereof. Assuredly, nothing could more lively express both the one, and the other, than the consideration of these two points, being so strange as they are. For if almighty God do take so great care about the affairs of others, how happeneth it, that the very persons themselves, to whom even the charge and travail of the affairs appertaineth, (together with the profit, commodity, loss, and damage of the same) do live with such carelessness, and negligence therein?

By this same care of our Savior, and carelessness of his disciples, thou mayst understand, how truly this Lord is our father, and how he hath indeed towards us the very bowels, and heart of a true, and loving father. How often times chanceth it, trow ye, that the daughter sleepeth very soundly, and quietly, when her father watcheth all the night, carking and caring for her relief, and provision. And even so doth this our most loving and merciful father for us, whiles we be so heavy asleep, and are utterly careless of our own salvation, as by this example is lively set out before our eyes, in that he continueth all the night watching, and sweating, and in great agony to take order for the redemption he intended to bestow upon us.

§. II. How Our Savior Was Apprehended.

Consider moreover, how when our savior had finished his prayer, Judas that counterfeit and false friend of his, came thither with that hellish company, where renouncing the office of an Apostle, he became now the very principal ringleader and Captain of Satan's army. Consider how without all shame he pressed, and set himself even the very foremost before all the rest of his malicious rout: and coming to his good master, sold him with a kiss of most traitorous, and deceitful friendship. It is certainly a great misery, that a man should be sold for money, but yet it is much more miserable, if he be sold of his friends, and of such, as to whom he hath been greatly beneficial before. Now our sweet Savior Christ is sold of him, whom he had made not only his disciple, but also his Apostle: yea, he is sold of him by deceit and plain treason, he is sold of him to most cruel merchants, that covet (you may be sure) nothing else of him, but only his blood, and life, to satisfy their greedy hunger. But for what price trow ye, is he sold? The baseness and smallness of the price increaseth the greatness and malice of the injury. Tell me, O Judas, thou naughty traitor, at what price dost thou set the Lord of all creatures? At thirty pence. O what a vile and slender price is this for a Lord of such majesty! Certainly, a very beast in the shambles is commonly sold for more. And dost thou o traitor, sell for so small a price almighty God himself? He setteth not thee at so small a price: forsomuch as he buyeth thee with his own most precious blood. O what a great price and estimation was that of man! And how base an estimation and price was this of God! God is sold for thirty pence: and man is bought even with the very precious blood of almighty God himself!

At the same time our savior said unto them that came to lay hands upon him: *Ye be come out, as it were against a thief, with swords, and spears, and I sat daily among you, teaching in the temple, and ye never laid hands upon me, but this is your hour, and the power of darkness.*[7] This is surely a mystery of great admiration. For what thing is more to be wondered at, than to see the very son of almighty God to take upon him the Image, and shape, not only of a sinner, but even also of a condemned person? *This (saith he) is your hour, and the power of darkness.* The which words give us to understand, that from that time, that most innocent lamb was given up into the power of the princes of darkness, which are the devils, to the intent that by means

7 Matt. 26:55; Luke 22:53.

of their members, and cruel ministers, they might execute upon him all the furious torments and cruelties they could devise. And like as holy Job, was by the permission of almighty God given up into the power of Satan, that he might use upon him all the cruelty he would, this only excepted, that he should not bereave him of his life:[8] even so was there power given to the princes of darkness, without any exception either of life, or death, that they might fully extend upon that sacred humanity all their fury and rage to the uttermost they could. Hereof rose those despiteful taunts, those slanderous and reproachful words, such as the like were never heard before that time, wherewith the devil pretended to satisfy his unsatiable rancor, and malice, to revenge his injuries, and to cast that blessed soul down into some kind of impatiency, if it had been possible. Almighty God (saith the Prophet Zacharie) shewed Jesus the high priest unto me, appareled with a spotted garment, and Satan stood at his right hand, ready prepared to speak against him.[9] But our Savior answered for his part, saying: *I did always set God before mine eyes, who standeth at my right hand, that I be not removed.*[10]

Consider then now o my soul, how much that high and divine majesty abased himself for thy sake, sithence he vouchsafed to come to the last extremity of all miseries, which is, to be given up to the power of devils. And because this was the pain, that was due to thy sins, it pleased him to put even himself to this pain, that thou mightest remain quite and free from the same. O holy Prophet, why dost thou wonder to see almighty God become inferior to his angels?[11] Thou hast now far greater cause to wonder, to see him given up into the power of devils. Undoubtedly both the heavens, and the earth, trembled, and quaked, at this so passing great humility, and charity of our Savior. So soon as these words were spoken, forthwith all that hellish rout, and malicious rabble of ravening wolves assaulted this most meek and innocent lamb, and some very furiously haled him

8 See Job 2.
9 See Zach. 3.
10 Ps. 15:8.
11 See Ps. 8.

this way, and some that way, each one to the uttermost of his power. O how ungently did they handle him! How uncourteously spake they unto him! How many blows and buffets gave they him! What a vile clamorous crying and shouting made they over him, even as conquerors use to do, when they have obtained their prey! They lay hold upon those holy hands (which not long before had wrought so many wonderful miracles,) and do bind them very hard, and fast, with certain rough, and knotty cords: and that in such force, that they gall the skin of his arms, and make the very blood to spring out. Our savior being thus bound, they lead him openly through the high common streets, with great despite, and ignominy. O what a strange and wonderful sight is this! Consider now with thyself, what thou wouldst think, if thou knewest some man of great authority, and worthiness, and shouldest see him led openly by the officers through the common streets, with an halter tied about his neck, his hands manacled and fast bound, in a great hurly burly, and concourse of people, with great clashing, and noise of men of arms, and soldiers guarding him: Imagine (I say) with thyself, what thou wouldst think in this case: and then lift up thine eyes, and behold this Lord, worthy of so great reverence, and honor, that had wrought such wonders in that land, that had preached such divine sermons among them, whom all the sick and impotent persons, did honor, and reverence, and besought to have remedy for all their diseases, and griefs. Consider now, how they lead him, as one deprived of all authority, and to put to open shame: partly going, and partly hauled forwards, and enforced to hasten his pace: not in such wise, as became a man of his gravity, and personage, but as it liked the outrageous fury of his unmerciful enemies, and the desire they had to pleasure the Pharisees, who had so great a longing to have that prey within their grips. Consider our savior well, how he goeth in this doleful way, abandoned of his own disciples, accompanied with his enemies: his pace hastened and disordered: his breath in a manner gone: his color changed: his face chafed, and inflamed, by reason of his so quick, and hasty passage. And yet in all this evil entreating of his person, behold the modest behavior of his countenance, the comely gravity of his eyes, and that divine resemblance, which in the midst of all the discourtesies in the world could never be obscured. Ascend also yet a little higher, and consider diligently what he is, whom thou seest thus led, and carried away, with such great contumely, and dishonor. This is he, that is the word of the father: the everlasting wisdom: the infinite virtue: the chief goodness: the perfect felicity: the true glory: and the clear fountain of all beauty. Consider then, how for thy salvation, and redemption, virtue is here tied with bands: innocence apprehended: wisdom flouted, and laughed to scorn: honor contemned: glory tormented: and the clear wellspring of all beauty troubled with weeping, and sorrow. If Heli the priest felt such an inward grief, when the Ark of the testament was taken, that being astonished therewith, he fell from the seat whereupon he sat, and brake his neck, and forthwith gave up the Ghost?[12] How ought a Christian soul to be grieved, when he seeth the ark of all the treasures of the wisdom of almighty God, led, and taken in the possession of such unmerciful and cruel enemies? The heavens and earth praise him therefore, and all that is in them: for he hath heard the cries of the poor, and hath not despised the sorrowful bewailings of his afflicted, that were in captivity,[13] but was content to be taken captive himself, to deliver them out of their thraldom and to set them at liberty.

§. III. Of Those That Do Spiritually Bind the Hands of Our Savior Christ.

Wherefore (O most gentle, and sweet savior) sithence it was thy blessed will, and pleasure, to be bound, to the intent, thou mightest by thy bands unloose us, and deliver us from our captivity, I most humbly beseech thee, even by the bowels of thy tender mercy, that caused thee to abase thyself after this sort, that thou wilt not suffer me to commit any such great wickedness, as to bind thy hands, as the Jews did.

---

12 See 1 Kgs. 4.

13 See Ps. 68.

For it is not the Jews only, that do bind thy hands, but whosoever maketh resistance against thy holy inspirations, and will not go wither thou wilt guide, and conduct him, but refuseth to accept that grace, which thou dost most mercifully offer unto him.

That man likewise bindeth thy hands, that giveth any scandalous offence unto his neighbor, and by his evil example, and naughty counsel, withdraweth him from his godly purposes, and so hindereth the good work, that thou didst begin to work in him.

The mistrustful, and incredulous persons also, do bind O Lord the hands of thy liberality, and clemency. For like as confidence openeth the hands of thy grace: even so doth incredulity, and mistrustfulness close them up, and bind them: according to the saying of the Evangelist, that thou couldest not do many virtues, and miracles in thy country, by reason of the incredulity of the inhabitants therein.[14]

Moreover, the ungrateful, and negligent persons, do bind thy hands O Lord, and do put an impediment to let the working of thy grace: the one, because they render not thanks unto thee, for the grace they have received: and the other, because they will not use the grace, that is given unto them, but do keep it idle, and unoccupied, without taking any benefit, or commodity of the same.

Last of all, those that become vainglorious, and proud, by reason of the graces, thou hast given them, do also most strongly bind thy hands. For by this offence they make themselves altogether unworthy of thy grace. Wherefore it is not reason, that thou shouldest continue to be beneficial unto such persons, as take occasion thereof to become more vain: neither is it seemly, that thou shouldest bestow the treasures of thy grace upon such a one, as yieldeth not to thee again the tribute of glory: but doth rather like a traitor, and robber, wax insolent, and vaunting, with the same, and usurpeth to himself the right, and prerogative of glory, that appertaineth unto thee alone.

I might say also, O Lord, that those talkers, and prattlers, that keep not secret such consolations, and spiritual feelings, as thou

14 See Matt. 13.

givest them, do likewise bind thy hands: for like as wise, and discrete men, will not communicate their secrets any more unto them, who they have found unfaithful in publishing them abroad; even so dost thou also many times leave to make those persons partakers of thy secrets, who without any cause do publish, and reveal them to others, and take occasion thereby to make themselves more vain.

WEDNESDAY MORNING

THIS day, when thou hast made the sign of the Cross, and prepared thyself hereunto,) thou hast to meditate upon the presentation of our Savior before the bishops, and Judges. First, before Annas. Secondly, before Caiphas. Thirdly, before Herod. Fourthly, before Pilate. And afterwards, how he was most cruelly whipped, and scourged at the pillar.

The Text of the Holy Evangelists.

When our Savior was brought before Annas the bishop, he demanded him of his Disciples, and of his doctrine. Jesus answered him, and said: I spake openly to the world, I ever taught openly in the Synagogue, and in the temple, whither all the Jews resort continually, and in secret I said nothing. Why asketh thou me? Ask them that heard me, what I said unto them. When he had spoken these words, one of the officers that stood by, smote Jesus with his hand, saying. Answerest thou thus the bishop? Jesus answered him. If I have spoken evil, bear witness of the evil: But if I have spoken well, why smitest thou me.

And Annas sent him bound unto Caiphas,[1] where the doctors of the law, and the ancients of the people were gathered together. And the high priest, and the Scribes, and the whole council, sought for false witness against Jesus to put him to death, but found none,

[1] John 18:19–24.

though many false witnesses came thither, but their witness agreed not together. But at the last came two false witnesses, and said. This man said. I can destroy the temple of God, and build it up again in three days. Then the chief priest arose, and said to him: I conjure thee, in the name of the living God, that thou tell us, whether thou be Christ the son of God. Jesus said to him. Thou hast said it: Nevertheless I say unto you. Hereafter shall ye see the son of man sitting at the right hand of the power of God, and come in the clouds of the heaven. Then the high priest rent his clothes, saying: He hath blasphemed, what need we any more witnesses? Behold, ye have now heard his blasphemy. What think ye? They answered, and said: he is worthy to die. Then spat they in his face, and buffeted him, and others gave him blows on his face, saying. Areed O Christ, who is he, that smote thee?[2]

The next day in the morning, the whole multitude of them arose, and led our Savior unto Pilate. And they began to accuse him, saying: we have found this man perverting the people, and forbidding to pay tribute to Caesar: saying: that he is the king Messias. And Pilate asked him, saying: Art thou the king of the Jews? And he answered him, and said: Thou sayest it. And when he was accused of the chief priests, and elders, he answered nothing. Then said Pilate unto him. Hearest thou not, how many things they lay against thee? But he answered him not to one word, insomuch that the president marveled greatly. Then said Pilate to the high priests, and to the people. I find no fault in this man. But they were more fierce, saying: He moveth the people, teaching throughout all Judea, beginning at Galilee even to this place.

Now when Pilate heard of Galilee, he asked whether the man were of Galilee born. And when he knew he was of Herod's jurisdiction, he sent him to Herod, who was also at Jerusalem in those days. And when Herod saw Jesus, he was exceedingly glad. For he was desirous to see him of a long season, because he had heard many things of him, and trusted to have seen some sign done by him. The

2 See Matt. 26:59–68; Mark 14:55–65.

high Priests, and the Scribes stood forth, and accused him vehemently. And Herod with his men of war contemned, and mocked him, and put a white garment upon him, and sent him again to Pilate.[3]

And by reason of the solemnity of the feast of Easter, the president was wont then of custom to deliver unto the people a prisoner, whom they would demand. And there was at that time a notable malefactor in prison, called Barrabas. When they were then gathered altogether, Pilate said unto them: Whether of the two will ye that I let loose unto you, Barrabas, or Jesus, that is called Christ? And they answered: Not this man, but Barrabas. This Barrabas was cast into prison for a certain insurrection, and murder, committed in the city. Then said Pilate unto them: What shall I do then with Jesus, that is called Christ. They cried all: let him be crucified. Then Pilate took Jesus, and scourged him.[4]

Meditations upon These Points of the Text.

§. I. Of the Presentation of Our Savior before Annas: Caiphas: Herod: and Pilate: and of Our Savior's Whipping at the Pillar.

Many things hast thou (O my soul) this day to contemplate, and consider. This day must thou accompany our Savior to many stations, unless thou intend to run away with his disciples: or else feelest thy feet over heavy to tread those paths, which our Savior vouchsafed to tread for thy sake. This day is he brought five times before divers Judges, and for thy sake is evil entreated in each of their houses, and payeth that, which thou hast deserved. In one house he is buffeted: in an other spitted upon: in an other mocked, and scorned: in an other whipped, and crowned with thorns, and condemned by an unjust sentence to a most cruel death. Consider whether these stations be

3 Luke 23:1–8, 10–11; Matt. 27:12–14.
4 See Matt. 27:15–26; Luke 23:17–25; John 18:39–19:1.

not of force to break and rive thy heart, and to make thee to go barefoot with him, with the blood running about thy feet.

Let us go then to the first station, which was in Annas house, and mark there, how whilst our Savior answered very courteously unto the demand, that the Bishop made unto him concerning his disciples, and doctrine, one of those wicked caitiffs that stood there by, gave him a great blow upon the face, saying: *Answerest thou thus the Bishop*. Unto whom our Savior very gently answered: *If I have spoken evil, shew me wherein, and if I have spoken well, why strikest thou me?*[5]

Consider here now (O my soul) not only the mildness of this gentle answer, but also that divine face, which beareth the print, and is changed very red in color with the force and violence of the blow. Consider also that most constant and modest look of his clear eyes, which were nothing at all distempered in that so fierce and shameful assault. Consider withal that most holy soul, that was inwardly so humble and ready to have turned the other cheek, if the naughty wretched caitiff had required it. O cursed and unfortunate hand, that durst thus strike, and beray that divine face, before whose reverent aspect the very heavens do stop, and bow! At whose majesty even the Seraphines and all things created do tremble, and quake! What sawest thou in him, that thou shouldest thus be provoked to disfigure him, who is the lively Image of the glory of the father? What moved thee to use this despiteful kind of most villainous reproach unto him, who is the most beautiful among all the sons of men.[6]

But this was not the last injury our Savior suffered that night: For from the house of Annas, they lead him to the house of the Bishop Caiphas, whither reason would that thou shouldest go with him to keep him company: and there shalt thou see the son of justice darkened with an Eclipse, and that divine countenance defiled most unreverently with spittle, which the Angels desire to behold.[7] For

5 John 18:22–23.
6 See Ps. 44:3.
7 See 1 Ptr. 1:12.

when our Savior was conjured in the name of the father to tell them what he was, he answered truly unto their demand, as it was meet he should: but those wicked men that were so utterly unworthy to hear such a high and excellent answer, being blinded with the brightness of so great light, assaulted him like mad dogs, and disgorged upon him all their malice, and fury. There each one to the uttermost of his power gaveth him buffets, and strokes: There they spit upon that divine face with their devilish mouths: There they hoodwink his eyes, and strike him on the face, scoffing, and jesting at him, saying: *Areed, who hath smitten thee?* O marvelous humility, and patience of the son of almighty God! O beauty of the angels! Was that a face to spit upon? Men use commonly when they are provoked to spit, to turn away their face towards the foulest corner of the house: and is there not to be found in all that palace a fouler place to spit in, than thy face O sweet Lord! O earth, and ashes, why dost thou not humble thyself at this so wonderful example? How is it, that there should yet remain in the world any token of pride, after this so great and marvelous example of humility? Almighty God holdeth his peace whilst he is spitted upon, and buffeted: the angels and all creatures hold their hands, and revenge not the injuries done unto their creator, beholding him thus contemned and reviled with most despiteful reproach, and villainy: and yet thou being a poor seely miserable worm, turmoilest the world upside down, with a malicious chiding, brawling, and fighting, in case thou be but touched in any small point appertaining to thy estimation? Why wonderest thou (O man) to see Almighty God thus beaten, and evil entreated in the world: sith the very cause of his coming was to cure the pride of the world? If the sharpness of the medicine do cause thee to wonder: Consider the greatness of the wound, and thou shalt see, that such a wound required so sharp a medicine as this was: especially considering that all this notwithstanding, the wound is not yet whole. Thou wonderest to see how almighty God hath humbled himself: And I wonder to see thee (for all this example) so proud and insolent in all thy talk, dealings, and behavior, seeing almighty God hath so humbled himself, to teach thee to be humble. Thou wonderest to see almighty God thus to abase himself under the dust of the earth: and I wonder to see, that dust and earth for all this advanceth itself above the heavens, and would be honored above almighty God himself.

How is it then, that this so wonderful example sufficeth not to subdue the pride of the world? The humility of Christ was sufficient to overcome the heart of God, to procure his favor, and to make him become gentle and mild towards us. And shall it not suffice to overcome thy heart, and to make it humble, and meek? The angel said to the Patriarch Jacob, *Thou shalt no more be called Jacob: but Israel shall be thy name. For seeing thou hast been mighty against God, how much more shalt thou be mighty against men?*[8] If then the humility and meekness of our Savior Christ prevailed against the fury, and wrath of almighty God: why doth it not prevail against our pride? If it were able to pacify and appease so mighty a heart, as the heart of almighty God, being then angry with us, why doth it not alter and mollify our stubborn hearts? Surely I am at my wit's end, and very much astonished, yea it passeth my reason to consider how this so great patience overcometh not thy anger, how this passing great abasing assuageth not thy pride, how these violent buffets beat not down thy presumption, and how this deep silence among so many injuries is not of force to make thee leave of thy quarrelings, and troublesome suits in law, wherewith thou vexest and turmoilest thy neighbors, about the vile muck, and transitory pelf of this world. It is a marvelous great wonder to see how almighty God would by means of these so terrible injuries overthrow the kingdom of our pride: and it is also greatly to be marveled at, that notwithstanding all this, there remaineth yet a fresh lively memory of Amelec under the heavens, and that to this day the relics of this wicked generation do for all that remain, and continue.[9]

Now therefore O sweet Jesus I beseech thee to cure in me with the example of thy great humility, the folly of my vain arrogancy,

8 Gen. 32:28.
9 See Ex. 17; 4 Kgs. 15.

and pride. And forsomuch as the greatness of thy wounds do give me plainly to understand, that I have great need of a helper, let it evidently appear by the operation of thy grace and remedy in me, that I do now presently enjoy the benefit of the same.

§. II. Of the Vexations, and Troubles, Our Savior Suffered the Night before His Passion: and of the Denial of Saint Peter.

Consider after this, what troubles our Savior suffered in that doleful night, when the soldiers that had him in custody, mocked and laughed him to scorn (as St. Luke saith,) and used as a mean to pass away the sleepiness of the night to scoff and jest at the Lord of majesty.[10] Consider how (O my soul) how thy sweet spouse is set here as a mark, to receive all the strokes and buffets they could give him. O cruel night! O unquiet night, in which thou (O good Jesus) tookest no rest at all, neither did the soldiers repose themselves, but accompted it even a pastime and recreation to vex, and torment thee! The night was ordained for this end, that all creatures should therein take their rest, and that the senses and members that are wearied with the toils and labors of the day might be refreshed, and relieved: but these wicked men use it now as a fit time to torment all thy members, and senses, striking thy body, afflicting thy soul, binding thy hands, buffeting thy cheeks, spitting in thy face, and lugging thee by the ears, that at such time as all members are wont to take their rest, all thy members might be in great pain, and trouble. O how far do these mattins differ from those, which the orders of angels sung at the same time in heaven unto thee! There they sing, Holy, Holy: but here these caitiffs cry out: put him to death: put him to death: crucify him: crucify him. O ye angels of Paradise, that heard both these voices, what thought ye, when ye saw him so despitefully contemned in earth, whom ye honor with so great reverence in heaven? What thought ye, when ye saw almighty God himself suffer such despites

10 See Luke 22:63.

even for their sakes, who did all this villainy unto him? Who hath ever heard of such a kind of charity, that one would suffer death to deliver the very same persons from death, that were the procurers of his death? Assuredly, the malice of man could not any further extend itself in committing a more wicked deed, than thus to presume to lay hands upon almighty God himself: neither could the goodness and mercy of almighty God appear more plainly in any thing, than in this, that he was content to suffer such a cruel death for that very creature that conspired his death.

The painful griefs and turmoils of this troublesome night were increased far the more by the denial of St. Peter. For he, who was so familiar a friend of our Savior: he, whom our Savior chose to see the glory of his transfiguration: and he, who above all the rest of his Apostles was honored and chosen by our Savior, to have the principality, and chief rule of the whole Christian Church:[11] this very chief Apostle (I say,) first before all others, not once, but three several times together, even in the very presence of his Lord, and master, sweareth, and forsweareth, that he knoweth him not, and that he wist not who he is.

O Peter, is he that standeth there by thee so wicked a man, that thou accomptest it so great a shame only to have known him? Consider, that this is a condemnation of him by thee, before he be condemned by the high priests: sithence by this denial thou gavest the world to understand, that he is such a manner of man, that even thou thyself dost accompt it as a great reproach and dishonor unto thee, ever to have known him. Now what greater injury could be done, than this?

Our Savior then hearing this denial turned back, and beheld Peter, and cast his eyes upon that sheep, which there was lost from him. O look of wonderful virtue! O silent look, but yet full of mystery, and signification! Peter understood right well the language

---

[11] Christ promised St. Peter in Matt. 16:18 that he would build his Church upon him. And in Luke 22:32 he was bid (after he should repent his denial) to confirm his brethren. And in John 21:17, Christ after his resurrection made St. Peter pastor of all his sheep, without exception of any person, or country.

and voice of that look, and although the crowing of the Cock was not able to awake his spirits, yet was this able, as indeed it did. For the eyes of our Savior Christ do not only speak, but also work, as it plainly appeared by the tears of Peter, which albeit they gushed from the eyes of Peter, yet did they much more proceed from the look, and eyes of Christ.

Wherefore when thou shalt at any time awake again out of thy sinful life, and with grief and sorrow call thy sins to mind, wherein thou hast offended almighty God, thou must understand, that this benefit proceedeth from the merciful eyes of our Lord, which do then look upon thee. The Cocks had already crowed, but Peter remembered not himself, because our savior had not as yet looked upon him. But when our Savior Christ looked upon him, then he remembered himself, and repented and bewailed his offence. For the eyes of Christ do open our eyes, and those are the eyes that do awake such as are asleep.

The holy Evangelists St. Matthew, and St. Luke say, that Peter went out forthwith, and wept bitterly:[12] to give thee to understand, that it is not enough for thee to be sorry, and bewail thine offence, but that it is requisite also to avoid and eschew the very place, and occasions of sin. For otherwise to lament and be sorry always for thy sins, and always to reiterate and commit the same sins again, is to provoke always the wrath and anger of almighty God against thee.

And note well and diligently this point especially, that the principal sin that Peter had committed, was for that he shrunk back, and feared to be accompted one of Christ his disciples: and in this his doing he is said to have denied Christ. Now if this be to deny Christ, how many Christians (trow ye) may ye now find in the world, that do after this sort deny Christ? Alas! How many be there at this day that refuse to confess their sins, to communicate, to fast duly the holy time of lent, and other fasting days commanded in the Catholic Church, to pray, to talk of God, and of spiritual matters, to use conversation with such as be good, and virtuous Catholics, and to suffer

12 See Matt. 26:75; Luke 22:62.

injuries, and troubles, because the world should not the less esteem them, or have them in contempt for the same? And what is this else, but to deny Christ, as St. Peter denied him, when he was ashamed to be accompted his disciple? What other thing may those that behave themselves after this sort hope and look for at the dreadful day of Judgement, but that punishment and sentence threatened by our savior Christ himself: saying: *He that is ashamed to be accompted my disciple before men, the son of the virgin will be ashamed to acknowledge him as one of his, when he shall come in his majesty, and in the majesty of the father, and his holy Angels.*[13]

How Our Savior Was Brought before King Herod, and Mocked, and Accompted for a Fool by Him, and His Courtiers.

When this painful and troublesome night was ended, they led our Savior forthwith to the house of Pilate the president. And Pilate (understanding that he was born in Galilee,) sent him unto Herod, that was king of that country, who took him for a fool, and as such a one caused him to be appareled in a white garment, and so returned him back to Pilate again.

Whereby it appeareth, that our Savior was taken in this world not only for a malefactor, but also for a very fool. O mystery worthy of great reverence! The principal virtue of a Christian man is not to make any accompt of the judgements and reputations of the world. Wherefore thou hast here (good Christian brother) an occasion given thee, whereby to learn this heavenly philosophy, and by this example to comfort thyself, whensoever thou shalt see thyself to be unjustly despised, mocked, and persecuted of the world. For the world cannot do thee any injury, nor bear false witness against thee, but it hath done the like unto our Savior Christ before. He was accompted as a malefactor, and stirrer of sedition, and for such a one they accused him before the judges, and accordingly demanded sentence of death

---

13 See Luke 9:26. See also Luke 12:9; Matt. 10:33; Mark 8:38; 2 Tim. 2:12.

upon him.[14] He was taken to be a nigromancer, and as one possessed with a devil, and so they said: *That in the power of Belzebub he cast out devils.*[15] He was taken for a glutton, and great eater, and so they reported of him, saying: *Behold this man is a glutton, and a drinker of wine.*[16] He was taken for a man of evil behavior, and as one that kept evil company, saying: *That he kept company with publicans, and sinners, and that he did eat with them.*[17] He was taken as one, that was come of a wicked generation, and of a naughty race: and so they termed him, saying: *Thou art a Samaritan, and art possessed with a devil:*[18] He was taken for an heretic, and blasphemer: and so they said, that he made himself God, and forgave sins as God.[19] There wanted nothing else, but after all this to accompt our Savior as a fool, and so is he now taken, and that not of every common person, but even of the ruffling nobility, and gentlemen, yea and of the chiefest counsellors, magistrates, and officers, in king Herods court. And so they apparel our Savior like a fool, that he might be also taken of all men for such a one. O wonderful humility of our sweet savior Christ! O example of all virtue! O comfort of all troubled, and persecuted Catholics! Wherefore o thou Christian, that art persecuted by Turks, Moors, or Heretics, for thy public zealous profession of the Catholic religion, be of good comfort, as a true Christian ought to be, in bearing patiently, and willingly, thy cross in this world, as a faithful disciple of our Savior Christ. And to the intent thou mayst make the less accompt of the judgements, and estimations of the world, and very evidently perceive, how foolish and frantic the world is, in his sayings, doings, opinions, and judgements, fix thine eyes upon this lively portraiture of all virtues: look upon this general comfort of all miseries: and behold here, how the wisdom of almighty God is holden for folly: virtue for vice: truth for blasphemy: temperance for gluttony:

---

14 See Luke 23:2.
15 See Luke 11:15; Matt. 9:34.
16 Matt. 11:19.
17 See Matt. 11:19; Luke 15:2.
18 John 8:48.
19 See Mark 2:7.

the peace maker of the world, for a seditious disturber of the world: the reformer of the law, for a breaker of the law: and the Justifier of sinners, for a sinner, and a follower of sinners.

In all these goings, and comings, and in all these demands, and answers, made before the Judges, consider diligently, and note the constancy, and modesty of our Savior: the gravity of his countenance: and the integrity of his mind: which was never overcome, nor once dismayed, for all these great conflicts. And when he saw himself in the presence of so many officers, and Judges, sitting in their Judgement seats: when he saw himself in the midst of so many injurious villainies, and furious blows, and in such a confusion of outcries, and clamors, thundered out vehemently by the accusers, and conspirers of his death: when he saw himself in such a throng of outrageous and cruel enemies, his death and Cross standing (as it were) present before his face: when our savior (I say) saw himself thus tossed, and turmoiled, up , and down, with so many tempestuous waves, and blustering storms of all adversity, and persecution, it was wonderful to behold his constancy, his patience, and his temperance, insomuch as whatsoever he did, or spake, made a plain demonstration of a noble heart, and courageous mind in him. There came no one bitter or sharp word out of his mouth: He never yielded, or submitted himself so much as to frame any manner of supplication, or entreaty to his enemies for his life: neither shed he any one tear, or made any lamentation unto them, in that behalf. But in all points, and respects, he observed such a comely gravity and majesty, as was seemly for the dignity of so high, and worthy a personage. What silence kept he among so many, and those so false accusations? How circumspect was he in his words, whensoever he spake? How wisely behaved he himself in all his answers? To conclude, such was the form and shew of his countenance, and mind, in these his troubles, that even that alone, without any further testimony might have sufficed to justify his cause, if the grossness of their wicked, and malicious understandings, had been able to conceive the highness, and excellency, of such a proof.

§. III. Of the Cruel Scourging and Whipping of Our Savior at the Pillar.

After all these injuries, consider what scourgings and whippings our savior suffered at the pillar. For when the Judge perceived that he was not able to pacify the furious rage of those his most cruel enemies, he determined to punish our savior with such a severe kind of punishment, as might suffice to satisfy the malicious outrage of such cruel hearts, that they being content therewith should cease, and seek no more after his death.

This is one of the greatest, and most wonderful sights, that ever was seen in the world. Who would ever have thought, that whips, and lashes, should have been laid upon the shoulders of almighty God. The Prophet David saith: that the place of thy habitation O Lord is most high, and that there shall none evil approach near unto thee: he saith that there shall no whip be felt in thy tabernacle.[20] Now what thing is farther from the high majesty and glory of almighty God, than to be villainously whipped, and scourged? This is surely a punishment rather for bondslaves, and thieves: yea it was accompted generally so vile, and infamous, that in case the offender were a Citizen of Rome, though his offence were never so heinous, he was thereby quit, and exempted, from that most slavish, and villainous kind of punishment. All which notwithstanding, behold here, how the Lord of the heavens, the creator of the world, the glory of the angels, the wisdom, power, and glory of the living God, vouchsafeth for our sakes to be punished with whips, and scourges? Certainly I do believe, that all the orders of angels were wholly amazed, and astonished, when they beheld this so strange, and wonderful sight: and that they adored and acknowledged the unspeakable goodness of almighty God, which was very manifestly discovered unto them in this act. Wherefore, if they filled the air with high lauds, and praises, upon the day of his nativity, when as yet they had seen nothing else, but only the swaddling clothes, and the manger, where he was laid:[21]

20 See Ps. 90.
21 See Luke 2.

what did they now (trow ye,) when they beheld him so villainously and most cruelly whipped, and scourged at the pillar. Consider thou therefore (o my soul,) unto whom this business appertaineth much more, than to the angels: Consider I say, how much more oughtest thou to be inwardly moved in thy very heart, with this so wonderful, and most pitiful doleful sight of thy sweet Savior: and to acknowledge unto him much more humble thanks, and praises, for his so passing great love shewed hereby unto thee.

Go now therefore, and enter with thy spirit into Pilates consistory, and carry with thee great store of tears in a readiness, which in that place shall be very needful, to bewail such things, as there thou shalt both hear, and see. Consider on the one side, with what rudeness those cruel, and bloody tormentors, do strip our Savior of his garments: and see on the other side, with what humility he suffereth himself to be stripped by them, never so much as once opening his mouth, or answering one word to so many despiteful scoffs, and blasphemous speeches, as they uttered there against him. Consider also what haste they make to bind that holy body to a pillar, that being fast bound, they might fetch their full strokes more at pleasure and strike him where, and how they list. Consider, how the Lord of angels standeth there post alone among so many cruel tormentors, having on his part neither friend, nor acquaintance to entreat, or defend him from injury: no not so much as eyes to take compassion upon him. Mark now with what furious cruelty they begin to discharge their whips and scourges upon his most tender flesh: and how they lay on lashes upon lashes, strokes upon strokes, and wounds upon wounds.

There mightest thou see that sacred body swollen with weals, all black, and blue, the skin rented, and torn, the blood gushing out, and streaming down on every side, throughout all parts of his body.

But above all this, what a pitiful sight was it to behold that so great, and deep open wound, that was given him upon the shoulders, where chiefly all their lashes and strokes did light? Verily I am persuaded, that that wound was so large, and deep, that if they had laid on a little longer, they had discovered the white bones, between the bloody flesh, and made an end of his holy life at the pillar, before he had come to the Cross. To be short, they so strook, and rent, that most amiable, and beautiful body: they so bound him, and laid on such lode of stripes, and lashes, upon him: they so tormented and filled his blessed body, with most cruel strokes, and wounds, that he had now clean lost the form, and shape, he had before: yea (and to say further) they so foully disfigured him, that he scarcely seemed to have the shape of a man. Consider now O my soul, in what a doleful plight that goodly and bashful young man stood there, being as he was in that pitiful case, so evil entreated, so reproachfully used, and set out so nakedly to the utter shame of the world. Behold, how that most tender, and beautiful flesh, yea even the flower of all flesh, is there most cruelly rent, and torn in all parts of it.

The law of Moses commanded, that malefactors should be beaten with whips, and that according to the quality of their offences, so should the number of the lashes be: Howbeit with this condition, that they should never pass forty lashes: to the end (saith the law) that thy brother fall not down before thee foully torn, and mangled: seeming to the law maker, that to exceed this number, was a kind of punishment so cruel, that it could not stand with the laws of brotherly love.[22] But against thee (O good Jesus,) that didst never break the law of justice, were broken all the laws of mercy: yea, and that in such sort, that in steed of forty lashes, they gave thee five thousand, and above, as many holy fathers do testify. If then a body would seem so foully berayed, being scourged not passing with forty stripes: in what plight was thy body my sweet Lord, and Savior, being scourged with above five thousand stripes? O joy of the angels, and glory of the saints, who hath thus disfigured thee? Who hath thus defiled thee with so many spots, being the very glass of innocency? Certain it is O Lord, that they were not thy sins, but mine, not thy robberies, but mine, that have thus evil entreated thee. It was even love, and mercy, that compassed thee about, and caused thee to take upon thee this

[22] See Deut. 25.

so heavy a burden. Love was the cause, why thou didst bestow upon me all thy benefits: and mercy moved thee, to take upon thee all my miseries. Wherefore, if love, and mercy, have caused thee to enter into these so cruel, and terrible conflicts, who can now stand in doubt of thy love? If the greatest testimony of love, be to suffer pains for the beloved, what else are each one of thy pains, but a several testimony of thy love? What else are all these wounds of thine, but as it were certain heavenly voices, that do all preach, and proclaim unto me thy love, and require me to love thee again. And if the testimonies be so many, as the stripes, and blows were, that thou sufferedst for my sake, who can then put any doubt in the proof being as it is so plainly avouched, and proved, by so many witnesses? What meaneth then this incredulity of mine that is not yet convinced with so manifold and so great arguments? St. John the Evangelist wondered at the incredulity of the Jews, for that our Lord wrought so many miracles among them, for confirmation of his doctrine, and they nevertheless would not believe in him.[23] O holy Evangelist, wonder no more at the incredulity of the Jews, but rather at mine. Forsomuch as to suffer pains is no less argument to cause me to believe the love of Christ, than is the working of miracles to cause me to believe in Christ. If then it be a great wonder, that after so many miracles wrought by our savior Christ, his words are not yet believed: how much more wonderful is it, that having suffered for our sakes above five thousand stripes, we believe not yet that he loveth us?

But what shall we say, if to all these strokes, and wounds, which he received for us at the pillar, we add moreover all the other pains, and travails of his whole life, all which proceeded of love? What brought thee down O Lord from heaven unto the earth, but only love? What thing pulled thee out of thy father's bosom, and laid thee in thy mother's womb? What thing caused thee to take the garment of our frail nature upon thee, and to become partaker of our miseries, but only love? What thing placed thee in an ox stall, and swaddled thee in a manger, and chased thee into strange countries, but only

[23] See John 12.

love? What thing made thee to carry the yoke of our mortality for the space of so many years, but only love? What thing made thee to sweat, to travail, to watch, to continue waking all the long night, and to pass over both sea, and land, seeking after lost souls, but only love? What thing bound Sampson hand, and foot, shaved his hair, spoiled him of all his force, and caused him to be mocked, and scorned of his enemies, but only the love of his spouse Dalida?[24] And what thing hath bound thee our true Sampson, and shaved thee, and spoiled thee of thy force, and strength, and given thee into thine enemies hands, to be so reproachfully laughed, spited, and scoffed at, but only the love, that thou bearest unto thy spouse the Catholic Church, and unto each one of our souls? Finally, what thing hath brought thee to be crucified upon the tree of the cross, there to stand so cruelly tormented from top, to toe, thy hands nailed, thy side opened, thy members racked one from another, thy body all of a gory blood, thy veins exhausted, and void of blood, thy lips pale, and wane, thy tongue bitter: to be short, all thy body wholly rent, and torn? What thing could have wrought such a most cruel foul mangling, and butchery of thee, as this was, but only love? O passing great love! O gracious love! O love, seemly for the great unspeakable mercy, and infinite goodness of him, who is infinitely good, and loving, yea wholly love!

Having therefore so great, and so many testimonies of thy love (O my sweet Lord, and Savior) as these be, how can I but believe, that thou lovest me? Sith it is most certain, that thou hast not changed that most charitable loving heart, being now in heaven, which thou hadst when thou didst walk here upon the earth? Thou art not like that cup bearer of king Pharao, who when he saw himself in prosperity, forgot his poor friends, that he had left in prison:[25] but rather the prosperity, and glory, that thou dost now enjoy in heaven, moveth thee to have greater pity, and compassion, upon thy children, whom thou hast left here in earth. Now then, sith it is certain, that thou lovest me so much, as I see very evidently thou dost, why do not I

24 See Jgs. 16.
25 See Gen. 40.

love thee again? Why do not I put my whole trust, and affiance, in thee? Why do not I esteem myself very happy, and rich, having even almighty God himself, so constant, and loving a friend unto me? It is undoubtedly a great wonder, that any thing in this life doth make me careful, and heavy, having on my side so rich, and so mighty a lover, through whose hands all things do pass.

THURSDAY MORNING

THIS day (when thou hast made the sign of the Cross, and prepared thyself hereunto) thou hast to meditate, and consider: How our Savior was crowned with thorns: How Pilate said of him to the people, ECCE HOMO: Behold the man: And how he bare the Cross upon his shoulders.

The Text of the Holy Evangelists.

When our Savior had been thus whipped, and scourged, the soldiers of the president took him into the common hall, and there gathered about him the whole band. And they stripped him, and put upon him a purple robe, and platted a crown of thorns, and put it on his head, and a reed in his right hand. And they bowed their knees before him, and mocked him, saying: Hail O king of the Jews: and they spitted upon him, and took the reed he held in his hand, and smote him on the head therewith.[1] Then Pilate went forth again, and said unto them: Behold I bring him forth to you, that ye may know, that I find no fault in him at all. Then came Jesus forth, wearing a crown of thorns, and a purple garment. And Pilate said to them: Behold the man. Then when the high priests and officers saw him, they cried, saying: Crucify him, Crucify him. Pilate said unto them. Take ye him, and crucify him. For I find no

1 See Matt. 27:27–30; Mark 15:16–19.

fault in him. The Jews answered, and said: We have a law, and by our law he ought to die, because he made himself the son of God. Then when Pilate heard that word, he was the more afraid, and went again into the common hall, and said unto Jesus. Whence art thou? But Jesus gave him no answer. Then said Pilate unto him. Speakest thou not unto me? Knowest thou not, that I have power to crucify thee, and have power to loose thee? Jesus answered: Thou couldest have no power at all against me, except it were given thee from above: Therefore he that delivered me unto thee hath the greater sin. From thenceforth Pilate sought to loose him.[2] But the Jews cried out, requiring to have him crucified, and their cries prevailed. And Pilate determined to accomplish their request. And he let loose unto them him, that for an insurrection, and murder, was cast into prison, whom they desired, and delivered Jesus unto them, to do with him what they would.[3]

And they took Jesus, and led him away. And he bare his Cross, and came into a place, that was called Calvary[4] And there followed him a great multitude of people, and women, which bewailed, and lamented him. But Jesus turned back unto them, and said: Daughters of Jerusalem, weep not for me, but weep for yourselves, and for your children. For behold, the days will come, when men shall say. Blessed are the baren, and the wombs that never bare, and the paps that never gave suck. Then shall they begin to say to the mountains: fall upon us: and to the hills: Cover us. For if they do these things to the green tree, what shall be done to the dry?[5]

---

2 John 19:4–12.
3 Luke 23:23–25.
4 John 19:16–17.
5 Luke 23:27–31.

Meditations upon These Points of the Text.

§. I. How Our Savior Was Crowned with Thorns: How Pilate Said of Him to the People, Ecce Homo: and How He Bare the Cross upon His Shoulders.

Come forth O ye daughters of Sion, and behold king Salomon with the crown, wherewith his mother crowned him at the day of his espousals, and upon the day of the joyfulness of his heart.[6] O my soul, what dost thou? O my heart, what thinkest thou? O my tongue, how is it, that thou art become dumb? What heart is not broken? What hardness is not mollified? What eyes can abstain from tears, and lamentation, beholding such a pitiful and doleful sight, as this is? O my most sweet Savior, and redeemer, when I open mine eyes, and do behold this dolorous Image, which is here set before me, how is it, that my heart doth not even cleave and rent in sunder, for very anguish, and grief? I see the most tender head of my Lord, and Savior, pierced with cruel thorns, at whose presence the powers of heaven do tremble, and quake: I see his divine face spitted upon, and buffeted: I see the light of his goodly bright forehead obscured: I see his clear eyes dimmed, or rather blinded with showers of blood: I see the streams of blood, trickling down from his head: which fall over his eyes, and stain the beauty of his divine face. How happeneth it (O Lord,) that the cruel whippings thou didst suffer before, and the death that ensueth, and the great quantity of blood that was so cruelly shed, did not suffice, but that the sharp thorns also should now perforce let out the blood of thy head, which the whips and scourges before had pardoned? If thou didst receive those reproaches, and buffets, to make satisfaction by them for such blows, and buffets, as I through my sins have laid upon thee, hadst thou not received enough of them all the night before? If thy death alone was sufficient to redeem us, what needed so many kinds of most shameful villainies, and reproaches? To what end

6 Cant. 3:11.

were all these new inventions, and strange devices of contempts, and mockeries? Who hath ever heard, or read of such a kind of crown? Or of such manner of torments? Out of what heart came this new invention into the world, that one punishment should serve in such wise, as both to torment a man, and withal to dishonor him? Were not those cruel torments sufficient, that had been used in all former ages, but that they must also invent these new and strange punishments at the time of thy most bitter passion? I see well (O Lord) that these so manifold injuries were not necessary for my redemption, (for even one only drop of thy most precious blood was sufficient for the same:) howbeit it was very convenient, that they should be so many, and so great, that thou mightest thereby declare unto me, the greatness of thy love: and by means of them link me unto thee with chains, and fetters of perpetual bond, and duty: and confound the gay braveries, and fond shews of my pride, and vanities: and teach me thereby to despise the pomp, and glory of the world.

Wherefore O my soul, that thou mayst conceive, and have some feeling of this so doleful passage, set first before thine eyes, the former shape of this Lord, and withal the excellency of his virtues: and then incontinently turn thyself, and behold him in such pitiful sort, as he is here represented unto us. Consider therefore the greatness of his former beauty, the modesty of his eyes, the sweetness of his words, his authority, his meekness, his mild behavior, and that goodly countenance of his, so full of gravity, and reverence. Behold how humble he was towards his disciples: How fair spoken towards his enemies: How stout towards the proud: How sweet towards the meek: and how merciful towards all sorts of persons. Consider how mild he hath always been in suffering: how wise in answering: how pitiful in his judgements: how merciful in receiving sinners: and how free, and bountiful in pardoning their offences.

When thou hast thus beholden our Savior, and delighted thyself with beholding such a perfect form, turn thine eyes, and behold him in this pitiful plight, wherein he is here set out to the world, clad in most scornful wise with an old purple garment, holding a reed in his hand in steed of a royal scepter. Behold that horrible and painful diadem of thorn on his head, those hollow and wane eyes, and that dead countenance. Behold that strange form of his, wholly disfigured, and begored with blood, and defiled with the spittle, which they had besmeared all over his face. Behold him in all parts, both inwardly, and outwardly, his heart pierced with sorrows: his body full of wounds: forsaken of his own disciples: persecuted of the Jews: scorned of the soldiers: contemned of the Bishops: basely rejected of the wicked king: accused unjustly: and utterly destitute of the favor of all men.

And think upon this, not as a thing past, but as a thing present: not as though it were any other man's pain, but as though it were thine own. Imagine thyself to be in the place of him, that suffereth: and think with thyself what a terrible pain it would be unto thee, if in so sensible and tender a part as the head is, they should fasten a number of thorns (yea and those very sharp) which should pierce even to the skull. But what speak I of thorns? If it were but one only prick of a pine, thou couldest hardly abide the pain of it. And therefore thou mayst well think what a sore grievous pain that most tender, and delicate head of our Savior felt at that time, with this strange kind of torment.

Wherefore O brightness of the glory of the father, who hath thus cruelly delt with thee? O unspotted glass of the majesty of almighty God, who hath thus wholly bespotted thee? O River that flowest out of the paradise of delights, and with thy streams rejoicest the City of God, who hath troubled these so clear, and sweet waters? It is my sins (O Lord) that have so troubled them, and my iniquities have made them so muddy. Alas poor wretch, and miserable caitiff, that I am. Woe is me: how have my sins bespotted mine own soul, seeing the sins of others have here so foully bespotted and troubled the very clear fountain of all beauty? My sins O Lord, are the thorns that prick thee: My follies are the purple, that scorn thee:

My hypocrisy, and feigned holiness, are the ceremonies, wherewith they despise thee: My gay garments, and vanities, are the crown, wherewith they crown thee. So that I O Lord am thy tormentor, and I am the very cause of thy pains, and griefs. The king Ezechias purified the temple, that had been profaned by wicked persons, and commanded that all the filth that was therein should be cast into the river of Cedron.[7] I O Lord am this lively temple, that is profaned by the devils, and defiled with infinite sins: and thou art the clear river of Cedron, that dost with thy running streams sustain all the beauty of heaven. In this river O Lord are all my sins drowned: In this river are my iniquities washed away: insomuch as by the merit of that unspeakable charity, and humility, with which thou hast humbled thyself, to take upon thee all my sins, thou hast not only delivered me from them, but also made me partaker of thy graces, and treasures. For in taking upon thee my death, thou hast given me thy life: in taking upon thee myself, thou hast given me thy spirit: and in taking upon thee my sins, thou hast given me thy grace. So that (O my merciful redeemer,) all thy pains are my treasures, and riches: Thy purple clotheth me: thy crown honoreth me: thy strokes beautify me: thy sorrows comfort me: thy anguishes sustain me: thy wounds heal me: thy blood enricheth me: and thy love maketh me drunk. And what wonder is it, if thy love make me drunk, seeing the love thou barest towards me, was able to make thee also drunken, and to leave thee like an other Noe to appear dishonored, and naked, to the open sight of the world? The purple of burning love causeth thee to sustain the purple of shame, and reproach: the earnest zeal thou hast of my profit, and furtherance, causeth thee to be content to hold this reed in thy hand: And the compassion thou hast of my loss, and damnation, moveth thee to bear this dolorous crown of ignominy upon thy head.

---

7 See 2 Par. 29.

§. II. Of Those Words of the Gospel, Ecce Homo: Behold the Man.

When they had thus crowned, and scorned our Savior, the Judge took him by the hand, in such evil plight as he was, and leading him out to the sight of the furious people said these words unto them: ECCE HOMO, *Behold the man*. Which is as much as if he had said: If for envy ye seek his death, behold him here in what a pitiful and doleful case he is. A man undoubtedly not to be envied, but to be pitied. If you were afraid least he should have become a king, behold him here so wholly disfigured, that scarcely he seemeth to be a man? Of these hands so fast, and strongly bound, what cause is there, why ye should fear? Of a man in this wise so sore whipped, and scourged, what would ye require more?

By this mayst thou understand (O my soul) in what a lamentable case our Savior was at his going out of the judgement hall, seeing that even the Judge himself verily believed, that the pitiful case in which he was, might have sufficed to mollify, and break the unmerciful cruel hearts of his enemies. Whereby thou mayst well perceive, what a dangerous, and unseemly thing it is for a Christian, not to have compassion of the most grievous, and bitter pains, and sorrows, of our savior: seeing they were so great, that they were able (as the Judge was persuaded) to mollify those most savage and cruel stony hearts of the Jews. Where love is, there is also sorrow. How can he then say, that he loveth our Savior Christ: that beholding him tormented in this most pitiful, and doleful plight, hath no compassion of him?

And if it be so wicked a thing not to have compassion of our Savior Christ, what a heinous matter is it to increase his pains, and martyrdoms, and to add thereunto sorrow upon sorrow? Surely there could not be any greater cruelty in all the world, than after that the Judge had shewed our Savior Christ unto them so pitifully berayed, for his enemies to answer with such cruel words: *Crucifige: Crucifige: Crucify him: Crucify him:* Now if this was so great a cruelty in the Jews, what a cruelty is that in a Christian, who in his deeds and works saith even as much as the Jews did, although he express it not in words.

For doth not St. Paul say? *That he that sinneth, crucifieth the son of God again.*[8] Forsomuch as touching his part, he doth a thing whereby he would bind him to die again, if his former death had not been sufficient. How is it then (O Christian) that thou hast thy heart, and hands, ready bent, to crucify our Lord and redeemer, so often times in this wise with thy sins? Thou oughtest to consider, that like as the Judge presented that so pitiful form to the Jews, supposing there was none other more effectual mean, to withdraw them from their fury, than that doleful sight: even so the heavenly father presenteth that same doleful sight daily unto all sinners: meaning thereby, that in very deed there is none other more effectual mean to withdraw them from sin, than to set before them this so pitiful a form. Make accompt therefore, that even now the heavenly father layeth also the same pitiful form of his most dear, and only begotten son before thy face, and that he saith unto thee: ECCE HOMO: *Behold the man:* As though he should say: Behold this man, in what a dolorous case he standeth, and remember withal, that he is God almighty, and that he standeth in this most doleful, and lamentable plight, as here thou seest him, not for any other cause, but for the very sins of the world. See into what plight God is brought by the sins of man. Consider, how necessary it was to satisfy for sin. And consider also, how abominable and horrible a thing sin is in the sight of almighty God: seeing it so disfigured his own only son to destroy it. Consider moreover, what a sore revenge almighty God will take of a sinner, for such sins as he himself committeth, sith he hath so sharply punished his own most dearly beloved and innocent son, for the sins of others. Last of all, consider the rigor of the justice of almighty God, and the foul staining malice of sin, which appeareth so dreadfully even in the very face of Christ the son of God. Now what thing could possibly be done of greater efficacy, both to cause men to fear God, and also to abhor sin?

It seemeth hereby, that almighty God hath shewed himself towards man, as a good loving mother is wont to do towards her wicked daughter, that seeketh leud means to play the harlot. For

[8] See Heb. 6:6.

when neither words, nor punishment be able to dissuade her from her wicked devilish purpose, she turneth her rage against her own self, she beateth her own face, and teareth her hair, and when she is thus disfigured, she setteth herself before her daughter, that thereby she may understand the greatness of her offence, and that at the least for very pity, and compassion of her mother, she may be moved to leave her wicked purpose.

Now it seemeth that almighty God hath used the very same remedy here for the chastising of men, setting before them his own divine Image: to wit, the face of his own most dearly beloved son, so evil used, and disfigured: to the end, that whereas they had been so many times admonished and rebuked by the mouths of his Prophets, and yet would not forsake their wickedness, they might at the least be moved for very compassion to forsake the same, beholding that divine form of our Savior Christ in such pitiful wise disfigured for their sins. So that before he laid his hands upon men, but now he came to lay them upon himself: which truly was the last refuge that could be devised, to withdraw men from sin. And therefore as it hath been at all times accompted a very great wickedness to offend almighty God, so now after that he hath taken such a shape upon him to destroy sin, it is not only a great wickedness, but also a very great ingratitude and horrible cruelty to offend him with any deadly sin.

If thou wilt continue in the contemplation of this point, (besides that thou mayst learn hereby to abhor sin) thou mayst also take great courage to put thy whole trust and affiance in almighty God, by considering this very doleful form of our Savior Christ, the which as it is of great force to move the hearts of men, even so hath it no less force, but rather far greater, to move the heart of almighty God. And therefore thou must think, that what doleful form our Savior took at that time upon him, in the sight of the furious people, the very same he presenteth now before the divine eyes of his most pitiful and merciful loving father, so fresh, and in such bleeding wise, as it was that very same day. Now what image and form can there be of greater efficacy to pacify the eyes of the heavenly father, than the pale, and wane countenance (so pitifully disfigured) of his only begotten son. This is the golden propitiatory: This is the rainbow of divers colors, placed among the clouds of heaven, with the sight whereof almighty God is pacified. With this, were his eyes fed: With this, was his justice satisfied: Here was his honor restored: Here was such service done unto him, as was answerable, and seemly unto his divine majesty.

Tell me now then, O thou weak, and mistrustful man, if the shape, and form of our savior Christ was such at that time, that it was able, as the Judge verily believed, to mitigate the cruel eyes of such enemies, how much more able is it to pacify the eyes of the most merciful heavenly father? Especially considering that whatsoever our savior there suffered, was for his honor, and under his obedience. Compare then eyes, with eyes: person, with person: and thou shalt see, how much thou art more assured of the mercy of the heavenly father, by presenting unto him this doleful form of our Savior Christ, than Pilate was of the mercy of the Jews, when he shewed our Savior thus pitifully disfigured unto them. Wherefore, in all thy prayers, and temptations, take this Lord for thy shield, and buckler: set him between thee, and almighty God: and present him before his divine majesty, saying: ECCE HOMO: *Behold the man*: I have here (O Almighty God) the man, whom thou hast so many years sought for, to be a mean between thee, and sinners. I have here the man, whose justice is such, that it answereth thy goodness in every point. I have here the man who is so much punished, as our sins and offences required. Wherefore O most merciful loving Lord, look mercifully upon us, I most humbly beseech thee. And that thou mayst so do, fix thine eyes upon the face of thy Christ. And thou (O our sweet Savior, and mediator) cease not to present thyself before the eyes of thy father for us. And forsomuch as thy love towards us was so great, that thou wouldst offer up thy body to the tormentors to be tormented for our sakes: vouchsafe (O Lord) with the same love, to present it unto the heavenly father, beseeching him, that it may please him, for thy sake to pardon us all our sins, and offences.

§. III. How Our Savior Carried the Cross upon His Shoulders.

Now when Pilate saw that all those extreme punishments that had been so cruelly executed upon that most innocent lamb, were not able to assuage the fury of his enemies, he entered forthwith into the judgement hall, and sat him down in his tribunal seat, to give final sentence in that cause. The Cross was in the mean time prepared and made ready at the gate, and that dreadful banner was hoised up on high in the air, which threatened the terror of a most cruel death to our Savior. Now when that sentence was given, and published, although it was of itself both unjust, and cruel, yet did his enemies add an other further cruelty upon it: to wit, they laid upon those tender shoulders, that were so pitifully rent, and torn, with unmerciful whips, and scourges, the heavy tree of the cross. All which notwithstanding, our most merciful Lord, and Savior, refused not to carry that heavy burthen, (whereupon were laid all our sins,) but embraced the same with an unspeakable great charity, and obedience, for the very love he bare unto us. And so he went on his way as an other true Isaac, with the cross upon his shoulders, to the place of his sacrifice. The carriage was divided between two. The son carried the wood, and the body, that should be sacrified: and the father carried the fire, and the knife, wherewith the sacrifice should be made.[9] For truly it was the fire of love, which he bare towards mankind, and the sharp knife of the divine justice, that put the son of God upon the cross. These two virtues contended together within the heavenly father's breast, each one demanding his right. Love requested him to pardon mankind: and justice required that sinners might be punished. Wherefore, to the end that men might be pardoned, and sin punished, a mean was found, that an innocent (to wit the son of God) should die for all mankind. This was the fire, and knife, that the Patriarch Abraham carried in his hands, to sacrifice his son. For it was the love of our salvation, and the zeal of justice, that caused the heavenly father to offer his own most dearly beloved son to the cross.

9 See Gen. 22.

Now goeth the sweet innocent Jesus forwards on his way, with that so heavy dolorous burthen upon his weak, and torn shoulders, great multitudes of people following after him, and many a pitiful and sorrowful woman accompanying him with grievous tears, and lamentations. What stony heart had been able to abstain from most bitter weeping, beholding the king of angels to go thus faintly, with such a great, and weighty burthen: his knees trembling under him: his body crouching under the cross: his modest eyes, and face, all bloody: with that dolorous garland of thorn upon his head: and besides all this, annoyed with those most shameful opprobrious exclamations, and outcries, which they gave out in the way against him?

But now in the mean time (O my soul) withdraw thine eyes a little while from this cruel sight, and hie thee with quick speed, with heaviness of heart, and great store of tears trickling down by thy cheeks, towards the house of the blessed virgin Mary. And when thou art come thither, cast thyself down at her feet, and speak these words in most doleful, and lamentable wise unto her. O Lady of angels, and Queen of heaven! O gate of paradise, and advocate of the world! O refuge of sinners, and health of the just! O joy of the Saints, and teacher of virtues! O mirror of cleanness! O pattern of patience, and example of all perfection! Woe is me (O blessed lady,) woe is me, why am I preserved alive, to see this present hour! How can I live, having now seen with mine eyes that doleful sight, which I have seen! What need more words? Alas dear virgin, and most blessed mother: I have left thy only begotten son, my sweet Lord and Savior in the cruel hands of his malicious enemies, with a cross upon his shoulders, whereupon he shall be crucified.

Now what understanding is able to comprehend how deeply these sorrowful news pierced the most tender heart of that most blessed virgin? Here her soul began to wax faint. Her face, and all the parts of her unspotted maidenly body were covered all over with a deadly sweat, which might have sufficed to end her life, saving that by divine dispensation, she was reserved for greater anguishes: and so consequently for a greater crown, and reward, in the kingdom of heaven.

Now the holy virgin walketh towards her sweet son and the great desire she hath to see him, restoreth unto her again the force, and strength, which sorrow, and grief, had taken away. She heareth afar of the clashing of armor, the troupes of the people, and those most shameful exclamations, and outcries which in most despiteful wise were thundered by his outrageous cruel enemies against him. And incontinently she seeth the glistering spears, and halberds, which were holden up a loft. She findeth in the way the drops and traces of blood, whereby she might easily trace him, which way he had gone, and she needeth none other guide to conduct her unto him. She approacheth nearer, and nearer, unto her dearly beloved son: She openeth her eyes, which were very sore dimmed with sorrowful weeping, to prove whether she might see him, whom her soul so exceedingly loved. O what a strange combat was there now of fear, and love, in the dolorous heart of the most blessed virgin Mary! In one respect she had a desire to see him, and in an other she was unwilling to see him thus miserably and most cruelly disfigured. At the length, when she was come where she might see him indeed, then those two lights of heaven, do behold one an other, and their hearts embrace sweetly together by means of their eyes. Howbeit the sight of one an other in this doleful wise was a very great corsie to both their afflicted souls. Their tongues were dumb, so that neither of them both for a while spake one word: but the natural affection of that most sweet son, spake privily to the heavy heart of the most blessed virgin, and said unto her. Why comest thou hither my dove, my beloved, and my dear mother? Thy sorrow increaseth mine, and thy torments do augment my pains, and be a great torment unto me. Depart my dear mother: depart I beseech thee, and return home again to thy house. For it is not seemly for thy virginal shamefastness, and purity, to be here in the company of murders, and thieves. And if it would please thee so to do, it would certainly assuage both thy sorrow, and mine. And I will remain here to be sacrificed for the world. For this office appertaineth not to thee, but unto me, and thy innocency deserveth not this torment. Return therefore my dove to the ark, until such time as the waters of the flood do cease: forsomuch as here thou shalt find no place, where thou mayst rest thy feet.[10] There mayst thou attend to thy accustomed devout prayer, and contemplation. And there by lifting up thy soul in godly meditations above thyself, thou shalt pass over more easily this thy doleful sorrow and grief.

Now this being said, the sorrowful heavy heart of the holy mother made answer to her son, and said unto him. Why dost thou command me to do thus my dear son? Why wouldst thou have me to depart away from this place? Thou knowest (O my Lord God) that in thy presence each thing is lawful unto me, and that there is none other Oratory but where thou art. How can I then depart away from thee, unless I should depart from myself? This grief and sorrow so possesseth my heart, that truly I can not think upon any other thing. I can go no whither without thee, neither can I seek, or receive comfort of any other, but of thee. Upon thee is fixed all my whole heart. Within thee have I made my habitation. And my life wholly dependeth of thee. Seeing therefore thou hast vouchsafed for the space of nine months to inhabit within my bowels, and to take my body for thy dwelling place, why may not I for these three days take thy bowels for my habitation? If thou wilt thus receive me within thee, when thou art crucified, then shall I be crucified with thee: and when thou art buried, then shall I be buried also together with thee. With thee should I drink of the gall, and vinegar. With thee would I suffer upon the cross. And with thee would I yield up my ghost.

Such words as these spake the blessed virgin in her doleful heart as she went. And after this sort, she passed over that painful, and irksome way, until she came to the place of the Sacrifice.

10 See Gen. 8.

FRIDAY MORNING

THIS day, (when thou hast made the sign of the Cross, and prepared thyself hereunto,) thou hast to meditate upon the mystery of the Cross: And upon those seven words, which our Savior spake being crucified on the same.

The Text of the Holy Evangelists.

Of the Mystery of the Cross: and of Those Seven Words Which Our Savior Spake upon the Cross

They came (saith the holy Evangelist) to the place called Golgotha, that is to say: the place of dead men's skulls. And they gave him vinegar to drink mingled with gall. And when he had tasted thereof, he would not drink. It was then three a clock. And they crucified him, and with him two thieves, one at the right hand, and the other at the left. And so was the scripture fulfilled, that saith. And he was reckoned among the wicked.[1] And Pilate wrote also a title, and put it upon the Cross. And it was written: Jesus of Nazareth king of the Jews. This title many of the Jews did read. For the place where Jesus was crucified, was near to the city: and it was written in Hebrew, Greek, and Latin. Then said the high priests of the Jews to Pilate: write not: The king of the Jews, but that he said, I am king of the Jews. Pilate answered: What I have written, I have written.

1 Is. 53:12; Matt. 27:33–4; Mark 15:22–23, 25–27.

Then the soldiers when they had crucified Jesus, took his garments, and made four parts, to every soldier a part. And they took his coat also, which was without any seam, woven from the top throughout. Therefore they said one to an other. Let us not divide it, but cast lots for it, whose it shall be. This was done, that the scripture might be fulfilled, that saith. They parted my garments among them, and upon my coat they cast lots.[2] So the soldiers did these things indeed.[3]

And they that passed by reviled him, wagging their heads, and saying: Fie on thee, thou that destroyest the temple, and buildest it in three days, save thyself. If thou be the son of God, come down from the cross. Likewise also the high priests, mocking him with the Scribes, and elders, and Pharisees, said. He saved others, but he cannot save himself. If he be the king of Israel, let him now come down from the Cross, and we will believe him. He trusteth in God. Let him deliver him now, if he will have him. For he said: I am the son of God. The very same words also, did the thieves, that were crucified with him, cast in his teeth.[4] But Jesus said: Father pardon them, for they know not what they do.

And one of the malefactors, that was crucified with him, blasphemed, saying: If thou be Christ, save thyself, and us. But the other answered, and rebuked him, saying: Neither dost thou fear God, being in the self same condemnation? We are justly punished: for we receive according to our doings. But this man hath done nothing amiss. And he said unto Jesus. Lord, remember me, when thou comest into thy kingdom. Then Jesus said unto him. Verily I say unto thee, This day shalt thou be with me in paradise.[5]

There stood by the Cross of Jesus, his mother, and his mother's sister, Mary the wife of Cleophas, and Mary Magdalene. And when Jesus saw his mother, and the disciple whom he loved standing by: he said unto his mother: Woman, behold thy son. Then he said to the

---

2 Ps. 21:19.

3 John 19:19–24.

4 Matt. 27:39–44.

5 Luke 23:34, 39–43.

disciple: Behold thy mother. And from that hour, the disciple took her for his mother.[6]

About the ninth hour, Jesus cried with a loud voice: saying: Eli, Eli, Lamasabacthani: that is: My God, my God, why hast thou forsaken me? And some of them that stood there, when they heard it, said. This man called Elias. Some other said: let us see, if Elias will come and save him.[7]

Afterwards, Jesus knowing that all things were fulfilled, that the scripture might be accomplished, said: I am a-thirst. And there was set a vessel full of vinegar, and they filled a sponge with vinegar, and put it about an hyssop stalk, and put it to his mouth. Now when Jesus had received of the vinegar, he said: It is finished.[8]

And he cried again with a loud voice, and said: Father into thy hands I commend my spirit. And from the sixth hour there was darkness over all the earth until the ninth hour. And the veil of the temple was rent in two parts, from the top to the bottom. And the earth quaked, and the stones were cloven. And the graves opened themselves, and many bodies of the Saints, which slept, arose. And there were many of his friends, and acquaintance, and women beholding him afar of. Among whom was Mary Magdalene, and Mary the mother of James the younger, and of Joseph, and Salome, who had followed him out of Galilee, ministering unto him: with many other women, that came in his company to Jerusalem.[9]

Meditations upon These Points of the Text.

We are now come (O my soul) to the holy mount Calvary, and we be now arrived at the top of the mystery of our redemption. O how wonderful is this place! Verily this is the house of God, the gate of heaven, the land of promise, and the place of salutation. Here is

6 John 19:25–27.
7 Matt. 27:46–47, 49.
8 John 19:28–30.
9 See Matt. 27:45, 50–52; Mark 15:40–41; Luke 23:46, 49.

planted the tree of life. Here is placed that mystical ladder that Jacob saw, which joineth heaven with the earth, whereby the angels do descend unto men, and men do ascend unto almighty God.[10] This is (O my soul) the place of prayer. Here oughtest thou to adore and bless our Lord, and give him most humble, and hearty thanks for this his most high and excellent benefit: saying thus unto him.

We worship and adore thee O Lord Jesus Christ, and we bless thy holy name, forsomuch as thou hast by means of this holy Cross redeemed the world. Thanks be given unto thee O most merciful Savior, for that thou hast thus loved us, and washed away our sins with thy most precious blood, and hast offered thyself for us upon the same Cross: to the end, that with the most sweet savour of this noble sacrifice, enkindled with the fire of thy most fervent love, thou mightest satisfy, and appease the wrath of Almighty God. Blessed be thou therefore for evermore, which art the Savior of the world: the reconciler of mankind: the repairer of Angels: the restorer of the heavens: the triumphant conqueror of hell: the vanquisher of the devil: the author of life: the destroyer of death: and the redeemer of them, that were in darkness, and in the shadow of death.[11]

All ye therefore that be a thirst, come unto the waters, and ye that have neither gold, nor silver, come, and receive all these precious treasures freely, without paying any thing.[12] Ye that desire the water of life, this is that mystical rock, that Moses stroke with his rod in the wilderness, out of which there sprang water in great abundance, to satisfy the thirst of his afflicted people.[13] Ye that desire peace, and amity with almighty God, know ye that this is also that rock, that the patriarch Jacob anointed with oil, and erected up for a title of peace, and amity, between almighty God, and men.[14] Ye that are desirous of wine, to cure your wounds, this is that cluster of grapes, that was brought out of the land of promise into this vale of tears, which is now crushed,

---

10 See Gen. 28.

11 See Luke 1.

12 See Is. 55:1.

13 See Ex. 17; Num. 20.

14 See Gen. 35.

and pressed upon the press of the Cross, for the remedy and redress of our offences.[15] Ye that desire the oil of the grace of God, know ye likewise, that this is that precious vessel of the widow of Elizeus, full of oil, wherewith we must all pay our debts. And albeit the vessel seem very little to serve so many, yet look not to the quantity, but to the virtue thereof: which is certainly so great, that so long as there be vessels to fill, so long will the vein of this sacred licour always run, and never cease.[16]

§. I. A Contemplation upon the Mystery of the Cross.

Awake, I pray thee now (O my soul,) and begin to contemplate upon the mystery of this holy Cross, by the fruit whereof the hurt of that poisoned fruit is repaired, which the forbidden tree caused unto us, through the offence of the first man Adam. As the bridegroom hath signified to his spouse in the Canticles, when he said: *I have raised thee up my spouse, from under the tree, because under an other tree thy mother was corrupted, when she was deceived by the ancient serpent.*[17]

Consider then, how when our Savior came to this place, his cruel enemies to make his death the more reproachful, stripped him of all his apparel, even to his innermost garment, which was wholly woven throughout without any seam. Behold now here, with what meekness this most innocent lamb suffereth himself to be thus stripped of all his garments, without opening his mouth, or speaking so much as one word against them, that handled him with such villainy: But shewed himself rather very willing, and ready, to be spoiled of his garments, and to remain naked to the shame of the world: to the intent that the nakedness of such as had through sin lost the garments of innocency, and grace received, might be covered after a better sort, than with the leaves of the fig tree.[18] Some holy fathers report, that the tormentors in plucking of our Savior's garments,

[15] See Num. 13.
[16] See 4 Kgs. 4.
[17] See Cant. 8:5.
[18] See Gen. 3.

took off his crown of thorn, which then stuck fast on his head, and that afterwards when they had stripped him stark naked, they set it on again, and fastened the sharp thorns to the brain pan afresh, and so made new holes, and wounds therein, which was an exceeding great grief, and pain unto him. And undoubtedly thought, that they would use this kind of cruelty against him, forsomuch as we are well assured, that they used many others, and those very strange, in all the process of his passion: especially considering, that the holy Evangelist saith, that they did unto him, whatsoever they would.[19]

Again, by reason of his garment, that stuck fast to the wounds of his scourgings, and blood, which was now congealed unto the same, at what time they pluck it of from his body, (as those caitiffs were far from all piety, and mercy) they haled it of with such furious haste, and force, that they loosed, and renewed, all the sores of his whippings in such rueful wise, that his blessed body was in all parts open, and as it were flain, and became all one great wound, out of which distilled blood on all parts.

Consider now here (O my soul,) the excellency of the goodness, and mercy of almighty God, which sheweth itself so evidently in this mystery. Consider, how he that clotheth the heavens with clouds, and adorneth the fields with flowers, and beauty, is here spoiled of all his garments. Consider how the beauty of the Angels is here defiled: how the height of the heavens is here brought low: how the majesty and omnipotency of almighty God is here abased, and put even to open shame, and reproach. Behold, how that royal blood distilling out from his brain, trickleth down all along by the hair of his head, and by his sacred beard, insomuch as it watereth, and dyeth the very ground under him. Consider what extreme cold that holy tender body of his suffered, standing as he stood, all rent, and spoiled, not only of his garments, but also even of his very skin, having withal so many gapes and wide holes of open sores, and deep wounds throughout all his blessed body. For if St. Peter notwithstanding he was both

[19] See Matt. 17:12; Luke 23.

clothed, and shod, felt cold the night before:[20] how far greater smart and cold did that most tender body of our Savior abide, being so naked, and full of sore bruises and wounds as it was?

Whereby it appeareth that albeit our Savior in all the whole course of his life gave unto us so wonderful examples of nakedness, and poverty: yet at his death he gave himself unto us, as a most perfect pattern and spectacle of this virtue. Forsomuch as at that time he was in such a poor case, that he had no place whereupon to rest his head. And to give us to understand, that he had taken nothing of the world, he died naked upon the cross, and had nothing of the world to cleave unto him.

According to this example, we read of the blessed holy father St. Francis, who was such a perfect and true follower of this poverty of our Savior Christ, that at what time he should give up the ghost, he stripped himself stark naked of all he had upon him, and threw himself from his bed upon the bare ground, and being thus naked, he embraced the earth, to imitate herein (as a faithful servant) the nakedness, and poverty, of his Lord, and Savior. Awake therefore (O my soul,) awake now I pray thee, and learn thou also hereby, to imitate our Savior Christ, poor and naked. Learn to despise all such things as this transitory world may give unto thee, that thou mayst be worthy to embrace our Lord naked, with naked arms, and be united unto him by love, which ought also to be naked, without mixture of any other strange love.

§. II. How Our Savior Was Nailed upon the Cross.

Consider after this, how our Savior was nailed upon the Cross, and how passing great grief, and torment, he suffered at that time, when those great, and square nails were driven in, and pierced through the most sensible, and tender parts of his most blessed body, which was of all bodies most tender, and delicate. And consider also, what an extreme grief it was to the blessed virgin, when she saw with her eyes,

---

[20] See John 18.

and heard with her ears, the mighty and cruel hard strokes, which were so often, and so thick laid on, and iterated one after an other upon his divine members. For certainly those hammers, and nails as they passed through the hands of the son: so did they also pierce the very heart of his most tender, and loving mother.

Consider moreover, how they hoised up the Cross on high, and how when they went about to ram it in the hole, which they had made for that purpose (such was the cruelty of those tormenting raging ministers) that at the very time of rearing it up, and placing it therein, they let it fall furiously from them, with a jump into the hole, with all the weight thereof. And so all his blessed body was sore shaken and jogged up and down in the air, and thereby his wounds were widened, and enlarged, and his pains and griefs more increased.

Now therefore (O my sweet Savior, and redeemer,) what heart is so stony hard, that will not rive in sunder for very sorrow, and grief, sith the very stones themselves were riven the same day, considering the extreme pain, that thou sufferedst on the Cross?

The sorrows of death O Lord, have compassed thee about, and the waves of the Sea have overwhelmed thee:[21] Thou art mired in the depth of the bottomless gulfs, and findest nothing whereupon to stay thyself.[22] Thy father (O Lord) hath forsaken thee: what hope mayst thou have of men? Thy enemies make outcries against thee: thy friends break thy heart: thy soul is afflicted: and for the love thou bearest to me, thou wilt not admit any manner of comfort. Undoubtedly (O Lord) my sins were very great, and heinous, and that doth thy penance well declare. I see thee O my king fastened to a tree, and there is nothing to sustain thy body, but only three iron nails, whereupon thy sacred flesh hangeth, without any other stay, or comfort. When the weight, and sway of thy body stayeth upon thy feet, then are the wounds of thy feet the more torn, and enlarged, with the nails wherewith they are pierced. Again, when the weight of thy body stayeth upon thy hands, then are the wounds of thy hands the more

21 See Ps. 17:5.
22 See Ps. 68.

rent, and enlarged also, with the poise of thy body. One of thy members cannot succor an other, but with equal prejudice, either of the one, or of the other. Now as touching thy holy head, being thus tormented, and weakened with the sharp crown of thorns, what pillow hath it to rest upon? O how well might thy arms (O most excellent virgin) be here employed to supply this office! But alas thine arms may not serve at this present, but only the arms of the Cross. Upon them must our Savior stay his sacred head when he will rest: and yet so, that the ease he taketh thereof is nothing else, but a further driving in of the thorns, and fastening of the same deeper into the brain. Besides all this, I see those four principal wounds, as it were four fountains, always distilling out blood. I see the ground all besprinkled and bedewed round about with blood. I see that most precious licour all betrampled, and shed upon the earth, which crieth much better, than did the blood of Able.[23] For his blood cried for vengeance against the murderer, but this most precious blood of thine O sweet Jesus, craveth pardon for sinners.

§. III. Of the Compassion the Son Had upon His Mother, and the Mother upon Her Son, Hanging upon the Cross.

The sorrows of the son were much increased, by reason of the presence of his most blessed mother, wherewith his doleful heart was no less crucified within, than his holy body without. Two crosses be here prepared for thee (O good Jesus) this day. The one for thy body, and the other for thy soul. The one is of passion, and the other of compassion: The one pierceth thy most blessed body with nails of iron: the other pierceth thy most holy soul with nails of sorrow. Who is able to declare (O sweet Jesus,) what an unspeakable grief it was unto thee, when thou didst consider the great anguishes of the blessed soul of thy holy mother, which thou knewest so certainly was crucified with thee on the cross! When thou sawest her pitiful heart

23 See Gen. 4; Heb. 12.

pierced, and thrust through with the knife of heaviness, and sorrow![24] When thou didst open thy bloody eyes, and beheldest her divine face, wholly overcast with paleness, and wanes of death! When thou sawest those most grievous pains, and anguishes of her mind, which was not resolved with death, and yet abode greater pains, than the very pains of death itself! When thou beheldest those rivers of tears, which gushed out from her most pure eyes, and heardest those so lamentable deep sighs, and sobs, which burst out of her sacred breast, being enforced with the vehemency of her most grievous heaviness, and sorrow! Certainly O Lord, it can not be expressed with words, how much this invisible cross tormented thy most pitiful heart.

And who is able to declare also (O most blessed mother,) the greatness of the sorrows, and anguishes of thy doleful heart. When thou sawest him die with such grievous torments, whom thou sawest born with so great joy? When thou sawest him scorned, and blasphemed of men, whom there thou sawest praised of the angels? When thou sawest that holy body, which thou hadst handled with so great reverence, and brought up with such motherly tenderness, and cherishings, so evil entreated and tormented by most wicked persons? When thou beheldest that divine mouth of his, (which thou hadst nourished with the milk of heaven) distempered with the bitter taste of gall, and vinegar? When thou didst also behold that divine head, (which thou hadst so often times laid and rested on thy virgins breast,) all to begored now with blood, and crowned with thorns? O how often didst thou lift up thine eyes on high, to behold that divine shape, that had so often times rejoiced thy soul in beholding the same! And how often again did thine eyes turn aside from him, because the tenderness of thy heart could not abide to see that doleful sight!

What tongue is able to express the greatness of this sorrow? If the souls that love our Savior Christ truly, and unfeignedly, when they meditate upon these sorrows being now past, have such a tender compassion upon him, what didst thou then O most blessed

---

[24] See Luke 2.

virgin, being his mother, yea and more than a mother, when thou sawest presently with thine eyes such a son, suffer such a most cruel, and painful passion? If those women that accompanied our Savior when he went with his Cross towards his death, being neither of kin, nor of acquaintance unto him, did weep, and lament, to see him go after such a pitiful sort? How great then was the abundance of tears that fell from thine eyes O blessed mother, when thou sawest him, who was so dearly beloved unto thee, not only carrying the Cross on his shoulders, but nailed also fast upon it, and hoised up aloft upon the same?

And albeit these thy griefs, and sorrows were so great, yet didst not thou (O blessed virgin) refuse the company of the Cross, neither wouldst thou turn thy back, but stoodest there even hard, and fast by the same, and not falling down in sounds, nor yet overthrown to the ground, but like a strong pillar standing upright upon thy feet, beholding with inestimable sorrow, and heaviness of mind thy dear son crucified on the cross: to the end, that like as Eve by beholding with delight that fruit, and tree of death, was the occasion of the perdition of the world:[25] even so thou (O blessed Lady) by beholding with great grief, and sorrow, the fruit of life, which then was hanging upon that tree of the Cross, mightest with thy presence, and eyes, there see the remedy, and redemption of the world.

§. IV. An Other Meditation of the Doctrine, That May be Learned at the Foot of the Cross.

The holy Evangelist saith, that there stood hard by the Cross, Mary the mother of Jesus: and his mother's sister, Mary the wife of Cleophas: and Mary Magdalene.[26] O that I were so happy, that I might stand in the company of these three blessed Marys always at the foot of the Cross! O ye blessed Marys, who hath caused you to stand so constantly at the foot of the Cross? What chain is this, that thus

---

25 See Gen. 3.

26 See John 19.

holdeth you so fast linked unto this holy tree? O sweet Christ, which being dead, dost mortify the living, and givest life to the dead! O ye Angels of paradise, be not offended with me, though I a sinner, and a very wicked person, be so bold to come, and join with this holy company: because the love I bear to my sweet Savior draweth me unto them, and the very same love enforceth me to embrace this cross. If these three Marys will not depart from the cross, how can I depart from thence, knowing that all my weal, and salvation, consisteth in the same?

Assuredly the fire shall first wax cold, and the water shall naturally become hot, before my heart shall depart from this cross: sithence I understand what a lesson the love of God teacheth me: to wit: How happy a thing it is, to stand always at the foot of the cross. O holy cross, thou drawest the hearts of men unto thee more strongly, than the Adamant stone draweth iron! Thou givest a more clear light to our understanding, than the sun doth to our eyes. Thou enkindlest a more fervent heat in our souls, than fire doth in the very coals. Draw me therefore (O holy cross) unto thee, with great force, and might. Illuminate me continually, and enflame me with thy mighty power, that my thought and mind may think upon none other thing, but only upon thee, and may never depart from thee. And thou O good Jesus, illuminate the eyes of my soul, that I may understand how to look and fix mine eyes, and thoughts, upon the cross: to the end, that I may not only behold the cruel pains, and torments, thou hast suffered for me, and so by beholding them, take compassion of them: But also consider the examples of so many wonderful virtues, as thereby thou hast discovered unto me, and invited me to imitate, and follow the same.

Wherefore O most wise master, and instructor of the world! O physician of souls! Here I come to the foot of thy cross to present unto thee my sores, and wounds. Heal me O my most merciful, and omnipotent Lord, and teach me what I ought to do. I do confess, and acknowledge plainly unto thee (O Lord) that I am very sensual, and given overmuch to the love of myself, and I see well that this greatly hindereth my profiting, and proceeding in virtue, and godliness. Many times for my recreation, and pastimes sake, or for fear of the pain of fasting, and rising up early in the morning, I pass over, and do leese the godly and devout exercises of prayer, and meditation, with other holy spiritual exercises: by the loss whereof, I leese myself also. This sensuality of mine is very importune upon me. It would fain eat and drink very finely, and delicately, at such hours, and times, as it liketh: and after dinner, and supper, it would gladly have some idle talk, or else some pastime, and recreation. It delighteth at such times to be walking in a fair green garden, or orchard, and there to take some solace, and pleasure. Teach me now (O my most loving Savior, and redeemer,) what I ought to do, whereby to follow thy example: and help me with thy grace, that I may perform my duty in this point. O what a great shame is it unto me, to see after what sort thou didst handle thy blessed body, which was more tender, and delicate, than all other bodies! In the midst of the most bitter anguishes, and grievous torments of thy death, thou didst not give unto thy body any other food, or electuary, but such as those cruel apothecaries had compounded of bitter gall, and sour vinegar for thee. Who then will from henceforth have any tongue to complain, that the meat set before him is either too cold, or too salty, or too fresh, or not well dressed, or that it was over late, or too timely made ready: considering what a table was here prepared for thee, O my almighty God: and that in the time of so great necessity? In steed of the mirth, and pleasant talk, and entertainment, which I seek to have at my suppers, and feasts, thou hadst none other, but only outcries and clamorous noises of them, which shaking their heads at thee, scorned, and blasphemed thee: saying: *Fie on thee, that destroyest the temple of God, and in three days buildest it up again.*[27] This was the music, and minstrelsy of thy banquet: and thy walking in a garden, was to be fast nailed hands, and feet to the cross. And albeit there was an other garden, into which thou wentest after thou hadst ended thy supper, yet was it not to walk in for pleasure, but to pray:

27 Matt. 27:40.

not to take the air, but to shed blood: not to recreate thyself, but to be pensive, and sad, and in a great agony of death. Now what shall I say of the other ease, and refreshings, which thy blessed flesh had? My flesh would gladly have a soft bed, curious and costly apparel, and a large and wide house. Tell me now (O my sweet Savior,) what manner of bed hast thou? What manner of house hast thou? And what is thy apparel? Thy apparel is nakedness, and a purple coat of mockery, and reproach. Thy house is none other, but to stand openly abroad in the sun, and air. And if I seek for any other, I find it to be nothing else, but only a stable for beasts. The foxes have their holes, and the birds of the air their nests, and thou that art the creator of all things, hast no place where to rest thy head.[28] O curiosity, and superfluity! How are ye two crept in, and so usually, and universally received in this our corrupt age, throughout all the countries, and nations, of Christendom! O what manner of Christians be we, that do not utterly abandon from us, all manner of fine daintiness, curiosity, and superfluities, knowing that our Lord, and master, utterly abandoned from him, not only all manner of daintiness, and superfluities, but also even such things, as were of necessity!

I desire now O Lord to see also what manner of thing thy bed is. Tell me (O sweet Savior) where dost thou lodge? Where sleepest thou at noon day?[29] Here I set myself at thy feet: Teach me I most humbly beseech thee, what I ought to do. For this my sensuality will not suffer me to understand well this language of thy cross. I desire a soft bed, and if I awake early in the morning at the hour of prayer, and divine service, I suffer myself to be overcome with sloth, and drowsiness, and I expect duly for the morning sleep, that my head may take an other nap, and so have his full ease, and rest. Tell me O my most gracious, and loving Lord, what rest hadst thou on that hard bed of the cross? When thou wast weary in lying on the one side, how didst thou turn thee on the other, to take the better rest? What heart is not overcome and broken in sunder herewith? What? Is this not enough

[28] See Matt. 8.
[29] See Cant. 1.

to kill all sensuality in us? O what a comfort is this to the poor! What a confusion to the rich! What an encouragement to the penitents! And what a condemnation to nice, delicate, and sensual persons! Certainly the bed of our Savior Christ is not for such fine delicate wantons, neither is his glory in heaven prepared for them. Give me grace (O Lord) that I may by thy example mortify this my sensuality. And if it be not thy blessed will to grant me this request, I beseech thee then even now out of hand to end my life. For it is not meet, nor seemly, that thou, (O my omnipotent Lord, and redeemer) being upon the cross, and having none other comfort, nor refreshing, but only bitter gall, and sour vinegar, I should seek for sweet savors, delicate fare, sugared sauces, with other curious dainties, pleasures, and ease, in this miserable life. It is not meet that thou being thus poor, and naked, I should go wandering and leesing myself after the transitory goods and riches of this world? It is not reason that thou having none other bed, but only the hard and painful cross, I should seek to have a soft bed, and other delicacy, and ease, for my wretched body.

Be thou therefore greatly ashamed, O my soul, beholding our Lord, and Savior, on the hard painful tree of the cross, and make accompt, that from the same cross he preacheth unto thee, and rebuketh thee: saying: O man I have for thy sake worn a crown of thorns: and dost thou in contempt of me wear a garland of flowers, with golden chains, aglets, brooches, and gay ostrich feathers? I for thy sake have stretched forth my arms to be nailed, and tormented upon the cross: and dost thou stretch forth thine to pleasant games, and pastimes? I being a thirst at my very death, had not so much as a little cold water, and seekest thou after precious wines, delicate meats, and dainty sugared sauces? I was on the cross, and in all my whole life time, full of dishonors, reproaches, and grievous labors, and pains, and dost thou spend all the days of thy life seeking after dignities, offices, promotions, estimations, pleasures, and delights? I was very willingly contented, that my side should be opened to give thee my very heart, and hast thou thine open to vain and dangerous loves of the world?

§. V. What Patience We Ought to Have in All Troubles and Adversities, Following the Example of Our Savior Christ.

Thou hast taught me now O Lord from the chair of the Cross the laws of temperance: teach me also at this present the laws of patience, whereof I have surely very great need. Thou hast cured that part of my soul, which is called concupiscible: Cure also I beseech thee, that part, which is called irascible. Forsomuch as thy cross is a medicine for all the whole man, and the leaves of that holy tree are the health of all nations.

Some times I have said, and purposed within myself: I will never from henceforth fall out, or be angry again with any man: I will surely keep peace with all persons: and therefore I think it good for me to avoid all company, and thereby to eschew all occasions of trouble, contention, and anger.

But now, O Lord, I understand my weakness in this point, For to flee from company, is not a mean to subdue anger, but rather to cover, and hide mine own imperfection. And therefore I will from henceforth carry ever with me a mind ready prepared to live not only with the good, but even with the wicked also, and to keep peace with such choleric, wayward, and forward contentious persons, as do abhor peace. Thus I purpose from henceforth to do: grant me thy grace therefore O almighty God, that I may duly accomplish this my good intent. If others shall take my lands, or goods away from me, grant me thy grace O Lord, that I be not angry nor grieved therewith: seeing I see thee thus spoiled, and naked, upon the Cross. If they shall take my credit, honor, and estimation from me, let not that cause me to break peace with them: seeing I see thee here O Lord, so despised, dishonored, and contemned. If my friends and acquaintance shall forsake me, let me not therefore be confounded, seeing I see thee thus left alone, and forsaken not only of thy disciples, and friends, but also of thine own heavenly father. And if it shall seem to me at any time, that I am forsaken of thee, yet let me not for all that lose my confidence, and trust in thee: seeing thou didst not lose thine, but after thou hadst made an end of saying those words. *My God, my God, why hast thou forsaken me?*[30] Didst forthwith recommend thy spirit into the hands of him, who had forsaken thee: saying: *O Father into thy hands, I commend my spirit.*[31] And therefore even now at this instant I request, that from henceforth all troubles and persecutions may come and fall upon me, and not to spare me, forsomuch as all such things can do nothing else unto me, but give me occasion to be a follower of thee my sweet Lord, and Savior Jesus Christ.

But now (O my Lord) what if the troubles and persecutions shall be very great, and long, wherewithal shall I then comfort myself? For thy passions although they were very great, yet it seemed that they continued not any long time, forsomuch as all the martyrdom of thy passion did not continue altogether twenty hours. Now he that hath been ten years bedridden, or lying in fetters in hard prison, or in continual necessity, trouble, and dissension, within his own house, and family, what comfort shall he find in thee for so long a combat, and tribulation? Answer (O Lord) I beseech thee, unto this demand, forsomuch as thou art the word, and the wisdom of the father. Tell me whether thou be the universal comforter in all miseries, be they never so long? Or else whether we need to seek any other comforter for them? Verily O Lord, we have no need of any other comforter, but only thee. For undoubtedly the cross whereon thou didst suffer, was not a martyrdom of one day only, but it continued all thy whole life. For even from the very first hour, and instant of thy most holy conception, there was represented unto thee, both the cross, and withal all the cruel bitter pains, and torments, that thou shouldest suffer upon the same: and so thou hadst them all continually very lively set before thine eyes all the days thou didst live here on earth. For like as all things both past, and to come, were present before the eyes of thy divine understanding: even so also were all the martyrdoms, and instruments of thy passion. There were the cross, the nails, the scourges, the thorns, the cruel spear, with all other thy most

30 Matt. 27:46; Mark 15:34; Ps. 21:2.

31 Luke 23:46; Ps. 30:6.

bitter pains, and torments, at all times as lively present before thy sight, as when thou sawest them with thy eyes the very same Friday, that thou wast crucified on the Cross. We, though we suffer never so great, and extreme pains, yet we have always some time of ease, either by means of physic, or other comfort: by thy pain was always in a manner continual, or at the least it did very often times torment thee in thy soul, during the time thou didst live here in this world. And albeit this consideration of thy bitter torments, and passion, had not tormented thee, yet was the very zeal of thy father's honor, and desire of the salvation of our souls, a continual torment unto thee: which undoubtedly did eat, and rent thy pitiful loving heart, and was a more cruel martyrdom unto thee, than the very death itself. Whereunto was also added the obstinate malice, which thou sawest in that rebellious people, (the Jews:) and withal the stubborns and ingratitude of all other sinners, (for whose remedy and redemption thou wast sent) which would not help themselves with the benefit thereof, nor yet acknowledge the time of their visitation. This was the cause of those pitiful tears, thou didst shed upon Jerusalem:[32] and hereof rose the complaint thou madest by the Prophet Isaias: *In vain have I travailed, and in vain have I consumed my strength.*[33]

Wherefore O my soul, thou hast here with whom thou mayest keep company, and take comfort in thy long pains and troubles. For although the last pains, and torments, of the holy body of our Savior were short, yet were the griefs, and pains, of his pitiful heart and soul very long, and continual.

---

32 See Luke 19.
33 Is. 49:4.

SATURDAY MORNING

THIS day (when thou hast made the sign of the Cross, and prepared thyself hereunto) thou hast to meditate upon the piercing of our Savior's side with a spear. Of his taking down from the Cross. And withal of the pitiful bewailing, and lamentation of our blessed Lady. And of our Savior's burial.

The Text of the Holy Evangelists.

When the Jews (because it was the feast of Easter) that the bodies should not remain upon the Cross on the Sabbath day, (for that day of the Sabbath was very solemn among them) besought Pilate that their legs might be broken, and that they might be taken down from the Cross. Then came the soldiers, and brake the legs of the first, and of the other, that was crucified with Jesus. But when they came to Jesus, and saw that he was already dead, they brake not his legs. But one of the soldiers with a spear pierced his side, and forthwith there issued out blood, and water. And he that saw it, bare witness, and his witness is true.[1]

And when the evening was come, there came a certain worshipful knight, called Joseph of Arimathea, (one that looked for the kingdom of God,) and entered boldly unto Pilate, and demanded the body of Jesus. And Pilate marveled, if he were already dead: and called unto him the Centurion, and asked of him, whether he had

[1] John 19:31–35.

been any while dead. And when he understood the truth of the Centurion, he gave the body to Joseph.[2]

There came also with him, one called Nicodemus, who was wont to resort to Jesus by night: and he brought with him of Myrrh, and Aloes mingled together, about a hundred pounds. And Joseph bought a linen cloth, and took him down from the cross, and wrapped him in that linen with those sweet savours, according to the custom, which the Jews observe in the burial of the dead.

And in that place where Jesus was crucified, there was a garden, and in the garden a new sepulcher, wherein was never man yet laid. There they laid Jesus, by reason of the Passover of the Jews: for the sepulcher was near.

And Mary Magdalene, and Mary the Mother of Joseph marked the place, where they laid him.[3]

Meditations upon These Points of the Text.

§. I. Of the Piercing of Our Savior's Side with a Spear.

Hitherto (O my soul) thou hast celebrated the death and grievous pains of the son: It is now time for thee to begin to celebrate, and bewail the grievous sorrows of the mother. Wherefore sit down a while at the feet of the prophet Jeremias, and taking the words out of his mouth, and sighing deeply with a bitter, and sorrowful heart, say thus unto her. How happeneth it (O most innocent virgin) that thou art now alone? How is it (O lady of the world) that thou art become a widow?[4] What? Have they set so sore a penalty upon thee, without having committed any offence at all? O most holy virgin, I would gladly comfort thee, and I know not how! I would gladly ease some part of thy great griefs, and anguishes, and I know not which way! O Queen of heaven, if the cause of thy sorrows, were

2 Mark 15:42–45.
3 See John 19:39–42; Mark 15:46–47.
4 See Lam. 1.

the sorrows of thy blessed son, and not thine own, (for that thou didst love him more than thyself,) his sorrows are now ended, forsomuch as his body suffereth no more, and his soul is now altogether glorious! Cease therefore (I beseech thee) the multitude of thy sorrowful sighs, and bewailings, seeing the cause of thy sorrow is already ceased, and gone. When he wept, thou didst weep also: reason it is therefore, that thou shouldest rejoice with him, now that he rejoiceth. Shut up the springs of thy most pure eyes, more clear than the waters of Esebon, and now sore troubled, and dimmed with the showers of so many tears.[5] The wrath and anger of almighty God is now pacified with the sacrifice of the true Noe.[6] Cease therefore the flood of thy most holy eyes, and let the earth be cleared again with new brightness.

The dove is now departed out of the ark, and when she returneth, she will bring with her signs of the mercy, and clemency of almighty God. Rejoice therefore O blessed virgin, and comfort thyself with this hope, and cease now I pray thee these thy mournful sobbings, and sighs. Thy own dearly beloved son himself putteth thy doleful mourning, and tears, to silence, and inviteth thee to a new joy in his Canticles: saying: *The winter is now past, the showers and tempestuous storms are ceased, the flowers do appear in our land. Rise up therefore my wellbeloved, my darling, and my turtle dove, that abidest in the holes of the rock, and in the clefts of the wall.*[7] That is to say, in the strokes and wounds of my body. *Leave now this habitation, and come and dwell with me.*

I see well O blessed Lady, that none of all these things are able to comfort thee: because thy sorrow, and grief is not hereby taken away, but only changed. One martyrdom I see is ended, and an other now beginneth. The torments of thy heart are renewed continually, and though some go away, yet others do succeed with new kinds of torments: that by such changes, the torment of the Passion

[5] See Cant. 7.
[6] See Gen. 8.
[7] Cant. 2:11–14.

may be doubled unto thee. Hitherto thou hast lamented his pains, and sorrows: now thou lamentest his death. Hitherto thou hast lamented his passion: now thou lamentest thine own solitariness. Hitherto thou hast lamented his griefs, and troubles: and now thou mournest for his absence. One wave is past, and an other cometh on to overwhelm thee. So that the end of his pain, is a beginning of thine.

And as though this thy pain were too little, I see that these cruel tormentors prepare yet an other pain for thee, no less than this. Close up thine eyes therefore O blessed Lady: close them up out of hand I beseech thee: and look not upon that long terrible spear, which goeth with great violence in the air, to strike the place whereunto it is leveled. Now hast thou O holy virgin thy desire fulfilled. For now art thou become a buckler to thy son, forsomuch as this blow striketh not him, but thee. Thou didst desire the nails, and thorns, and they were ordained for his body: but the piercing spear was reserved for thee. O ye cruel ministers! O ye hearts of iron! Were the pains, and torments too little (trow ye) which his body suffered being alive, that ye would not pardon it even after it was dead? What fury and rancor of enmity is there so outrageous, but that it is pacified when it seeth his enemy dead before him? Lift up your cruel eyes a little O ye unmerciful and cruel ministers, and behold our Savior? Behold I say his deadly face, his dim eyes, his falling countenance, his pale and wane color, and shadow of death. For though you be more hard than either iron, or the Adamant stone: yea though ye be more hard, than your own selves, yet it may be, that in beholding him, your fury and malice will be appeased. Wherefore are ye not contented with the wounds ye have given to the son, but that ye will wound his blessed mother also? Her ye do wound with that spear: unto her ye give the stroke: and against her sorrowful heart threateneth the sharp point of that cruel lance.

Now cometh the wicked minister with a long sharp spear in his hand, and pierceth the very naked side of our Savior with great fury.

The cross shaked in the air with the mighty force of the stroke: and from thence issued water, and blood, wherewith are washed the sins of the world. O river that runnest out of paradise, and waterest with thy streams all the face of the earth! O wound of the precious side of my sweet Savior, made rather with his fervent love towards mankind, than with the sharp iron of the cruel spear! O gate of heaven! O window of paradise! O place of refuge! O tower of strength! O sanctuary of just persons! O sepulcher of pilgrims! O nest of clean doves! O flourishing bed of the spouse of Salomon! All hail O wound of the precious side of our Savior, that woundest the hearts of devout persons! O stroke that strikest the souls of the just! O rose of inspeakable beauty! O ruby of inestimable price! O entrance into the heart of my sweet Savior Jesus Christ! O witness of his love, and pledge of everlasting life! Through thee do all living things enter into the Ark of the true Noe, to be preserved from the flood. Unto thee do all such as are tempted repair: In thee do all those that are heavy, and sad find comfort: by thee are the sick persons cured: through thee do sinners enter into heaven: and in thee do all banished persons, and pilgrims, sleep sweetly, and take their rest. O furnace of love! O house of peace! O treasure of the Catholic Church! O vein of lively water, that springest up even unto life everlasting![8] Open O most loving Lord, I beseech thee, this gate unto me: receive my heart into this most delightful habitation: give me passage through the same unto the tender bowels of thy love: let me drink of this sweet fountain: let me be washed with this holy water: let me be made drunk with this most precious licour. Let my soul sleep in this sacred breast. Here let it forget all the cares of the world: here let it sleep: here let it eat: here let it sing sweetly with the Prophet: saying: *This is my resting place for ever, and ever: here will I dwell: for this place have I chosen for my habitation.*[9]

8 See John 4.

9 Ps. 131:14.

§. II. How Our Savior Christ Was Taken down from the Cross.

After this, consider how the holy body of our Savior was taken down from the cross: and how the blessed virgin received it in her arms.

Now the very same day in the evening, there came those two holy men, Joseph, and Nicodemus, who reared up their ladders unto the cross, and took down the blessed body of our Savior into their arms. The holy virgin then perceiving that the torment of the cross was now ended, and that the sacred body of our Savior was coming towards the earth, she setteth herself in a readiness to give him a secure haven in her lap, and to receive him from the arms of the cross, into her own arms. And so she wringeth her hands very pitifully, and requesteth of those noble men with great humility, and instancy, that forsomuch as she had taken no leave of her dearly beloved son, nor received those last embracings of him upon the cross at the time of his departure, they would now suffer her to come unto him, and not increase her discomfort on every side. She beseecheth them, that they would not deal so straitly with her, as the enemies had done, taking her sweet son from her being now dead, as the enemies did, whiles he was yet alive. O blessed Lady, how void of comfort art thou on every side! For if they deny thee thy request, thou wilt be sore discomforted: and if they grant thee thy petition (according to thy earnest desire) yet shall thy discomfort be never a-whit diminished. Thy miseries have no comfort at all, but only in thy patience. If thou go about on the one side to diminish thy sorrow, on the other side it increaseth double. Now ye holy men, what will ye do in this case? What is your best advice, and counsel, in this matter? To give a flat denial unto such lamentable tears, and to so blessed a Lady, in so just and reasonable a request, were certainly an unseemly act: and to grant her the thing she demandeth, were peradventure to end her life. You are afraid on the one side to discomfort her: and on the other side you fear also least perhaps you should be murderers of the mother, as the enemies were of the son. In conclusion the pitiful earnestness of the holy virgin overcometh them, and those noble men thought best, that considering her great doleful bewailing, and lamentation, it should be a greater cruelty to take her own dear son from her, than to bereave her of her life. And so they were enforced to grant her request.

Now when the blessed virgin had by her pitiful intercession gotten the body of her dear son into her arms, what tongue is able to express the great inward anguish and sorrow which then she felt? O ye angels of peace, weep with this holy virgin! O ye heavens, lament with her! O ye stars of heaven, and all creatures of the world, accompany the blessed virgin Mary in her great heaviness and doleful lamentation! The blessed mother embraceth the torn, and rent body of her sweet son. She huggeth, and clippeth him fast to her breast, (her strength serving her to this thing only.) She putteth down her face between the thorns of his sacred head. She joineth countenance with countenance. The face of the mother is imbrued with the blood of the son: and the face of the son is bathed with the tears of the mother. O sweet mother, is this haply thy sweet son! Is this he, whom thou conceivedst with so great glory, and broughtest forth with so great joy! Where are now thy former joys become? Whither is thy wonted gladness gone? Where is now that mirror of beauty, wherein thou didst so often times behold thyself? Now thou takest no pleasure to behold him in the face, because his eyes have lost their light. Now it availeth thee not to speak, and talk with him, because his ears have lost their hearing. Now that tongue moveth not, which was wont to utter the words of heaven. Now are those eyes dimmed, which were wont with their sight to rejoice the whole world. How is it, that thou speakest not now (O Queen of heaven!) How happeneth it, that very sorrow, and heaviness, hath thus tied up thy tongue! True it is, that the tongue of the blessed virgin was as it were dumb for a time: but her heart might secretly with inward grief speak unto her sweet, and dearly beloved son, and say unto him.

§. III. The Pitiful Lamentation of the Blessed Virgin Mary.[10]

O Life dead! O light obscured! O beauty defiled! What bloody hands were those, that have so disfigured thy divine shape? What crown is this, that my hands do feel upon thy head? What wound is this, that I see in thy side? O high priest of the world! What doleful marks, and signs, are these, that my eyes do see in thy body? Who hath bespotted the clear glass, and beauty of heaven? Who hath disfigured the face of all graces? Are these the eyes, that were wont to dim the sun with their beauty? Are these the hands, that raised up the dead, whom they touched? Is this the mouth, out of which the four Rivers of paradise issued? Have the hands of men such power against God? O my sweet son, and blood of my body, from whence arose this terrible tempest? What raging storm hath this been, that hath so bereaved thee from me? O my dear son, what shall I do now without thee? Wither shall I go? Who shall be able to help me? Many fathers, and brothers, when they were afflicted, came to entreat thee for their children, and brethren, that were dead, and thou with thy infinite virtue, and clemency, didst comfort, and help them: But I (alas,) that see mine own dear son, my father, my brother, and my Lord, here dead before me, to whom shall I make suit for him? Who shall comfort me? Where is the good Jesus of Nazareth, the son of almighty God, which comforteth the living, and restoreth life unto the dead? Where is that great Prophet, so mighty both in words, and works?

O my sweet son, which heretofore hath been my comfort, and rest, but now a very sharp knife to my sorrowful and heavy heart. What hast thou done, why the Jews should thus crucify thee on the cross? What cause had they to put thee to so cruel and shameful a death? Is this the thanks for so many good works, as thou hast wrought among them? Is this the reward, that is given unto virtue? Is this the recompence, for such divine doctrine? Hath the wickedness

---

[10] Note, that the intention of the author is not to represent here exactly and precisely the affections of the blessed virgin: but only by expressing her doleful griefs, to move the readers to devotion, and piety.

of the world extended itself so far? Hath the malice of the devil been so furiously bent? Hath the goodness, and clemency of almighty God yielded so far forth? Is the horror, and hatred, which almighty God beareth against sin so passing great? What? Was so great a satisfaction requisite, to satisfy for the sin of one? Is the rigor of God's justice so strait? Doth almighty God make so great accompt of the salvation of men?

O my sweet son, what shall I do without thee? Thou art my son, my father, my spouse, my master, and all my company? I am now become, as it were an Orphan without a father: a widow without a husband: I am now alone, and deprived of such a master, and of such a sweet companion. Now shall I not see thee any more to enter in at my gates, wearied with the discourses, and preaching of the gospel. Now shall I no more wipe of the sweat from thy face, which was so often times sunburned, and tired with painful travails, and Journeys. Now shall I see thee no more sitting, and eating at my table, and ministering food to my soul with thy divine presence. Now Alas, this glory is finished: this day is this joy ended, and my solitariness beginneth presently.

O My dear son, why speakest thou not unto me? O tongue of heaven, that hast comforted so many with thy words, and given speech, and life, to so many persons: who hath put thee to such a great silence, that thou speakest not to thy loving mother? How is it, that thou hast not at the least left me some legacy, wherewithal I might comfort myself? Well, I will take it by thy license. This Royal crown shall be my legacy. Of these nails, and of this spear will I be thy heir. These so precious Jewels will I keep always in my heart. There shall thy nails be knocked in. There shall thy crown, and scourges, and thy cross, be kept, and preserved. This is the inheritance which I have chosen to enjoy all the days of my life.

O how little while do the joys of the earth endure! And how sore doth that grief smart, which cometh after much prosperity? O Bethlehem, O Jerusalem, how far do these days differ from those, which I have had in you! What a clear night was that! And what an obscure day is this! What a great joy, and riches had I then! And what a great grief and penury have I now! The loss of so great a treasure can not be little. O blessed Angel, where are now those great praises of thy old salutation! It was not in vain, that I was in such a great trouble, and fear, at that time. For after great praises, there must needs follow, either some great fall, or some great cross, and tribulation. Our Lord will not have his gifts to be in vain, Idle, and without exercise. He never giveth honor without charge: nor superiority without servitude: nor great abundance of grace, but to make us able to suffer great trouble, and persecution. Then thou didst call me *Full of grace*: and now am I full of sorrow. Then thou didst call me *Blessed among all women*: and now am I the most afflicted of all women. Then thou didst say, *our Lord is with thee*: now he is also with me, howbeit not alive, but dead, as I now hold him here in mine arms.[11]

O my sweet redeemer, and savior, was it any offence in me to hold thee in my arms with so great joy, when thou wast but newly born, that I should now come to hold thee in them so sore tormented? Was it any fault in me, to take so great pleasure in giving thee the sweet milk of my breasts, that now thou shouldest give me to drink of such a bitter cup? Was it any fault in me to behold myself in thy face, as in a bright glass, that thou hast thus ordained, that I should now see thee thus cruelly rent, and tormented? Was it any offence in me to love thee so entirely, that thou shouldest now cause my love to become my tormentor? And that I should now suffer so much the greater grief, be how much I loved thee more entirely?

O heavenly father! O lover of men! Which art merciful towards them, and rigorous towards thine only and dearly beloved son. Thou knowest O Lord how great the waves, and tempestuous surges are, which lie beating at this present against my doleful heart. Thou knowest that this heart of mine hath abidden so many deaths, as there have been whips, and strokes, given unto this holy body of thy sweet son. Howbeit, although I be the most afflicted of all creatures, yet do I give thee infinite thanks for this great sorrow, and grief, that

11 Luke 1:28.

I sustain. It is a sufficient comfort unto me, to understand that it is thy blessed will that it should so be. Any thing that cometh from thy hands I must needs take in good worth, though it were a sharp knife, and would thrust it even into my bowels. I give thee most humble, and hearty thanks, both for my prosperity, and adversity: and as well and even in as equal wise for the one, as for the other. And for the use, and commodity of thy benefits, which I have hitherto enjoyed, I bless thee: And I am nothing discontented, that thou dost now take them away from me. I mislike not of that, but I do rather restore to thee the thing again, that was committed to my custody, and do yield unto thee most humble and hearty thanks. Both for the one, and the other, the angels bless thee, and with them my tears also bless thee for evermore. Howbeit I beseech thee O my most loving and merciful father (if it may stand with thy blessed will, and pleasure,) that the martyrdom which I have already suffered for these thirty and three years may content thee. Thou knowest O Lord, that from the day, that holy Simeon signified this martyrdom unto me, all my pleasures have been mingled with bitter gall.[12] And from that time hitherto, I have had that sorrowful day ever lying overthwart my heavy heart. In the midst of my Joys, I have been always assaulted with the remembrance of this dolorous sorrow: and I never had any Joy so pure, but that it was mingled with the terrible sorrows, and fears of this day. I know well that all this was directed by thy divine providence, and that it was thy blessed will, that from that time I should have knowledge of this mystery, to the end, that as the son carried the cross evermore before his eyes, (even from the very day of his conception:) so should his mother carry it also. For thy will, and pleasure is that those that by thine should always suffer, and be afflicted in this transitory life: And thou wilt not that our joys should be great, or perpetual, in this vale of tears, though they be such as we take in thee.

Wherefore O my king, vouchsafe now I beseech thee, if it may so stand with thy blessed will, that this may be the very last of my martyrdoms: if not, thy holy will be fulfilled both in this, and in all

12 See Luke 2.

other things. If thou think one martyrdom be too little for a poor seely woman, thou knowest very well O Lord, that I have been so oftentimes a Martyr, as there have been wounds, and strokes, given to the most blessed body of my Savior. His martyrdoms are now all ended, but mine in beholding him thus cruelly tormented do begin afresh. Command death to return again, to take the spoil, which he hath left behind him: and let him carry the mother also with the son to the grave. O happy sepulcher that succeedest me in mine office! The crown that they take from me, they give unto thee, whom I have had enclosed in my bowels. My very bones would rejoice, if they might see themselves laid up there, and certainly there should my life be laid also. My heart, and my soul, will I bury there, (for that may I do,) but as for my body, bury thou it there also (O Lord) I beseech thee, for that I may not do without thee. O death, why art thou so cruel, as to separate me from him, in whose life my whole life consisteth? Thou art sometimes more cruel in pardoning, than in killing. Surely thou hadst shewed thyself very pitiful towards me, if thou hadst taken us both together: But now alas, thou hast been cruel in killing the son, but far more cruel in sparing the mother.

Such words as these would the blessed virgin speak privily in her heart: and the like might those holy Marys, that accompanied her speak also. All that were present wept very tenderly with her. Those holy Matrons wept: Those noble Gentlemen wept: Heaven and earth wept: Yea all the creatures accompanied the tears of the blessed virgin Mary.

The holy Evangelist also wept very lamentably, and embracing the blessed body of his master, said: O my good Lord, and master, who shall be my teacher from henceforth? To whom shall I resort to be resolved in my doubts? Upon whose breast shall I rest myself? Who shall impart to me the secrets of heaven? O what a strange change, and alteration is this! The last evening thou sufferedst me to rest upon thy holy breast, and gavest me the Joys of life: and now do I recompense that great benefit, with holding thee dead on my breast.

Is this the face, which I saw transfigured upon the mount Thabor? Is this that figure, which was more clear, than the sun at noon day?

Likewise that holy sinner Mary Magdalen wept full bitterly also, and embracing the feet of our Savior said: O light of mine eyes, and redeemer of my soul: if I shall see myself overcharged with sins, who shall receive me? Who shall cure my wounds? Who shall answer for me? Who shall defend me against the Pharisees? O how far otherwise held I these feet, and washed them, when thou receivedst me, lying prostrate at them! O my sweet heart root, and most entirely beloved, who could bring to pass, that I might now die with thee? O life of my soul, how can I say, that I love thee, seeing I see thee here dead before mine eyes, and yet do remain alive?

After the like manner did all that holy company weep, and lament, watering and washing his holy body with their tears. Now when the hour of his burial was come, they wind his holy body in a clean linen cloth: They bind his face with a napkin. And laying his body upon a bier, do carry it to the place of his burial, and there they lay in that most precious treasure. The sepulcher was covered with a stone: and the heart of the blessed mother with a dark cloud of heaviness, and sorrow. There is she once again bereaved of her son. There beginneth she a fresh to lament her solitariness. There she seeth herself dispossessed of all her treasure. And there her heart remaineth buried, where her treasure was left.

§. IV. A Declaration Why the Blessed Virgin Mary, and All Just Persons, Are Afflicted in This Present Transitory Life, with Divers Adversities, and Tribulations.

O Heavenly father, sith of thy infinite goodness, and mercy, thou wouldst that thy blessed son should thus suffer for our sins: why wouldst thou that this holy virgin his blessed mother should suffer also, who neither deserved death for the sins of others, (forsomuch as thy sons death sufficed for them:) neither yet for her own, seeing she never committed any manner of sin in all her whole life? How easily might this her tribulation have been tempered, if at that time she had been forth of the city of Jerusalem, where if she had been absent, she should not have seen with her eyes the cruel death of her only and dearly beloved son, neither have so greatly augmented her sorrow, and grief, with the sight of the present object, and with beholding him suffering his so manifold, and cruel torments upon the cross. O wonderful dispensation, and counsel of almighty God! Thy will was O Lord, that the blessed virgin should suffer, not for the redemption of the world, but because there is nothing in the world more acceptable unto thee, than to suffer for the love of thee. Among all things created there is nothing more precious than in heaven the glorious love of the blessed Saints, and in earth the troubled and afflicted love of just persons: I mean: than the love of just persons, that is tried with adversity, affliction, and tribulation. In the house of almighty God there is no greater honor, than to suffer for the love of God. Among all the good works, and services, that our savior did unto thee in this world, this was that which thou hast appointed, and accepted, for the most chief, and principal work, to be the mean of our reparation, and redemption. This was the jewel, and precious stone, that among all the riches of virtues, which that rich merchant laid before thee, liked thee best: for the which thou gavest unto him whatsoever he demanded: which was the redemption of the world. Now then, if this jewel be of so great value and estimation in the sight of almighty God, it were not meet, that such a rich piece as this is, should be wanting in our blessed Lady, who was of all perfect women, the most perfect, and most acceptable in the sight of almighty God.

Moreover there is no work in this world that maketh a more manifest, and perfect shew of true virtue, than to suffer tribulations for the love of God. For the proof, and trial of true love is to have true patience for the beloved. And there is no trial, and proof, so far from all suspicion, as this is. And like as almighty God himself did never discover the greatness of his love unto men so clearly, and perfectly, (though his other benefits which he bestowed upon them were very great) until he came to suffer for them: even so shall they never discover their love towards him fully, and perfectly, (be there other services they do unto him never so many, and great,) until they come to suffer tribulations for his sake. *Tribulation* (as St. Paul saith) *is the occasion, and matter of patience:*[13] And patience is the proof, and trial of true virtue. And this proof giveth us a hope of glory. For this cause therefore, a man ought always to suspect all virtue, and holiness, which he perceiveth in himself, until it be tried and proved with the testimony of tribulation. For as the Wise man saith: *The vessels of clay are tried in the furnace: but the hearts of the just in the furnace of tribulation.*[14]

Almighty God in all the works of nature hath not made any one thing that should be idle, or in vain: much less would he, that in the works of grace his gifts should be idle, and in vain, And therefore he divideth to every one of his elect the burthen, and charge, which he must bear, according to the forces, and talent of the grace he hath received. So that here in this short transitory life, it is not to be esteemed for the greater love, and friendship, if almighty God do give us greater pleasure, and ease: but rather if he give us greater tribulation, and adversity. *Thou shalt give us O Lord,* (saith the Prophet) *to drink tears by measure.*[15] And the measure is this, that he that is most and greatest in thy grace, and favor, is commonly most afflicted, and troubled in this transitory life. When Moses made that peace, and accord, between almighty God, and his people, the holy scripture saith, that he sprinkled all the people with an hyssop dipped in blood, and this being done, the rest of the blood that remained, he sprinkled upon the altar.[16] Wherefore let all those that determine to be the friends of almighty God understand hereby, that their love, and friendship with him must be celebrated, and dedicated with blood: and not only with the blood of Christ, but even also with the proper blood of every one: to wit: with patience, and suffering of troubles, and adversities. Our Savior Christ at that last supper which he made with his disciples, drank first himself of the Cup, but after he had

13 See Rom. 5:3.
14 See Ecclus. 27:6.
15 Ps. 79:6.
16 See Ex. 24.

drunk himself thereof, he gave the remnant unto his guests, which he had invited, and commanded them, to divide the same among them, and that every one of them should also drink his draught of that cup. So that it appertaineth to all persons to have their part of this cup: and it is also requisite, that they all, as members of Christ, do conform themselves with our Savior Christ in suffering. Howbeit herein standeth the difference, that as concerning the common sort of people, and those, that are imperfect, it is sufficient if they be sprinkled with blood: but those devout godly persons, that are more nearly approached, and joined unto almighty God, and be such, as are worthy to be called his altars, these must not only be sprinkled with blood, but they must also be dyed, and bathed in blood: forsomuch as to the strong are reserved the strongest battles, and so consequently a greater reward and greater crown in the kingdom of heaven.

Our Savior Christ, and his blessed mother, were the two persons, that of all others in this world were most entirely beloved of almighty God. Now these two as they far passed, and excelled all creatures in virtue: so did they likewise in suffering. And undoubtedly there were never in the world two better persons, nor more tossed, and turmoiled with adversities, afflictions, and tribulations, than these two were.

Be of good comfort therefore all ye Catholics that are in tribulation, assuring yourselves, that the more troubles, afflictions, imprisonments, and crosses you sustain, the more like you are unto our Savior Christ, and his holy mother. Be of good comfort all ye Catholics that are troubled: For you are not therefore the more forsaken of almighty God, but rather (if you have patience in your troubles,) you are certainly the more in his grace, and favor, and more singularly, and dearly, beloved of him. Be of good comfort again, and again, I say, all ye Catholics that are afflicted, and troubled: For there is no sacrifice more acceptable unto almighty God, than a troubled and afflicted heart:[17] neither is there any sign more certain of his love, and

17 See Ps. 50.

friendship, than patience in tribulation. Let no man therefore slander tribulation, for that were to slander our Savior Christ, and his blessed mother: yea it were to bring a slander upon almighty God himself, who always sendeth tribulations and afflictions to his friends.

What thing is tribulation, but only a cross? And therefore what other thing is it to defame tribulation, but to defame the cross? Again what is it else to fly from tribulation, but to fly from the cross? Now if we worship the dead cross, which is the figure of the Cross, why fly we than from the lively cross, which is, to suffer by the cross of tribulation? This is to imitate, and follow the Jews, of whom our Savior saith, that when they had persecuted the Prophets, they made for them afterwards very great, and sumptuous sepulchers: honoring them after they were dead, and persecuting them, whilst they were alive.[18] And even so it seemeth that those wicked Christians do likewise in a sort imitate them, which on the one side do worship the dead Cross, and on the other side do deny, and spit at the lively Cross: which is suffering by the cross of tribulation.

And let no man be discomforted, and say, that he suffereth for his sins, or without sin: for howsoever thou suffer, all is finally in effect to suffer upon the cross. For if thou suffer for thy sins, (and do heartily repent them) thou sufferest upon the cross of the good thief: But if thou suffer without sin, and without desert, thou oughtest to take the more comfort thereof, because this is to suffer even upon our Savior's own Cross.

---

18 See Luke 11.

SUNDAY MORNING

THIS day, when thou hast made the sign of the Cross, (and prepared thyself hereunto,) thou hast to meditate upon the mystery of the holy Resurrection: in which thou mayest consider these four principal points: to wit: Of the descending of our Savior into that place of hell, which is commonly called by the Learned divines: *Limbus Patrum*. Of the Resurrection of his holy body: Of his appearing first to our blessed Lady, and afterwards to St. Mary Magdalene, and to the disciples.

Nondum propalatam esse sanctorum viam, adhuc priore tabernaculo habente statum. Heb.9.vers.8.

Quod autem ascendit, quid est, nisi quia et descendit primum in inferiores partes terrae? Ephes.4.vers.9.

Descendit ad Inferos. In Symbolo Apostolorum. Christus descendit ad inferos solus, ascendit vero cum multitudine. St. Ignarius in Epist.2. ad Trallianos.

Quis nisi Infidelis negaverit fuisse apud inferos Christum. St. Augustinus. Tomo 2. Epist.99. ad Euodium.

The Text of the Holy Evangelists.

Upon the Sunday next ensuing after this Friday of the Passion, very early in the morning before the break of the day, Mary Magdalen came to the sepulcher: and saw the stone removed from the tomb, and perceived that the body was not there. The which, when she found not, she stood without the sepulcher in the garden weeping. And as she wept, she bowed herself down into the sepulcher, and saw two Angels in white, sitting the one at the head, and the other at the feet of the place, where the body of Jesus was laid. And they said unto her: Woman, why weepest thou? She made answer, and said: They have taken away my Lord, and I know not where they have laid him. When she had thus said, she turned herself back, and saw Jesus standing, and knew not that it was Jesus. Jesus said unto her: Woman, why weepest thou? She supposing that he had been the gardener of that garden, said unto him: Sir, if thou hast taken him away, tell me where thou hast laid him, and I will take him away. Then said Jesus unto her: Mary. And she said unto him, Master. Jesus said unto her. Touch me not, but go, and tell my brethren, that I ascend to my father, and your father, to my God, and your God. Mary Magdalen came forthwith away, and told these things unto the Disciples, saying: I have seen our Lord, and he told me these, and these things, that I should tell them unto you.

The same day, late in the evening, when the doors were shut, where the disciples were assembled for fear of the Jews, Jesus came, and stood in the midst of them, and said unto them. Peace be with you. And when he had so said, he shewed unto them his hands, and his side. Then were the disciples glad, when they had seen our Lord. Then said Jesus again unto them: Peace be with you. As my father sent me, so send I you. And when he had said those words, he breathed upon them, and said: Receive the holy Ghost. Whose sins so ever ye shall forgive, they be forgiven unto them: and whose sins so ever ye shall retain, they are retained.

At that time, Thomas one of the twelve, who was also called Didymus, was not with the Disciples when Jesus came. The other disciples therefore (when he came) said unto him: We have seen our Lord. But he said unto them. Except I see in his hands the print of the nails, and put my finger into the holes of them, and put my hand into his side, I will not believe. And eight days after, his Disciples were again within, and Thomas with them. Then came Jesus again, when the doors were shut, and standing in the midst of them: said: Peace be with you. And after he said unto Thomas. Put thy finger here, and see my hands, and bring hither thy hand, and put it into my side, and be no more incredulous, but faithful. Thomas answered, and said: My Lord, and my God. And Jesus said unto him. Thomas, because thou hast seen, thou believest. Blessed are they, that have not seen, and have believed. Many other signs did Jesus work also in the presence of his disciples, which are not written in this book: but these things are written, that ye might believe, that Jesus Christ is the son of God, and that believing, ye might have life by him.[1]

Meditations upon These Points of the Text.

§. I. Of the Descending of Our Savior into *Limbus Patrum*.

This is the day that our Lord hath made, let us rejoice, and be merry in it.[2] Our Lord who is the maker of all times, hath made every day: but this day especially he is said to have made, forsomuch as on this day he finished the most excellent of all his works, to wit, the work of our redemption. Now as this work is called (by way of excellency) the work of God, by reason that it far passeth all his other works: even so also this day is called the day of God, for that upon this day he finished this work, which was the most excellent of all his works.

It is also said that our Lord made this day, because whatsoever was done in it, was done only by his own hand. In other feasts and mysteries of our Savior, there is ever some thing that we have done ourselves, because there is always in them some thing of pain, which pain grew of our sin, and therefore there is some thing belonging unto us. But this day is not a day of travail, nor of pain, but a putting

1 See John 20:1, 11–31.
2 Ps. 117:24.

away, and banishment of all pain, and a fulfilling of all glory, and therefore it is wholly and purely the day of God. Who is he then that will not rejoice upon such a day as this is? This day all the humanity of Christ rejoiced: The blessed mother of Christ rejoiced: The disciples of Christ rejoiced: Heaven and earth rejoiced: Yea hell itself had his part of this joy. This day the sun shined more clearly than it did any other day: because it was meet that it should serve our Lord with his light on this day of his rejoicing, as it had served him before with his darkness on the day of his Passion. The heavens which before in the day of his passion became dark, because they would not see their creator naked, do now on this day shine with a singular clearness, to see him how he cometh forth as a conqueror out of the sepulcher. Let the heavens therefore rejoice, and thou O earth take part of this joy: because this day there shineth a greater brightness out of the sepulcher, than from the very son itself that giveth light in the heavens. A certain holy Father given much to contemplation saith, that every Sunday morning when he rose to matins, he took so great joy by calling to mind the mystery of this day, that it seemed to him, that all creatures both of heaven, and earth, did sing at that hour, with loud voices, and say: *In thy Resurrection O Christ, Alleluia. The heavens and earth rejoice, Alleluia.*

Now to understand somewhat of the mystery of this day, consider first of all, how our Savior having finished that painful journey of his passion, as he ascended with passing great charity upon the cross for our sakes, even so did he descend down into hell with the like love, and charity, to finish the work of our reparation. For as he took death as a mean to deliver us from death: even so did he likewise go down to hell, using that as a mean to deliver such as be his from hell.

Now therefore let us consider, how this noble triumphant conqueror goeth down into hell, clothed with brightness, and strength, whose entry Eusebius Emisenus describeth in these words. O beautiful light which shining from the highest part of heaven, didst give light with a sudden and unwonted brightness to them that were in darkness, and in the shadow of death! For at the very instant that our

Savior descended thither, immediately that everlasting dark night shined very brightly, and noise of them that there lamented ceased forthwith, and all that cruel rout of tormentors trembled, to behold our Savior Christ present. There were the princes of Edom troubled, and the mighty of Moab quaked for fear, and the inhabitants of the land of Canaan were sore amazed, and astonied.[3] Incontinently all those infernal tormentors began in the midst of their obscure darkness to murmur among themselves, and to say: Who is this, that is so terrible, so mighty, and withal so bright?[4] There was never seen any man like unto this in our quarters. There was never the like person sent into these dens from the beginning of the world unto this day. What? He looketh as one that would rather assault us, than pay here any debt: and as one that would sooner give us an overthrow, than be punished as a sinner. He seemeth to be a Judge, and no guilty person. He cometh with great might to fight, and not to suffer any pain. Where stood our guard, and the porters of our gates, when this conqueror brake our strong enclosures, and entered thus perforce upon us? What may he be, that is of such a mighty puissance? If he were faulty, he would not have been so hardy? And if he had brought with him any obscurity of sin, he could never have thus given light to our darkness with his brightness? If he be God, what hath he to do in hell? If he be a man, how is it that he is so bold? If he be God, what hath he to do in the sepulcher? If he be a man, how happeneth it, that he hath spoiled our strong prison?

O Cross that hast after this manner defeated our hopes, and been the cause of this our great loss, and damage! Upon a tree we gained all our riches, and now upon a tree we lose them all again.[5]

Such words as these murmured those infernal fiends among themselves, at what time the noble triumphant conqueror our Savior Christ entered therein, to deliver his prisoners. There stood all the souls of the just gathered together, that had from the beginning of the

[3] See Ex. 15:15.
[4] St. Augustine, Tom. 10. Serm 137. De tempore.
[5] See Gen. 3.

world until that hour departed out of this life. There might ye have seen one Prophet sawed asunder: an other stoned: an other having his neck broken with a bar or iron: and others that had with other kinds of death glorified almighty God. O glorious company! O most noble treasure of heaven! O most magnificent, and rich part of the triumph of our Savior Christ! There were those two first persons (to wit: Adam, and Eve,) who in the beginning peopled, and increased the world: which two, as they were the first in sin, so were they the first also in faith, and hope. There was that holy old man Noe, who by building of the great Ark, preserved seed that the world might be replenished, and peopled again, after the ceasing of the waters of the flood.[6] There was the Patriarch Abraham the first father of the believing people, who deserved before all others to receive the testament of God, and the sign and separation of his family from others, by the mark of Circumcision in their flesh. There was his obedient son Isaac, who in carrying upon his shoulders the wood wherewith he should be sacrificed, represented the sacrifice, and redemption of the world.[7] There was Jacob the holy father of the twelve tribes, who by putting upon him an others apparel, and strange garments, gained his father's blessing: which figured the mystery of the humanity and incarnation of the everlasting word.[8] There was the holy St. John Baptist also, as a guest, and new inhabitor of that land: and likewise the blessed old man Simeon, who would not depart out of this world, until he had seen with his eyes the redeemer of the world, and received him in his arms, and song like a swan before his death that sweet song: *Nunc dimittis: Etc.*[9] There had the poor seely Lazarus mentioned in the gospel his place also, who by means of his sores, and patience, deserved to be partaker of that so noble company, and hope.[10]

All this choir, and assembly of holy souls were there mourning, and sighing for this day. And in the midst of them (as master of the

6 See Gen. 6; 9.
7 See Gen. 22.
8 See Gen. 27.
9 See Luke 2.
10 See Luke 16.

chapel) was that holy king, and Prophet David, who without ceasing repeated his ancient lamentation. *As the heart longeth after the fountains of waters, even so doth my soul long after thee my God. My tears were bread unto me day, and night, whiles they say unto my soul, where is thy God?*[11] O holy king David, if this be the cause of thy lamentation, now mayest thou cease from singing this song: for here thy God is now present, and here is thy Savior, whom thou mayest now enjoy. Change this song therefore, and sing that other song which thou didst sing long before in spirit. *Thou hast blessed thy land (O Lord,) thou hast delivered Jacob out of captivity. Thou hast pardoned the iniquity of thy people, and hast dissembled the multitude of their sins.*[12] And thou holy Jeremias that wast stoned to death for the same Lord, shut up now thy book of lamentations, which thou didst write, when thou beheldest the destruction of Jerusalem, and the ruin of the temple of God. For even within these three days, thou shalt see an other temple builded up, far more beautiful than that was, and thou shalt see an other more goodly Jerusalem renewed throughout the world.

Now when those blessed fathers saw their darkness changed to a goodly bright light: when they saw the time of their banishment expired, and their glory now begone, what tongue is able to express the passing inward joy that they felt? O how glad were they to see themselves now delivered out of the captivity of Egypt, and their enemies drowned in the red Sea?[13] How heartily did they sing altogether, and say: *Let us sing unto our Lord, for he hath gloriously triumphed. He hath overthrown both the horse, and the horsemen into the sea.*[14] With what inward affection (trow ye) did the first father of all mankind prostrate himself before the feet of his son, and Savior, and said unto him. Thou art now come my dearly beloved Lord, whom I have so long time looked for to redeem my sin. Thou art come to fulfill thy promise, and hast not forgotten them that did put their trust in thee. The difficulty of the way thou hast overcome with thy great

11 Ps. 41:2, 4.
12 Ps. 84:2–3.
13 See Ex. 14.
14 Ex. 15:1.

pity, and mercy: and with thy passing great love thou hast overcome also the painful travails, and torments of the Cross.

No tongue is able to express the great joy of these holy fathers. But the joy that our Savior had to see such a multitude of souls redeemed by the merits of his passion was far greater without all comparison. O sweet Lord, how well wouldst thou then accompt the great labors, and pains of thy cross employed, when thou sawest what goodly fruit, that most blessed and sacred tree began to yield. The Patriarch Joseph when he had two sons born unto him in the land of Egypt, made none accompt of all his pains, and travails past: and in signification thereof, he called the first son that was born in that country Manasses, saying: God hath caused me to forget all my travails, and the house also of my father.[15] If Joseph rejoiced so much at the birth of one son: What might our Savior now think, when he saw himself beset on every side, with such a number of sons, after the end of his torments, and Martyrdom upon the cross? What might that precious olive think, when it saw round about her so many, and such goodly branches shooting out on every side?

§. II. Of the Resurrection of the Body of Our Savior.

But O my Savior what meanest thou, that thou givest no part of this thy glory to thy most holy body, that lieth waiting for thee in the sepulcher? Thou knowest well (O Lord) that the law, that was made concerning the division of spoils saith, that there should be given as great a portion to him that remaineth in the tents, as to him that entereth into the battle.[16] Thy holy body hath remained waiting for thee in the Sepulcher, whilst thy most holy soul entered into hell to give the battle. Make therefore an equal division of thy glory to thy body, forsomuch as thou hast now won the battle.

The holy body of our Savior lay in the sepulcher in such a pitiful form as he had left it, stretched out along upon that cold stone:

15 Gen. 41:51.
16 See Num. 31; 1 Kgs. 30.

wound up in his winding sheet: his face covered over with a napkin: and all the parts of his body wholly rent, and torn. It was now after midnight, and the dawning of the day approached near at hand, when the son of Justice had determined to prevent the sun of the morning, and to be before him in this day's Journey. In this blessed time therefore entered that glorious soul into his sacred body. And how (think you) did it adorn the same? Surely there is no tongue able to express it in words: Howbeit by an example we may perceive somewhat thereof. We see sometimes towards the west a very obscure, and dark cloud: and if haply the sun do take it before his going down, and beat upon it, and cover it all over with his beams, it is wont to cause it to appear all beautiful, and goodly, and all glistering like gold: insomuch as it seemeth to be the very son itself. Now in like manner did that glorious soul after it was invested in that holy body, and entered into the same. For it converted all the darkness of the body into light, and all his filthiness into beauty, and caused the body that was the foulest of all bodies, to become the fairest, and most beautiful of all bodies. After this sort our Savior riseth again out of the sepulcher, altogether perfectly glorious, as the first begotten of the dead, and the figure of our resurrection.

This is that holy Patriarch Joseph, who is now delivered out of prison, the hair of his mortality being cut off, and appareled with the garments of immortality, and made Lord of the land of Egypt.[17] This is that holy Moses, who was taken out of the waters, and out of the poor rush basket,[18] and is now come to destroy all the power, and chariots of king Pharaoh. This is that holy Mardocheus, who after he had put off his sackcloth, and ashes, and was appareled with royal garments, overcame his enemy, and crucified him upon his own cross, and delivered all his people from death.[19] This is that holy Daniel, who is now come forth out of the lions' den, and hath not received any damage at all of the furious, hungry, and ravenous

17 See Gen. 41.
18 See Ex. 2.
19 See Esther 6–8.

beasts.[20] This is that strong Sampson, who being environed about with his enemies, and enclosed within the city, riseth up at midnight, and breaketh up their strong gates, and locks, and so defeateth the malicious purposes, and designments of his adversaries.[21] This is that holy Johnas, that was allotted to die, to deliver his companions from death, who entering into the belly of that great beast, is the third day cast up again upon the coast of Nineveh.[22]

Who is this, that being between the hungry Jaws of the devouring beast, could not be eaten of her? Who is this, that was swallowed down into the bottom of the waters, and enjoyed nevertheless the air of life? Who is this, that being sunk down into the depth of perdition, caused even death itself to serve him? This is our glorious Savior, who was snatched away by that cruel beast, which is never satisfied (to wit, by death,) which after she had him in her mouth, and perceived the worthiness of the prey, trembled, and quaked for fear, and could not hold it. For although the earth swallowed him after he was dead, yet finding him free from all fault, and sin, she was not able to detain him in her house. For it is not the pain, that maketh a man guilty, but the cause, which could not be found in him.

§. III. How Our Savior Christ after His Resurrection Appeared to the Holy Virgin His Blessed Mother.

Now hast thou O Lord glorified, and rejoiced thy most holy flesh, that suffered with thee upon the cross. Remember likewise that the flesh of thy mother is also thy flesh, and that she also suffered with thee, when she saw thee suffer upon the cross. She was crucified with thee, it is reason therefore that she also rise again with thee. It is a saying of thy Apostle, that whosoever have been thy companions in thy pains, shall be thy companions likewise in thy glory.[23] Forsomuch therefore, as this blessed Lady hath been thy faithful

20 See Dan. 6; 14.
21 See Jgs. 16.
22 See Jon. 1–2.
23 See Rom. 6:8; 2 Tim. 2:11–12.

companion in all thy pains, even from the manger to the cross, reason it is, that she should be now partaker of thy joys also. Wherefore clarify that heaven, that is now obscured: discover that moon, that is now eclipsed: dissolve those clouds of her heavy soul: dry up the tears of her maidenly eyes: and now after the stormy winter of so many floods, command the flowering spring to return again.

At this time of the resurrection of our Savior, the holy virgin had withdrawn herself into her oratory, expecting there the coming of this new light. She cried inwardly in her heart, and called like a pitiful lioness the third day unto her dead son, saying: Arise up my glory, arise my harp, and my viole.[24] Return (O triumphant conqueror) unto the world. Gather together (O good pastor) thy dispersed flock. Give ear (O my dear son) unto the clamors of thy heavy and afflicted mother. And seeing by these clamors thou wast moved to descend down from heaven into the earth, let the same move thee now also to ascend up again from hell into the world. In the midst of these clamors, and cries of the blessed virgin, behold that poor cottage of hers was suddenly brightened all over with a heavenly light, and her son being now gloriously risen again from death to life, presenteth himself to the sight of his holy mother. The morning star appeareth not so beautiful, the bright sun at noon day shineth not so clear, as did that face full of all graces, and that unspotted glass of divine glory in the eyes of his holy mother. She beholdeth the body of her sweet son, risen up again from death, and glorified, all the disfigures of the former deformity being clean wiped away, the comely grace of those divine eyes returned, and his former beauty was restored again, and increased.

She also beholdeth those gaps of his wounds, which as they were before very swords of sorrow to her heavy, and tender heart, so are they now become fountains of love. Whom she saw before to suffer between two thieves, she seeth now accompanied with Saints, and Angels. Whom she saw before to commend her from the cross unto his disciple, she seeth now stretching forth his loving arms, and

[24] Ps. 56:9.

giving unto her the sweet kiss of peace. Whom she held before dead in her arms, she seeth now risen up again before her eyes. The blessed mother now holdeth him, and will not leave him, she embraceth him, she desireth and prayeth him most instantly not to depart away from her. Heretofore she was made speechless for sorrow, and knew not what to say: But now she is become speechless for very joy, and cannot utter her inward gladness unto him.

Now what tongue can tell, or what understanding is able to comprehend, the exceeding joy that this blessed virgin conceived inwardly in her mind? We cannot understand the things that do exceed our capacity, unless we compare them to other less things, and frame by them as it were a ladder, to ascend by degrees from the lower unto the higher, and so make a conjecture of the one by the other. Now that we may understand somewhat of this her exceeding joy, consider what a great joy the Patriarch Jacob felt, when after he had bewailed his dearly beloved son Joseph with so great abundance of tears, supposing him to be dead, tidings were brought him, that he was alive, and Lord over all the land of Egypt. The holy scripture saith, that when these news were told him, he conceived so great joy, and astonishment therewith, that as a man newly awaked out of a heavy sleep, he could not call his wits perfectly together, nor yet believe the news that his sons had told him, no more than if it had been a very dream. But afterwards, when he was fully resolved that it was true: the holy scripture saith, that his spirit revived again, and that he spake these words following. *It is enough for me, if my son Joseph be yet alive: I will go, and see him, before I die*:[25] Now then, tell me I pray you, if Jacob that had eleven other sons in his house, conceived yet so great a joy in his heart to understand that even one only, whom he supposed to be dead, was yet alive, what an exceeding great joy conceived the blessed virgin, who having no more but one son, and that one such a son as our blessed Savior was, so notable, and so dearly beloved, as he was unto her, after she had seen him with her eyes both dead, and buried, saw him now again risen up from death, and withal glorified,

[25] Gen. 45:28.

and made Lord not only of all the land of Egypt, but also of all things created? Is there any understanding able to comprehend this? Undoubtedly her joy was inwardly so great, that her heart had not been able to sustain the force thereof, had it not received some supernatural strength, and comfort, by special miracle of almighty God for that end. O blessed virgin, this benefit alone may suffice thee! It is enough for thee, that thy dear son is alive, and that thou hast him in thy presence, and seest him before thy death: so as now there remaineth nothing else for thee to desire. O Lord, how well knowest thou how to comfort them, that suffer for thy sake! The former pain of thy blessed mother seemeth not now to be great, being compared with this passing great joy. If thou O Lord, dost comfort such as suffer for thee after this sort, blessed and happy are their persecutions, and troubles, seeing they shall be thus rewarded.

In like manner we have to consider, how our Savior appeared unto his disciples, and especially to St. Mary Magdalen, whereof presently we do not intreat, because we would not make this meditation over long.

The end of the first seven meditations, for the seven days of the week in the mornings.

✝

HERE BEGIN OTHER SEVEN MEDITATIONS FOR THE SAME SEVEN DAYS IN THE NIGHTS

And although these Meditations be placed in the second place, yet are they first to be used in the order of exercise: Forsomuch as with them they must first begin, that are but newly converted to the service of almighty God.

MONDAY NIGHT

Of the Knowledge of Ourselves: and of Our Sins.

THIS day (after thou hast made the sign of the Cross, and prepared thyself hereunto,) thou must attend to the knowledge of thyself: and thou must use diligence to call to mind thy sins, and offences. And this is the way to obtain true humility of heart, and repentance, which are the two first gates, and foundations of a Christian life.

For the better performance whereof, thou must think first of all upon the multitude of the sins of thy former life, and especially upon those offences, that thou didst commit, at what time thou hadst least knowledge of almighty God. For if thou canst well view, and examine them, thou shalt find, that they have exceeded in number the very hairs of thy head, and that thou didst live at that time like an heathen, that knoweth not what God is.

This done, run over briefly the ten commandments, and the seven deadly sins, and thou shalt see, that there is no one of them, wherein peradventure thou hast not offended more, or less, divers and sundry times, by thought, word, or deed. Our first father Adam did eat but of one only tree forbidden him, when he committed the greatest sin of the world:[1] But thou hast set thy eyes, and hands infinite times upon all sins.

1 See Gen. 3.

In like manner run over all the benefits of almighty God, and all the times of thy life past, and consider wherein thou hast employed them: forsomuch as thou must undoubtedly give an accompt at the very hour of thy death of all these things.[2] And therefore it were well done, that thou shouldest first take an accompt of thine own doings, and enter into judgement with thyself, that thou be not afterwards judged of almighty God.

Wherefore tell me now, wherein hast thou spent thy childhood? Wherein thy infancy? Wherein thy youth? To be short, wherein hast thou spent all the days of thy life past? Wherein hast thou occupied thy bodily senses, and the powers of thy soul, which almighty God hath given thee, to this end, that thou shouldest know him, and serve him? Wherein hast thou employed thine eyes, but in beholding of vanities? Wherein thine ears, but in harkening after lies? Wherein thy tongue, but peradventure in all kind of swearing, backbiting, and most unhonest talk? Wherein hast thou occupied thy taste, thy smelling, and thy touching, but only in pleasures, and delights, and in sensual, and fleshly allurements? What benefit hast thou taken by the Sacraments, which almighty God hath ordained for thy remedy, and comfort? How thankful hast thou been unto him for his benefits? How hast thou answered unto his inspirations? Wherein hast thou spent thy health, thy natural forces, and habilities? How hast thou employed the goods, which are termed the goods of fortune? How hast thou used the means and opportunities, which almighty God hath given thee to lead a holy, and virtuous life? What care hast thou had of thy neighbor, whom almighty God hath commended unto thee? And of those works of mercy, which he hath appointed thee to use towards him? Now what answer wilt thou make at that dreadful day of thine accompt, (to wit, at the hour of thy death,) when almighty God shall say unto thee. *Give me an accompt of thy stewardship,*[3] and of the lands, and goods, that I have committed to thy charge: For now I will that thou shalt have no more to do

---

2 See Matt. 12:36; Heb. 9:27.
3 Luke 16:2.

therewith? O dry and withered tree, ready for the everlasting horrible torments in hell fire! What answer wilt thou make at that terrible day, when an accompt shall be required of thee, of all the time of thy life, and of all the minutes, and moments of the same?

And assure thyself, that it will so certainly come to pass: for even our Savior Christ himself (who shall be our Judge) hath plainly protested it, and forewarned us beforehand thereof: saying: *Every idle word that men have spoken, they shall render an accompt of the same at the day of Judgement.*[4]

Secondly, call to mind what sins thou hast committed, and dost commit every day, since the time thou art come to a further knowledge of almighty God. And thou shalt find that even now presently (all that knowledge notwithstanding) old Adam liveth in thee, with many of thy lewd corrupt manners, and ancient customs. Whereupon thou mayest take occasion to run over the negligences, and defects, wherein thou dost daily offend against almighty God, against thy neighbor, and against thyself. For in each of these points, thou shalt find thyself to have failed very much in thy duty. Consider then how unreverent thou art towards almighty God: how unthankful for his benefits: how rebellious, and stiff-necked to yield to his inspirations: how slothful, and negligent in matters appertaining to his service: which either thou hast left undone, or else if thou hast done them, it was not with such a readiness, and diligence, as the things required, nor with such a pure intention as thou oughtest to have had: but the very true cause why thou didst them, was for some other respect of worldly commodity.

Consider likewise, how hard and severe thou art towards thy neighbor: and contrariwise how pitiful and favorable towards thyself: what a lover of thine own proper will, of thy flesh, of thy estimation, and of all thy worldly profits, and commodities. Consider moreover, that whereas thou sayest in words, that thou art now converted unto almighty God, thou art yet notwithstanding in thy deeds very proud, ambitious, angry, rash, vainglorious, envious, malicious, delicate,

4 Matt. 12:36.

inconstant, light, sensual, a great lover of thy pastimes, or pleasant company, laughter, jesting, idle talk, and of vain babbling, and prattling. Consider also, how unconstant thou art in thy good purposes: how unadvised in thy words: how headlong in thy deeds: how cowardly, and faint hearted to do any matter of weight, and importance.

Thirdly, when thou hast considered in this order the multitude of thy sins, consider forthwith the grievousness of them, that thou mayest perceive how thy miseries be increased on every side. The which thing thou shalt the better see, if thou consider these three circumstances in all such sins, as thou hast committed in thy former life: to wit: Against whom thou hast sinned: For what cause thou hast sinned: And in what manner thou hast sinned: If thou consider against whom thou hast sinned, thou shalt find that thou hast sinned against almighty God, whose goodness and majesty is infinite: whose benefits and mercies towards mankind do exceed the sands of the Sea: in whom alone are all excellencies, and titles of honor to be found: and to whom all duties and homages due to any creature, are due in the highest degree of bounden duty. If thou consider the cause that moved thee to sin, it was for a point of estimation, for a beastly delight, for a trifling world commodity, and for other things of no weight: whereof almighty God himself most grievously complaineth by one of his Prophets, saying: *They have dishonored me, in the presence of my people, for a handful of barley, and for a piece of bread.*[5] But if thou consider after what manner thou hast sinned? Surely it hath been done with such facility, with such boldness, so without all scruple, so without all fear, yea some times with such contention, and joy, as if thou hadst sinned against a God of straw, that neither knew, nor saw, what passeth in the world. Now is this the honor that is due unto so high a majesty? Is this the thankfulness that thou yieldest for his so manifold, and so great benefits? Is this the recompence that thou makest unto him for the precious blood, which he hath shed for thee upon the cross? Is this the repayment for those lashes, and buffets, which he suffered for thy sake? O miserable and wretched

---

5 Ezech. 13:19.

creature that thou art! Wretched undoubtedly in consideration of that thou hast lost: and more wretched in respect of the sins thou hast committed: but most wretched, and miserable, if thou be so blinded, that even yet for all this thou perceive not thine own perdition, and damnation.

Consider moreover what a wonderful hatred almighty God beareth against sin: and what great punishments he hath sent to the world for the same: that hereby thou mayest more clearly understand, how great, and how abominable the wickedness thereof is, as it shall be declared hereafter.

When thou hast considered all these things aforesaid, the next point is, that thou think of thyself as basely, as thou canst possibly. Think that thou art no better than a very wavering reed, which is blown up and down with every light blast of wind: without weight, without strength, without firmness, without stay, and without any manner of being. Think that thou art a Lazarus, that hath lain dead four days together,[6] and that thou art a stinking and abominable carcass, so full of worms, and of so vile a stench, and savour, that as many as pass by thee do stop their noses, and shut their eyes, that they may not behold thee. Think with thyself, that thou dost stink in this wise in the sight of almighty God, and of his holy angels. And esteem thyself, as unworthy to lift up thy eyes towards heaven:[7] unworthy that the earth should bear thee: unworthy that any creature should serve thee: unworthy of the very bread that thou eatest: and unworthy even of the light, and air that thou receivest. And if thou be unworthy hereof: consider how much more unworthy thou art to speak and talk with almighty God: yea and far more unworthy of the comforts and consolations of the holy Ghost, and of the cherishings, and delights of the children of God.[8] Accompt thyself for one of the most poor, and miserable creatures of all the world: and that none doth so much abuse the benefits of almighty God, as thou dost.

6 See John 11.
7 See Luke 18.
8 See Luke 15.

Think that if almighty God had wrought in Tyre, and Sidon, (that is, in other very great sinners) those things, which he hath wrought in thee, they would have done penance ere this, even in sackcloth, and ashes.[9] Acknowledge thyself to be far more wicked than thou canst imagine, and that notwithstanding thou dost sink very deep into this mire, and howsoever thou imaginest thyself to be at the very bottom, yet mayest thou find every day how to sink deeper and deeper therein. Cry out therefore earnestly unto almighty God, and say unto him: O Lord I have nothing, I am worth nothing, I am nothing, and nothing can I do without thee. Cast thyself down prostrate with the public sinner at our Savior's feet,[10] and covering thy face for very shame, and confusion, look with what shame a woman will appear before her husband, when she hath committed treason, and adultery against him, with the very same present thyself before that heavenly spouse, against whom thou hast committed so many, and so shameful adulteries. And with great sorrow, and repentance of heart, desire him to pardon thy sins, and offences, and that it may please him of his infinite pity, and mercy, to receive thee again into his house.

The First Treatise: Of the Consideration of Sins. Wherein This Former Meditation is Declared More at Large.

The first table after shipwreck, (as St. Jerome witnesseth) is penance. This is the first step of this ascending, and the first stone of this spiritual building.

Now to obtain this virtue of penance, (besides the grace of God, whose gift true penance is,) it helpeth very much to consider the multitude of our sins, as well present, as past: and withal the grievousness and malice of them. For this consideration proceedeth compunction, and repentance for sins.

9 See Matt. 11.
10 See Luke 7.

And out of this consideration proceedeth not only the virtue of penance, but also many other virtues, yea and those very excellent. For hereof cometh the knowledge of ourselves, (of which point we mind to treat in the meditation next following.) Of this consideration also cometh the contempt of ourselves: the fear of God: the abhorring of sin: with divers and sundry other like affections, wherein consisteth a very great part of perfection. Now that this exercise may be the more profitable unto thee, thou must apply and direct the same unto all these ends: and labor to suck all these sweet fruits out of the bitter root of this consideration. But because towards the obtaining of such fruits, it is needful to have the grace of God, (which is principally given to such as be humble, and devout,) it shall be requisite for thee, to desire of our Lord this gift of humility, and devotion, to the end that recollecting thyself in the inward part of thy heart, thou mayest imitate that holy king, who said: *I will recite before thee O Lord, all the years of my life, in the bitterness of my heart.*[11]

§. I. Of the Multitude of the Sins, That Thou Hast Committed in Thy Former Life.

Now if thou wilt know the number of thy sins, that thou hast committed in times past, run over briefly all the commandments, and deadly sins: and undoubtedly thou shalt find, that there is scarcely a commandment, that thou hast not broken, nor a deadly sin, wherein thou hast not offended.

The first commandment is to honor almighty God, who (as St. Augustine saith) is honored with those three Theological virtues: FAITH: HOPE: AND CHARITY. Now what manner of Faith had he, that hath lived so loosely as if he had believed that all those things which his faith teacheth him had been stark lies? What Hope had he, that neither remembered the life to come: neither knew what it was to call upon almighty God in his troubles, and adversities: nor yet how to put his assured trust, and affiance in him? What Charity

11 Is. 38:15.

had he, that hath more loved a point of honor, more accompted of the chaff of his worldly lucre, and commodity, and more regarded the filthiness of his pleasures, and delights, than almighty God himself: sith that for every one of these things he hath contemned, and offended almighty God. What reverence hath he born to that most high, and divine majesty, that hath been accustomed to rent that name of so great reverence, and to tear it in pieces, in swearing, and forswearing by it upon every light occasion, and that for every trifle, and matter of none importance? How hath he sanctified and kept holy his Feasts, that hath gaped for these days to none other end, but only to offend almighty God the more in them: to use dicing, carding, playing at tables, bowling, and other games: to jet and gaze up and down in the streets: to give scandal and offence to innocent young maidens, and virgins: and to keep evil company, and conversation?

After this, consider how froward, and obstinate thou hast been towards thy parents? How disobedient to thy superiors: How negligent in overseeing thy family, and servants, to instruct them in Catholic doctrine, and prayers: to train them up in honesty, virtue, and goodness: and to direct them with thy good counsel, and virtuous example, in the way of God? As for the hatreds, displeasures, grudges, passions, and desires of revenge, which thou hast had, who is able to number them? And if these things cannot fully be expressed, who is then able to declare the number of the dishonesties, and uncleanness, wherein thou hast fallen by works, words, and desires? What hath thy heart been, but a filthy puddle, and stinking dunghill, meet for beastly swine? What hath thy mouth been, but (as the Prophet saith) An open sepulcher, from whence have issued the evil savours of thy soul, that lie dead within thee?[12] What hath thine eyes been, but as it were certain windows of perdition, and death? What thing hath been presented to the sight of thine eyes, that thou hast not coveted, and procured, never so much as once remembering that almighty God was present, and looking upon thee, and that he had given thee an inhibition that thou shouldest not taste of that tree? Unto the fornicator

[12] See Ps. 5.

(the Wise man saith) all bread is sweet.[13] Because his appetite, and greedy desire is so unsatiable, that he tasteth all things, and findeth savor in all things, never remembering that there is a God unto whom he must be accomptable for them. Moreover, who is able to declare the greatness of thy covetousness, and the robberies, and thefts of thy desires, which have been so far of from being contented with that, that almighty God hath given thee, that all the whole world hath seemed to little for them. And if he that desireth an other man's lands, or goods, be (as in very deed he is,) a very thief in the sight of almighty God, how often times hast thou deserved to be hanged, that in thy heart hast committed so many thefts? Now as touching thy lies, thy backbitings, and rash judgements, as hardly may they be numbered, as the rest. For in a manner thou never hadst scarcely communication with others, but that the principal part of thy talk hath been of other folks' lives, of the widow, of the virgin, of the priest, and of the lay man, without sparing any order or estate whatsoever.

After this sort hast thou observed the commandments of almighty God. Let us now see how thou hast refrained thyself from sin. The pride of thy heart, how great hath it been? Thy desire of honor, and praise, how far hath it extended? Thy presumption, thy estimation of thyself, and thy contempt of others, who is able to express? Now what shall I say of the vain glory, and lightness of thy heart, sith that even a light feather in thy cap, or a strait pair of hose on thy legs, or a guard of velvet upon thy cloak, or a few silk cuts, and jags, have been able to make thee to strout, jet, and advance thyself very proudly, fondly, and peacocklike in the streets? Yea, and to make thee desirous to be gazed upon of all men? What steps hast thou made, what work hast thou done, what word hast thou spoken, that hath not been set forth with vanity, and desire of thine own estimation? Thy apparel, thy service, thy conversation, thy table, thy bed, thy entertainment, to be short in a manner all thy dealings, and demeaner, have savored of pride, yea, they have been wholly clothed with mere vanity. Furthermore, thy anger hath been like a Serpent:

13 Ecclus. 23:24.

thy gluttony, like a ravening wolf: thy sloth, like a lazy Ass: thy envy, far passing any viper: And herein finally (if thou do well consider thyself,) thou shalt find that thou hast gone very far wandering out of the way, and lived in a very dangerous state.

Consider likewise of thy senses, and not only of them, but also of all the gifts, graces, and benefits, that almighty God hath given thee. And consider after what sort thou hast employed them, and undoubtedly thou shalt find, that of all these things, (wherewith thou shouldest have done the more service unto him, who is the giver of them all,) thou hast made weapons, and instruments, wherewithal to offend him the more. Herein hast thou consumed thy strength, thy health, thy substance, thy life, thy understanding, thy memory, thy will, thy sight, thy tongue, with all the rest.

These and many other worse wicked acts hast thou committed in thy life past. Wherefore thou mayest very well say with that great sinner, (who as he was a great sinner, so was he also a repentant sinner,) *I have sinned (O Lord) above the number of the sands of the sea: my transgressions (O Lord) are multiplied, my offences are exceeding many.*[14] And whereas there were so many things, that might somewhat have bridled thee, and made thee afraid of almighty God: as the multitude of his benefits: and his exceeding great goodness, and justice: yet for all his benefits thou wouldst never acknowledge him, nor for his goodness love him, nor for his justice fear him, but utterly forgetting all these things, and closing fast thine eyes from beholding them, as one that had been stark blind, thou hast willfully wallowed thyself in all kind of vices. Now if it had so been, that the commodities, and provocations, thou hadst to allure thee to sin had been great, then peradventure thine offences might have had some pretensed colour of excuse. But what canst thou say for thyself, seeing that even for trifling matters of no importance, for childish toys, yea many times without any commodity at all, thou hast voluntarily sinned, as it were only in mere contempt, and despite of almighty God? Other men when they sin, are wont to do it with some fear, and remorse of

[14] See The Prayer of Manasses.

conscience, or at the least after the sin is committed they are very sorry for it. But thou perhaps hast been so blind, and so unsensible, that thou hast committed a thousand sins without any kind of fear, or remorse of conscience, even as if thou hadst thought that there had been no God at all. Or if thou hadst believed that there was a God, yet thy belief was like unto theirs, that said. *Our Lord shall not see our doings, neither shall the God of Jacob understand them.*[15] This is one of the greatest wickedness in all the world. For among those six things, which (as Solomon saith) are abhorred of almighty God, one is: *To have swift feet to run to do wickedness:*[16] That is: to have a facility, and swiftness, which the wicked have in offending almighty God.

§. II. Of the Sins, and Defects, That a Man May Fall into after He Is Come to the Knowledge of Almighty God.

In these and many other sins it is certain thou hast fallen before thou knewest almighty God. But after thou didst come to the knowledge of him, (if haply thou hast yet known him,) desire him that he will a little open thine eyes, and thou shalt find that even still for all this knowledge there are many relics of the old man, and many Jebusees yet remaining in the land of promise: because thou hast dealt so favorably with them, and hast been so well affected towards them.[17]

Consider then how in all things thou art full of defects, to wit: in thy duty towards God, towards thy neighbor, and towards thyself. Consider how little thou hast profited in the service of thy creator, being so long a time as it is, since he called thee. Consider how lively thy passions are even yet to this day: How little thou hast increased in virtues: And how thou hast continued evermore at one same stay, even like unto an old knotty tree, that never thriveth, but rather perhaps thou hast turned backward: Forsomuch as in the way of God, the not going forward is a turning backward. At the least wise consider as touching thy fervor, and devotion of spirit. Is it well (trowest

15 Ps. 93:7.
16 See Prov. 6.
17 See Jos. 15; Jgs. 1.

thou) that thou art now very far of from that fervent devotion, which peradventure thou hast had in times past?

Consider also, how little penance thou hast done for thy sins, and how little love, fear, and hope, thou hast had in almighty God. Thy little love towards him is seen by the little pains thou hast taken for his sake. Thy little fear of him is perceived by the manifold sins thou hast committed against him. Thy little confidence, and trust in him, is evidently declared in the time of tribulation, by the great raging storms, and troubles of mind, which thou sufferedst in that tempest, for that thou hast not perfectly stayed and settled thy heart with the anchors of hope.

Furthermore, consider how evil thou hast answered to his divine inspirations: how unwilling thou hast shewed thyself to receive the light of heaven: how thou hast grieved the holy Ghost,[18] and sufferest him to cry and call upon thee so often times in vain. For in that thou art loath to gainsay and resist thine own will, thou dost gainsay and resist the will of almighty God. He calleth thee to one way, and thou followest an other. He would have thee to serve him in one work, and thou wilt serve him in an other work. And although thou seest clearly what the will of almighty God is: yet if haply thine own will be set on the contrary, thou servest him in such things, as thine own will liketh, and not in such things as he would have thee to serve him. He peradventure calleth thee to inward exercises, and thou turnest to those that be outward. He calleth thee to prayer, and thou givest thyself to reading. His will is that thou shouldest first attend to thine own souls health before any others: but thou forgettest thyself, and settest aside thine own profit to profit others. Whereupon it cometh to pass, that thou neither dost profit thyself, nor them. To conclude, as often as thy will is contrary to the will of almighty God, thine always prevaileth, and is the conqueror, and the will of almighty God hath the overthrow.

And if perhaps thou do any good work, (good Lord,) how many defects are there intermingled therein? If thou be given to prayer,

[18] See Eph. 4.

how often times art thou there distracted, heavy, irksome, drowsy, and slothful, without any reverence to the majesty of almighty God, unto whom thou speakest. And thou thinkest the time of prayer very long, and tedious unto thee, and art never in quiet until thou hast given it over, that thou mayest attend to thy other business, that be more agreeable to thy taste, and liking. Now when thou dost any other good work, O with what coldness and faintness is it done? With how many defects and imperfections is it fraughted? If this be certain, that almighty God looketh not so much unto the substance of the good work that is done, as to the intention wherewith it is done, how many good works (I pray thee) hast thou done in such sort, as they passed away pure and clean from dust, and chaff: and that neither vanity, nor the world have plucked at the least one lock of wool from them? How many hast thou done moved only by the importunity of others, or for custom, or manners sake? How many hast thou done only in regard of thine own estimation, and credit? How many only to satisfy thine own taste, and contentation? And how few hast thou done sincerely and purely for the love of God, without having some kind of vain respect to the world?

Now if thou consider how thou hast done thy duty towards thy neighbors, thou shalt find, that thou hast neither loved them as almighty God commandeth thee, nor been sorry for their adversities as for thine own, nor endeavored to help them in their troubles, neither yet hast thou had so much as even pity and compassion upon them: yea peradventure in steed of taking compassion upon them, thou hast disdained and grudged at their doings, though it be certain that true justice taketh pity, and compassion, and false and counterfeit justice disdain, and indignation. At the least as touching that bond of love which the Apostle so often times requireth of us, commanding us to love one an other, as members of one same body, (sith we be all partakers of one same spirit)[19] consider how far of thou hast been from having that love? How often times hast thou omitted to relieve the poor, to visit the sick, to help the widow, and to be a

[19] See Eph. 4.

proctor and mediator for him, that could do very little for himself? Unto how many persons hast thou gave offence with thy words, with thy deeds, and with any answers? How often times hast thou preferred thyself before thy equals, despised thy inferiors, and flattered thy superiors, crouching, and creeping down like a seely emmet to the one sort, and strutting, and advancing thyself very proudly like an Elephant to the others?

But now if thou wilt take a view of thyself, and put thy hand into thine own bosom, O how leprous shalt thou pluck it out again? And what deep festered wounds shalt thou find within thee? How green and lively shalt thou find within thee the roots of pride, the love of honor, and estimation, the tickling of vain glory, and hypocrisy privily dissembled, wherewith thou laborest to cover thy defects, and wouldst gladly seem to be an other manner of man, than in very deed thou art? What a lover art thou of thine own worldly gain, and commodity, and of the pleasures, and delights of thy flesh? Whereunto often times under the colour of necessity, thou dost not only provide, but also serve: thou dost not only sustain it, but also pamper and cherish it with great delicacy. Again, if one of thine equals do but take the right hand of thee, or set his foot somewhat before thee, or sit above thee at the table, how quickly do the roots of envy bud forth, and shew themselves? And if an other do but a little touch thee in a point of estimation (good Lord) what a sudden, and furious choleric rage dost thou fall into.

But among all other evils, who is able to express the looseness of thy tongue, the lightness of thy heart, the stubbornness of thine own will, and the inconstancy in good purposes? How many waste, and void words do issue from thy tongue? How much vain and needless language dost thou fondly lavish out in a day? How much dost thou babble and talk to the derogation and hinderance of thy neighbor, and to the praise and commendation of thyself? How seldom times dost thou deny thine own will, and give over the prey whereupon it feedeth, to fulfill either the will of almighty God, or of thy neighbor? Consider this point attentively, and thou shalt find that it is very rare and seldom that thou hast obtained the victory over thyself, and thine own perverse will. Whereas in very deed it is always necessary for thee to have this victory, in case thou mind to be perfectly virtuous. Now what shall I say of thy inconstancy in thy good purposes, but (to conclude in few words,) that there is no weathercock that so lightly turneth with every wind, as thou dost with the least puff of every trifling occasion, that is offered unto thee? What else is all thy whole life but very childish toys, and as it were a weaving, and unweaving, purposing a thing in the morning, and breaking it at evening, yea and some times thou tarryest not so long, but changest and alterest thy determinations, if not out of hand, yet the very same hour? Now what other thing is this, but to be like unto that Lunatic man mentioned in the gospel, whom the disciples of our Savior could not heal, for that this disease was so great.[20]

In like manner the lightness of thy heart, the fickleness, mutability, unsteadfastness, and pusillanimity thereof are such, as they can hardly be expressed. For it is manifest, that thy heart changeth and varieth into so many divers shapes, and forms, as there chanceth divers occasions and accidents unto it every hour of the day and that without any firmness or constancy at all. How soon is it distracted with every trifling business? How lightly poureth it out all that it hath? And how little trouble and adversity is able to vex and torment it, yea and utterly to overwhelm it?

To conclude, when thou hast well examined and made thine accompt aright, and seest what thou hast, and what thou wantest, thou shalt surely find, that thou hast good cause to be afraid, least all that thou hast be but only a very deceit, and a mere shadow of virtue, and even a false and counterfeit justice: forsomuch as thou hast no more in thee, but a little taste of almighty God, which may perhaps savour more of the flesh, than of the spirit. And yet it may so be, that herewith thou thinkest thyself to be safe, and secure: yea peradventure thou wilt not stick to say with the proud Pharisee: *That thou art*

20 See Matt. 17.

not as other men be:[21] Because they have not that taste and feeling that thou hast. Whereas on the other side, thou hast the bosom of thy soul full of self love, and of thine own obstinate will, and of all the other foul defects, and inordinate passions before mentioned. So that all the substance of this thy gay shew of virtue, and goodness, is no more in effect, but to say, Lord! Lord! And not to do the will of our Lord. This is to imitate the counterfeit Justice of the Pharisees, and to be that lukewarm man, (to wit, neither hot nor cold in the service of God,) which is spoken of in the Apocalypse, whom almighty God vomiteth out of his mouth.[22]

All these things (Christian brother) thou oughtest to consider very diligently with thyself, and to direct this consideration to this end, that thou mayest hereby procure sorrow, and grief for thy sins, and attain to the knowledge of thine own misery: that by the one thou mayest desire pardon of our Lord for thine offences past: and by the other virtue, and grace, never to offend him any more.

§. III. Of the Accusation of a Man's Own Conscience: and of the Abhorring and Contempt of Himself.

When a man hath thus considered the multitude of his sins, and seen himself how he is on every side very sore loden, and overcharged with the burthen of the same, his part is to humble himself, and to have as great a sorrow and compunction as he may possibly, and to desire to be contemned, and despised of all creatures, for that he hath thus despised the creator of them all. For the furtherance of which desire he may help himself with a very devout consideration of St. Bonaventure, wherein speaking of this confusion of conscience, and of the contempt of ourselves, he saith thus.

Let us consider my brethren our own great vileness, and how greatly we have offended almighty God, and let us humble ourselves before him, as much as we can possibly: let us be afraid to lift up our

---

21 See Luke 18:11.
22 See Apoc. 3.

eyes towards heaven, and let us strike our breasts with that publican of the gospel, that almighty God may take pity and compassion upon us:[23] let us enforce ourselves, and take arms against our own malice and wickedness: let us become judges over ourselves:[24] and let every one of us say within himself: If our Lord hath been so reproachfully handled for my sake, if he have suffered so great torments and most grievous pains for the sins that I have committed, why should not I abase and despise myself, being the very person that hath sinned? God forbid, that I should ever presume any thing more of myself than of a most vile, and filthy dunghill, whose horrible stench even I myself cannot well abide. I am he that hath despised almighty God: I am he, that hath sought means to crucify him again upon the cross: and me thinketh that all the whole frame of this world crieth out with open voice against me: saying: This is he, that hath offended and despised our common Lord. This is that wicked and ungrateful wretched creature that hath rather been moved with the guileful baits of the devil, than with the great benefits of almighty God. This is he, that hath been more delighted with the malice of the devil, than with the bountiful goodness and favor of almighty God. This is he, that could never be induced to virtue and goodness with the fatherly loving cherishings, and entertainments of almighty God: neither could he ever be made afraid with his dreadful and terrible judgements. This is he, that hath (so much as lieth in him) defaced the power, wisdom, and goodness of almighty God, and brought them in contempt. This is he, that hath been more afraid to offend a seely weak man, than the omnipotency of God. This is he, that hath been more ashamed to commit a filthy act before a rude plough man of the country, than before the presence of almighty God. This is he, that hath rather loved, and chosen to enjoy a little stinking dung and mire here upon the earth, than the everlasting chief felicity in the kingdom of heaven. This is he, that hath fixed his eyes upon rotten, and corruptible creatures, and utterly neglected the creator. What shall I

23 See Luke 18.
24 See 1 Cor. 11.

say more? There is nothing so filthy, nothing so abominable, that he hath refrained to commit in the presence of almighty God, without having any respect, or shame, of so great a majesty.

Wherefore all creatures do cry out after their manner against me, and say: This is that lewd Caitiff, that hath abused us all. For whereas he ought to have employed us in the service and glory of our Creator, he hath made us to serve the will and pleasure of the devil, perverting all such things to the injury, and reproach of the creator, as he had created for his service. His soul was beautified with the image of God, and he hath disfigured this divine image, and clothed it with our vile image, and likeness. He hath been more earthly than the earth itself: more slippery than the water: more mutable than the wind: more enkindled in his appetites, than the fire: more hardened than the very stones: more cruel against himself, than the wild beasts: more spiteful and venomous against others, than the very Cockatrice. What need I to use many words? He hath neither feared almighty God, nor made accompt of men, and therefore he hath cast abroad his poison (as much as in him lay) upon many persons, alluring them to bear him company in his sins, and wickedness. He hath not been content to be himself alone injurious, and reproachful against almighty God, but would have many others also to be partners, and companions with him in his sinful, wicked, and injurious doings.[25] Now what shall I say of his other abominable naughtiness? His pride hath been so great, that he would not be subject unto almighty God, nor submit his neck under the sweet yoke of his obedience, but would rather live as he himself thought best, and fulfil his own will in each point, rebelling (so much as lay in him) against almighty God. If almighty God did not fulfil his appetites and desires, or if he sent him any troubles, or adversities, he was in as great an anger, and rage against him, as he would have been against one of his own servants. In all his doings he would be praised, as well in the wicked, as in the good, as though

[25] Transliterators Note: Pages 319–322 missing from copy of George L'Oiselet's 1584 printing. Used corresponding pages from Thomas Brumeau's 1582 printing to complete transliteration, which correspond to pages 345–348 in this printed transliteration.

he had been almighty God himself, to whom only it appertaineth to be praised in all his works: forsomuch as all that he doth is good, or ordained to goodness. What shall I say more? He hath been more proud in some degree than lucifer: more presumptuous than Adam: For they being (as they were) full of clearness and beauty, had some motive and provocation to presume of themselves, but this ungracious sinful caitiff being in very deed a filthy, and stinking dunghill, what should move and provoke him to esteem himself in any respect?

All creatures do therefore justly cry out against me, and say: Come let us destroy this wicked sinful wretch that hath done such great wrong and villainy to our creator. The earth saith: Why do I bear him? The water saith: why do I not drown him? The air saith, why do I give him breath? The fire saith, why do I not burn him? Hell saith, why do I not swallow him up, and torment him? Alas! Alas! Miserable wretch that I am, what shall I do? Whither shall I go? Seeing all things are in arms against me? Where shall I hide myself? Who will receive me, seeing I have offended all things? Almighty God I have despised: the Angels I have made angry: the saints I have dishonored: men I have offended and scandalized: and all creatures I have most wickedly abused. But to what end do I make so long a discourse? For in that I offended the Lord and creator of all things, I have also offended all creatures together in him. I know not therefore (poor wretched sinful caitiff that I am) whither I may go: forsomuch as I have made all things to become enemies against me. Amongst all the things that I see about me, I can find nothing that will take my part, insomuch as even mine own very conscience barketh against me, and all my bowels do accuse me, and rent me in pieces.

Wherefore I will weep continually: I will lament my wretchedness like a poor miserable creature: I will never cease weeping, so long as I live in this vale of misery: I will expect if perhaps my most merciful Savior will vouchsafe to turn his pitiful eyes towards me: I will cast myself down at his feet: and with all the humility, and shame that I can, I will say unto him. O Lord I am that great enemy of thine, which in presence of thy divine eyes have committed most wicked, and abominable offences. I acknowledge myself to be guilty here before thee. I confess my wickedness to be so great, that although I alone should suffer all the pains and torments that both the devils, and damned persons do suffer in hell, yet should I not be able with all this to make a sufficient satisfaction for that, which my sins have deserved. Wherefore I beseech thee (O Lord) to cast the cloak of thy mercy over me thy poor, wretched, and sinful creature: and let the greatness of thy goodness overcome, and cover my wickedness. Let the most sweet loving father rejoice at the coming home again of his prodigal son. Let the good shepherd rejoice at the recovery of his lost sheep. Let the pitiful woman rejoice at the finding of her lost groat.[26] O how happy and joyful shall that day be, when thou shalt cast thine arms about my neck, and give me the sweet kisses of peace!

Howbeit to obtain this gracious benefit, I know now what I will do. I will take arms even against myself: And I will be more cruel, and rigorous against myself, than any other. I will afflict and punish myself all manner of ways with labors and pains: and I will despise myself as a most stinking, and filthy dunghill. Yea I will rejoice when so ever I shall be despised, and dishonored, how soever the same shall happen unto me. I will be glad also, when my shame shall be discovered, and published abroad. And because I alone am not sufficient to abhor, and despise myself, I will join all creatures in the whole world unto me, and will desire to be punished, and despised by every one of them, forsomuch as I have despised the Creator of them all. This shall be unto me a treasure, which I will very earnestly desire: to wit: to heap pains and despites against myself, and to love them with hearty affection, that shall help me herein. All the consolations, and honors of this life, shall be a torment unto me: and I will accompt them all to be my most deceitful, and flattering enemies. I believe assuredly, that in case I shall thus do, I shall provoke all things (notwithstanding I have offended them) to take pity, and compassion upon me: and that those creatures, which before cried out against me will now after their manner pray, and entreat in my

[26] See Luke 15.

behalf. Wherefore I am contented that all dishonors, reproaches, and punishments do run upon me on every side, so that by them I may be brought to my most sweet, and merciful Lord. And as for all honor, pleasure, and delight, they shall be banished away quite from me: insomuch as the very names of them shall no more be heard in my house. In all things I will seek nothing else, but only the honor of my Lord God, and the contempt and confusion of myself.

Hitherto are the words of St. Bonaventure. Which will undoubtedly be a very great help unto him, that shall devoutly meditate upon them, to procure, and engender in him these four noble affections. To wit, sorrow for sin: the fear of God: a holy hatred of himself: and a desire to be contemned and despised for God's sake. Of the first affection proceedeth penance, which washeth away all our sins past. In the second is contained the fear of God, which excludeth all sins that are to come. By the third is obtained a hatred of himself, against the love of himself. And by the fourth is obtained true humility, against the desire of the glory of the world. Whosoever is desirous to obtain these four virtues, must exercise himself in these, and such like considerations. But especially hereby is obtained this holy hatred of a man's self, whose office is, not only to eschew the cherishings, and delicacies of the body, and to procure to himself pains, and labors, but also much more to despise all manner of dignity, honor, and estimation of the world, and to love all kind of contempt and dishonor for God's sake. And this affection appertaineth properly unto humility, which is a very inward, and hearty contempt of ourselves: Which contempt cometh of the true knowledge of ourselves, and of the consideration of our own sins. I speak this, to the intent that such as be lovers of true humility may understand, that out of this very same fountain, from whence that water is drawn that may cause in us an hatred and abhorring of ourselves, is that other water drawn also, that sustaineth, and watereth the tree of true humility, out of which tree all virtues do spring.

TUESDAY NIGHT

Of the Miseries of This Life.

THIS day (when thou hast made the sign of the Cross, and prepared thyself,) thou hast to meditate upon the condition, and miseries of this life: that thou mayest by them understand, how vain the glory of this world is, seeing it is built upon so weak a foundation: and how little accompt a man ought to make of himself, being (as he is subject) unto so many miseries.

Now for this purpose thou hast to consider first of the vileness of the original, and birth of man, to wit: the matter whereof he is compounded: the manner of his conception: the griefs, and pains of his birth: the frailty, and miseries of his body: according as hereafter shall be entreated.

Then thou hast to consider the great miseries of the life that he liveth, and chiefly these seven.

First, consider how short this life is, seeing the longest term thereof passeth not threescore and ten, or fourscore years.[1] For all the rest (if any man's life be drawn a little longer) is but labor, and sorrow. And if thou take out of this the time of our infancy, which is rather a life of beasts, than of men and withal the time that is spent in sleeping, at which time we have not the use of our senses, and reason, thou shalt find that our life is a great deal shorter, than it seemeth unto us. Besides all this, if thou compare this life with the eternity

[1] See Ps. 89.

of the life to come, that endureth for evermore, it shall scarcely seem so much as a minute: Whereby thou mayest perceive, how far out of the way those persons are, who to enjoy the little blast of so short a life, do hazard to lose the quiet rest of the blessed life to come, which shall endure everlastingly.

Secondly, consider how uncertain this life is, (which is an other misery besides the former.) For it is not only of itself very short, but even that very small continuance of life that it hath, is not assured, but doubtful. For how many (I pray thee) do come to the age of those threescore and ten, or fourscore years, which we spake of? In how many persons is the web cut off, even at the first, when it is scarcely begun to be woven? How many do pass away out of this world, even in the flower (as they term it) of their age, and in the very blossoming of youth. *Ye know not* (saith our Savior) *when our Lord will come, whether in the morning, or at noonday, or at midnight, or at the time of the cock crowing:*[2] That is to say: Ye know not whether he will come in the time of infancy, or of childhood, or of youth, or of age. For the better perceiving of this point, it shall be a good help unto thee to call to mind, how many of thy friends and acquaintances are dead, and departed out of this world. And especially remember thy kinsfolk, thy companions, and familiars, and some of the worshipful and famous personages of great estimation in this world, whom death hath assaulted, and snatched away in divers ages, and utterly beguiled, and defeated them of all their fond designments, and hopes. I know a certain man, that hath made a memorial of all such notable personages, as he hath known in this world in all kind of estates, which are now dead: and some times he readeth their names, or calleth them to mind: and in rehearsal of every one of them, he doth briefly represent before his eyes the whole tragedy of their lives, the mockeries, and deceits of this world, and withal the conclusion and end of all worldly things. Whereby he understandeth what good cause the Apostle had to say: *That the figure of this world*

2 See Mark 13:35.

passeth away.[3] In which words he giveth us to understand, how little ground, and stay, the affairs of this life have, seeing he would not call them very things indeed, but only figures, or shews of things, which have no being, but only an appearance, whereby also they are the more deceitful.

Thirdly, consider how frail, and brickle this life is, and thou shalt find, that there is no vessel of glass so frail as it is. Insomuch as a little distemperature of the air, or of the sun, the drinking of a cup of cold water, yea the very breath of a sick man is able to spoil us of our life, as we see by daily experience of many persons, whom the least occasion of all these that we have here rehearsed, hath been able to end their lives, and that even in the most flourishing time of all their age.

Fourthly, consider how mutable and variable this life is, and how it never continueth in one self same stay. For which purpose thou must consider the great and often alterations, and changes of our bodies, which never continue in one same state, and disposition. Consider likewise, how far greater the changes, and mutations of our minds are, which do ever ebb and flow like the Sea, and be continually altered and tossed with divers winds, and surges of passions, that do disquiet, and trouble us every hour. Finally, consider how great the mutation in the whole man is, who is subject to all the alterations of fortune, which never continueth in one same being, but always turneth her wheel, and rolleth up and down from one place to an other. And above all this, consider how continual the moving of our life is, seeing it never resteth day, nor night, but goeth always shortening from time to time, and consumeth itself like as a garment doth with use, and approacheth every hour nearer and nearer unto death. Now by this reckoning what else is our life, but as it were a candle that is always wasting, and consuming, and the more it burneth, and giveth light, the more it consumeth and wasteth away? What else is our life, but as it were a flower, that buddeth in the morning, and fadeth away at noon day, and at evening is clean dried up? This very comparison maketh the Prophet in the Psalm, where he saith.

---

3 1 Cor. 7:31.

The morning of our infancy passeth away like an herb, it blossometh in the morning, and suddenly fadeth away, and at evening it decayeth, and waxeth hard, and withereth away.[4]

Fifthly, consider how deceitful our life is (which peradventure is the worst property it hath.) For by this mean it deceiveth us, in that being in very deed filthy, it seemeth unto us beautiful: and being but short, every man thinketh his own life will be long: and being so miserable (as it is in deed) yet it seemeth so amiable, that to maintain the same, men will not stick to run through all dangers, travails, and losses, (be they never so great,) yea they will not spare to do such things for it, as whereby they are assured to be damned for ever and ever in hell fire, and to lose life everlasting.

Sixthly, consider how besides this that our life is so short (as hath been said,) yet that little time we have to live is also subject unto divers and sundry miseries, as well of the mind, as of the body: insomuch as all the same being duly considered, and laid together is nothing else, but a vale of tears, and a main Sea of infinite miseries. St. Jerome declareth of Zerxes that most mighty king, (who threw down mountains, and dried up the Seas) that on a time he went up to the top of a high hill, to take a view of his huge army, which he had gathered together of infinite numbers of people. And after that he had well viewed and considered them, it is said that he wept: and being demanded the cause of his weeping, he answered, and said: I weep because I consider that within these hundred years, there shall not one of all this huge Army, which I see here present before me, be left alive. Whereupon St. Jerome saith these words: O that we might (saith he) ascend up to the top of some tower, that were so high, that we might see from thence all the whole earth underneath our feet. From thence shouldest thou see the ruins and miseries of all the world: Thou shouldest see nations destroyed by nations: and kingdoms by kingdoms. Thou shouldest see some hanged, and others murdered: some drowned in the Sea, others taken prisoners. In one place thou shouldest see marriages, and mirth: in an other doleful

4 Ps. 89:6.

mourning, and lamentation. In one place thou shouldest see some born into this world, and carried to the Church to be Christened: in an other place thou shouldest see some others die, and carried to the Church to be buried. Some thou shouldest see exceeding wealthy, and flowing in great abundance of lands, and riches: and others again in great poverty, and begging from door, to door. To be short, thou shouldest see, not only the huge army of Zerxes, but also all the men, women, and children of the world, that be now alive, within these few years to end their lives, and not to be seen any more in this world.

Consider also all the diseases and calamities that may happen to men's bodies, and withal all the afflictions, and cares of the mind. Consider likewise the dangers, and perils, that be incident as well to all estates, as also to all the ages of men: and thou shalt see very evidently the manifold miseries of this life. By the seeing whereof thou shalt perceive how small a thing all that is, that the world is able to give thee, and this consideration may cause thee more easily to despise and contemn the same, and all that thou mayest hope to receive from it.

After all these manifold miseries, and calamities, there succeedeth the last misery, that is death, which is as well to the body, as to the soul, of all terrible things the very last, and most terrible. For the body shall in a moment be spoiled of all that it hath. And of the soul there shall then be made a resolute determination what shall become of it for ever, and ever.

The Second Treatise.

§. I. Of the Miseries of Man's Life.

How great the miseries are, that the nature of mankind is subject unto by reason of sin, there is no tongue able to express. And therefore St. Gregory said very well, that only our two first parents, Adam, and Eve, (who knew by experience the noble condition, and state, wherein almighty God created man,) understood perfectly the miseries of man. Because they by calling to mind the felicity and prosperous estate of that life, which they had once enjoyed, saw more clearly the miseries of the banishment, wherein they remained through sin. But the children of these our two miserable parents, as they never knew what thing prosperity, and good hap was, but were always fostered, and brought up in misery: so they know not, what thing misery is, because they never knew what prosperity was. Yea many of them are as it were persons in a mere frenzy, so far void of sense, as they would (if it were possible) continue perpetually in this life, and make this place of banishment their country, and this prison their dwelling house, because they understand not the miseries thereof. Wherefore like as they that are accustomed to dwell in places of unsavory and stinking air, do feel no pain nor trouble of it, by reason of the custom, and use, they have thereof: even so these miserable persons understand not the miseries of this life, because they are so enured, and accustomed to live in them.

Now that thou mayest not likewise fall into this foul deceit, nor into other greater inconveniences that are wont to follow hereof, consider (I pray thee with good attention) the multitude of these miseries: and before all other, consider and weigh the miseries, that are in the first beginning, and birth of a man, and afterwards the conditions of the life he liveth.

To begin this matter therefore at the very original: Consider first of what matter man's body is compounded. For by the worthiness, or baseness of the matter, often times the condition of the work is known. The holy scripture saith, that almighty God created man of the slime, or dirt of the earth.[5] Now of all the elements, earth is the most base, and inferior: and among all the parts of the earth, slime is the most base, and vile. Whereby it may appear, that almighty God created man of the most vile, and basest thing of the world. Insomuch as even the Kings, the Emperors, and the Popes, be they never so high, famous, and royal, are even slime, and dirt of the earth. And this thing understood the Egyptians right well, of whom it is

5 See Gen. 2.

written, that when they celebrated yearly the feast of their nativity, they carried in their hands certain herbs, that grow in miry and slimy ditches: to signify thereby, the likeness, and affinity, that men have with weeds, and slimy dirt: which is the common father both to weeds, and to men. Wherefore if the matter of which we are made be so base, and vile, whereof art thou so proud, thou dust, and ashes? Whereof art thou so lofty, thou stinking weed, and dirty slime?

Now as concerning the manner, and workmanship, wherewith the work of this matter is wrought, it is not to be committed to writing, neither yet to be considered upon, but to be passed over with silence, and closing up our eyes, that we behold not so filthy a thing as it is. If men knew how to be ashamed of a thing which they ought of reason to be ashamed of, surely they would be ashamed of nothing more, than to consider the manner how they were conceived. Concerning which point I will touch one thing only, and that is, that whereas our merciful Lord, and Savior, came into this world to take upon him all our miseries, for to discharge us of them, only this was the thing, that he would in no wise take upon him. And whereas he disdained not to be buffeted, and spitted upon, and to be reputed for the basest of all men, only this he thought was unseemly, and not meet for his majesty, to wit, if he should have been conceived in such manner, and order, as men are. Now as touching the substance and food wherewith men's bodies are nourished, before they be born into this world, it is not so clean a thing, as that it ought once to be named. No more ought a number of other unclean things, that are daily seen at the time of our birth.

Let us now come to the birth of a man, and first entry into the world. Tell me I pray thee, what thing is more miserable, than to see a woman in her travail, when she bringeth forth her child? O what sharp agonies and bitter pains doth she then feel! What painful tossings and throes doth she make! What dangerous grips and qualms is she in! What pitiful skrikes and groanings doth she utter. I omit here to speak of many monstrous, strange, and overthwart births. For if I should make rehearsal of them, I should never make an end. And yet all this notwithstanding when the seely creature cometh into the world, it cometh (God wot) weeping, and crying, poor, naked, weak, and miserable: it is utterly destitute and in necessity of all things, and unable to do any thing. Other living things are born with shoes upon their feet, and apparel upon their back: some with wool: others with scales: others with feathers: others with leather: others with shells: insomuch as the very trees come forth covered with a rind, or bark, yea and sometimes for feeling they be double barked: only man is born stark naked, without any other kind of garment in the world, but only a skin, which is all riveled, foul, and loathsome to behold, wherein he cometh lapped at the time of his birth. With these ornaments creepeth he into the world, who after his coming, groweth unto such fond ambition, and pride, that a whole world is scarcely able to satisfy him.

Moreover, other living things at the very hour of their coming into this world, are able immediately to seek for such things as they stand in need of, and have ability to do the same: Some can go: others can swim: others can fly: to be short, each one of them is able without any instructor to seek for such things, as it hath need of: only man knoweth nothing, neither is he able to do any thing, but must of necessity be carried in other folks arms. How long time is it before he can learn to go? And yet he must begin to crawl upon all four, before he can go upon two. How long time is it before he can speak so much as one word? And not only before he can speak, but also before he can tell how to put meat into his own mouth, unless some others do help him? One thing only I must confess he can do of himself, that is, he can cry, and weep. This is the first thing he doeth, and this is the thing only he can do without any teacher. And although he can also laugh of himself, yet can he not do it, before he be forty days old, notwithstanding that he is ever more weeping from the first hour of his coming into this world. Whereby thou mayest understand, how far more prompt, and ready our nature is to pewling, and weeping, than to joy, and mirth. O mere folly, and madness of men, (saith a

Wise man) who of so poor, naked, and base beginning, do persuade themselves, that they are born to be proud!

Now as concerning the very body of man, (whereof men esteem themselves so much, and take such a vain conceit) I would thou shouldest consider with indifferent eyes, what our bodies are in very deed, how gay and beautiful soever they appear to our outward sight. Tell me (I pray thee) what other thing is the body of a man, but only a corrupt and tainted vessel, which incontinently soureth, and corrupteth whatsoever licour is poured into it? What other thing is a man's body, but only a filthy dunghill, covered over with snow, which outwardly appeareth white, and within is full of filth, and uncleanness? What muckhill is so filthy? What sink avoideth out of it such filthy gear through all his channels, as a man's body doth by several means, and ways? The trees, the herbs, yea and certain living beasts also do yield out of them very sweet and pleasant savours: but man yieldeth, and avoideth from him, such loathsome, and foul stinking stuff, as he seemeth truly none other thing, but only a fountain of all sluttishness, and filthiness.

It is written of a great wise philosopher called Plotinus, that he was ashamed of the condition, and baseness of his body, insomuch as he was very unwilling to hear any talk of his lineage, and pedigree: neither could he ever be induced with any persuasions to give his consent that any man should portrait him out in picture: saying, that it was sufficient, that he himself carried with him all the days of his life a thing so filthy and so unworthy of the nobleness of his soul, although he were not bound to leave behind him a perpetual remembrance of his own dishonor.

It is written also of the holy Abbot Isidorus, that upon a time whilst he was at meat he was not able to refrain from weeping, and being demanded why he wept, he answered: I weep, because I am ashamed to be here feeding upon the corruptible meat of beasts: whereas I was created to be in the company of Angels, and to feed upon heavenly food with them.

§. II. Of the Miseries and Conditions of This Life: and First of the Shortness of the Same.

After this, consider the great and manifold miseries of man's life, and especially these seven: to wit: How short this life is: How uncertain: How frail: How inconstant: How deceitful: and finally, how miserable it is. This done think upon the end thereof, which is death.

Consider then first of the shortness of our life, which thing the holy man Job considered, when he said: *O Lord the days of man are very short, and thou knowest the number of the months, that he hath to live.*[6] We see at this day, what a great matter it is for one to live threescore and ten, or fourscore years, and this is commonly the ordinary rate of man's life: Insomuch as when they live so long, they accompt themselves not to be evil dealt withal. As the Prophet signifieth, when he saith: *The days of man are at the uttermost but threescore and ten years: and if the strongest do reach to fourscore, all that followeth is but labor, and grief.*[7]

Now if thou wilt divide this accompt into parts, and not reckon it thus in a gross sum, it seemeth unto me, that thou canst not well reckon the time of our infancy for any part of our life: and much less the time, that is consumed in sleep. Because the life of infancy when we are not as yet come to the use of reason (which only sheweth us to be men) can not well be called the life of men, but rather the life of beasts, even as it were the life of a young goat, that goeth here and there skipping, and leaping: especially because we see that in all that age, there is nothing either learned, or done, that may well beseem the dignity of a man. Now as touching the time that is spent in sleep, I see not how it may be called the time of life, seeing the principal part of our life is to have the use of our senses, and reason, which as then both the one and the other are suspended in us, and as it were dead.

And therefore a certain Philosopher said, that in the half of a man's life there is no difference between the happy man, and unhappy: forsomuch as during the time of sleep all men are equal, because they

---

6 Job 14:5.

7 See Ps. 89:10.

be then as it were dead. It is clear, that if a king should be detained as a prisoner for the space of one or two years, we can not say (and say truly) that he reigned during that time, seeing he enjoyed not the kingdom, nor governed the same like a king. How then can it be said, that a man liveth whiles he sleepeth, seeing during that time the Seignory and use of his reason, yea and of his senses also, by which he liveth, stand as it were in suspense? For this cause a certain Poet termed sleep the cousin germane of death, for the likeness and resemblance, which he perceived to be between the one, and the other. Now then if so great a part of our life be spent in sleep, what a great part is that wherein it cannot be said that we do live at all. And if it be the common custom of men to sleep the third part of the day, and night, which is eight whole hours, (although there be a great sort, that do not content themselves therewith) it followeth by this accompt, that the third part of our life is consumed in sleep, and so consequently, that during that time we do not live. So that hereby thou mayest perceive, what a great part of our short life is spent in sleep every day. This accompt therefore being thus made, (which undoubtedly is a very true accompt) how much is that, that remaineth of a man's very life in deed, even of such I mean, as live longest?

Certainly that philosopher had very great reason to do as he did, who being demanded what he thought of the life of a man, turned himself about before them that made the demand, and suddenly departed out of their sight. Giving them thereby to understand, that our life is no more, but only a turn about, and of short continuance. Our life is no more, but as it were the shooting of a star, that passeth at a trice, and flasheth quickly away, and within a little while after, even that very sign that was left behind, vanisheth out of sight also. For within very few days after a man is departed out of this life, the very remembrance of him dieth with his life, be the personage never so great, or honorable. To conclude, this life seemed so short to many of the ancient wisemen, that one of them termed it a dream: and an other not contented therewith, called it the dream of a shadow, seeming to him that it was overmuch to call it the dream of a true thing in deed, being as he thought it none other than a dream of a vain and frivolous thing.

Again, if we compare this small remnant of the life that we here live, with the life to come, how much less will it yet appear? Ecclesiasticus saith very well: *If the number of a man's days be an hundred years, it is much.*[8] Now what is all this (being compared with the life everlasting) but as it were a drop of water compared with all the whole Sea? And the reason hereof is evident. For if a star (which is far greater than all the whole earth) being compared with the rest of heaven, seemeth so small a thing, how small shall this present life (which is so short) seem to be, being compared with the life to come, that shall never have end? And if (as the astronomers affirm) all the whole earth in comparison of heaven be but as it were a little pin's point, because the inestimable greatness of the heavens causeth it to seem so small a thing, what shall this little puff of our short life seem to be, if it be compared with life everlasting, which is infinite? Undoubtedly it will seem nothing at all. For if a thousand years in the sight of almighty God, be no more but as it were yesterday, which is now past, and gone,[9] what shall the life of one hundred years seem to be in his sight, but only a very nothing?

And thus it seemeth unto the damned persons, when they make comparison between this life, which they have left behind them, with the eternity of the torments, which they shall suffer for evermore. As they themselves do confess in the book of wisdom in these words: *What hath our pride availed us, and the pomp of our riches? All these things are past away, as it were a shadow that flieth, and as one that rideth swiftly in post, or as the ship that passeth by the waters, and leaveth no sign where it hath gone, or as an arrow shot at a certain mark, which so soon as the air hath once opened, and made him his way, forthwith it closeth up again, and it is not known which way it went.*[10] Even so it fareth with us. For at that very instant when we are born, we begin

8 Ecclus. 18:8.
9 See Ps. 89.
10 Sap. 5:8–10, 12.

to decay, and we leave no memory or sign of virtue behind us. Consider then how short all the time of this transitory life shall seem there to all those miserable damned wretches, seeing they do plainly confess, that they lived not at all, but that so soon as they were born, forthwith they began to fade and vanish away. Now if this be so, what greater folly, or madness, can be imagined, than that a man for the enjoying of this short dream of so vain pleasures, and delights, should go to suffer everlasting damnation and torments in hell fire for ever, and ever. Furthermore, if the time and space of this life be so short, and the life to come so long, to wit, everlasting, what a mere folly is it, to take so great labor and pains to provide so many things for this life being so short, and not to make any provision at all for the life to come, which is so long, that it shall never have end? What a fond part were it for a man that minded to live in Spain, to spend, and consume all he hath in buying roots, and building houses in the Indies, and to make no provision for the country, whereunto he goeth to dwell, and make his abode? Now how much more foolish and mad are they, that spend all their goods, and substance, in making provision for this present life, where they shall live so short a time, and make no provision at all for the everlasting life to come, where they must dwell, and make their abode for evermore? Especially considering that they have so good means for their provision there, by transporting all their goods thither by the hands of the poor. As the Wiseman witnesseth, saying: Throw thy bread upon the running waters, for a long time after shalt thou find it again.[11]

§. III. Of the Uncertainty of Our Life.

But although our life endure but a short space, yet if this short space were so certain, that we might be assured thereof, (as king Ezechias was, unto whom almighty God granted fifteen years of life) our misery were the more tolerable.[12] But truly it is not so. For as our life

[11] Eccles. 11:1.
[12] See Is. 38.

is very short, even so that very time we have to live (how short or long so ever it be) is also uncertain, and doubtful. For as the Wise man saith: Man knoweth not the day of his end, but like as fishes when they think themselves in most safety are taken with the hook, and as birds are caught in a snare, when they think nothing less: even so death assaulteth men in an evil season, when they think least of it.[13] Truly that is a very wise and approved sentence, which is commonly said. *That there is nothing more certain than death, nor nothing more uncertain than the hour of death.* And therefore a certain philosopher compared the lives of men to the bells, or bubbles, that are made in water pits, when it raineth: of the which, some do vanish away suddenly even at their very rising, others do endure a little longer, and out of hand are decayed, others also do continue somewhat more, and others less. So that although they do all endure but only some little time, yet in that little there is great variety.

Wherefore if the end of our life be so uncertain: If it be so uncertain also when the dreadful hour of our accompt shall come: why do we live with such looseness, and negligence? Why do we not consider those words of our Savior, where he saith unto us: *Watch, because ye know not when the son of man will come?*[14] O that men would weigh the force of this reason! Because ye know not the hour (saith our Savior) watch ye, and be always in a readiness. As if he had said in express words: because ye know not the hour, watch every hour: because ye know not the month, watch every month: and because ye know not the year, be still in a readiness every year. For although ye know not certainly what year he will call you, yet most certain it is, that a year shall come in which undoubtedly he will call you.

But that the force of this reason may the better be perceived, let us put an example. Tell me, if there were set before thee upon a table thirty or forty several dishes of meat, and thou hadst a certain warning given thee by some of thy friends, that in one of them there were poison, durst thou give the adventure to eat of any one

13 See Eccles. 9:12.

14 See Matt. 24; Mark 13; Luke 12.

of them, although thou were very much a hungered? Undoubtedly thou wouldst not do it. For the very fear thou wouldst have, least thou mightest peradventure light upon that dish that were poisoned, would make thee to abstain from all the rest. Now let us examine how many years at the uttermost thou mayest hope yet to live. Thou wilt say peradventure (after thou hast well considered the matter) that thou mayest live thirty or forty years. Well then if it be certain, that in one of these years thou art assured to die, and thou knowest not in which of them, why art thou not then afraid in every one of them, seeing thou art well assured, that in one of them thy life shall be taken from thee? Thou wouldst not be so hardy, as to put thy hand into any one of the foresaid forty dishes, although thou were in a very sore hunger, because thou knowest that in one of them there is death present. And wilt thou not also be afraid of every one of these forty years, seeing thou art so well assured, that thou shalt die in one of these years? What answer canst thou make to this reason?

Harken yet to an other reason, which is of no less efficacy than the other. Tell me, why do men keep a continual watch in a Castle that standeth in the frontiers upon the enemies? Is it for any other cause, but only for that they now not when the enemies will come to assault it? Assuredly for none other. So that because they know not certainly at what time the enemies will come, therefore do they continually watch it at all times. For if they knew certainly the time of their coming, they might be careless in the mean while, and reserve the diligence of their watch until that very time. Now I require thee heartily for the love of God, to be an indifferent Judge touching that, which I shall say unto thee. Let us consider well this point. If thou watch thy Castle every night, because thou art uncertain when thy enemy will come, whether today, or tomorrow, this year, or the next: why dost thou not then keep a continual watch over thy soul, seeing thou knowest not what hour death shall come to give the assault upon thee? The very same uncertainty that is in the Castle, is in thy soul also: yea this uncertainty is far more, and the matter is without all comparison of greater importance. Now what judgement have they that are always so vigilant in watching their castle, and so careless always about their souls: so careless I say, as to sleep always, without ever thinking upon them? What thing can be more against reason? Consider that thy soul is of greater value, than all the castles and kingdoms in the world. Yea if thou consider the price wherewith it was bought, thou mayest well judge that it is of more value than all the angels in heaven. Consider also that thou hast greater enemies, that do endeavor continually both day and night to assault it. Consider that thou canst by no means understand the day, or the hour of thy assault. Consider that the whole substance of the salvation or damnation of thy soul consisteth in this point, whether thou be taken provided or unprovided at that dreadful hour. Forsomuch as according to the parable of the Gospel, the virgins which were found ready, and prepared, entered into the marriage with the bridegroom, and such as were found unprovided tarried without.[15] To conclude therefore, what cause is there why thou shouldest not always watch as well over thy soul, as over thy castle, seeing the uncertainty is greater, the danger greater, the cause greater, and all the rest without any comparison far greater, and of more importance?

§. IV. Of the Frailty of Our Life.

Howbeit our life is not only uncertain, but also very frail, and brickle. For I pray thee, what glass is so brickle, and so subject to knocks, and breaking, as the life of man? Some times the very air, and heat of the sun (if it be vehement) is able to spoil us of our life. But what speak I of the sun? Seeing the very eyes, yea the only looking of some person is able some times to bereave a creature of his life. It shall not need to draw any sword, or to use any kind of armor or munition for the matter, seeing the only look of some one man is able to bereave an other of his life. Consider now what a sure castle this is, wherein the treasure of our life is kept, seeing the only beholding of it afar off, is able to batter it clean down to the ground.

15 See Matt. 25.

But this were not so much to be wondered at in the age of infancy, when the building is as yet but new, and green: but the greater wonder is, that after that the work is settled, and hath continued many years together, there happeneth some accident of no greater importance than these beforenamed that is able utterly to overthrow it. If thou enquire and ask whereof died this man, or whereof died that man, they will answer thee, that he died by drinking a cup of cold drink in a sweat: or by surfeiting at a supper: or of some other great pleasure, or grief: and some times they can give no cause at all, but that he went to his bed safe, and sound, and the next day in the morning was found stark dead at his wife's side. Is there any glass or earthen vessel in the world more brickle, or subject to breaking than this? And certainly it is not to be wondered at, that man is so brickle, considering that he is also made of earth: but it is rather to be wondered at, that being of such stuff, and making as he is, he is able to endure so long a time as he doth. Why is a clock so often times disordered, and out of frame. The reason is, because it hath so many wheels, and points, and is so full of artificial work, that although it be made of iron, yet every little thing is able to distemper it. Now how much more tender is the artificial composition of our bodies, and how much more frail is the matter of our flesh, than is the iron whereof a clock is made? Wherefore if the artificial composition of our bodies be more tender, and the matter more frail, why should we wonder, if some one point among so many wheels have some impediment, by reason of which defect it stoppeth, and endeth the course of our life? Truly, we have rather good cause to marvel, not why men do so quickly end their lives, but how they endure so long, the workmanship of their bodies being so tender, and the matter and stuff whereof they be compounded so frail, and weak.

This is that miserable frailty, which the Prophet Isaias signifieth in these words. *Almighty God said unto his prophet: Cry: the Prophet answered: what shall I say? God said unto him: All flesh is hay, and all the glory thereof is like unto the flower of the field. The hay withereth, the flower fadeth away, but the word of God continueth for ever.*[16] Upon which words St. Ambrose saith thus. Truly it is even so: for the glory of man flourisheth in the flesh like unto hay, which although it seem to be great, it is in very deed but little like an herb: it buddeth like a flower, and fadeth like hay. So that it hath no more but a certain flourishing in appearance, and no firmness nor stability in the fruit. For what firmness can there be in the matter of flesh, or what good things of any long continuance are to be found in so weak a subject? Today thou mayest see a young stripling in the most flourishing time of his age, with great strength, lusty, and jetting up and down in the streets in great bravery, with a jolly lofty countenance: and if it so fall out that this very next night he be taken with some disease, thou shalt see him the next day with a face so far altered, and changed, that whereas before he seemed very amiable, and beautiful, he will now seem evil favored, miserable, and very loathsome to behold. Now what shall I say of the other accidents, and alterations of our bodies? Some are sore broken with trouble and adversities: others are weakened with poverty: others are tormented for want of good digestion: others are distempered with drinking of wines: others wax feeble with age: others become tender, and over delicate, by much cherishing themselves: and others mar their complexion with using riotous behavior. Now then according to this reckoning, is it not true (trow ye) that our flesh withereth like hay, and that the flower thereof fadeth, and vanisheth away?

Thou shalt see some other, who being descended of a very honorable parentage, of noble blood, and of a very ancient house, and family, well friended, and having good store of kindred both by father, and mother, and keeping a great house, and attended upon with a great train of his tenants and servants, and ruling the whole country where he liveth, and who there but he? Yet nevertheless if a contrary wind of fortune blow but a little against him, then is he forthwith utterly forsaken of his friends, evil entreated of his equals, and little regarded of all the world: insomuch as then very few or

16 See Is. 40:6, 8.

none will put of a cap unto him, but rather contemn him. Thou shalt see an other that hath now abundance of lands, and riches, and is generally reported in all men's mouths to be a very courteous, liberal, and bountiful man, and of great renown, and estimation, exalted to honorable dignities , and promotions, and preferred so high in the common wealth that he is a great ruler, and mighty governor, and hath the commendation of all persons to be a very wise, happy, and fortunate man: thou shalt see (I say) the times so to alter, and change, that even this man who is now so highly exalted to great dignities, and offices, and magnified in the mouths of all men, shall be utterly disgraced, and thrust into that very prison, where he himself had heretofore imprisoned many others, and shall there end his life in very great infamy, misery, and wretchedness. Unto how many also doth it happen to be waited upon, and brought home to their houses this day with a number of golden chains, footclothes, and serving men, and with all the gay pomp in the world, and the very next night following, either by means of treason of some one of his own household, or familiar acquaintance, or by other misfortune, to have all this glorious pomp obscured? Yea it may so fall out, that even a little stitch coming in his side, may mar the fashion of all this gay ruffling shew, wherein he took so great delight. O how deceitful are the hopes of men (saith Tully,) how frail is fortune, how vain are all our contentions, and strifes, which many times do break, and fall in the middle way, and are overwhelmed, and drowned in sailing, before they can come to the sight of the haven! Now what a fond madness is this in the children of Adam, upon so weak foundations to build such high castles, and towers? They consider not, that they build upon sand, and that even when the weather is most fair a wind will come, and blow down all that standeth not upon a sound and strong foundation. O what fond accompts do men make often times, because they will not turn their eyes, and look into their own consciences, and take first an accompt of themselves!

And if this be thought so great a blindness, how much greater is the blindness of those wicked persons, that are so bold, as to continue many years in sin, knowing that there is no greater distance between them and hell gates, but only this brickle and short life? Let us imagine now, that there were a man hanging by a small twined thread, and that there were directly under him a very great deep well, and he hanging in such wise over it, that when the thread happened to break he should forthwith fall into it. In what evil case (trow ye) would this man think himself to be? O how fearful, and how sore troubled would he be! How willingly would he offer all the substance he hath, to be delivered of that danger! Now thou miserable wretch that darest continue so many days and years in sin, contrary to the laws of almighty God, why dost thou not consider, that thou hangest in the like danger? Dost thou not plainly see before thy face, that whensoever the thread of this frail, and short life breaketh in sunder, thou art assured (continuing still in this thy wicked and sinful life) to fall into the deep bottomless pit of hell fire? How canst thou then sleep? How canst thou play? How canst thou laugh, or be in any quiet? How is it, that thou art so stone blind, as not to see such a terrible peril and danger as hell, and everlasting damnation, to be ready every hour to fall upon thee?

§. V. Of the Mutability of This Life.

Our life hath yet an other defect, which is to be mutable, and never to continue in one stay: according as the holy man Job affirmeth in a pitiful discourse which he maketh of the miseries of man's life in these words. *A man born of a woman, living but a small time, is replenished with many miseries, he cometh forth like a flower, and withereth away out of hand: his days pass away like a shadow, and he never continueth in one state.*[17] But now to pass over all other miseries, what thing is there in the world more fickle and mutable than man? They say that the Chameleon changeth himself in one hour into many and divers colors: And the Sea called Euripus is by reason of his often changes accompted very infamous: The Moon hath likewise

---

17 Job 14:1–2.

for every day a peculiar form, and shape: But what is all this in comparison of the alterations of man? What proteus was ever changed into so many forms, as man changeth every hour? Some times he is sick, some times whole: Some times contented, some times discontented: Some times sorrowful, some times merry: Some times in good hope, some times in despair: Some times suspicious, some times secure: Some times pleased, some times angry: Some times he will, and some times he will not: yea many times he knoweth not himself what he would have. To be short, he altereth, and changeth himself so often, as there be accidents happening unto him every hour. For all such accidents do toss and turmoil him, each one in his several kind. That which is past is irksome unto him: that which is present troubleth, and molesteth him: and that which is to come vexeth, and disquieteth him. If he have neither lands, nor goods, he liveth in travail. If he have them, he liveth in pride: And if he lose them, he liveth in great grief, and sorrow. Now what Moon, or Sea, is subject to so many changes, and alterations, as the life of man? The Sea changeth not but when the winds turn contrary unto it. But in man's life whether it be windy, or calm weather, there be evermore divers alterations and storms.

Now what shall I say of the continual moving and wasting of our life? What minute of an hour passeth, but that we go one step forward towards our death? What other thing (trowest thou) is the moving of the heavens, but as it were a very swift wheel, which is continually spinning, and winding up our life? For like as a roll of wool is spun upon a wheel, of the which at every turning about some part is wound up, at the first turn a little, at the second turn a little more, and so forth at every turn, until all be ended: so doth the wheel of the heavens continually spin, and wind up our life, in that at every turning that it maketh, a piece of our life is spun, and wound up. And therefore holy Job said: *That his days were more swift, than one that rideth in post.*[18] For he that rideth in post, though his message require never so much haste, yet some times necessity causeth him to stay.

---

[18] See Job 9:25.

But our life never stayeth, neither will it give us so much liberty, as the space of one hour of rest.

Whereunto St. Jerome agreeth very well, saying: Whatsoever I go about, whatsoever I write, whatsoever I read over again, and correct, each thing taketh away from me some part of my life. And look how many points and minumes the notary writeth, so many are the losses and decreasings of my life. Insomuch that like as they that sail in a ship, whether they stand, or sit, are always going, and sailing, and do ever approach nearer and nearer to the end of their navigation: even so in this life all the time that we live, we walk, and sail still forwards, approaching nearer, and nearer, to the common haven, and end of our navigation, which is death.

Now then if our life be nothing else but a continual walking towards death? If the hour of death be also the dreadful hour of our judgement? What other thing is our whole life, but only a continual walking towards the tribunal seat of almighty God, and an approaching every hour nearer and nearer unto his judgement? Now what greater madness may there be, than for us going actually to be judged, to offend him (as we be going in the way thitherwards) that must give sentence upon us: and so by our offences provoke his anger more and more against us? Open thine eyes therefore (O thou miserable man,) and consider the way that thou takest: think well with thyself whither thou art going: and be ashamed, or at least take compassion of thyself, and consider how evil this that thou doest, agreeth with that which thou goest to do.

§. VI. Of the Deceitfulness of Our Life.

I could well bear with all these miseries of our life, if it had not yet an other misery (in my judgement) far greater and worse than all these: which is, that it is deceitful, and seemeth in appearance otherwise, than it is in very deed. For as it is true, that is commonly said: that *Feigned holiness is a double iniquity*: even so is it also most certainly true: that *Deceitful felicity is a double misery*. For if this life would shew itself plainly as it is in deed, and make no lie at all unto us, undoubtedly we would neither lose ourselves for it, nor yet trust unto it, but would always live ready prepared against it. But verily it is so full of hypocrisy, and deceit, that whereas it is indeed filthy, it is nevertheless sold unto us for beautiful, and being short, it seemeth unto us very long, and whereas it changeth itself every hour, it beareth a countenance as though it continued always firm and stable in one same state. Dost thou perceive (saith St. Jerome) when thou wast made an infant? Canst thou tell when thou wast made a stripling? Or when thou camest to man's state? Or when thou beganest to wax an old man? Good Lord, what a wonder is this, that every day we die, and every day we alter, and change, and yet for all this we persuade ourselves very fondly that we shall live here for evermore.

Upon this affiance were those proud, and sumptuous buildings of the Magarences built, of whom a certain Philosopher saith, that they builded as though they should live for ever, and they lived as though they should die the next day. Whereof (I pray you) cometh so great forgetfulness of almighty God? So great covetousness? So great vanity? So great carefulness in purchasing, and heaping together of lands, and riches? And so great negligence in preparing ourselves to die? But that we believe and persuade ourselves that our life shall be very long, and endure a great time? This false imagination maketh us to believe, that we have time enough for all things: for the world, for pleasures, for vanities, for vices, and for many other vain, and curious exercises: and that yet after all this, we shall have time enough also before we die, to provide our accompt ready, and to make our atonement with almighty God. Insomuch that like as we make our accompt of a piece of cloth when it lieth upon a table before us, appointing one piece for one purpose, and an other piece for an other: even so do we make an accompt of our lives, as though we ourselves had the seignory and government of times, and might dispose both of them, and of our life, at our own will, and pleasure. This fond deceit growth of a secret persuasion, and affiance, that every man hath within himself, grounded not upon any reason, or true foundation, but only upon self love. The which as it hateth and abhoreth death exceedingly, so will it in no case have any remembrance of it, nor be persuaded that it will come so soon to his house as to other men's. And all this is for avoiding of the great pain, and grief, which he would conceive if he believed it in very deed. And hereof it cometh, that he is easily induced to believe, that other folk shall die within a short space. For as he is not greatly in love with them, so is not the knowledge of that truth so sour, and unliking unto him, but that he can easily believe it. But as touching himself, he maketh an other manner of accompt. For as he loveth himself exceedingly, so is he very loath to believe a thing, that may be occasion of so great pain, and grief unto him, as the same would be. But we see daily that such persons are often times foully deceived, and that their dreams turn clean contrary to their fond imaginations. For as touching others, of whose lives they had small hope that they should have any long continuance, they live a longer time, than they ever imagined they could have done: And they themselves that thought to live, and remain here a long while, do lead the dance, and depart out of this world before them. So that it fareth with them, as with young sea men, that begin to sail in the Sea, who when they come forth of the haven mouth, it seemeth unto them, that the land and houses do depart away from them, (which is nothing so,) but contrariwise, it is they themselves that move, and depart away, and the land remaineth still in his old place.

§. VII. Of the Miseries of Man's Life.

Although our life be subject to all these miseries before rehearsed, yet if that little time of life were wholly life indeed, it were somewhat: but the greatest misery of all is, that the life which a man hath to live, whether it be short, or long, is altogether subject to such a number of miseries and calamities, both of body, and mind, as it may more truly be termed death, than life.

Wherefore according as a Poet said very well: *Not to live, but to pass the life well, is life.* So that although this life be very sparing and short in all other things: yet in troubles and miseries it is very plentiful, and long. Undoubtedly our life is but short, respecting the life itself: and if we respect the time of enjoying it, it is yet much shorter: but if we consider, how insufficient it is towards the obtaining of wisdom, it is little, or nothing at all. Howbeit although it be indeed very short for all good things: yet in one thing only I find it long, that is, in the bearing of pain, and misery. O dangerous strait, in which the less time thou hast to pass the more peril and danger thou hast in the passage! Certainly if we had eyes to consider ourselves, and to see our own case, we should always go weeping, and lamenting our own state, as men condemned by the just judgement of almighty God to suffer such great miseries. But that our misery might be yet more increased on every side, this misery is added to all the rest, that being in miserable case, we live like men in a frensy, and do neither feel nor understand our own misery, and wretchedness. Those two Philosophers Heraclitus, and Democritus, although they were infidels perceived the same better than we do, of whom it is reported, that the one passed his life always weeping, and the other always laughing: forsomuch as they saw clearly, that all our life was nothing else, but mere vanity, and misery.

If thou doubt of this, tell me (I pray thee) what mean all these carks, and cares, wherein men do live? What a number of infinite sorrows, griefs, anguishes, fears, passions, suspicions, malices, with other the like tribulations, and afflictions, is the soul of man subject unto? Unto all which passions man is so prone, that many times he is in a passion without any cause: and feareth, where there is no cause at all to fear: and when there is no other man to vex and torment him outwardly, he then vexeth, and tormenteth himself inwardly: as holy Job confessed in these words, when he said: *Why hast thou (O Lord) set me against thee? I am become irksome, and burdensome even to mine own self.*[19]

Now as touching the external miseries of the body, who is able to number them? How great labor and pain must we take to gain a piece of bread, whereby to sustain our lives? The very birds and brute beasts are fed without any occupation, labor, or pain: but man is constrained

19 Job 7:20.

to sweat day, and night, and to turmoil both by Sea, and land, to get his living. This is that misery, which the Prophet lamented, when he said: *The days of our life consume away like the spider's web.*[20] For like as the spider laboreth day, and night, in spinning of her web, wasting even her own bowels, and consuming herself to bring it to an end, and all this long and costly travail is ordained to none other purpose, but only to make a fine and tender net, to catch flies withal: even so the seely miserable man doth nothing else, but labor, and toil, night both with body, and mind: and all this his travail serveth to none other end, but only to catch flies: I mean, to procure vain and trifling things, and of very small value. And some times it falleth so out, that after much travailing up, and down, and great labor and pains taken therein, when the web is fully finished, and brought to an end, there cometh suddenly a blustering blast of wind, that carrieth away the web, and the owner withal: and so both the work and the workman perish wholly together at one instant.

And yet were it so, that with all these painful travails, and labors, our life were safe, and secure, then our misery should not be so great as it is, but though our life be secure from famine, and hunger: yet is it not from the plague, and pestilence, and from infinite other dangers, and diseases, that do daily and hourly assault us. Who is able to number how many kinds and diversities of diseases nature hath ordained for man's body? The books of the physicians are full fraught with the declaration of divers diseases, and remedies for the same. And yet we see, that their science increaseth every day with the coming of new and strange diseases, insomuch as the number of the diseases, whereof we have presently experience, were utterly unknown unto the ancient physicians, that were in times past. And yet among all these remedies scarcely shall ye find one that is pleasant, or delectable: yea, and there be many of them that are more irksome and painful, than the very sickness, or diseases themselves. Insomuch as one great torment can not be remedied, without an other greater than it.

---

20 See Ps. 89.

And if there be any complexions so happy, as that they have not been assaulted with these kinds of miseries, yet are they not secure and exempt from other calamities, and mischances, wherewithal we see those men to be daily molested, that have not been much vexed with sickness and diseases. How many thousands of men (trow ye) are drowned every day in the Sea? How many are devoured in wars? How many are endangered by earthquakes? How many with overflowing of rivers, and great waters? How many with falling down of houses? How many with the stinging and striking of venomous beasts? How many woeful women in travail of their children do purchase full dearly the children's lives, with their own painful deaths?

Now although it be so, that the brute beasts do fight against us, and although in a manner all things that were made to serve us, be no less noisome than serviceable unto us, (yea rather it seemeth that they all have as it were conspired against us:) yet for all this (I say) there might be some remedy found, if men would accord and agree together among themselves, and were as conformable in peace, as they are in nature. But alas it is far otherwise. For even they themselves are in arms against themselves: and among all creatures in the world, there is none against whom man is more cruelly bent, than against the companion of his own nature. How many kinds of engins, artillery, munition, and weapons have men invented to defend themselves, and to offend others? How many threatenings, robberies, injuries, wounds, deaths, reproaches, slanders, and imprisonments, do men daily sustain by the malice, and cruelty of other men? We see that neither the land, nor the sea, nor the high ways, nor the common streets, are free from thieves, robbers, murderers, pirates, and enemies. The cruel anger and rage of the furious man is at all times ready to be revenged of his enemy: yea and he taketh great pleasure in it. What mean so many kinds of weapons? Such diversity of artillery? Such store of munition? Such abundance of gunpowder? So many devisors and inventors of new kinds of stratagems, and cruel practices of war, but only to multiply, and increase on every side the miseries, and calamities of mankind? Insomuch as when we are not molested with the air, nor with the elements, we are persecuted by the companions of our own very nature. It is written of one only man called Julius Ceasar, (who among all the Emperors was most commended for clemency,) that even he alone with his armies slew in divers battles above a million, and a hundred thousand men. Consider now, how many more would he have slain, if he had been cruel, seeing he slew so many being commended, and praised for a very gentle, and merciful prince?

Tully also maketh mention of a notable Philosopher, who wrote a book concerning the deaths of men, wherein he rehearseth many occasions of men's deaths, that have happened in the world: as by floods, plagues, pestilences, destructions of Cities, concourse of wild beasts, which coming suddenly upon some nations, have utterly slain and devoured them. And yet after all this he concludeth, that a far greater number of men have been destroyed by men, than be all the other kinds of calamities, though they were all joined together. Now what thing can be more ruthful, and of greater grief and admiration than this? This is that politique and sociable creature, that is born without nails, without weapons, and without poison, to live in peace and concord with other living creatures: and yet he is full of hatred, cruelty, and desire of revengement.

But now if we would make a discourse, and run throughout the miseries that are incident to all the ages, and states of this life, we should find ourselves to be yet in far worse case. How full of ignorance is the time of our infancy? How light, and wanton are we, when we grow to be striplings? How rash, and headlong be we in the time of our youth? How heavy, and unwieldy, when we wax old men? What else is an infant, but a brute beast in the form of a man? What is a young boy, but as it were a wild untamed colt, and unbridled? What is a heavy, and unwieldy old man, but even a sack stuffed with griefs, and diseases? The greatest desire that men have, is to live until they be old: at which age a man is in far worse case, than in all his life time before, and then he standeth in most need, and hath least help, and succor. For the old man is forsaken of the world: He is forsaken of his own kinsfolk, friends, and acquaintance: He is forsaken of his own members, and senses: yea he forsaketh himself, in that the very use of reason forsaketh him. And he is only accompanied with his painful aches, griefs, and diseases. For his company and conversation is then very irksome and troublesome unto the whole house where he dwelleth. This is the mark forsooth whereupon the eye of man is so earnestly fixed: This is the happy state, which all men do so greedily desire: and hereunto tendeth the worldly felicity, and the ambition of long life.

As concerning the states of men we should never make an end, if we should rehearse the little contentation that is to be found in each of them, and the great desire that every one hath to change his own state, and condition, with the state of others: thinking that he should have greater hearts ease in an other man's state, than he hath in his own. And thus do men continually vex, and turmoil themselves like unto a sick man, that doth nothing else but tumble and toss in his bed from one side to an other, persuading himself that by means of these often changes and removings he shall find more ease and rest than he had before, and yet he findeth in very deed that he is foully deceived: Forsomuch as the cause of his disquietness resteth within himself, which is his own grief, and disease.

To conclude, such is the miserable state and condition of this life, that the Wise man had good cause to say: Great and heavy is the yoke, that the children of Adam carry on their necks, even from the day they come forth of their mother's womb, until the day of their burial, which is the common mother of all.[21] And St. Bernard was not afraid to say, that he thought this life little better than the life of hell itself, were it not for the hope we may here have to attain unto the kingdom of heaven.

And albeit all these miseries do come unto us as a punishment for sin: yet was it a very merciful and medicinable punishment. For the providence of almighty God did so ordain it, meaning thereby to withdraw and separate our hearts from the inordinate love of this

---

[21] See Ecclus. 40.

life. The very cause why he put so much bitter mustard upon the breasts of this life, was to wean us from it. The cause why he suffered our life to become so filthy, was that we should not set our love upon it. The cause why he would have us to be molested and vexed so often times in this life, was that we might the more willingly forsake it, and sigh continually for the true life, which is in the world to come. For if we be so unwilling to forsake this life, being wholly so miserable as it is: if we be now ever whimpering, and whining for the fruits, and fleshpots of Egypt, what would we do, if all our life were sweet, and pleasant?[22] And what would we do, if it were wholly liking and delightful to our taste, and appetite? Who would then (trow ye) contemn it for God's sake? Who would then exchange it for heaven? Who would then say with St. Paul, I have a desire to be loosed from this flesh, and to be with Christ?[23]

§. VIII. Of the Last Misery of Man: Which is Death.

After all these miseries, succeedeth the last, and of all others most terrible, which is death. This is that misery, whereof a certain Poet lamented, saying: The best days of mortal men are those that pass first away, and then succeedeth a number of sicknesses, and diseases, and with them heavy and doleful age, and continual trouble, and above all, the sharpness of cruel death. This is the lodge and end of man's life, whereof holy Job said: *I know well O Lord, that thou wilt deliver me over to death, where there is a house prepared for all men living.*[24]

How many the miseries are that be included in this misery alone, I will not take upon me to declare at this present. Only I will rehearse what a certain holy father saith by way of exclamation against death in this wise. O death, how bitter is the remembrance of thee? How quickly and suddenly stealest thou upon us? How secret are thy paths, and ways? How doubtful is thy hour? And how universal is

22 See Ex. 16.
23 See Phil. 1.
24 Job 30:23.

thy seignory, and dominion? The mighty can not escape thy hands: the wise can not hide themselves from thee: and the strong lose their strength in thy presence. Thou accountest no man rich: forsomuch as no man is able to ransom his life of thee for money. Thou goest every where: thou searchest every where: and thou art every where. Thou witherest the herbs: thou drinkest up the winds: thou corruptest the air: thou changest the ages: thou alterest the world: thou stickest not to sup up the sea: all things do increase, and diminish, but thou continuest always at one stay. Thou art the hammer that always striketh: thou art the sword that never blunteth: thou art the snare whereinto every one falleth: thou art the prison wherein every one entereth: thou art the sea wherein all do perish: thou art the pain that every one suffereth: and the tribute that every one payeth.[25]

O cruel death, why hast thou not compassion of us, but comest stealing suddenly upon us, to snatch us away in our best times, and to interrupt our affairs when they are well begone, and brought to a good forwardness! Thou robbest from us in one hour, as much as we have gained in many years. Thou cuttest of the succession of kindreds, and families: Thou leavest kingdoms without any heirs. Thou fillest the world with widows, and orphans: Thou breakest of the studies of great clerks: Thou overthrowest good wits in their ripest age: Thou joinest the end with the beginning, without giving place to the middle: To conclude, thou art such a one, as almighty God washeth his hands of thee, and cleareth himself in plain words, saying: *That he never made thee, but that thou hadst thine entry into the world by the very envy and craft of the devil.*[26]

§. IX. What Fruit, and Commodity, May Be Taken of the Foresaid Considerations.

These are the miseries of our life, with infinite others: the consideration whereof a man ought to direct unto two principal ends among

[25] See Job 13.

[26] See Sap. 1:13; 2:24.

others: the one, to the knowledge and contempt of the glory of this world: and the other, to the knowledge and contempt of ourselves. For this consideration serveth very well both for the one, and the other. But wilt thou understand in one word what the glory of this world is? Mark and consider with attention the state and condition of man's life, and thereby shalt thou perceive, what the glory of this life is. Tell me (I pray thee) can the glory of man be more long or more stable than the life of man? It is most certain that it can not. For this glory is an accident, which is grounded upon this life, as upon his subject, or foundation, and therefore when the foundation and subject faileth, the accidents must needs fail withal. And for this very cause no riches, no pleasures, no delights can continue any longer time with a man until his grave. Forsomuch as then faileth the foundation, whereupon all these things are built, and have their stay: which foundation is our life. Now tell me then, if this life be such as thou hast now heard described unto thee: to wit: short, uncertain, frail, inconstant, deceitful, and miserable, how long can the building endure, that shall be framed upon this foundation? How long can the accidents continue, that shall be grounded upon so weak a substance? When thou hast considered this point well with thyself, thou must needs say, that they shall endure no longer than the foundation and substance itself endureth: and thou must needs confess, that many times they endure not so long: as we see by daily experience in the goods of fortune, which with many men have an end before their life endeth.

Now if that saying of the Poet Pindarus be true: to wit, That this life is no more but a dream of a shadow: What thinkest thou then is the glory of this world, which is of shorter continuance then our life? What accompt wouldst thou make of a goodly building, in case it stood upon a false foundation? What accompt wouldst thou make of an image of wax, very richly and curiously wrought, in case it were set against the sun, where it is certain that so soon as the wax should be molten, forthwith the form of the image would utterly be defaced, and leese his beauty? Why do we make so little accompt of the beauty of a flower, but because it groweth upon so weak a subject? For so soon as it is nipped of from the stalk, incontinently it loseth his fair gloss, and beauty? It is not possible to have beauty of any firm continuance in a matter so frail, and corruptible. It followeth therefore that the glory of man is such as the life of man is. For although glory do continue after the end of our life, yet what shall that glory avail him that hath no sense, nor feeling thereof? What doth it avail Homer now whilst thou so highly praisest and commendest his Iliads? Undoubtedly no more, but as St. Jerome saith speaking of Aristotle, Woe be unto thee Aristotle, that art praised where thou art not, to wit, here in the world: and art tormented where thou art indeed: to wit, in hell.

Other inestimable commodities mayest thou gather out of this consideration. For if thou consider all these miseries with good attention, thine eyes shall be opened forthwith, and thou shalt wonder at the great blindness of men, yea the very strangeness of it shall cause thee to say to thyself: Good Lord, what cause is there, why this miserable lineage of Adam should wax proud! From whence cometh such puffing and arrogancy of mind, such haughty and lofty courages, so great contempt of others, such estimation of ourselves, and so great forgetfulness of almighty God? What cause hast thou to be proud thou dust, and ashes? Why dost thou magnify, and advance thyself, thou seely wretch of the earth? Why dost thou not hold down thy peacock's tail, beholding thy foul feet, to wit, the vileness of thy state, and condition? What cause hast thou to seek so carefully for the glory of this world, seeing it is mingled with so many miseries? What thing is there so sweet, but that it may be made bitter with the mixture of so many sour, and bitter sauces?

Moreover, if this life be a vale of tears, a prison of guilty persons, and a banishment of them that be condemned, how canst thou settle so great vanity, so great pomp, and pride of the world, such gay ornaments, and stately furniture of houses, and families, in the place of tears? How canst thou imagine to make this a place of pastimes, and pleasures, of feasts, and banquets? How canst thou be so diligent to heap so greedily together for the provision of this world, and be so forgetful of the world to come, as if thou were born only to live here in earth with brute beasts, and hadst no part in heaven with the Angels. Surely I must needs say, that thou art very much wedded to misery, and that thou camest out of a marvelous miserable stock, if so many arguments of the miseries of this world be not able to open thine eyes, and make thee to discern so gross and so palpable a blindness.

WEDNESDAY NIGHT

Of the Hour of Death.

THIS day (when thou hast made the sign of the Cross, and prepared thyself hereunto,) thou hast to meditate upon the hour of death: which is one of the most profitable considerations, that a Christian man may have, as well for the obtaining of true wisdom, and eschewing of sin: as also to move him to begin to prepare himself in time for the hour of death.

But to the intent that this consideration may be profitable unto thee, it shall behoove thee to make thy petition unto almighty God, beseeching him to grant thee some feeling of such things as are wont to pass in this last conflict: that thou mayest dispose of thy lands, and goods accordingly, and direct thy life in such sort, as at that time thou wouldst wish thou hadst done. Now therefore that thou mayest have the better feeling in this matter, think upon it, not as thou wouldst of a thing that were to come, but as it were even now present: and think upon it, not as of a thing, that appertaineth to others, but as of a thing that belongeth properly to thine own self, making this accompt, that thou liest now very sickly and weak in thy bed, and in such a dangerous case, that thou art utterly forsaken of thy physicians, and that they are all persuaded, that thou wilt die within a few hours.

Consider now first, how uncertain that hour is, in which death will assault thee. For thou knowest not, neither what day, nor in what place, nor how thou shalt be disposed when death shall come unto thee. Only this thou knowest for most certain, that die thou shalt: all the rest is uncertain, saving that ordinarily this hour is wont to steal upon us at such a time, as a man is most careless, and thinketh least of it.

Secondly, consider what a separation shall then be made, not only between us and all the things we love in this world, but also even between the soul, and the body, which have been such ancient, and loving companions. If it be thought so grievous a matter, to be banished out of our native country, and from the natural air in which a man hath been bred, and brought up, although the banished man might carry away with him whatsoever he loveth: how much more grievous then shall that universal banishment be from all things that we have, from our lands, from our goods, from our house, from wife, father, mother, children, kinsfolk, friends, and acquaintance, from this light, and common air, yea (to be short) from all things of this world? If an ox make so great a bellowing at what time he is separated from an other ox, with whom he hath been used to be yoked, and to draw in the plough: what a bellowing will thy heart then make, when death shall separate thee from all those things, wherewith thou hast been yoked, and carried the burthens of this life?

Consider also, what a grievous pain it shall then be to a man, when a certain representation shall be made unto his mind foreshewing in what case his body and soul shall be after his death. For as touching the body, he knoweth for certain already, that though it hath been heretofore neversomuch cherished, and honored, yet there shall no better provision be made for it, but only a hole seven foot long, where it shall remain in company of other dead bodies. But as concerning the soul, he knoweth not certainly what shall become of it, nor what lot shall fall unto it. For although the hope which he hath in the mercy of almighty God may strengthen and comfort him: yet the consideration of his own sins may dismay him, and make him afraid: especially if he consider withal the great justice of almighty God, and the profoundness of his judgements, who useth often times to cross his hands, and to alter the lots of men. The thief went up from the cross to paradise: and Judas fell down from the honorable dignity of Apostleship into hell fire.[1] Manasses also after his so many abominations, and wickedness, obtained grace to become repentant:[2] And as yet we know not whether Salomon obtained the like for all his virtues. This is one of the greatest griefs, and anguishes, that men are commonly troubled withal at the hour of death: to understand, that there is to ensue glory everlasting, and pain everlasting and that then a man is so near both unto the one, and to the other, and yet knoweth not whether of these two lots being so far different as they are, shall fall unto his share.

After this anguish there followeth an other no less than this: to wit: the particular accompt of all our whole life, which at the very hour of every man's death must be made unto almighty God. This accompt is so dreadful, that it causeth even the most stoutest men that are to tremble and quake for very fear. It is written of the famous holy father Arsenius, that being at the point of death he began to be afraid, whereat his scholars marveled, and said unto him: What father, are you now afraid of your accompt? Unto whom he answered: yea yea my sons, this fear is no new thing in me: for I have always lived with the same. At that time all the sins of a man's former life are represented unto him, like a squadron of enemies ready set in battle array to assault him. Then are the greatest sins and those wherein he hath taken greatest delight represented most lively unto him, and are the cause of greater fear: Then cometh the young virgin to his mind, which he hath dishonored: Then come the maids, and household servants, whom he hath solicited and provoked to lewdness: Then come the poor folks whom he hath injured, and evil entreated: Then come his neighbors whom he hath offended: Then shall there cry out against him, not the blood of Abel,[3] but the precious blood of our Savior Jesus Christ, which he shed, when he gave scandal and offence

1 See Luke 23; Matt. 27.
2 See 2 Par. 33.
3 See Gen. 4.

to his neighbor. And if his cause must be judged according to the law, that saith: Eye, for eye: tooth, for tooth: and wound, for wound:[4] what shall he look for, that by his evil counsel or lewd example hath been the occasion of the loss of a Christian soul, if he be judged by that law? O how bitter shall the remembrance of the delights and pleasures past be at that time unto him, which at other times seemed so sweet? Undoubtedly the Wiseman had very good cause to say: *Look not upon the wine when it is red, and when it sheweth his colour in the glass: for although at the time of drinking it seem delectable, yet at the end it will bite like a serpent, and poison like a cockatrice.*[5] O that men would understand how true a saying this is, that we have here rehearsed! What serpents sting is there that doth so prick and vex a man, as the dreadful remembrance of his pleasures past shall do at the hour of his death? These are the dregs of that poisoned cup of the enemy. These be the leavings of the cup of Babylon, that seemeth so gayly gilted in outward appearance.[6]

After this there followeth the Sacrament of Confession, the blessed Sacrament of the Altar, and last of all the Sacrament of extreme Unction, which is the last succor and relief that our mother the Catholic Church may help us withal in that troublesome time. And as well herein, as in the other things, thou hast to consider what great grief and anguish of mind the sick person shall then abide in calling to mind his wicked and sinful life: and how gladly he wisheth at that time that he had taken a better way: and what an austere kind of life he would then determine to lead, if he might have time to do the same: and how fain he would then enforce himself to call upon almighty God, and to desire him of help, and succor. Howbeit the very pain, grief, and continual increasing of his sickness and death will scarcely permit him so to do.

Consider then also those last accidents, and pangs of the sickness, (which be as it were the messengers of death) how fearful and

4 See Ex. 21.
5 Prov. 23:31–32.
6 See Jer. 51; Apoc. 14.

terrible they be. How at that time the sick man's breast panteth: his voice waxeth hoarse: his feet begin to die: his knees wax cold, and stiff: his nostrils run out: his eyes sink into his head: his countenance looketh pale, and wane: his tongue faltereth, and is not able to do his office: finally, by reason of the haste of the departure away of the soul out of the body, all his senses are sore vexed, and troubled, and do utterly leese their force, and virtue.

But above all, the soul is then in most pain, and suffereth greatest griefs, and troubles. For at that time she is in a very great conflict, and agony: partly for her departure from the body: and partly for fear of her dreadful accompt, which is then to be made. Because she is naturally loath to depart from the body, and she liketh well her lodging, and is in very great dread to come to her accompt before almighty God.

Now when the soul is thus departed out of the flesh, yet there remain two voyages for thee to make with him: the one, to accompany the body until it be laid in his grave: the other, to follow the soul until her cause be determined. And thou hast to consider diligently what shall become of each one of these two parts.

Consider now in what plight the body is after the soul hath forsaken it: and what a worthy garment they provide to wind it in: and what haste his friends and executors do make to get him quickly rid away out of the house. Consider also the funerals, with all the other circumstances that are wont to happen therein: The often ringing of the bells: the going about of the bellman crying unto the people to pray for his soul: the questioning in the streets one of an other who is dead: the diriges, and doleful Service of the Church: the accompanying of his corpse to the Church: and the sorrowful weeping, and mourning of his wife, children, kinsfolk, servants, and friends for him: and finally all the other particulars, that are then wont to happen until the body be laid and left in the grave, where it shall lie buried until it be raised again by the terrible sound of the trumpet at the general day of Judgement. And such is the great change and alteration in worldly affairs that it may so come to pass, as a time may happen, when some building may be made near unto thy grave, (be it never so gay, and sumptuous,) and that they may dig for some earth out of the same to make mortar for a wall, and so shall thy seely body (being now changed into earth) become afterwards an earthen wall, although it be at this present the most noble body and most delicately cherished of all bodies in the world. And how many bodies of Kings and Emperors trowest thou have come already to this promotion.

Now when thou hast left the body in the grave, go from thence forthwith, and follow after the soul: and consider what way it taketh through that new region: whither it goeth: what shall everlastingly become of it for ever, and ever: and what judgement it shall have. Imagine that thou art now present at this judgement, and that thou seest all the whole court of heaven to expect the end of this sentence, where the soul shall give a particular accompt, and be charged and discharged of all that he hath received, even to the value of a pin's point: yea, and (as our Savior himself affirmeth) of every idle word.[7] There an accompt shall be required of his life, of his lands, and riches: of his household, and family: of the inspirations of almighty God: of the means and opportunity he hath had to lead a virtuous, and godly life: and above all, he shall be straitly examined what estimation he hath made of the most precious blood of our Savior Christ: and of the use of his Sacraments. And there shall every man be judged according to the accompt he shall make of the gifts and graces he hath received of almighty God.

---

[7] See Matt. 12:36; see also Job 14:13; 31:14, 23; Eccles. 12:14; Matt. 19:17; Rom. 2:6; 1 Cor. 4:4–5; 9:27; 2 Cor. 5:10; Eph. 6:8; Phil. 2:12; Heb. 9:27; 1 Ptr. 4:18; 2 Ptr. 1:10; Apoc. 2:23; 14:7–13; 22:12.

The Third Treatise: Wherein Is Treated of the Consideration of Death: Where the Former Meditation is Declared More at Large.

The consideration of death is very profitable for many purposes, and especially for three. First for the obtaining of true wisdom: that is, to know how a man ought to govern and frame his life. For (as the Philosophers do say) in things that are ordained to any end, the rule and measure whereby to direct them, is to be taken of the same end. And therefore when men do either build, or Sail, or do any thing, they have always their eye fixed upon the end which they pretend, and according to the same do frame and direct all the rest of their doings. Now considering that among the ends and terms of our life, death is one of them (whither we go all to take our rest) he that will endeavor to direct his life in good order, let him fix his eyes upon this mark, and according to the same let him dispose and direct all his affairs. Let him consider how poor and naked he must depart out of this world, and what a strait judgement he must pass at the hour of his death, and how he shall lie in his grave all betrodden, and quite forgotten of all men: and according to this end let him consider how to frame and direct the whole order and course of his life. By this rule a certain Philosopher governed and directed his life that said: Naked came I out of my mother's womb, and naked must I return again to my grave:[8] To what purpose then should I lose my time, in purchasing and heaping together lands, and riches, seeing nakedness shall be my end. For want of consideration of this our end do grow all our errors, and deceits. Hereof cometh our presumption, our pride, our covetousness, our pleasures, our niceness, and delicateness, and the vain castles and towers of wind, which we build upon sand. For if we would consider, in what case we shall be after a few days when we are once lodged in that poor seely cottage of our grave, we should be more humble, and more temperate in our life. How could he possibly have any spark of presumption, that would consider, that

8 See Job 1.

he shall be there dust, and ashes? How could he find in his heart to make a God of his belly, that would consider that he shall become there worms' meat? Who could ever be persuaded to occupy his grain in such lofty and fantastical thoughts, and devices, if he did but consider and weigh how frail and weak the foundation is, whereupon all his fond designments are grounded? Who would endanger the loss and destruction of himself, in seeking for riches both by land, and Sea, if he considered that at his death he should carry no more with him, but a poor winding sheet? To conclude, all the works of our life would be duly corrected, and framed in good order, if we would measure and square them out by this rule.

For this cause the Philosophers said, that the life of a Wise man was nothing else but only a continual cogitation and thinking of death: forsomuch as this consideration teacheth a man what thing is somewhat, and what is nothing, what he ought to follow, and what to eschew, according to the end whereunto he must certainly arrive. It is written of those Philosophers called Brackmanni, that they were so much given to think upon their end, that they had their graves always open before the gates of their houses, to the intent that both at their entry and going forth by them they might always be mindful of this journey and passage of death.

Almighty God said unto the Prophet Jeremias, that he should go down into a house where earth was wrought, for that he would there speak with him.[9] Almighty God could have spoken with his Prophet in any other place, but he chose to speak with him in that place, to give us to understand, that the house of earth (which is our grave) is the school of true wisdom, where almighty God is wont to teach those that be his. There he teacheth them how great is the vanity of this world: There he sheweth unto them the misery of our flesh, and the shortness of this life. And above all, there he teacheth them to know themselves, which is one of the most highest points of Philosophy that may be learned. Wherefore (O thou man) descend down with thy spirit unto this house, and there shalt thou see, who thou

9 See Jer. 18.

art: whereof thou art come: where thou shalt rest: and wherein the beauty of thy flesh and glory of this world do end. So shalt thou learn to despise all those things, that the world hath in reverence for want of due knowledge how to consider them. Because the world considereth no more but only the painted face of Jezabel, that shined very beautifully and gayly at the window. It considereth not the miserable extreme parts of her, which after that her body was devoured with dogs, almighty God would have to remain whole,[10] that thereby we might see, that the world is an other manner of thing in deed than it appeareth in outward shew, and that we should in such wise consider the face of it, as to be mindful also of the extreme griefs, and sorrows wherein the glory of it endeth.

Secondly, this consideration is a great help to cause us to eschew and forsake sin: according as Ecclesiasticus witnesseth, saying: *Remember the last end, and thou shalt never sin.*[11] It is a great matter not to sin, and a great remedy also for the same is for a man to remember that he must die. St. John Climacus writeth of a certain Monk, that being sore tempted with the beauty of a woman, whom he had seen abroad in the world, and understanding that she was dead, went to the grave where she was buried, and rubbed a napkin in the stinking body of the dead woman. And he used always afterwards whensoever the devil troubled him with any evil thought of her, to take the stinking napkin, and to put it to his nose, and say to himself: Behold here thou miserable wretch the thing thou lovest, and behold here what end the delights and beauties of the world have. This was a great remedy to overcome this sin. And the deep consideration of death is of no less importance than it, as St. Gregory saith: *There is nothing that doth so mortify the appetites of this our perverse flesh, as to consider in what plight the same shall be after it is dead.*

The same holy father rehearseth a like story of an other Monk, who having his table ready provided to go to dinner, to eat somewhat for the refreshing of his weak and weary body, chanced suddenly to

10 See 4 Kgs. 9; 3 Kgs. 21.

11 Ecclus. 7:40.

have a remembrance of death, which cogitation (even as though it had been a constable or other like officer there ready to attach him) put him in such a terror, and fear, that it caused him to refrain from his meat. Consider therefore how much the remembrance of the dreadful accompt that we must make at the hour of our death is able to work in the heart of a just man, seeing it caused this holy Monk to abstain from a thing that is so lawful and necessary to be done.

Certainly this is one of the most wonderful things in all the world, that men knowing so assuredly, that at the very hour of their death, a particular accompt shall be required of them of all their whole life, yea and of every idle word,[12] will notwithstanding run headlong with such facility into sin. If a wayfaring man having but one farthing in his purse should enter into an Inn, and placing himself down at the table, should require of the host to bring in Partridges, Capons, Pheasants, and all other delicates that may be found in the house, and should sup with very great pleasure, and contentation, never remembering that at the last there must come a time of accompt: who would not take this fellow, either for a jester, or for a very fool? Now what greater folly or madness can be devised, than for men to give themselves so loosely to all kinds of vices, and to sleep so soundly in them, without ever remembering, that shortly after at their departing out of their Inn, there shall be required of them a very strait and particular accompt of all their dissolute and wicked life?

Wherefore it is verily to be thought, that the devil laboreth all he can to make us utterly to neglect and forget the remembrance of our accompt, that we must make at the very hour of our death, because he knoweth full well, what great profit and commodity would arise unto us by the continual remembrance of the same. For otherwise how were it possible that men should forget a thing that is so terrible, and fearful, yea such a thing, as they know most assuredly will come, and steal very shortly upon them at their own houses? If we have but the least doubt or suspicion in the world of losing a little worldly riches, or of some other like thing, it maketh us often times

12 See Matt. 12:36; Heb. 9:27; 1 Ptr. 4:17–18; Apoc. 14:7.

very careful, and watchful, and causeth us to lose both our sleep, and our health. How happeneth it then that the remembrance of death which as well to the body, as to the soul, is the most horrible and dreadful thing that may come unto us, causeth us not to be likewise very careful and watchful in making provision beforehand for the coming of it? Surely it seemeth unto me a thing very much to be marveled at, that men should be so careful as they be in trifles, and matters of small importance, and live so negligently, and without all care in things that are of so great importance unto them as is their everlasting salvation, or damnation.

Thirdly, this consideration of our death is a great help not only to provoke us to live a good life, (as it hath been said,) but besides that to die well. In things that be hard, and difficult, foresight and preparation beforehand is a very great help to bring them well to pass. Now so great a leap as is the leap of death, (which reacheth from this life to the everlasting life to come) can not well be leaped unless we make a great course, and fetch a long race to run the same. No great thing can be well and perfectly done at the first time. Seeing therefore it is so great a matter to die, and so necessary to die well, it shall be very expedient for us to die often times in our life, that we may die well at the very time of our death. The soldiers that be appointed to fight do first practice themselves in such feats, and exercises, as whereby they may learn in time of peace, what they must do in time of war. The horse also that must run at the Tilt traverseth all the ground before, and trieth all the steps thereof, that at such time as he cometh to make his course he be not found new and strange in doing his feat. Wherefore sith we all must needs run this course (forsomuch as there is no man alive but must die,) considering also that the way is so obscure and stony (as all men know,) and the danger so great, that whosoever falleth shall be tumbled down headlong into the bottomless pit of hell fire, it shall be requisite that we do now tread diligently beforehand all this way, and consider particularly all the steps and places thereof one by one, forsomuch as in every one of them there is much to be considered.

And let us not think it enough to consider only what passeth outwardly about the sick man's bed, but let us endeavor much more to understand what passeth inwardly within his heart.

§. I. Of the Uncertainty of the Hour of Death: and What a Grief It Is at That Time to Depart from All Things of This Life.

To begin now even from the beginning of this conflict: Consider how when death shall come upon thee, it will come at such a time, as when thou thinkest thyself in most safety, and suspectest least of the coming thereof, as we see by experience it is wont to happen unto many. *The day of our Lord* (saith the Apostle) *shall come like a thief*:[13] Which watcheth always to come at such times, as men are most careless, and think themselves in most safety, that it may take us upon a sudden at unwares. And so we see it happeneth most often, that even at that time when men do least think to die, and when they are least mindful of their departure out of this life, yea when they cast their accompts beforehand to make great purchases, and buildings, and to set upon great enterprises of many days, and years, then cometh death suddenly upon them, and disappointeth them of all their vain hopes, and designments, and utterly overthroweth all their fond imaginations, and buildings, which they made in the air. And so is that saying fulfilled of the holy king. *My life* (saith he) *was cut of like as the weaver cutteth of his thread: while I was as yet in the beginning he cut me of: from morning to evening thou wilt make an end of me.*[14]

The first stroke wherewith death is wont to strike, is the fear of death. Surely this is a very great anguish unto him that is in love with his life: and this forewarning is such a great grief unto a man, that oftentimes his carnal friends do use to dissemble it, and will not have the sick man to believe it, least it should vex and disquiet him: and this they will do some times although it be to the prejudice and

---

13 1 Thess. 5:2.

14 Is. 38:12.

destruction of his miserable soul. King Saul had a very stout and valiant courage, but after that the shadow of Samuel appeared unto him, and had told him, that he should die in the battle, adding moreover these words: *Tomorrow both thou and thy sons shall be here with me*:[15] The fear and terror which he conceived at these tidings was so great, that at that very instant he lost all his force, and courage, and fell down to the ground as a dead man. Now what a grief will it be to a man, that is in love with this life, when such like news shall be signified unto him? For immediately upon this denunciation there shall be represented unto him his departure and perpetual banishment from this world, and from all things that be in the same. Then shall he see that his hour is now come, and that the dawning of that dreadful day appeareth now at his house, wherein he shall depart from all things that he hath loved in this life. His body shall die but once, but his heart shall die as often as he shall remember the loss of all those things whereunto it beareth love, and affection. Forsomuch as death shall put the knife between him, and them all, and make an everlasting division. The deeper root the tooth hath in the jaw, the greater grief it causeth at what time it is plucked out. Now the heart of a wicked man being so fast rooted in the love of the things of this life, it cannot be, but that it must needs be a very great grief unto him, when he seeth the hour is now come wherein he must depart from them all. At that time those things whereunto he beareth most affection shall wound his heart most grievously: and that thing which was wont to be a comfort unto him in his trouble shall be then a most cruel torment in vexing him. St. Augustine declareth that at what time he determined to separate himself from the world, and from all the pleasures and delights thereof, it seemed unto him that they all represented themselves lively unto him, and said: What wilt thou leave us for ever? And wilt thou never have any more to do with us? Consider now then with thyself, what a grief it will be to a carnal heart, when those things that he hath most loved, do represent themselves at that hour unto him, and when he seeth that he shall be

15 1 Kgs. 28:19.

spoiled of them all in such wise, that he shall be enforced to say. Now shall this world have no more to do with me, neither this air, nor this sun, nor this element. Now shall I have no longer conversation and comfort of my children, my wife, my house, my lands, my goods, my pleasures, and delights. Of all things I am now left naked, and bare. Now will death spoil me of them all. Now is my old age at an end: Now is the number of my days fulfilled: Now shall I die unto all manner of things, and they all unto me. Wherefore O thou world, I bid thee farewell: ye my lands, my goods, and riches, I bid you farewell: my friends, my acquaintance, my kinsfolk, my loving wife, and my dear young children I bid you all farewell. For now alas shall we never see one an other any more in this mortal flesh.

There is yet an other separation after this more terrible and dreadful than this is: to wit, between the soul, and the body, which have kept company so long time together, and have been such hearty friends. The devil had spoiled the holy man Job of all manner of things saving only of his life, and it seemed unto him, that in comparison of the spoil thereof, all the rest were of none accompt and therefore he said: *Skin for skin, and all that a man hath he will give for his life.*[16] This is the thing that naturally is most loved, and the separation whereof causeth most grief. If the separation of one wayfaring man from an other, when they have travailed in journey together any time, do cause such grief, and solitariness: what a grief shall it be, when two such entire friends, and companions, as the soul, and the body have been, are separated the one from the other, which have travailed together from their mother's womb until that very hour, and have had so many knots, and bonds of friendship between them? What a grief will it be when the spirit shall say unto the flesh: I must now remain all alone without thee. And the flesh shall likewise make answer unto the spirit, saying: And in what case then shall I be without thee, seeing all the being I have, I received of thee?

---

16 Job 2:4.

§. II. Of the Horror and Loathsomeness of Our Grave.

After this it cometh naturally to a man's mind to think what shall become of his body, when his soul is departed out of it. And in thinking hereupon, he seeth that the best hap his body may have, can be no better than to be laid in a little grave of earth. The baseness of which condition maketh him to be as it were astonied. For considering on the one side what great estimation he hath made of his body in times past, and seeing on the other side what a base and vile place that is, wherein it must now be laid, he cannot but wonder exceedingly at it. He considereth and weigheth with himself, that the lodging which they will prepare for him in the earth shall be strait, and narrow, that it shall be also obscure, stinking, full of worms, maggots, bones, and dead men's skulls, and withal so horrible, that it shall be very irksome to them that be alive only to look upon it. And when he seeth that his body which he was wont to make so much of, his belly which he esteemed for his God, his mouth for whose delights the land and sea could scarcely serve, and his flesh for which gold and silk was wont to be woven with great curiosity, and a soft bed prepared to lay it in, must now be laid in such a filthy and miserable dunghill, where it shall be trodden upon, and eaten with foul worms, and maggots, and within few days be of as ugly a form, as a dead Carion that lieth in the fields, insomuch that the wayfaring man will stop his nose, and run away in great haste to avoid the stinking savour of it: when (I say) he considereth all this, and seeth that in steed of his soft bed, he must lie there upon the hard ground: and in steed of his precious and gorgeous apparel he must have there but only a seely poor winding sheet: and in steed of his sweet odoriferous perfumes, and musks, filthy rottenness, and horrible stenches: and in steed of his multitude of delicate dishes, and waiting serving men, he must have there such an infinite number of crawling worms, and filthy maggots feeding upon him, he cannot choose (if he have any sense of Judgement remaining in him) but marvel to see unto how base a condition such a noble creature is now come, and to consider with whom he must now keep company there, even fellow, and fellow like, who in his life time had no fellow, nor equal. It is not the part of wise men to wonder at things: and the customable seeing of things every day taketh away from them (be they never so great) all admiration, and wonder. And yet all this notwithstanding, the great Wise man wondered at this misery (though it be a matter whereof we have daily experience) when he said: If man and beast do die both after one sort, what availeth me that I have travailed so much in seeking for wisdom?[17] If it were so, that the body in this separation should end in some thing that were of any price, or profit, it would be some kind of comfort unto us. But this is a thing to be wondered at, that so excellent a creature shall end in the most dishonorable and loathsome thing in the world. This is that great misery whereat the holy man Job wondered, (and surely not without good cause) when he said. The tree after it is cut, hath hope to revive, and spring again, and if the root of it do rot in the ground, and the stock be dead in the earth, yet with the freshness of water it springeth again, and bringeth forth leaves, as if it were newly planted. But man after he is once dead, withered, and consumed, what is become of him?[18] Great (undoubtedly) was the tribute that was laid upon the children of Adam for sin. And the everlasting Judge understood very well, what penance he gave unto man, when he said: *Thou art dust, and into dust thou shalt return again.*[19]

§. III. Of the Great Fear and Doubt the Soul Hath at the Hour of Death, What Shall Happen unto It after It Is Departed out of the Body.

Howbeit this is not the greatest cause of fear, that a man hath at the hour of his death, but there is yet one far greater: and that is, when the soul casteth her eyes further, and beginneth to think upon the dangers of the life to come, and imagineth what shall become of her hereafter. For this is now as it were to depart from the haven mouth,

17 See Eccles. 2; 3.
18 See Job 14.
19 Gen. 3:19.

and to launch into the main Sea, where none other thing is to be seen on what side so ever ye look, but only heaven, and the water, the which is wont to be occasion of greater fear in such as are but new Seamen. For when a man considereth that eternity of worlds, which followeth after death: and withal casteth his eye into that new and strange region, which was never known nor travailed by any man alive, where he must now begin to take his journey, when he considereth also the everlasting glory or pain which there must fall to his lot, and seeth that wheresoever the tree falleth, there it shall remain for evermore,[20] and knoweth not on which of the two sides he shall fall, when he considereth (I say) all these things, he cannot but be in a very great fear, and trouble of mind. We read that when Benadad king of Syria was sick, he was in so great anguish and grief of mind, for that he knew not whether he should die of that sickness or not, that he sent the general of his army with forty Camels loden with treasure unto the Prophet Elizeus, requesting him with words of great humility, to rid him out of that perplexity he was in, and to put him out of all doubt, whether he should recover of that sickness, or not.[21] Now if the love of so short a life as this is be able to cause a man to be in such a great care and pensiveness, how great care will a Wise man take, when he perceiveth himself to be in such a case, as that he may truly say, that within two hours he shall have one of these two lots: to wit, either life everlasting, or else death everlasting: and that he knoweth not certainly whether of these two shall come unto him? What martyrdom may be compared to such a painful anguish and grief as this is? Put the case now, that a king were taken prisoner among the Turks and when his Ambassadors should come to ransom him, the Turks would propound, that the matter should be determined by casting of lots, and that if he happened to have a good lot, he should be ransomed, and go home with his Ambassadors to his kingdom, but if contrariwise, that then immediately he should be thrown into a great fiery furnace, which were there prepared burning

20 See Eccles. 11.
21 See 4 Kgs. 8.

and flaming before him. Tell me I pray thee, at the time when they should be casting the lots, and putting their hand into the vessel to take them out, and all the world in great expectation, waiting what should be the end thereof, and the king himself standing there present, beholding the doubtful hap that must be allotted unto him, in what a doleful case (thinkest thou) would he then be! How troubled? How fearful? How quaking, and trembling? And how ready to promise and vow unto almighty God all he could possibly do, to be quite rid out of that terrible anguish? Now what is all this (be it never so great) but as it were a shadow, if it be compared with this danger that we speak of? How far greater is the kingdom that we seek? How far greater is the fiery furnace that we do fear? How far more grievous is the perplexity and doubtfulness of this matter, than of the other? For on the one side the angels shall be there expecting for us, to carry us to the kingdom of heaven, and on the other side the devils, to cast us into the horrible furnace of hell fire, and no man knoweth whether of these two lots shall happen unto him, which shall be determined either the one way or the other within the space of one hour after his death. Consider therefore in what a heavy plight thy heart shall be at this last instant: how fearful, how humble, how abased before the face of him, who only can deliver thee out of this danger. Surely I am of this opinion, that there is no tongue in the world able to declare this matter as it is indeed.

§. IV. How We Come to Understand Hereby the Errors and Blindness of Our Life Past.

After this anguish there followeth yet an other as great as it, (namely in such persons as have lived a wicked and dissolute life,) which is, to come so late to think upon the accompt they have then forthwith to make of all the disorders, and offences of their former life. O how wonderfully shall the wicked be confounded at that time, when the grief of their pain shall cause them to open their eyes, which heretofore the delight and pleasure of sin had closed up! Insomuch as they shall then clearly perceive what false gods those were which they have served, and how deceitful those riches were which they have so greedily gaped after, and how by following that way, whereby they thought to have found rest, they find in conclusion their utter ruin, and destruction. The servants of the king of Syria came to apprehend the Prophet Eliseus, and when almighty God had stricken them all blind by means of the prayer of the Prophet, the Prophet said unto them: *Come, go with me, and I will shew you him whom you seek.* And when he had thus said, he carried them with him unto Samaria, and brought them into the market place of the city, in the midst of all their enemies. And then made his prayer again, and said. *O Lord, open the eyes of these miserable men, that they may see where they are.*[22] Now tell me I pray thee, when those men opened their eyes, and saw whither they were come, (believing certainly before, that they went to find the party they sought for,) how amazed and ashamed were they, when they saw how foully they were deceived. Now what thing in the world could make a more lively resemblance of the process and deceits of our life? We all do walk here in this world by the way of our appetites, and desires. Some seek after gold: others to purchase lands: others to make great buildings: others seek for pleasures, and delights: others for offices, and dignities: and each one is fully persuaded, that he taketh the best and wisest way to obtain the thing he desireth. But when the terrible presence of death, and the danger of our accompt discovereth the vanity of our hopes, then finding ourselves to be in arrearages for our accompt, we shall clearly perceive how foully we have been deceived: and we shall see that by following that way, whereby we thought to have found quietness, and rest, we find our perdition. O what miserable men are we! How blindly do we now wander up and down in the world? What eyes shall we then have? How shall our judgement be then altered? How far different shall it be from that it was before? Then shall we plainly see, how all the things of this world are miserable, her goods false, her ways crooked, her hopes vain, her promises lying, her pleasures bitter, her glory short, and vain. Then shall we perceive (though too late) how

22 See 4 Kgs. 6.

her riches were thorns, and her delights poison. To be short, then shall we see how our eyes have been closed up, and that we never knew whither we went: and at the end of our journey we shall find ourselves in the streets of Sameria, and in the snare of the judgement of almighty God, and compassed about with all our enemies, to wit, the devils, and our sins. O how shall the wicked be confounded at that hour, and how foully shall they see themselves beguiled! How truly may every one of them say at that time: O miserable wretch that I am, what other commodity have I now by all my pleasures past, but only that I have provoked at this dreadful hour the indignation of the judge against me, who must give sentence upon me? Now my pleasures are all ended, and gone, and there remaineth of them neither relic nor memory to comfort me withal, no more than if they never had been: yea contrariwise they remain as thorns that lie pricking all about my heart, they make my cause doubtful, they torment my woeful soul now presently, and peradventure shall torment it everlastingly for ever, and ever. This is the fruit that I have gathered of my dissolute and wanton life, and of all my carnal delights: This is the setting of my teeth on edge, that my gluttonies past do cause me now to have. My pleasures and delights have now forsaken me: They are quite gone away, and will never return again: yea perhaps in steed of pleasures that continued but a moment, there are prepared for me everlasting horrible torments in hell fire. Now what blindness can be greater than this? How much better had it been for me never to have been born, than to have offended him, of whose help and favor I have at this present so great need? How much better had it been for me that the earth had opened, and swallowed me up, before I had once thought to offend him? O unfortunate day! O cursed hour, wherein I offended thee O Lord! Why did I not consider beforehand of this dreadful hour? Why was I not sooner mindful of this terrible judgement? How were mine eyes blinded with so small a glimpse? Is this the way that I took to be so certain, and sure? Is this the end that all the honors of the world come unto? What? Are all those things which I have so greatly esteemed heretofore of so little accompt at this present?

§. V. Of the Terror of the Dreadful Accompt We Must Make at the Hour of Our Death unto Almighty God of All Our Life Past.

After this grief there followeth also an other as great as this: which is, the fear of the accompt that shall then be required of us.

This is one of the greatest troubles, and griefs, we shall have at that time. For besides this that it is so terrible a matter to enter into judgement with almighty God, the very devils also, and fiends of hell will increase this fear at that hour, which before they were wont to extenuate, and dimmish unto us, with the hope and colour of God's mercy. Then will they put us in mind of the greatness and profoundness of the judgements of almighty God, and of his justice, which they will then shew to be so great, that he pardoned not his own only son for the sins of others. *If this then be done in green wood, what shall be done* (say they) *in dry wood?*[23] Then the wicked man shall begin to tremble, and quake for fear, and say to himself. O miserable wretch that I am! If that be true, which all the scripture reporteth, to wit, that almighty God will give to every one according to his works, what may I hope to receive at his hands, that have done so many wicked works?[24] If the Gospel say, That the tree shall be judged according to the fruit that it yieldeth, what judgement may I look for, that have brought forth so many wicked fruits?[25] If it be true, which the Prophet saith: That none shall ascend up to the hill of God, unless he have innocent hands, and an undefiled heart:[26] whither shall I then go, that have had such wicked hands, and such a filthy heart? If the saying of the Wiseman be true: That whosoever shutteth his ears and will not hear the law, shall cry, and not be heard:[27] what may I look for, that have had mine ears shut against almighty God, and yet have had them so open to harken after lies,

---

23 Luke 23:31.

24 See Matt. 16:27; Rom. 2:6; 2 Cor. 5:10.

25 See Matt. 3:10; 7:16–20.

26 See Ps. 23:3–4.

27 See Prov. 28:9.

and vanities of the world. Wherefore (O my omnipotent God) with what face shall I now appear before thee, and desire thee to give ear unto me, seeing thou hast so often times called me, and I would give no ear unto thee? How can I request thee to receive me into thy house, seeing thou hast so often times called at my house, and I have shut my gates against thee? How shall I find thee now at the time of my need, seeing thou hast had so often times need of me in thy poor and impotent members, and hast not found me? By what title or right may I request thee now at the end of my journey to grant me heaven, seeing I have spent all my life time in the service of the devil thine enemy? O how justly mayest thou now (O Lord) say unto me: Thou hast served the world, and the devil, get thee therefore unto them, and let them give thee thy hire. The like answer made the Prophet Eliseus to king Joram the son of Achab. Who when he had spent and employed all his life in the service and worshiping of Idols, and came in the time of his necessity to the Prophet of God, requesting him of help, and remedy, the holy Prophet answered, and said: O king Joram, what hast thou to do with me? Get thee hence to the Prophets of thy father, and mother, and desire them to help thee at this time.[28] O how many of us do follow this wicked king both in our life, and death! In our life we serve the world, and at the point of death we call upon almighty God. What answer may we look to have at that dreadful hour, but even the same that he hath already given in the like case? Which is: What hast thou to do with me, sith thou didst never service unto me? Get thee hence to thy counselors whom thou hast followed, and to thy idols whom thou hast loved, served and adored, and speak unto them to give thee thy wages for thy service.

When ye shall cry (saith almighty God by his prophet Isaias) *let them that ye have gathered together deliver you, but the wind shall take them all away.*[29]

---

[28] See 4 Kgs. 3:13.
[29] Is. 57:13.

At this time the sick man beginneth to wish that he might have some space to do penance for his former wicked life. And he thinketh then with himself, that if he might obtain it, O how he would fast, and pray, and do great works of mercy: Yea, he would not content himself with every common kind of penance, but would live the most strait, and austere kind of life of all men in the world. But alas, when he perceiveth by the increasing of his sickness, that his request will not be granted: and calleth to mind what time opportunity and means he hath had to prepare himself for this dreadful hour, and how fondly he hath suffered the same to pass in vain, then is he wonderfully grieved and vexed for this loss, and acknowledgeth himself to be well worthy of such punishment, for that he would not be mindful beforehand of his dreadful accompt, but omitted to do penance for his sins when he had time and space to do it. O unto how many of us doth it happen to be beguiled after this sort, spending and consuming the time (which almighty God hath given us to do penance for our sins,) in vanities, and pleasures, and afterwards when we stand in most need of it we want it! And so it happeneth unto us, as it doth commonly to the pages, and servitors in the Court, who being allowed a candle to light themselves to bed, do spend their candle in play all the night, and afterwards are constrained to go to bed darkling.

§. VI. Of the Sacrament of Extreme Unction: and of the Agony of Death.

Now approacheth the sick person to his last end: and the Catholic Church as a very loving and pitiful mother, beginneth then to help her Children with prayers, and Sacraments, and with all the means she may possibly do. And because his necessity is so great (for at that instant it shall be determined what shall become of him for ever, and ever,) great haste is made to call upon all the Saints in heaven, that they all will help the sick man in this his great peril, and danger. For what other thing is the Litany which then by commandment of the Church is to be said over him that is at the point of death, but that the Catholic Church as a pitiful mother, being very careful for the danger of her sick child, knocketh at all the gates of heaven, and crieth unto all the Saints, desiring them to be intercessors before the divine majesty for the salvation of him, that standeth now in so great need of their help, at the time of his passing out of this world.

Then the Priest out of hand anointeth all the senses and members of the sick person with the holy Oil, (according as the holy Scripture commandeth in the Epistle of St. James chap.5.vers.14.) And desireth almighty God to pardon the sick person all that he hath offended by any of his senses. And then anointing his eyes he saith: *Almighty God by this Unction and of his divine mercy pardon thee all the sins that thou hast committed by means of thine eyes.* And in this wise he anointeth all the other parts of the sick person. Now if the miserable sinner have been dissolute in his eyes, or in his tongue, or in any other of his bodily senses: If all his former dissolute disorders and wanton pleasures be represented unto him at that time, in such sort that he seeth well what little fruit he is like to find then by all his former delights, and pleasures: If he perceive withal into what a narrow strait he is brought by means of his wicked and licentious life, how can he choose but feel an extreme anguish and grief therewith? What would he give at that time (trow ye) that he had never lifted up his eyes from the ground to behold any woman with any wanton look, and that he had never opened his mouth to speak any words of lying, slander, detraction, or any other wicked word?

After this follow the pangs and agony of death, which is surely the greatest of all the conflicts we have in this life. Then is the holy Candle lighted, and his friends and executors begin to provide his winding sheet, and other things for his funerals: Then they begin to say to the sick man, that the hour of his departure out of this world is now come: and therefore they counsel him to recommend himself unto almighty God, and to call upon the holy virgin Mary his blessed Mother, who is wont at that hour to help all them that call upon her. Then the sick man beginneth to hear the woeful cries and pitiful lamentations of his poor wife, who now presently beginneth to feel the discommodities of her new widowhood, and solitary life. Then the soul of the sick man is ready to depart from the body: and at the time of her going every one of his members is sore grieved and vexed therewith. Then are the cares of the soul renewed afresh. Then is the soul in a marvelous great conflict, and agony, not so much for her departure, as for fear of the hour of her dreadful accompt, approaching so near unto her. Then is the time of trembling, and quaking, yea even of such as be most stout, and courageous. The blessed holy father Hilarion, as he was passing out of this world, began to tremble, and fear, and was loath to die, howbeit the holy man encouraged himself, saying, Go forth my soul: go forth out of this body: whereof shouldest thou be afraid? It is threescore and ten years that thou hast served Christ, and art thou yet afraid of death? Now if this holy man were afraid of his passing out of this world, who served Christ so many years, what shall he do, who peradventure hath offended him so many years? Whither shall he go? Whom shall he call upon? What counsel shall he take? O that men understood how great this perplexity and anguish is at this dreadful hour? Imagine now (I beseech thee) in what a doleful case the heart of the Patriarch Isaac was, when his father held him bound hands, and feet, and had laid him upon the wood to sacrifice him, when he saw his father's glistering sword over his head, and underneath him the flames of fire burning, and the servants that might have succored him staying at the foot of the hill, and he himself bound hands and feet in such sort that he could neither flee, nor defend himself, in what plight trow ye was the heart of this blessed young man, when he saw himself in so narrow a strait?[30] And surely in far greater perplexity is the soul of the wicked man at this dreadful hour: because he can turn his eyes on no side, where he shall not see occasions of great terror, and fear. If he look upward, he seeth the terrible sword of the justice of almighty God threatening him: If he look downward, he seeth the grave open ever gaping, and tarrying for him: If he look within himself, he seeth his own conscience gnawing, and biting him: If he

[30] See Gen. 22.

look about him, there be Angels, and devils, on both sides of him, watching and expecting the end of the sentence, whether of them shall have the prey: If he look backward, he seeth his doleful wife, his little young children, his poor servants, his kinsfolk, his friends, his companions, his acquaintance, his house, his lands, and the goods of this life to remain all behind, and are not able to succor him in this his great distress: forsomuch as he must depart all alone out of this life, and they all must remain still here. To conclude, if after all this he take a view of himself, and consider what he is inwardly, he shall be wonderfully amazed, and afraid, to see himself in such a dangerous and terrible state: insomuch as if it were possible, he would fly away even from himself. Now alas, to depart from the body is a thing intolerable? To continue still therein is a thing impossible: And to differ his departure any longer will not be granted. All the time past seemeth unto him but as a blast of wind: and that which is to come appeareth (as it is in deed) infinite. Now what shall the miserable soul do being thus compassed and environed about with so many straits? O how fond and blind are the sons of Adam, that will not provide in time for this terrible passage!

§. VII. How Filthy, and Loathsome the Body Is after It Is Dead: and of the Burying of It in the Grave.

Last of all, when this great conflict is ended, the soul is violently taken away from the body, and departeth from her ancient habitation, the body remaining utterly spoiled of all the beauty, and qualities it had.

Now let us consider what lot each one of these two parts must have. First consider, in what case the body is, after the soul is departed out of it. What thing is more esteemed than the body of a prince whiles he is alive? And what thing is more contemptable, and more vile, than the very same body when it is dead? Where is then that former princely majesty become? Where is that royal behavior, and glorious magnificence? Where is that high authority, and sovereignty? Where is that terror, and fear, at the beholding of his presence? Where is that capping, and kneeling, and speaking unto him with such reverence, and subjection? How quickly is all this gay pomp utterly overthrown, and come to nothing, as if it had been but a mere dream, or a play on a stage, that is dispatched in an hour?

Then out of hand the winding sheet is provided, and brought forth, which is the richest jewel he may take with him out of this life. And this is the greatest recompence that the richest man in this world shall have of all his goods at that hour. I wish this point were well considered by every covetous man, and by those that make their money their God: whose blindness and folly the Prophet reprehendeth in these words: *Be not afraid when a man waxeth rich, and when thou seest the glory of his house very much multiplied, and increased: for when he dieth he shall not carry his goods away with him, neither shall his glory go down with him.*[31]

Then do they make a hole in the earth of seven or eight foot long, (and no longer though it be for Alexander the great, whom the whole world could not hold) and with that small room only must his body be content. There they appoint him his house for ever: There he taketh up his perpetual lodging until the last day of general Judgement, in company with other dead bodies: There the worms crawl out to give him his entertainment: To be short, there they let him down in a poor white sheet, his face being covered with a napkin, and his hands and feet fast bound: which truly needeth not, for he is then sure enough for breaking out of prison, neither shall he be able to defend himself against any man. There the earth receiveth him into her lap. There the bones of dead men kiss, and welcome him: There the dust of his ancestors embraceth him, and inviteth him to that table, and house, which is appointed for all men living. And the last honor that the world can do unto him at that time, is to cast a little earth upon him, and to cover him well therewith, that the people may not feel his stinking savour, and behold his dishonor. And the greatest pleasure that his very dear and special friends can do then unto him (besides praying for his soul,) is to honor him with casting a handful of earth upon him. And therefore the faithful people are

31 Ps. 48:17–18.

wont to use this ceremony towards the dead, that almighty God may dispose others to do the same unto them, when they shall be in the like case. Now what greater confession and acknowledging of our misery can we devise, than to see how men do prevent beforehand that they may not want after their death so small a benefit as this is? O greedy covetousness of the living, and great poverty of the dead! Why should a man desire and gape after so many things for this present life, being so short as it is, seeing so little will content him at the hour of his death?

Then the grave maker taketh the spade, and pickaxe into his hand, and beginneth to tumble down bones upon bones, and to tread down the earth very hard upon him. Insomuch that the fairest face in all the world, the best trimmed, and most charily kept from wind, and sun, shall lie there, and be stamped upon by the rude grave maker, who will not stick to lay him on the face, and rap him on the skull, yea and to batter down his eyes and nose flat to his face, that they may lie well and even with the earth. And the fine dappered gentleman who whiles he lived might in no wise abide the wind to blow upon him, no not so much as a little hair or mote to fall upon his garments, but in all haste it must be brushed of with great curiosity, here they lay and hurl upon him a dunghill of filthiness, and dirt. And that sweet minion gentleman also that was wont forsooth to go perfumed with Amber, and other odoriferous smells, must be contented here to lie covered all over with earth, and foul crawling worms, and maggots. This is the end of all the gay braveries, and of all the pomp, and glory of the world.

In this plight do all his friends now leave him, lying in that strait lodging, in that earth of oblivion, and in that dark prison, where he shall remain accompanied with perpetual solitariness until the general day of Judgement. O world what is become of thy glory? O ye my houses, lands, and riches, where is your power? O my wife, my children, my friends, and kinsfolk, where have ye now left me? How happeneth it, that ye my old friends and companions do so quickly forsake me, and leave me here in the earth thus solitary alone? How chanceth it, that the wheel of my so great prosperity and felicity is so quickly overturned, and defaced? They that saw Queen Jezabel when she was (by the just judgement of God) eaten with dogs, when they saw that there remained nothing else of her beauty, but only her skull, and the extreme parts of her feet, and hands, those (I say) that had known her before in so great flourishing and royal estate, and saw her at that time in such a miserable plight, wondering at that so great alteration, and change, demanded, and said: Hæccine est illa Jezabel? Is this that Jezabel?[32] And as many as passed by that way, and beheld her thus eaten with dogs, repeated the same exclamation, marveling at so great a change, and said: Is this that Jezabel? Is this that great Queen, and Lady of Israel? Is this she that was so mighty, that she usurped and seized the lands and goods of her subjects, by shedding of their blood? Is death able to bring the mighty and puissant Princess to such a base and miserable calamity?

Now therefore my dear brother go down I pray thee with thy spirit into the graves and Sepulchers of such Princes, and great noble personages, as thou hast, either heard of, or known in this world: and consider what a horrible and deformed form of their bodies is there to be seen. And thou shalt see, that thou hast good cause to make the like exclamation, and to use the same words, and say: Is this that Jezabel? Is this that amiable face, which I knew so fair, and lively? Are these those eyes, that were so clear, and bright to behold? Is this that pleasant rolling tongue, that talked so eloquently, and made such goodly discourses? Is this that fine and neat body, that was so trimly polished, and adorned? Is this the end of the majesty of Princes' scepters, and royal crowns? Is this the end of the glory of the world? O how often times (saith a Wise man) hath it been my chance to enter into the sepulchers of some dead bodies, where wondering or rather being greatly astonished at the sight that I saw, I fixed mine eyes advisedly upon the shape of the dead corpse: I set the bones in order, I joined the hands together, and set the lips in their proper places, and spake thus secretly to myself. Behold these feet, that have

32 4 Kgs. 9:37.

travailed such crooked paths, and ways: These hands also, that have committed so many wicked acts: These eyes, that have beheld so many vanities: This mouth, that hath eaten and devoured so many delicate, and superfluous meats. Behold this skull of his head, that hath built so many vain castles, and towers in the air: This dust, and filthy skin for whose pleasure, and delight he hath committed so many sins, and wickedness: and for which cause the soul of this body doth and shall perhaps suffer everlasting horrible torments in hell fire. This done, I departed out of that place wholly astonied, and amazed: and meeting with certain persons both men, and women, young, and old, I beheld them likewise, and considered, that both they and I should shortly appear in the like ugly form, and seem as vile, and loathsome to behold, as those dead bodies are now presently. Wherefore what a fond wicked wretch am I to live in such wise as I do? To what end is my purchasing, and heaping together of lands, and riches, and my building of such sumptuous houses, seeing I shall shortly be here so poor, and naked? To what end are my gay braveries, and gorgeous ornaments in my apparel, and furniture of household stuff, seeing I shall shortly be here so filthy, and loathsome to behold? To what end are my delicate dishes, my sugared sauces, and dainty fare, seeing I shall shortly be here meat for the worms and maggots of the earth?

§. VIII. Of the Way, That the Soul Taketh after It Is Departed out of the Body: and of the Dreadful Judgement, and Sentence, That Shall Be Given upon It at That Time.

Statutum est hominibus semel mori, post hoc autem Judicium. Hebr.9.vers.27.

Omne verbum otiosum quod loquti fuerint homines reddent rationem de eo in die Judicii. Matth.12.vers.36.

Let us now leave the body lying thus buried in the grave, and let us see what way the soul taketh through that new world, which is as it were an other hemisphere, where it findeth a new heaven, a new earth, an other kind of life, and an other manner of understanding, and knowledge.[33] The soul then after it is departed out of the body entereth into this new region, where those that by living never entered: a place full of fear and terror, and of shadows of death. But now what shall this new stranger do in this so strange a country, unless it be so, that he hath deserved in this life to have the guard and defense of Angels for this time. O my soul (saith St. Bernard) what a terrible day shall that be, when thou shalt enter all alone into that unknown region, where those hellish monsters that are so horrible and ugly to behold, shall encounter and assault thee in the way? Who will then take thy part? Who will then defend thee? Who will then deliver thee from those ramping lions, which being raging mad for hunger, do lie there in wait to devour thee?

Undoubtedly this is a very fearful way, but the judgement that shall then so solemnly be given, is far more terrible. Who is able: to declare, how strait the decision of this particular judgment shall be? How righteous the judge? How busy, and solicitous the devils our accusers? How few intercessors on our side? What a particular examination shall then be made of every point of our accompt? And what a long process shall be drawn of all our whole life? And as our Savior affirmeth: *We must then render an accompt of every idle word.*[34] Wherefore, *if the just man* (as St. Peter saith) *shall hardly be saved, where shall the sinner and wicked man shew themselves?*[35] It is a thing truly very worthy to be noted, that whereas a man would think that those things that we have most loved, and for which we have taken most pains, should most help us in this great distress, it falleth out quite contrary. For they shall not only not help us, but also be an occasion at that time of more pain and grief unto us. The thing that Absalom loved, and esteemed above all things was his goodly hair of

33 Note, that there be two judgements: one is at the hour of every man's death, which is called the particular judgement: And the other is at doomsday, which shall be the universal judgement of all mankind together.

34 See Matt. 12:36.

35 1 Ptr. 4:18.

his head, and that very hair almighty God ordained by his just judgement to be the cause of his death.[36] Now the very same judgement is prepared for all wicked persons at that hour: that those things that every man most loved in this life, and for which he committed most heinous offences against almighty God, the very same things shall make his accompt more doubtful, and be occasion of greater torment unto him. There shall our children (whom we sought to enrich, not passing whether it were by right or wrong) accuse us. There shall the naughty harlot (for whose wanton love we have broken the laws and commandments of almighty God,) plead against us. There shall our lands, our goods, or offices, our dignities, our pleasures, and delights, (which were our idols) be our hangmen, and torment us most cruelly. There shall almighty God give judgement upon all the gods of Egypt, ordaining the matter in such sort, that those very things wherein we have put all our glory, shall at that time be the cause of our ruin.

Now if the severity of the dreadful sentence of almighty God be answerable to our sins, Alas, who shall be able to abide it? One of those ancient holy fathers that lived in the wilderness was wont to say, that of three things he lived continually in great fear. The first was, when his soul should depart out of his body. The second, when it should be presented before the judgement seat of almighty God. The third, when the sentence of his cause should be given, and pronounced. But now (which is most terrible of all) what if almighty God shall give this most terrible sentence against thee, that thou shalt be damned for ever and ever to the horrible torments of hell fire, there to continue infinite millions of years, and world without end? In what a terrible strait shalt thou then be? What sorrow? What grief? What anguish shalt thou then feel? Again, what joy, and triumphs, will the devils thine enemies make at that time? Then shall that sentence of the Prophet be fulfilled: saying: *All thine enemies shall open their mouths upon thee, they shall laugh thee to scorn, and gnash their*

[36] See 2 Kgs. 14; 18.

teeth at thee, and say: we will devour him: this is the day we have so long looked for, we have found him, we have espied him.[37]

But thou O sweet Jesus, *Illuminate the eyes of my soul* (I beseech thee) *that I sleep not in death, that mine enemy may never say: I have prevailed against him. Amen.*[38]

---

37 See Lam. 2:16.
38 Ps. 12:4–5.

THURSDAY NIGHT

Of the General Day of Judgement.

THIS day (when thou hast made the sign of the Cross, and prepared thyself hereunto,) thou hast to meditate upon the day of the general judgement, that by means of this consideration those two principal effects may be stirred up in thy soul, which every faithful Christian ought to have, to wit: the fear of God, and the abhorring of sin.

Consider first what a terrible day that shall be, in which the causes of all the children of Adam shall be thoroughly examined, the process of all our lives diligently perused, and a general definitive sentence given what shall become of us all for evermore.

That day shall comprise in it all the days of all ages, and times, both present, past, and to come. For upon that day the world shall render an accompt of all these times. And then shall almighty God pour out the anger, and indignation, which he hath gathered together in all ages. How violently shall the main flood of God's wrath, and indignation break out at that day, which containeth in it so many floods of anger, and wrath, as there have been sins committed since the beginning of the world until that day. And therefore the Prophet had good cause to say: *That day shall be a day of anger: a day of calamity, and misery: a day of obscurity, and darkness: a day of clouds, and tempestuous storms: a day of the trumpet, and alarm against the strong cities, and against the high towers.*[1]

Secondly, consider what fearful and terrible signs shall go before this day. For (as our Savior saith,) Before the coming of this day, there shall be signs in the Sun, in the Moon, and in the Stars, and in all creatures both of heaven, and earth. For they shall all have as it were a certain feeling and understanding of their end, before they come to their end in deed: And shall tremble, and quake, and begin to fall before they fall in deed. But as for men they shall (saith he) go up and down dry, and withered, in great anguish, and fear of death, hearing the terrible roarings of the Sea, and seeing the great outrageous storms, and tempests, that shall then be stirring.[2] And by those dreadful signs they shall conjecture what great calamities and miseries are threatened to the world. And in this wise shall they go wholly amazed, and astonied: their faces pale, and wane: their hearts dead before death come: and as persons condemned before the sentence be given. For they shall measure the perils and dangers to come, by the great fear and terror they be presently in. And every one shall be so thoroughly occupied with his own affairs, that none shall think of others: no not so much as the father of the son, or the son of the father. No man shall have to do for any other man: because no man shall be sufficient for himself alone. The Sybilles do affirm, that at that time the beasts shall go bellowing and roaring through the fields, and cities: and that the trees shall sweat blood: and that the Sea shall cast up the fishes on the dry ground. But if this seem incredible to any man, let him consider, that there is much more spoken in the gospel. For it is a greater matter for men to be dried up, than for the sea to be dried up. And it is a greater matter that the virtues of the heavens should be moved, than that all creatures in the earth should be altered.[3]

1 Soph. 1:15–16.
2 See Luke 21:25–26.
3 See Luke 21.

Thirdly, consider that universal flood of fire, that shall come before the judge, and that dreadful sound of the trumpet, which the Archangel shall blow, to summon and call all the generations of the world to assemble together in one place, and to be present at their general and universal judgement. And above all this, consider with what a dreadful majesty the Judge shall come. Whose coming is described by the Prophet Nahum in these words: Our Lord shall come like a tempest, and furious whirlwind, and the clouds are the dust of his feet. He shall take indignation against the Sea, and it shall wax dry, and all the rivers of the earth shall be dried up: The hill Basan, and Carmelus, shall be withered, and the flower of the mount Libanus shall fade, and fall away. The mountains shall quake before him, and the hills shall melt: The earth shall tremble at his presence, and the world, and all the inhabitants thereof. Who shall stand before the face of his indignation? And who shall abide the fierceness of his fury? His wrath shall be poured out like a fire, and the very rocks shall become dust before him.[4]

After this, consider what a strait accompt shall be there required of every man. *Verily* (saith Job) *no man can be justified, if he be compared with almighty God, and if he contend with him in judgement, of a thousand things that he shall charge him withal, he shall not be able to answer unto one.*[5] Now then what shall every wicked person think at that time, when almighty God shall enter with him in this examination, and shall there within his own conscience say thus unto him: Come hither thou wicked and naughty man. What hast thou seen in me, that thou shouldest thus despise me, and go to mine enemies side? I have raised thee from the dust of the earth, and created thee after mine own image, and likeness. I have given thee virtue, and strength, wherewith thou mightest have obtained my glory. But thou despising the benefits and commandments of life, which I have given thee, wouldst rather follow the lies of the deceiver, than the wholesome counsel of thy Lord, and creator. To deliver thee form

4 See Nahum 1.
5 Job 9:2–3; see Job 31:14.

this foul fall I went down from heaven into earth, where I suffered the greatest pains, torments, and reproaches, that ever were suffered in the world. For thee have I fasted: For thee have I travailed from place to place: For thee have I watched, labored, and sweat drops of blood: For thee have I suffered persecutions, scourgings, blasphemies, reproaches, buffetings, dishonors, torments, and even death itself upon the Cross. To be short, for thee I was born in much poverty: For thee I lived in great pain: For thee I died with intolerable torments, and griefs. Witness hereof are this cross, and nails, which thou here now seest: Witness hereof are these wounds both of my hands, and feet, which are here to be seen in my body: Witness hereof are heaven, and earth, before whom I suffered: Witness hereof are the sun, and moon, which were eclipsed at the same hour. Now what hast thou done with this thy soul, which I with the shedding of mine own blood purchased to be mine? In whose service hast thou employed that which I bought so dearly? O foolish wicked and adulterous generation, why wouldst thou rather serve thy enemy with pain, than me thy creator, and redeemer, with joy? Be ye astonied (O ye heavens) at this strange case, and let your gates fall down at the strangeness hereof. For two abominations hath my people committed: They have forsaken me, that am the fountain of lively water, and refused me for an other Barrabas.[6] I called you very often times, and ye would not answer me. I knocked at your gates, and ye would not awake. I stretched out my hands on the cross, and ye would not behold them. Ye have despised my counsels, with all my promises, and threatenings. Wherefore speak ye now O ye Angels: be you judges between me, and my vineyard: what could I have done more for it, than I have done?

Now what answer can the wicked make hereunto? Such as be scoffers at holy and divine things? Such as be mockers of virtue? Such as be despisers of simplicity? Such as make more accompt of the laws and statues of the world, than of the laws of almighty God? Such as have been deaf to hear the callings of God: unsensible to understand

6 See Jer. 2.

his inspirations: rebellious against his commandments: obdurate and unthankful for all his chastisements, and benefits? What can they say? What answer will those persons make, that have lived in such sort, as if they had believed that there were no God? And such as have made none accompt of any other law, but only how to procure their own worldly interest, and commodity? What will ye do (saith the Prophet Isaias) in the day of the visitation, and calamity, that shall come upon you from afar? Unto whom will ye fly for succor, and help?[7] What shall the glory and abundance of your lands and riches at that time avail you, but that ye may be carried away prisoners into hell, and there fall among the dead?

After all this, consider the terrible sentence, which the Judge shall thunder out against the wicked: And that dreadful saying, which shall make the ears of all that shall hear it to glow and tingle. His lips (saith the Prophet Isaias) are full of indignation, and his tongue is like a consuming fire.[8] What fire shall burn so hot, as those words: *Depart from me ye cursed into the everlasting fire.*[9] This is the most terrible saying that can be said to a creature. For by this departure and separation is understood the pain which the divines call Penam damni: that is the loss of all losses. Which is a universal spoil of all things, and a deprivation of that chiefest goodness (to wit of almighty God) in whom all good things do consist. Now whither shall those cursed wicked persons go O Lord, that shall depart from thee? In what haven shall they arrive? What master shall they serve? Whosoever they be that shall depart from thee, shall be written in earth, because they have forsaken the vein, and spring of the water of life, which is almighty God.[10] The greatest punishment that the Romans used to put a Citizen unto for certain grievous offences, was to banish him out of the noble city of Rome, and to confine him into some Island apart among some Barbarous nation. Now if it were thought so great a punishment to be banished out of the city

---

7 See Is. 10.

8 Is. 30:27.

9 Matt. 25:41.

10 See Jer. 17.

of Rome, what a punishment shall this be, to be banished out of the company of almighty God, and of all his elect? Yea, and to be banished for ever and ever into the company of Satan, and of those Barbarous hellhounds.

Depart from me (saith Christ) *ye cursed*:[11] As if he should say: I have invited you with my blessing, and ye would not come, now therefore take ye my curse to your despite. *The wicked man,* (saith the Prophet) *loved malediction, and it came upon him, and he refused the blessing,* (that almighty God offered unto him,) *and therefore it shall be kept far enough from him.*[12] Our Savior Christ cursed the figtree, and immediately not only the leaves, but even also the body, and roots of the tree withered away, so as it never brought fruit any more.[13] In like manner shall those miserable damned persons be accursed and utterly deprived of all hope of salvation, and of all fruit, and merit for evermore.

But whither dost thou send them O Lord? Unto everlasting fire. O what a bed is this for delicate, and tender persons! *Which of you* (saith the Prophet) *is able to dwell in the burning fire? Which of you is able to continue in the everlasting flames?*[14] What greater curse and malediction can there be than this? What calamity, what sentence, what adversity, may be compared with the only shadow of this? This is that terrible and fearful fire, which the Prophet Isiah setteth forth in these words: The streams thereof shall be turned into melting pitch, and the dust of the earth into sulfur, and brimstone, and the very earth of it shall be wholly burning pitch. It shall not be quenched night, nor day: The smoke of it shall go up evermore. It shall be desolate from generation to generation. No man shall ever pass through it.[15]

---

11 Matt. 25:41.
12 Ps. 108:18.
13 See Matt. 21:19; Mark 11:14.
14 Is. 33:14.
15 See Is. 34.

The Fourth Treatise: Of the Consideration of the General Day of Judgement: Wherein the Former Meditation Is Declared More at Large.

Great are the effects undoubtedly which the fear of God worketh in the soul. *Who so feareth God* (saith Ecclesiasticus) *it shall go well with him at his last end, and on the day of his death he shall be blessed.*[16] And in an other place he saith: *How great is that man, that hath attained unto wisdom, and knowledge, but be he never so great, he is no greater than he that feareth God. For the fear of God hath placed his seat above all things. Blessed is that man, to whom it is given to fear our Lord. He that hath this fear, with whom shall we compare him? For the fear of God is the beginning of his love.*[17] All these be the words of Ecclesiasticus. Whereby it appeareth plainly, that the fear of God is the beginning of all goodness, (sithence it is the beginning of his love.) And it is not only the beginning, but also the key, and preservation of all good things. As St. Bernard witnesseth, saying: *I know this for a most certain truth, that there is nothing of so great force and efficacy to keep us in the grace of God, as to live at all times in the fear of him, and to eschew always all manner of proud and presumptuous thoughts.*

Now to obtain this so precious a Jewel, it availeth very much to occupy our mind in the consideration and continual remembrance of the judgement of almighty God, and above all other things, in the consideration of that supreme and final general judgement, that shall be given in the end of the world. This judgement is the most dreadful thing of all that the holy scriptures declare unto us. For the things that are there signified unto us of this day are so terrible, that were it not that almighty God himself reported them, they would seem altogether incredible. And therefore our Savior after he had preached, and set out certain of them to his disciples, the greatness of them was such, that they seemed to exceed the common credulity, and faith of men, in regard whereof he ended the matter with this

16 Ecclus. 1:13.

17 Ecclus. 25:13–16.

affirmation, saying: *Verily, verily, I say unto you, that the world shall not end before all these things be fulfilled. For heaven and earth shall fail, but my word shall never fail.*[18]

It is written in the Acts of the Apostles, that when St. Paul preached before the president of Judea of the terrible things of this day, the same president began to tremble, and quake, at the words which the Apostle spake, notwithstanding that he was an infidel, and had no belief at all in this mystery.[19] Whereby it may appear, what terrible things those were, that the Apostle then spake of, sith the only sound of them was able to cause such a great fear and trembling in a man that did not believe them. Now the Christian that believeth them, and holdeth them for a matter of faith, what a lively sense and feeling should he have in these things, when he heareth, readeth, or considereth them?

And let no man think to excuse himself, pretending innocency, and saying, that these threatenings are not spoken unto him, but to unjust and wicked persons. For St. Jerome was a just man, and yet for all that he said: *That so often as he remembered the day of judgement, both his heart and body trembled for very fear.* The Prophet David also was a just man, yea, he was a man according to God's own heart, and yet for all this he had so great a fear of the accompt of this day, that he said in a certain Psalm: *O Lord enter not into judgement with thy servant, for in thy sight no man living shall be justified.*[20] The holy man Job likewise was a most innocent, and just man, and yet for all that he lived in such exceeding fear all the days of his life, that he reporteth thus of himself: and saith: *Like as he that saileth in the midst of a stormy tempest is in great fear when he seeth the furious raging waves coming upon him: even so have I trembled always before the majesty of almighty God, and my fear hath been so passing great, that I was not able to abide the heavy burthen thereof.*[21] But above all these, the Apostle St. Paul was a very just man, and yet for all that he said thus

18 See Mark 13:30–31.
19 See Acts 24.
20 Ps. 142:2.
21 See Job 31:23.

of himself: *I feel no remorse of conscience of any thing I have done amiss, and yet I accompt not myself safe, and secure, forsomuch as our Lord is he that shall be my judge.*[22]

As if he had said in express words: Many times it may happen, that in our own sight we find ourselves to be without blemish in our works, and yet in the sight of almighty God we be far otherwise. For that which lieth hidden from the eyes of men, is not hidden from the eyes of almighty God. Unto a rude and unskillful painter the work that he hath drawn seemeth to be very perfect: but a conning and skillful painter will find many defects worthy to be noted in it. Now how far greater defects and imperfections shall the most high goodness and wisdom of almighty God find in a creature so evil inclined as man is: *Who* (as Job saith) *drinketh sin, and iniquity, as it were water.*[23] Again, if the sword of almighty God did find so much to be pared of in heaven, how much more shall it find in earth, which bringeth forth nothing else but brambles, and briers? And who is he that hath all the corners of his soul so pure, and clean, but that he shall have need to say with the Prophet: *Ab occultis meis munda me Domine: Cleanse me O Lord from my secret sins.*[24]

Wherefore it behooveth all men to live in great fear and dread of this day of judgement, be their life never so just: seeing the day is so dreadful, our life so faulty, and the Judge so just: and above all, seeing his judgements be so secret, and profound, that no man knoweth what lot shall fall unto him. But (as our savior saith:) *Two shall be in the field, the one shall be taken, and the other forsaken: Two in one bed, the one shall be taken, and the other forsaken: Two grinding in one mill, the one shall be taken, and the other forsaken.*[25] In which words we be given to understand, that of such persons as are all of one same state, and matter of life, some shall be carried up to heaven, and some thrown down into the bottomless pit of hell: insomuch as by this and many other places of the holy scriptures it plainly appeareth, that no man

22 1 Cor. 4:4.
23 Job 15:16.
24 Ps. 18:13.
25 See Matt. 24:40–41; Luke 17:34–35.

can accompt himself secure, and assured to be saved, so long as he liveth in this frail and transitory life.[26]

§. I. How Rigorous the Day of Judgement Shall Be.

To consider well of the greatness of this judgement, thou must first presuppose, that there is no tongue in the world able to express the least part of the troubles that shall be upon this day.

And therefore the Prophet Joel being desirous to speak of the greatness thereof, found his wits and senses so weak, and confounded, that he began to stut and stammer like a child, and to say, A! A! A! What a day shall that be?[27] The like manner of speech used the Prophet Jeremias, when almighty God would send him to preach: to signify that he was an infant, and altogether unable to discharge so great an embassy, as he was appointed by almighty God to do.[28] And the same manner doth the Prophet Joel use even at this time, to give us to understand, that there is no tongue in the world, that will not stut and stammer like a child, when it shall go about to signify what things shall happen upon this dreadful day.

Upon this day almighty God will reduce all such filthiness as the wicked have caused in the world through their wicked works, to his first due form, and comeliness. And as their filthy and wicked acts have been many, and great, even so must the purifying of them be proportionable to the acts committed. And so shall the world be so much beautified by the punishment of the wicked, as it hath been defiled and disfigured through their offences. When a man hath by reason of some great fall put his arm out of joint, the more it is out of joint, the more grief and pain must he afterwards abide, before it can be set in joint again, and brought to his due proper place. Now

---

[26] See Ps. 18:13–14; Job 31:14, 23; Eccles. 9:1; 12:14; Ecclus. 5:5; Dan. 4:24; Matt. 12:36; John 8:31; 15:7, 14; Rom. 2:13; 8:17; 1 Cor. 4:4; 9:27; 10:12; 13:2–3; 2 Cor. 5:10–11; Gal. 5:24; Phil. 2:12; Jas. 2:14–24; 1 Ptr. 1:17; 2:21; 2 Ptr. 1:10; 1 Jn. 2:3–6; 3:7, 24; 4:12; 5:3; Apoc. 3:11; 14:7.

[27] See Joel 1:15.

[28] See Jer. 1:6.

whereas the wicked have disordered all things in this world, and set them out of joint, and wrenched them out of their natural places, when that heavenly reformer shall come to restore the world by punishment of so many disorders, how great shall the punishment be, where so many and so great disorders have been?

This dreadful day is called not only the day of Anger, but also the day of our Lord, as the Prophet Joel termeth it.[29] Giving us thereby to understand, that all other days have been the days of men, in which they have fulfilled their own wills against the will of God, but this day is called the day of our Lord, because upon this day our Lord will do his will against the will of men. Thou dost now swear, and forswear, and blaspheme, and almighty God in this mean while holdeth his peace, and saith nothing unto it: but be thou well assured the day shall come when almighty God will break of his long silence of so many days, and of so many injuries, and will answer for his own honor. So that there be no more but two days in the world: the one is the day of our Lord, and the other is the day of men. Man whiles his day endureth may do whatsoever he listeth, and almighty God will hold his peace, and as it were wink at all his doings. Upon this day the King Sedechias may command the Prophet of God to be cast into a well, and bread to be given unto him by ounces.[30] He may use and abuse the Prophet at his pleasure, and at all those injuries almighty God will hold his peace. But after this day there will come an other day, and almighty God will take king Sedechias, and deprive him of his kingdom: he will destroy Jerusalem, and bring king Sedechias in fetters before the king of Babylon, and there shall all his sons and friends be murdered before his face. There shall he command his eyes (which were preserved to see so many mysteries) to be plucked out of his head: which done, he shall cause him to be carried in fetters to Babylon, and confine him into a prison, there to remain all the days of his life. So that as man hath liberty to do upon his day whatsoever he listeth, without any restraint, or impediment

29 See Joel 1:15.
30 See Jer. 37–38.

at all: even so will almighty God have free liberty to do upon his day whatsoever his will and pleasure shall be, and no man shall be able to let or disturb him.

§. II. Of the Terrible Signs That Shall Go before the Day of the General Judgement.

Finally, if thou desire to understand what manner of day this shall be, consider what signs shall go before it. For by the signs thou shalt perceive what the thing shall be that is signified: as by the evening, and Vigil, thou mayest understand what the feast of the day shall be.

First of all, when that day shall be, no man knoweth: no, not the Angels in heaven, nor yet the son himself (to reveal it to any other) but the father only.[31] Howbeit certain signs shall go before it, whereby men may prognosticate not only of the nearness of the day, but also of the greatness and dreadfulness thereof. For as our Savior saith: Before the coming of this day there shall be great wars and troubles in the world. Nation shall rise against nation, and kingdom against kingdom: And there shall be great earthquakes in many places, and pestilence, and famine, and terrible things appearing in the air, and other great signs, and wonders.[32]

And (which is more dreadful than all this) there shall come that great horrible persecution so oftentimes mentioned in the holy Scriptures, which shall be executed by the most cruel persecutor that ever the Catholic Church hath had, to wit, by Antichrist, who shall impugn the Catholic Church most maliciously, not only with most cruel wars, and horrible torments, but also with apparent and feigned miracles.[33] *Consider now therefore with thyself* (as the blessed holy Pope St. Gregory saith) *what a terrible time that of Antichrist shall be, when the godly martyr shall offer his body to the tormentor: and the tormentor shall work miracles before his face.* To conclude, the tribulation

---

[31] See Mark 13.

[32] See Matt. 24:7.

[33] The Jews shall receive and worship Antichrist for their Messias: as appeareth in John 5:43 and 1 John 2:22.

of these days (as our Savior saith) shall be so great, as the like was never since the beginning of the world, nor never shall be: insomuch that if almighty God of his great mercy did not provide to shorten these days, all flesh should not be saved: But for the elect's sake, the days (of Antichrist) shall be shortened.[34]

After these signs (as this day of the general judgement draweth nearer, and nearer) there shall appear other signs more dreadful than these, in the Sun, in the Moon, and in the Stars. Of which dreadful signs our Lord spake by his Prophet Ezechiel, saying: *I will cause the stars of heaven to be darkened over thee, and I will cover the Sun with a cloud, and the Moon shall not shew forth her light. And I will cause all the lights of heaven to mourn, and lament over thee. And I will send darkness over all the land.*[35] Now when these great signs and alterations shall appear in the heavens, what may we look for upon the earth, which is wholly governed by the heavens? We see in a common wealth, that when the heads that govern it are in any tumult, all the other members and parts thereof are also in a like tumult, and uproar, and the whole commonwealth is tossed and turmoiled with arms, and dissention.

Now if all this body of the world be governed by the virtue and influences of the heavens, in case both the heavens and this body be altered, and out of their natural order, in what ruthful case then shall all the members and parts be, that depend of them? The air shall be full of lightenings, whirlwinds, and blazing stars: The earth shall be full of wide yawning clefts, fearful tremblings, and quakings. And these earthquakes (as it is thought) shall be so great, and violent, that they shall be able to overthrow not only the sumptuous palaces, high towers, and strong Castles, but even the very mountains and rocks themselves shall be also shaken and overwhelmed by them, and quite removed out of their places. But most of all other elements the Sea shall at that time shew greatest rage, and fury, and the waves

34 See Matt. 24:21–22; Mark 13:19–20. Antichrist's reign and persecution shall not continue but three years and a half: as appeareth in Dan. 7:25; 12:7, 11; Apoc. 11:2–3; 13:5.

35 See Ezech. 32:7–8.

thereof shall be so high, and so furious, that it shall seem that they will utterly overwhelm all the whole earth. Such as dwell by the Sea side shall be in great dread, and terror, by reason of the great rising waters: and such as dwell further of shall be wonderfully afraid of the horrible roarings, and noises of it, which shall be so extremely outrageous, that they shall be heard many miles off.

In what a pitiful case then I pray you shall men be in these days? How shall they be astonied, confounded, yea utterly bereaved of their senses, of their speech, and of their taste of all things? Our Savior saith that at this time the people shall be in great anguish, and distress, and that men shall go as though they were withered, and dried up, and had no life in them, by reason of the great fear of those things that shall happen to the world.[36] Then shall they say one to an other: What meaneth this: What do these terrible prognostications signify? What will the world at the length bring forth, that it now swelleth and rageth in such furious wise? What shall the end be of all these so great tossings and alterations of all things? Now after this sort shall men go up and down sore afraid, and dismayed, their hearts failing them, and carrying their arms a cross, and one of them looking pitifully upon an other. And they shall be in so great dread, and fear, beholding one an other to be so far changed, and disfigured, that even that alone were enough to dismay them, although there were nothing else to be feared. All occupations and trades of the world shall then cease every where: and so shall in like manner all study, and desire of purchasing, and gaining. For the greatness of the fear shall hold men's hearts so thoroughly occupied, that they shall not only forget these things, but they shall also forget even to eat, and drink, and to do such things as are necessary for the maintenance and sustentation of their lives: Their chiefest care shall be where to seek out sure and safe places to defend themselves from earthquakes, and from the tempestuous storms of the air, and from the inundations of the Sea. And so men shall go to hide themselves in the caves and dens of wild beasts: And the wild beasts shall seek

[36] See Luke 21.

likewise to save themselves in the lodgings and houses of men. And so all things shall be tossed and turmoiled up side down, and be full of terror, and confusion. The present calamities shall afflict them very sore: but the great dread and fear of those that are to come shall vex them worse, because they know not what the end shall be of such doleful and lamentable beginnings. I want words to declare this matter, as it were requisite to be declared. And all that is said is much less then that which shall be in deed. We see even now by experience when any outrageous tempest riseth in the Sea, or when any stormy whirlwind or earthquake happeneth upon the land, how wonderfully men are dismayed, how they tremble, and be astonied, and how both their strength and wits do fail them. Now then, when the heaven, and earth, the Sea, and the air shall be wholly distempered, and disordered, when in all regions and elements in the world there shall be peculiar storms, and tempests, when the Sun shall threaten with mourning, the Moon with blood, and the Stars with their fallings, who shall be able to eat? Who shall be able to sleep? Who shall be able to take so much as one minute of rest, being compassed on each side with so many outrageous storms, and tempests? O how miserable and unhappy is the state and condition of the wicked, who are threatened with all these fearful prognostications! And contrariwise how blessed is the state of the good, and Godly, unto whom all these things are favors, comforts, and good tidings of the happy prosperity so near at hand approaching then unto them! How joyfully shall they then sing with the Prophet: *God is our refuge, and our strength, and therefore we will not fear though the whole earth be tossed, and turmoiled, and the mountains be removed, and fall into the bottom of the Sea.*[37] Like as you understand (saith our Savior) when the fig tree and all other trees begin to blossom, and to bring forth their fruit, that then the spring time draweth near at hand, even so when ye shall see these things come to pass, then may ye perceive that the kingdom of God is at hand.[38]

---

[37] Ps. 45:2–3.
[38] See Luke 21:29–31.

Then may ye open your eyes, and lift up your head, because the day of your redemption approacheth. O how joyful shall the good and virtuous then be! How well shall they think all their travails, and labors employed? And contrariwise, how woeful and sorrowful shall the wicked be, and how sore shall they then condemn all the steps, and ways, of their sinful lives?

§. III. Of the End of the World: and of the Resurrection of the Dead.

After all these signs shall the coming of the Judge approach near at hand, before whom there shall go an universal flood of fire, which shall burn and consume to ashes all the glory of the world.

This fire shall be to the wicked a beginning of their pain: to the good a beginning of their glory: and unto them that have not made full satisfaction, it shall be a purgatory for their offences. Then shall all the glory of the world have an end. Then shall the movings of the heavens, the course of the planets, and the generation of things cease. Then shall the variety of times, with all other things that depend of the heavens, have an end. And so St. John writeth in the Apocalypse: That he saw a mighty Angel clothed with a bright cloud. His face was like the sun: he had a rainbow for a crown on his head: his feet were like pillars of fire: of the which one he set on the Sea, and the other upon the land. And he saith, that this Angel lifted up his arm towards heaven, and swore by him that liveth everlastingly world without end, that from thenceforth there should be no more time.[39] That is to say: that there should be no moving of the heavens, nor of any other thing that is governed by them. And (which is more than all this) no place of penance, nor any time to merit or demerit for the life to come.

After this fire there shall come (as the Apostle saith) an Archangel with great power, and majesty, and he shall sound a trumpet,[40]

[39] See Apoc. 10.

[40] See 1 Thess. 4.

(to wit: a great and terrible voice,) whose sound shall be heard over all the parts of the world, and with this trumpet he shall summon all nations to come to the general judgement. This is that fearful voice, whereof St. Jerome speaketh: saying, *Whether I eat, or drink, or whatsoever I do, me seemeth always that I hear that voice sounding in mine ears, which shall say, rise up all ye that are dead, and come to judgement.* Who shall appeal from this summons? Who shall be able to avoid this judgement? Whose heart shall not tremble and quake for fear, at the terrible sound of this voice? This voice shall take from death all her spoils, and cause her to restore again all that she hath taken away from the world. And so St. John saith, that then, *The Sea shall restore the dead bodies, which it hath had. And likewise both death and hell shall restore all those bodies that they have.*[41] Now what a wonderful sight shall that be, to see the Sea, and the earth, to bring forth in all parts such variety of bodies, and to see so many huge armies, and so many sorts and diversities of nations and people assemble together? There shall the Alexanders appear: There the Zerxes, and Artaxerxes: There the Dariies, and the Emperors of Rome, and the most mighty Kings and puissant Princes of the world, with an other manner of habit, and behavior, and with other kind of thoughts, much differing from those, that they had in this life. To be short, there shall all the children of Adam meet together, every one to give up an accompt of his own life, and to be judged according to his works.

Howbeit although all persons shall rise again at that day never to die any more, yet shall there be a great difference between bodies, and bodies. For the bodies of the just shall rise very beautiful and bright like the Sun. But the bodies of the wicked shall rise very black, and filthy, even like unto death itself. Now what a great joy shall it be then unto the souls of the just, to see their desire now fully accomplished? What a joy shall it be, to see themselves after so long a banishment to be united and joined everlastingly in company with their most dear and loving brethren? With what joy may the soul say then unto the body? O my body, and faithful companion, that hast holpen me to

41 See Apoc. 20.

gain this crown, that hast so oftentimes fasted, watched, and suffered with me the painful strokes and lashes of discipline, the travail of poverty, the cross of penance, and the contradictions and reproaches of the world? How often times hast thou spared the meat from thine own belly to give it to the poor? How often hast thou lacked cloths thyself to clothe the naked? How often hast thou renounced and lost thine own right, and title, for that thou wouldst not break peace, and be at dissention with thy neighbor? Wherefore it is meet that thou shouldest now be partaker of this heavenly treasure, seeing thou hast holpen me to gain the same: And it is meet that thou shouldest be my companion in this my glory, seeing thou hast been my companion in all my pains, and labors. Then shall these two faithful friends be joined together in one subject, not (as they were in this life) with contrary appetites, and desires, but with a league of perpetual peace, and conformity. So as they may sing, and say for ever. *Behold what a good and joyful thing it is for brethren to dwell together in one.*[42] But contrariwise, what a heaviness and grief shall it then be to the soul of the damned person, when he shall see his body in an ugly form, as there it shall be given unto him, to wit: black, filthy, stinking, and horrible. Then shall he say: O cursed body! O beginning, and end of my pains, and sorrows! O cause of my damnation! Now art thou no more my companion, but mine enemy: Now art thou no more my helper, but my persecutor: Now art thou no more my habitation, but the chain and snare of my destruction. O cursed taste! How dearly do I pay now for thy delicacies, and delights? O stinking flesh, that hast thus brought me to these painful horrible torments, by yielding to thy lusts, and pleasures! What? Alas! Is this the body for whose sake I committed so many sins? Were these the delights of this body, that caused me utterly to cast away myself? Was it for this stinking muckhill, that I have lost for ever the kingdom of heaven? Was it for this vile and filthy carcass, that I have lost for ever the glory of life everlasting? O ye infernal furies rise up now against me, and tear and rent me in pieces, for I have well deserved these horrible torments!

---

42 Ps. 132:1.

Cursed be the day of my unfortunate birth, seeing my hap must be so miserable, as to suffer everlasting torments in the most horrible pit of hell, for so short pleasures, and delights.

These and other more desperate words shall the damned soul speak unto that body which she loved so exceedingly in this transitory world. But tell me O miserable soul, why dost thou now so much abhor that thing, which heretofore thou lovedst so well? Is not this flesh thy dearly beloved? Is not this the belly, which thou madest thy God? Is not this the face, which thou didst keep so charily from the sun, and wind? Is not this the visage, which thou didst paint with so many artificial colors? Are not these the arms, and fingers, which glistered with rings of gold, and diamonds? Is not this the body, for whose sake search was made both by land, and Sea, to furnish a table for it with all delicate and dainty dishes, to have a fine and soft bed, to procure curious and costly garments? Who hath now so altered thy affection? Who hath made thy body to look now so horrible, and ugly, which before seemed so fair, and amiable? Thou seest here now Christian brother, what end the glory of the world hath, with all the vain pleasures and delights of the body.

§. IV. Of the Coming of the Judge: of the Matter of the Judgement: and of the Witnesses, and Accusers, That Shall Be There against the Wicked.

Now when all mankind shall be raised again, and assembled together in one place, expecting the coming of the Judge, then shall he whom almighty God hath appointed to be judge over the quick and the dead come down.[43] And like as at his first coming he came with very great humility, and meekness, inviting men upon peace, and calling them unto penance: even so at his second coming he shall come with very great majesty, and glory, accompanied with all the powers and principalities of heaven, threatening all those with the fury of his anger, that refused to use the meekness of his mercy. At this time the

43 See Acts 10.

fear and terror of the wicked shall be so great, that as the Prophet Isaias saith: they shall seek the clefts of stones, and the hollow places of the rocks, to hid themselves therein, for the great fear they shall have of our Lord, and of the glory of his majesty, when he cometh to judge the world.[44] To conclude, this fear shall be so great, that as St. John saith, both the heavens and the earth shall fly from the presence of the judge, and shall find no place where to hide themselves.[45] Now O ye heavens, why do ye fly away? What have ye done? Why are ye afraid? And if by the heavens be understood the blessed spirits that are in heaven: O ye blessed spirits that were created and confirmed in grace, why do ye fly away? What have ye done? Why are ye afraid? Undoubtedly they are not afraid for any danger that is towards themselves, but they be afraid to behold in the judge such a great majesty, and indignation: the greatness whereof shall be able to strike all the heavens with terror, and admiration. When the Sea is outrageous, and tempestuous, even he that standeth safe upon the shore is in a kind of fear, and admiration. When the father goeth like a lion about his house in punishing his bond slave, his innocent son is also afraid, although he know right well that his father's rage is not bent against him, but against the slave. Now what shall the wicked do at this time, when even the just shall be so greatly afraid? If the heavens fly for fear, what shall the earth do? And if those that be wholly spirit do tremble, and quake, what shall they do that have been wholly flesh? *And if* (as the Prophet saith) *the mountains shall melt in this day before the face of almighty God*:[46] What stony hard hearts then have we, that for all this be nothing at all moved?

Before the Judge there shall come that royal standard of the cross, to be a witness of the redemption and remedy which almighty God sent to the world: and that the world would not receive it. And so the holy cross shall there justify the cause of almighty God, and leave the wicked void of all manner of comfort, and excuse. *Then shall*

[44] See Is. 2:19.
[45] See Apoc. 20.
[46] See Is. 64.

all nations of the earth (saith our Savior) *weep, and lament:*[47] and they all shall strike and beat upon their breasts. O how great cause shall they then have to weep, and wail! They shall weep, because at that time they can neither do penance, nor fly from the justice of almighty God, nor appeal from his sentence. They shall bewail their sins past, their shame present, and the torments that are to come. They shall bewail their miserable hap, their unfortunate birth, and their cursed end. For these and many other causes they shall weep and wail very bitterly: and as persons wholly dismayed and fettered in all parts, and without all manner of comfort, and remedy, they shall wring their hands, and strike themselves upon their breasts.

Then shall the Judge make a division between the evil, and the good: and place the goats at his left hand, and the sheep at his right hand.[48] O how happy and blessed shall those persons be, that shall be thought worthy to have a place among those elected sheep! O Lord, I most humbly beseech thee, let me have tribulation here in this world: Punish me here: cut me in pieces here: burn me here, so that I may there be placed at thy right hand. Then shall the general judgement begin to be solemnized: and the causes of each one shall be thoroughly scanned, and examined: According as the Prophet Daniel writeth in these words. *I stood* (saith he) *attentively, and I saw certain seats set in their places, and the ancient of years sat down, whose garment was white as snow, and the hair of his head like the pure wool. The throne wherein he sat was like flames of fire, and the wheels thereof like burning fire. And a river of raging fire issued and came forth from before him. Thousand thousands were attendant to serve him, and ten hundred thousand thousands stood waiting before him, etc. I beheld all this in the vision of the night, and I saw one coming in the clouds, who seemed to be the son of man.*[49] Hitherto are the words of the Prophet Daniel. Whereunto St. John addeth, and saith. *I saw all the dead both great and small standing before this throne, and there the books were opened: and an other*

---

47 Matt. 24:30.

48 See Matt. 25.

49 Dan. 7:9–10, 13.

book opened, which is the book of life, and the dead were judged according to the contents in those books, according to their works.[50]

Behold here dear Christian brother the measure whereby thou shalt be judged. Behold here the tax, and prices, whereby all things that thou dost shall be valued, and esteemed, and not by the fond judgement of the world, which hath the false and counterfeit weights of Canaan in their hands, in whose balance virtue and vice are judged to be of small weight, and accompt[51]. In these books are written all our whole life, and that with such care, and diligence, that a word hath no sooner passed thy mouth, but it is forthwith noted, and set in his proper register.

But of what things (trow ye) will the Judge require an accompt of us? O Lord (saith Job) *thou hast numbered all the steps of my life.*[52] Certainly, there shall not be somuch as one idle word, nor one only thought whereof an accompt will not be required in that judgement.[53] Yea, and not only of those things that we either think, or do, but also of those that we leave undone: of such things I mean, as we are bound to do. If thou say at the day of Judgement: O Lord, I have not sworn: the Judge will answer, that thy son, or thy servant hath sworn, whom thy duty was to have chastised, and corrected. And we shall give an accompt not only of our evil works, but also even of our good works, with what intention and after what manner we did them. Finally, as St. Gregory saith: *An accompt shall there be required of us of every point and moment of our life, how and after what sort we have spent them.* Considering therefore that such a strait accompt shall be required of us, how happeneth it, that we that believe this as a most certain truth, do nevertheless live with such security, and negligence as we do? Wherein do we put our affiance? Wherewithal do we persuade and flatter ourselves in the midst of so many dreadful perils, and dangers? How cometh this to pass, that those persons that have most cause to fear this dreadful day, do least fear it, and those

50 Apoc. 20:12.
51 See Osee 12.
52 Job 31:4.
53 See Matt. 12:36.

that have least cause to fear it, do live in greatest fear thereof? Holy Job was a just man (for so almighty God witnessed of him with his own mouth,)[54] and yet for all this he lived in so great fear and dread of his accompt at the day of Judgement, that he said: *What shall I do, when almighty God cometh to judge, and when he beginneth to question with me, what answer shall I make unto him?*[55] Surely these be words that proceed from a very sore afflicted, and troubled heart. *What shall I do,* saith he: As if he had said: One care I have that troubleth me continually: One nail I carry always fixed in my heart, that will not suffer me to take any rest. What shall I do? Whither shall I go? What answer shall I make, when almighty God shall enter into judgement with me? But O holy and blessed man Job, why art thou thus afraid? Why art thou thus troubled, and vexed? Art not thou he that said: *I have been a father unto the poor, an eye unto the blind, and feet unto the lame.*[56] Art not thou he that said, that *In all thy life time thy heart never reproved thee of any wicked deed.*[57] Now being a man of so great innocency, why O holy Job art thou thus afraid? Truly the cause is for that this holy man knew right well that almighty God looked not with fleshly eyes, and that he judged not according to the judgement of men, in whose eyes often times that thing shineth very gay, and bright, which in the sight of almighty God is very abominable. Thou art O holy Job very just indeed, yea even for this cause thou art very just, because thou livest in so great fear. This fear of this holy man Job (my dear brethren) condemneth our false security. These words of his overthrow our vain confidence. For which of us hath at any time respect of this care of our dreadful accompt at the day of Judgement once refrained from his dinner, or supper, or broken his sleep? Whereas those devout godly persons that think hereupon as they ought to think, do often times lose their sleep, and their appetite to their meat, yea, and some times more than that also. We read in the lives of the ancient holy fathers, that when one of those holy men

54 See Job 2:3.
55 Job 31:14.
56 See Job 29:15–16.
57 See Job 27:6.

saw one of his scholars laughing, he reprehended him for it, and said: *What? Knowing as thou dost, that thou must yield an accompt to almighty God before heaven and earth, art thou that notwithstanding so bold as to laugh?* This holy father thought that that man which looked earnestly for this dreadful accompt could hardly laugh.

Now as touching accusers, and witnesses, there shall not want in this behalf. For our own very consciences shall be witnesses and cry out against us: All creatures which we have abused shall be witnesses against us: And above all, our lord himself whom we have offended shall be also a witness against us: As he himself hath signified by one of his Prophets, saying: *I will be a swift witness against enchanters, adulterers, perjured persons, and against those that seek cavels to defeat the laborer of his day wages, and against them that do evil intreat the widow, and Orphan, and oppress pilgrims, and strangers. For they do not fear me, saith our Lord.*[58]

Neither shall there want accusers against the wicked. For the devil himself shall be a sufficient accuser: who (as St. Agustine writeth) shall allege very exactly before the judge his right, and title, and shall say unto him. O most just and righteous judge, thou canst not of justice but give sentence and adjudge these wicked traitors to be mine: forsomuch as they have been always mine, and have in all things fulfilled my will. Thine they were, (I grant,) because thou didst create them, and make them after thy Image, and likeness, and redeem them with thy blood. But they have defaced thy Image, and put on mine. They have refused thine obedience, and embraced mine. They have despised thy commandments, and observed mine: They have lived with my spirit. They have imitated my works. They have walked in my steps. And in each thing have followed my counsels. Consider how much more they have been mine than thine, as appeareth herein, that notwithstanding I gave them nothing, I promised them nothing, nor laid my shoulders on the Cross for them, yet have they always obeyed my commandments, and not thine. If I commanded them to swear, and forswear, to rob, and to kill, to commit adultery,

[58] See Mal. 3:5.

fornication, simony, and usury, and to deny thy holy name, all this they did willingly, and with great facility. If I commanded them to bestow their lands, their goods, their life and their soul, for a point of honor, and estimation, which I persuaded them in any wise to maintain, or for a false delight whereunto I invited them, they did forthwith very willingly hazard all this for my sake. But for thee, that art their God, their creator and their redeemer, that gavest them their lands, their goods, their health, and life, that hast offered unto them thy grace, and promised them thy glory, and above all this, hast suffered most cruel death upon the cross for them, they never took the least pain and labor in the world. How oftentimes hast thou come to their doors in great poverty, nakedness, and full of sores? And what alms hadst thou of them, but a wayward answer, and shutting their doors in a great fury and anger upon thee, they being then more careful to feed their hawks, their dogs, and their horses, and to clothe their walls with hangings of tapestry, silk, and gold, than to relieve, clothe, and help thee? Wherefore seeing thou art a most just Judge, and knowest that this is most certainly true, the very order of justice requireth, that they should be now punished for their injuries, and contempts, done to so great a majesty.

Now this accusation being found most true, Christ the judge will pronounce that terrible sentence against the wicked, saying: *Depart ye cursed into the everlasting fire, which is prepared for Satan, and his angels. For I was hungry, and ye gave me not to eat: I was thirsty, and ye gave me not to drink: etc.*[59] And then shall the good go to life everlasting, and the wicked to fire everlasting. Now who is able to express what an intolerable anguish, and grief, it will be to the damned persons, when they shall hear those most terrible words pronounced against them? There shall they cry out to the mountains, to come, and fall upon them, and to the hills to cover them. There shall they blaspheme, and renay, and open their sacrilegious mouths even against almighty God. There shall they continually curse the day of their birth, and their unhappy state. There shall their day wholly end.

[59] Matt. 25:41–42.

There shall their glory be finished. There shall their prosperity be utterly extinguished, and overthrown. There shall the day of their horrible pains and griefs begin in their bodies to continue for ever, and ever. As St. John signifieth in his Apocalypse under the name of Babylon, in these words: The kings of the earth shall weep and wail over themselves, that have enjoyed the pleasures and delights of Babylon, and have committed fornication with her, when they shall see the smoke that riseth up from their tormentors, and they shall endeavor to keep themselves afar of for fear of them, and say: Woe, woe, be unto that great City of Babylon, for in one hour is her judgement come. And the merchants of the earth shall lament, because now there be none to buy their merchandises of gold, and silver, and precious stones. And they shall lament over her, and say: woe, woe, be unto that great City, that was clothed with garments of purple, scarlet, silks, and velvets, and was covered over with gold, and precious stones. For in one hour all this great riches shall perish, and come to naught.[60]

Wherefore O my dear Christian brethren, if this must pass in this wise, let us provide for ourselves (I beseech you) whilst we have time here in this life, and let us follow the counsel which he giveth to us, who would rather be our advocate, than our judge: and there is none that knoweth better what is required for that day, than he who must be the judge of our cause. Christ then our judge teacheth us briefly what we ought to do, in these words: *Take heed* (saith he in the gospel of St. Luke chap.21.ver.34–36.) *that your hearts be not burthened with over much eating, and drinking, and with the cares of this life: and beware that that sudden day come not upon you at unawares. For it shall come like a snare upon all that dwell upon the face of all the earth. And therefore watch and pray at all times, that ye may be worthy to be delivered from all these evils that are to come, and that ye may appear before the son of man.* Now considering this my dear brethren, come I most heartily pray you, and let us arise whiles we have time out of this so heavy sleep, before that dark night of death fall upon us, and

60 See Apoc. 18.

before this dreadful cay come, whereof the Prophet Malachy chap.3. saith: Now he cometh, and who dare abide his coming? And who shall be able to behold the day thereof? Undoubtedly that man shall be able to abide this dreadful day of judgement, that shall prevent the judge, and judge himself before hand, according as St. Paul forewarneth and counseleth us.[61]

[61] See 1 Cor. 11:31.

FRIDAY NIGHT

Of the Pains of Hell.

THIS day (when thou hast made the sign of the Cross, and prepared thyself hereunto,) thou hast to meditate upon the pains of hell: to the intent that as well by means of this meditation, as by the former, thy soul may be the more confirmed in the fear of God, and abhorring of sin, as we have there declared.

These pains, (as St. Bonaventure saith) are to be conceived under some such corporal forms, and similitudes, as the saints have taught us. Wherefore it shall do well to imagine the place of hell (as he himself saith) to be as it were an obscure and dark lake under the earth, or a passing deep pit full of fire, or as a horrible and dark City wholly burning with terrible flames of fire, in which none other noise were there to be heard, but only the furious raging of hellish tormentors, and ruthful lamentations of damned persons tormented with continual weeping, and wailing, and gnashing of teeth.

Now in this cursed place there be two principal kinds of pains. The one, which the divines call, *Poenam sensus*: a sensible pain: And the other, *Poenam damni*: the pain of the loss of all losses. As touching the first pain, to wit, the pain of sense: consider that there shall be no sense, neither within nor without a man, but that it shall suffer his proper torment. For like as the wicked have offended God with all their members, and senses, and have made armour of them all to serve sin: even so will he ordain, that they all shall there be tormented, each one of them with his peculiar torment, and pay according to his desert. There shall the wanton and lecherous eyes be tormented with the terrible ugly sight of devils. The ears, with the confusion of such horrible cries, and lamentations, as shall there be heard. The nose, with the intolerable stench of that filthy and loathsome place. The taste, with a most ravenous hunger, and thirst. The touching, and all the members of the body, with extreme cold, and fire. The imagination shall be tormented with conceiving of the griefs present. The memory, by calling to mind the pleasures past. And the understanding, by considering what benefits are lost, and what miseries are to come.

Finally, there shall all the miseries and torments that possibly may be imagined be heaped together upon the damned person. For as St. Gregory saith. *There shall be cold intolerable, fire unquenchable, the worm of conscience that cannot die, and a most horrible stench that cannot be abidden. There shall be palpable darkness: whips of tormentors: vision of foul fiends, and ugly devils: confusion of sins: and desperation of all goodness.* Now tell me, I pray you, if the least of all these pains that are suffered here in this world though it were but for a very small time, do seem notwithstanding so intolerable a thing, what shall it be, to suffer there at one time all these multitude of horrible torments, in all the members, and senses, both inward, and outward, and that not for the space of one night alone, nor of a thousand nights, but for ever, and ever, during infinite worlds. What sense, what words, what judgement is there in the world, that is able to conceive and express this matter as it is indeed?

And yet this is not the greatest pain that is there suffered. For there is an other pain far greater without any comparison than all these: to wit, that pain which the divines term, *Poenam damni*: the pain of loss, or deprivation. Which is to be deprived of the sight of almighty God, and of his glorious company, for ever, and ever. And albeit this pain be common to all the damned persons, yet shall it be much more grievous unto them, that have had better means and opportunity than others, whereby to enjoy this felicity: As namely all Christians to whom the Gospel hath been preached, and especially all naughty religious persons, and priests, who as they have had greater means and provocations to obtain this everlasting felicity: even so shall they be more vexed and grieved for the loss thereof.

These are the pains that do generally appertain to all the damned. But besides these general pains, there be other particular pains, which every one of them shall also suffer according to the quality of his sin. For there shall be one kind of pain for the proud man, an other for the envious: one for the covetous, and an other for the lecherous: and so in like manner for all other sins. In which punishment the wisdom and justice of almighty God shall wonderfully appear, in that among such an infinite number of sins, and sinners, he shall be able to judge very perfectly all the excess of each one, and shall measure unto them as it were in a balance the pains proportionable to their sins. As the Wiseman saith: *The judgements of our Lord are by weight, and measure.*[1] O what a doleful thing shall it be to the wicked, when they shall see how almighty God will then pay them home in the very joints!

And what a delight shall it then be to the just, when they shall see such a wonderful just proportion observed, in allotting pains, and torments, among such a great multitude of sins! There shall the pain be taxed according to the pleasure and delight received. And the confusion according to the presumption, and pride: The poverty according to the superfluity, and abundance. The hunger and thirst according to the gluttony and delicate dainty fare in their life past. And in this wise did almighty God command that naughty woman to be punished, which is mentioned in the Apocalypse, who sat upon the waters of the Sea, holding a Cup in her hand full of poisoned pleasures, and delights. Against whom was thundered out from heaven that terrible sentence, which said: *Look how much she hath extolled herself, and enjoyed her pleasures, and delights: even so proportionably give her torments, and wailing, and lamentation.*[2]

---

1 Prov. 16:11.
2 Apoc. 18:7.

Unto all these pains and torments there is added an eternity or everlastingness of suffering them. And this is as it were the seal and key of them all. For all the rest were yet somewhat tolerable, if they might have some end. Forsomuch as nothing is great that hath an end. But to be tormented with most horrible pains that have neither end, nor ease, nor mitigation, nor declination, nor change, nor hope that ever they will finish, and have an end, neither the pains, nor he that giveth them, nor he that suffereth them, but to be as it were a perpetual banishment never to be remitted, this is a matter able to make a man besides himself, that should consider it deeply, and with good attention.

Of this eternity and everlasting suffering of these pains and torments in hell, cometh that horrible hatred, which the damned have against almighty God, and those blasphemies which they shall utter with great despiteful rage against him. For when they shall be in utter despair of his amity, and friendship, when they shall know that they shall never be received again into his grace, and favor, and that none of all their most grievous and horrible torments shall ever be diminished, or assuaged, again, when they shall consider that almighty God is he, that doth thus torment, and punish them, and that it is he, that fettereth them from above, and keepeth them prisoners in that fiery tormenting chain, they will be in such an exceeding anger, and rage, against him, that they will never cease day, nor night, blaspheming his holy name.

The Fifth Treatise: Of the Consideration of the Pains of Hell: Wherein the Former Meditation is Declared More at Large.

The consideration of the pains of hell is greatly profitable for divers and sundry respects. First, it moveth us to sustain the labors and austerity of penance. As we read that it moved the blessed holy man St. Jerome, who saith of himself, that by reason of the great fear he conceived of the terrible pains and most grievous torments of hell, he condemned himself to do that austere penance, which he writeth he did in the desert.

It helpeth us also to overcome the temptations of the enemy, when at the first entry of any evil thought, we do forthwith call to mind the horror of these pains. For by this mean we do quench the flame of the delight (before it burn) with the remembrance of the horrible flames of hell fire, which shall burn everlastingly. According hereunto it is written of one of those ancient fathers, that lived in the desert, that being upon a time tempted by the enemy of mankind with an evil thought, he laid his hand upon certain burning coals, to try whether he could abide that little heat, and perceiving that he was not able to abide it, he said unto himself: What? If I can not abide this little heat for so short a time, how shall I be able to abide the horrible fire of hell, which shall endure for ever, and ever, world without end?

This consideration helpeth also to provoke and stir up in our hearts the fear of God, which is the beginning of wisdom, and the original of charity: and next after charity itself it is the greatest bridle we can have to keep us from all sin, and wickedness. Above all this, this consideration helpeth very much to make us to be afraid of sin, considering what a miserable reward is ordained for it, to wit, death everlasting. Wherefore it is much to be marveled how the Christians that do both believe and openly confess this to be true, dare commit any one deadly sin against almighty God. Two great wonders have happened in the world in these kind of things. The one is, that whereas our Savior hath wrought so many miracles as he did here among men, there be yet a number of men that do not believe in him. The other is, that of such as be Christians, and do believe in him, there be yet nevertheless so many of them that dare offend him. Certainly, it was a wonderful matter, that when our Savior among other wonders had wrought that great miracle in raising up Lazarus from death, when he had been dead for the space of four days, yet there were many of them that were there present at the doing thereof, that would not believe in him.[3] And it is also wonderful, that whereas men do now believe by reason of his preaching, that there is pain and glory everlasting, (all this belief, and preaching notwithstanding,) there be yet so many Christians that dare offend him. It is a wonderful matter to see after so great miracles so great infidelity. And it is no less wonderful also, to see after so great faith such corrupt and wicked life.

But because this proceedeth rather of the want of consideration, than of the want of faith, it is therefore a very profitable exercise, to consider and weigh diligently those things that our faith telleth us: to the end that by understanding the grievousness of the pains of hell, we may live more warily, and be the more afraid to commit any deadly sin, whereby to deserve such great and everlasting pains.

§. I. Of Two Kinds of Pains That Are in Hell.

And although the pains in hell be innumerable, yet they all in conclusion (as we have said) are reduced to two. Which are, *Poena sensus*: and *Poena damni*: the pain of sense, and the pain of loss. The pain of sense, is that which tormenteth the senses and bodies of the damned. And the pain of loss, is to be deprived for ever of the sight and company of almighty God. These two kinds of pains are answerable to two enormities, and disorders, that are in sin: whereof one is the inordinate love of the creature: and the other is the contempt of the creator. Now unto these two enormities do answer these two kinds of pains in hell. To the love and sensual delight which is taken in the creature, doth answer the pain of sense: that like as the sense hath taken delight against the commandment of almighty God, even so with the grief of the pain it may make recompence for the enormity of his offence. And to the contempt of God doth answer the leesing of God for evermore. For seeing that man doth first forsake God, reason it is, that he should likewise be forsaken for ever of God. And because among these two evils, the last (which is the contempt of

3 See John 11:43–46.

God) is without all comparison greater than the first, therefore the pain of loss, which is answerable to this iniquity, is without all comparison far greater than the pain of sense.

And to begin now with the pains of the outward senses. The first pain is the horrible fire in hell, which is of such a great vehement heat, and strength, that (as St. Augustine saith:) *This fire here in this world in comparison of it is as it were but a painted fire.*

This fire shall torment not only the bodies of the damned, but even the souls also, And it shall torment them in such sort, that it shall not consume them. Which is so provided, to the intent that the pain may be everlasting, and continue for ever, and ever. The which everlasting continuance (as St. Augustine saith) is wrought by a special miracle. For almighty God (who hath given to all things their natural properties) hath given this special property unto the fire of hell, that it shall in such wise burn, and torment, that it shall not consume.

Consider then what an intolerable pain it shall be to the damned to be always lying in such an horrible everlasting tormenting bed, as this is. And that thou mayest the better conceive the same, imagine with thyself what a grievous pain it would be unto thee, if thou shouldest be cast into a great scalding caldron, when it boileth most fervently, and is in greatest heat, or into some hot glowing oven, such a one as that was, which Nabuchodonosor caused to be set a fire in Babylon, the flames whereof ascended forty and nine Cubits in height.[4] And hereby shalt thou have some kind of conjecture and guess of that raging hot fire which is in hell. For if the fire here in this world which (as we have said is in comparison of that fire, but as it were a painted fire,) do so sore burn, and torment, what shall that fire in hell do, which is a very lively tormenting fire indeed? Me thinketh it were not needful to pass any further in the consideration of the pains of hell, but even to leave here, if a man would stay himself a little while in consideration of this point, and make a station

4 See Dan. 3.

here, until such time as he hath considered this matter, as the thing itself requireth.

Unto this pain is joined an other directly contrary unto it, although no less intolerable, that is, an horrible extreme cold, far exceeding without comparison all the cold in this world, which shall be given as a miserable refreshing unto those that burn in that raging fire. And they shall pass (as it is written in Job) from the snowy waters, unto the fiery heats:[5] that there might be no kind of torments whereof they should not taste, that would be tasting of every kind of wanton pleasure, and delight.

And they shall not only be tormented with extreme fire, and cold, but also by the very devils themselves, which shall torment them with most horrible shapes of wild beasts, and terrible monsters, wherein they shall appear unto them. And they shall with their most horrible and ugly looks torment the adulterous, and lecherous eyes, and such as have painted themselves with artificial colors, to become the beautiful snares, and nets of Satan.

This pain of the horrible and ugly sight of devils, is far greater than any man can imagine. For if it be evidently known unto us, that some persons have lost their wits, and that some have been also stricken stark dead by means of the dreadful sight or imagination of fearful things, yea, and that some times the very suspicion thereof alone hath caused many men to tremble and quake in such sort, that the very hair of their heads did stare, and stand up an end: what shall the terror and fear of that dark lake be, which is full of so many horrible fiends, and dreadful hellish monsters, as there the damned persons shall behold with their eyes. And we may the better consider how ugly and horrible the form of the devil is, in that almighty God himself describeth him unto us by such terrible shapes in the holy scriptures. As in the book of Job he saith thus: Who shall discover the face of his garment? And who shall be so hardy as to look into his mouth? And who shall open the gates wherewith his face is covered? His teeth are terrible round about. His body is as it were a shield of

5 See Job 24.

steel covered all over with scales, and that so close riveted, and joined together, that not so much as a little air can pierce through them. His sneezing is like a lightning of fire, and his eyes are glowing red, like the eyelids of the morning. He casteth out of his mouth flakes of fire, like burning torches: and out of his nostrils reeketh smoke, as it were from a boiling pot. With his breath he is able to set coals a fire, and raging flames do issue out of his mouth.[6] Now what a terrible sight will this be to the damned persons in hell, to behold such an horrible and ugly monster, as is here figured unto us by these similitudes.

Unto the torment of the eyes is added an other very terrible pain for torment of the nose, to wit: an intolerable stench, which shall be there ordained to punish carnal and worldly persons, that used sweet savours and perfumes superfluously here in this life. And so doth almighty God threaten by his Prophet Isaias, saying: Because the daughters of Sion are haughty, and walk with stretched out necks, and with rolling eyes, walking and mincing as they go, and making a tinkling with their feet, because they make ostentation of their pomp and riches among the poor, and naked, therefore our Lord will pluck of their hair from their heads, with all their other profane attires, and give them in steed of their sweet odors, horrible stench: and in steed of their gorgeous girdle, a rope: and in steed of their curled hair, a bald skull: and in steed of their stomacher, a rough haircloth.[7] This is the pain that is due unto the odoriferous savours, and gay ornaments of worldly men, and women.

That we may the better conceive somewhat of this kind of pain, consider that terrible kind of torment which a certain cruel Tyrant invented, to put men to death withal, who took a dead body, and caused it to be laid a long upon him that was living, and binding the dead body and the living body very fast together he let them continue both joined thus together, until such time as the dead body had killed the living body with the filthy stench, and vermin, that issued from it. Now if this seem to thee so horrible a torment, what a torment

---

6 See Job 41.
7 See Is. 3.

shall that be (trowest thou) that shall proceed from the stench of all the bodies of the damned, and from that abominable place, where the wicked shall remain in a most horrible continual stench for evermore. There shall those works of Isaias be verified in every one of the damned: Thy pride sinketh down into hell, and there fell thy dead body: the worm is spread under thee, and the crawling worms do cover thee.[8]

And if this pain be appointed for the nose, with what pains shall the ears be tormented wherewith greater sins are committed? The ears shall be tormented with hearing of perpetual horrible cries, clamors, lamentations, and blasphemies, which shall sound in that place. For like as in heaven there shall be none other sound heard, but only a continual Alleluia, and praises of almighty God: even so shall there none other sound be heard in this infernal house of tormentors, but only blasphemies, cursings, and bannings of almighty God, and a disordered horrible melody of infinite jarring noises, roaring, crying, squeaking, and howling, at the terrible sound of the hammers, and strokes of the hellish tormentors, wherein shall such confusion, and variety of noises, such great howlings, and lamentations, among all of that miserable prison, that all the noise that was made at the destruction of Troy, or burning of Rome, was nothing in comparison of that, which shall be heard among the damned in hell.

And that thou mayest conceive somewhat of this horrible pain, imagine with thyself that thou didst pass by a very great deep valley, that were full of an infinite number of prisoners, some hurt, some wounded, and some sick, and that they were all crying, roaring, and howling, each one in horrible wise after his manner, both men, and women, young, and old: tell me I pray thee, what wouldst thou think of this so great roaring, and confusion? Now what may we think of that most horrible crying and roaring in hell, of such an infinite number of damned persons, which shall do nothing else but cry, and roar, blaspheme, and renye almighty God

---

8 See Is. 14:11.

and his Saints everlastingly? What Galley is there in the world so full fraught with renegades, and bond-slaves, as that horrible place of hell is? These are the matins which there are sung. This is the miserable chapel of the prince of darkness. These be his musicians, and singing men. Of whose brotherhood and fraternity shall all slanderers, and backbiters be, with all such as have given ear to the lies of the enemy.

Neither shall the tongue and delicate taste fail of their torments in hell. For what a great thirst was that, which the rich glutton mentioned in the Gospel suffered among the flames of his torments? What doleful cries and clamors did he make to the holy patriarch Abraham, requesting of him but only one drop of water, to cool his tongue, that burned so terribly?[9]

§. II. Of the Torments of the Inward Senses, and Powers of the Soul.

All these pains of the outward senses of the body are certainly very grievous. But the pains of the inward senses of the soul shall be much more grievous. For those inward senses shall be more or less tormented, according as the sinners have been more or less negligent in this life in eschewing the occasions of sins. First of all therefore the imagination shall there be tormented with such a vehement apprehension of those pains, that it shall not be able to think upon any thing else, but only upon the pains that they suffer. For if we see by experience, that when a grief is very intensive, and sharp, we be not able (though we would) to separate our cogitation from the same, because the very grief itself occupieth the imagination so vehemently, that it can not think upon any other thing, but only upon that which is the cause of our grief: how much more may we assure ourselves this to be true in hell, where the grief and pain is without all comparison much more intolerable, than all the griefs and pains of this world? By this mean therefore shall the imagination continually quicken and

9 See Luke 16.

renew the grief: and likewise the grief the imagination: and so the torment of the damned person shall be renewed and increased on every side. These shall be the continual meditations of them, that would not (whiles they lived) call to mind these pains. So as they that would not think upon these pains here, and so by thinking upon them bridle their affections in this life, shall suffer them there as a punishment for their offence.

The memory shall likewise torment the damned persons, when they shall there call to remembrance their old felicity, and prosperous state, and withal the pleasures and delights of the life past, for which they do then abide such horrible torments. There shall they plainly perceive how dearly they pay for their miserable gluttony, and delicate belly cheer, and what a sharp sauce is ordained for their dainty sugared morsels, which seemed before so sweet and delightful unto them. Among all kinds of adversities, one of the greatest is (as a Wise man saith) to have been once in prosperity, and afterwards to fall into misery. Now when the rich and mighty personages of this transitory world do look backward, and call to mind their former prosperity, and abundance of their lives past: when they see how after that abundance there succeedeth such a great bareness, and dearth, that they shall not have so much as one only drop of cold water given unto them: when they see all their pleasures turned into pains, all their delicacies into miseries, all their sweet perfumes into loathsome stenches, all their music into lamentation, what torment can be so great as the very remembrance of these things shall be at that time unto them.

Howbeit they shall yet have a far greater torment, when they shall compare the continuance of their former pleasures past, with the continuance of their pains present: when they shall see how their pleasures have endured but a moment, whereas their pains shall endure everlastingly world without end. Now what a terrible grief and anguish of mind shall that be unto them, when by casting their accompt they shall perceive that all the whole time of their life was but a mere shadow of a dream, and that for their wanton delights, and pleasures, that were so quickly at an end, they shall suffer most horrible pains, and torments, that shall never have an end.

These are the pains that the damned persons shall suffer in the memory by calling to mind their former prosperity. But the pains which they shall suffer in their understanding when they shall consider the everlasting glory that they have lost shall be far greater. Hereof cometh that worm that is always gnawing at their conscience: which (as the holy scripture doth so oftentimes threaten) shall lie day and night biting, and gnawing, and feeding continually upon the bowels of the damned persons. And as the worm breedeth in the wood, and is always eating the wood wherein it was bred: even so this worm of conscience proceedeth of sin, and is evermore striving and setting itself against the same sin, whereof it was engendered.

This worm of conscience is a certain despite, and raging repentance, which the damned shall have for ever, and ever, when they consider what they have lost, and what good opportunity and means they have had in this life not to lose it. This opportunity shall continually be before their eyes.

This worm is always gnawing their bowels, (howbeit in vain,) and it causeth them to say evermore: O what an unfortunate wretch am I, that had time and opportunity to gain that so blessed state which the virtuous do enjoy in the kingdom of heaven, and would not use the benefit thereof! Alas! Alas! A time there was when this felicity was offered unto me, and I was exhorted and desired to receive it, yea it was frankly given me, and I would not accept it. For the only confessing and pronouncing of my sins with sorrow, and contrition, they had been all forgiven me. For the only asking of forgiveness of almighty God, it had been granted me. For the only giving of a cup of cold water to the poor, I had had life everlasting granted unto me. And now alas cursed caitiff that I am, I shall fast for ever: now alas shall I weep and wail for ever: and repent me of that which I have done for ever: and all shall be utterly without any fruit. O how idly and wickedly hath my time passed away, which shall never return again! What great benefits received I of the world that might alure me to hazard and lose the everlasting felicity and bliss of heaven? Although the world should have given me all the rich offices, manors, lordships, kingdoms, pleasures, and delights that it had, although I might have enjoyed them so many years as there be sands in the Sea, all this were nothing in comparison of the least pain and torment which I now here alas do suffer. And whereas I have not had the true fruition of any of these things, but only a little shadow of a fugitive vain pleasure for this must I now suffer everlasting horrible torments here in hell. O unhappy pleasure! O cursed change! O unfortunate hour, and moment, wherein I thus blinded myself! O what a blind buzzard have I been! O what a miserable wretch and villainous caitiff am I! O a thousand, yea a hundredth thousand times unhappy, that have so fondly deceived myself! Cursed be he that deceived me. Cursed be he that should have corrected me, and did not. Cursed be my father, and mother, that so wantonly brought me up. Cursed be the milk that I sucked. Cursed be the bread that I did eat, and the life that I have lived. Cursed by my birth, and my nativity. And cursed be all creatures that were any helps or means to bring me to any being. O how happy and fortunate are they that had never any being, and they that were never born! Happy are the wombs that never conceived: and happy are the breasts that never gave suck.

After this sort shall the miserable damned wretches curse and banne all creatures, and chiefly them that were the cause of their damnation. And so we read in the lives of the holy fathers, of a blessed holy man that saw by revelation a very deep well, full of great and horrible flames of fire, and in the midst of them were the father, and the son, both of them manacled together, and cursing one an other, with great furious rage, and despite. The father said unto his son. *Cursed be thou my son. For I to leave thee wealthy, and rich became an usurer, and for usury am I now here in hell damned.* And the son said likewise unto his father: *Cursed be thou my father, for that imagining to enrich me hast been the cause of my damnation: in that thou didst leave me evil gotten lands, and goods, and I for the wrongful keeping of them and not making due restitution to the right owners am here now alas damned everlastingly.*

Above all this, how great shall the pains and torments of the malicious and evil disposed will of the damned be? There shall be in the will a continual and outrageous malicious envy against the glory of almighty God, and his elect, which shall be evermore biting and gnawing at their entrails, no less than the worm of conscience, whereof we spake before. Of this pain saith the Psalm: *The sinner shall see and be angry: he shall gnash with his teeth, and consume. And the desire of the wicked shall perish.*[10] They shall have also such a great abhorring and hatred against almighty God, because he detaineth and punisheth them in that place, that like as a mad dog stroken with a spear, turneth again in great fury to bite and gnaw it: even so would the damned persons (if they might possibly) tear and rent almighty God in pieces: because they know that it is he, that pricketh them with his terrible spear, and that it is he, that striketh and tormenteth them from above with the dreadful sword of his justice. They have also a very great obstinacy in wickedness: for they are not sorry, either because they are wicked, or because they have been wicked, but rather they wish that they had been worse. And if they be sorry for their wicked life, it is not for any love they bear unto almighty God, but for the love of themselves, that so they might have escaped these horrible torments, if they had lived otherwise. Besides this, they have also a perpetual desperation: For that they think so evil of almighty God, and of his mercy, that they have no manner of hope therein, that ever he can pardon them: and also for that they know for certain that their most grievous pains and torments shall never have any mitigation, or end. This is the cause of their so horrible blasphemies, and of their despiteful railings against almighty God. For as they have no hope in him, so do they seek to be revenged of him as much as they can with their outrageous and malicious railing tongues.

---

10 Ps. 111:10.

§. III. Of the Pain, Which Is Termed by the Divines, Poena Damni: That Is, the Pain of Loss of Almighty God.

Who would think that after all these pains here before rehearsed there were yet more to be suffered? And yet nevertheless it is certain that all these pains in comparison of that which we have now to speak of, are as it were nothing. Consider then what a wonderful pain this is like to be, seeing that such horrible torments as we have before mentioned may be termed nothing, if they be compared with this torment. For all the pains that we have hitherto spoken of, appertain for the most part to the pain of the sense. But besides all these, there is yet an other pain called the pain of loss (which we touched before) the which without all comparison is far greater than all the other, as it may well appear by this reason. For pain is nothing else, but only a privation of some good thing that was either had, or in hope to be had. Now the greater this good thing is, the greater pain and grief we have when it is lost. As it appeareth plainly in the loss of temporal things, the which the greater they are in value, the greater is the grief that they cause. Now then, considering that almighty God is an infinite good thing, and the greatest of all good things, it followeth necessarily that the wanting of him shall be an infinite misery, and the greatest of all miseries.

Besides this, almighty God is the center of the reasonable soul, and the place where it hath his perfect rest. And thereof it cometh that the separation of the soul from almighty God is the most grievous and painful separation of all that may possibly be devised. And therefore St. Chrysostom saith: *That if a thousand fires of hell were joined together in one, they should never be so great a pain to the soul, as it is to the soul to be separated in this wise for ever from almighty God.*

It is not possible for any man to express by words the exceeding greatness of this grief. That separation that is wont to happen in time of war, when the sucking babes are taken from their mothers' breasts, is nothing in comparison of the perpetual division, and separation, which shall be from the fruition of almighty God. And that thou mayest understand somewhat hereof, consider what a horrible kind of death that was, which certain tyrants caused some of the martyrs to be put unto. They caused two tops or great boughs of two great trees to be bowed down violently to the ground, and at the two ends of them they commanded the feet of the holy Martyr that should suffer death to be bound, this done, they commanded that the two boughs should suddenly be loosed with all violence, that when they should recoil and mount up again to their natural places, they should hoise up the body on high, and so rent and tear it asunder in the air, each one of the boughs carrying with it that part of the body, that was bound unto it.

Now if this cruel separation of the parts of a man's body one from an other seem so great a torment, what a torment think ye shall that be, when the soul shall be separated from almighty God, which is not a part but the whole of our soul, especially seeing the separation and torment must endure, not only for so small a time, as whilst the bough of a tree may ascend from the ground up on high, but so long as God shall be God, which is for ever, and ever, world without end.

§. IV. Of the Particular Pains of the Damned in Hell.

Besides all these pains before rehearsed, there be yet divers and sundry others. For these pains are general, and common unto all the damned in hell, but over and besides these, there are certain other pains that be particularly and especially appointed and proportioned to every damned persons, according to the quality of his sin. As the Prophet Isaias signified when he said. *Measure shall be given against measure, for so hath our Lord determined in his hard heart, in the day of his heat.*[11] This heat signifieth the enkindling and fury of the wrath of almighty God. The hard heart signifieth the terribleness of his sentence, that shall punish temporal offences with everlasting pains. The measure against measure shall be the quantity and proportion of the pain, answerable

[11] See Is. 27:8.

to the quality of the offence. For therein shall the beauty, and order of God's justice wonderfully shew itself, when he shall give to every one of the damned his desert, according to the quality of his sin.

After this sort (as a holy father saith) The covetous shall there be punished with miserable necessity. The slothful and negligent shall be pricked with burning hot bodkins, and needles. The gluttons shall be tormented with passing great hunger, and thirst. The lecherous, and licentious livers shall be wrapped in flames of stinking brimstone. The envious shall howl and cry like mad dogs, with most inward pains, and griefs. The proud and presumptuous shall be full of perpetual shame, and confusion: and so in like manner of all the rest.

Wherefore O ye Idolators of the world! O ye lovers of honor, and promotion! O ye greedy purchasers and scrapers together of lands, and riches! O ye devisors of new fashioned garments, and of strange meats, pastimes, and delights! O thou wicked and miserable City of Babylon, Who will now weep, and bewail thy case! Who will lament again thy miserable state with such pitiful tears, as our Savior did, saying: *Si cognovisses et tu: etc.* If thou knewest now, etc.[12] O that thou knewest how dearly these dainty delicate morsels will cost thee, and what fierce tormentors these same Idols that thou now adorest, will be there unto thee! If a man do eat fruit before it be ripe, it must needs set his teeth on edge. And in like manner forsomuch as worldly men will now enjoy ease and rest before their time, and have their paradise here in this place of banishment, certainly the day will come, when their dainty morsels will set their teeth sore on edge: According as almighty God hath threatened by his Prophet: saying: Whosoever will eat sour grapes before they be ripe, let him be well assured, that they shall be bitter unto him.[13] Now that man eateth grapes before they be ripe, that will prevent and taste before hand here in this life the delights that are to be enjoyed in the life to come: who afterwards shall feel the bitterness of that morsel, when by the

12 See Luke 19:42.
13 See Jer. 31:30.

just judgement of almighty God he shall be punished, because he would be so hasty to enjoy rest and delights before his time.

§. V. Of the Eternity of All These Pains Before Rehearsed.

Now if all these pains be of themselves so grievous, and so passing great, how much greater and more grievous shall they appear, if unto the greatness and grievousness of all these pains we join also the eternity, and everlasting continuance of them, and that they shall never have an end. When ten thousand years be gone, and past, there shall be added unto them a hundred thousand years, and after those hundred thousand, there shall succeed so many thousand millions of years as there be stars in the Sky, and sands in the Sea, and after all these numbers of years are past, and gone, then shall the damned begin to suffer afresh and so shall the everlasting wheel of their most horrible torments go continually turning about for ever, and ever, world without end. *The valley of Tophet* (saith Isaias) *is prepared long since as yesterday, it is prepared at the king's commandment, and it is very deep, and large. The nutriment thereof is fire, and much wood: and the blast of our Lord being as it were a running flood of brimstone doth enkindle it.*[14] This valley is the bottomless pit of hell, prepared as yesterday, (to wit, from the beginning of the world,) for the punishment of the wicked. The nutriment thereof is fire, which burneth, and never consumeth. And the matter that preserveth this fire can never possibly end, nor consume, nor be diminished with any continuance of time. And that the damned may be assured that this horrible fire shall never be quenched, the devils have always in charge to blow it, and to keep it continually burning, who as they be immortal, so shall they never cease, or be weary of blowing therein. And though they should be weary, yet is there the blast of the almighty and eternal living God, which shall never be weary. Surely it should be to great purpose, and very much it were to be wished, that men had some

[14] Is. 30:33.

understanding of the continuance and eternity of these most horrible grievous torments, in such sort as they be indeed. For undoubtedly this would be a great bridle for our life. And therefore it shall not be from our purpose, if we bring here some examples of like things, to the intent that thereby we may have some understanding thereof.

Consider then with thyself that so horrible kind of torment, that is used in some countries, where malefactors be burned alive, and the greater their offences are, the less is the fire wherewithal they are burned, which is done in this wise, that their torment may be the longer prolonged. But what is the longest time ordinarily that the torment of a man may continue, that is thus executed by this artificial cruelty? Truly it can scarcely continue one whole natural day. Well then, tell me I pray thee, if this be so terrible and so horrible a kind of torment that endureth not one whole day, the fire being also but small, what an exceeding horrible torment shall that be in hell, that shall endure everlastingly, for ever, and ever, with such an extreme great and fervent fire as that is? Is there any man in the world so well skilled in the Mathematical sciences, that he can declare by any demonstration how far the one exceedeth the other? Now if a man to escape that torment would not stick to put himself to all dangers, labors, and pains, be they never so great, what then ought all we to do, to escape this most horrible extreme torment of hell fire?

Consider also what a terrible kind of torment that was, which Phalaris that cruel Tyrant invented, of whom it is written, that he used when he would put men to death, to cause them to be enclosed within the belly of a bull made of metal, and then caused a fire to be made underneath it, and this cruel manner of punishment he devised, that the miserable man by the heat of the iron should burn within the same by little and little, and not be able to escape, nor defend himself, nor have any other remedy, but only to burn, and roar, and tumble, and toss himself within that strait place, until he were dead. What heart can hear of this cruelty, but that his flesh will tremble, and quake, only in thinking of it? Wherefore tell me now (O thou Christian) what is all this in comparison of that most grievous and horrible torment which we here treat of, but only a mere dream, or shadow? Now if the very imagination and thinking of these horrible pains of hell do make us afraid, what shall it be, not to think of them only, but even to suffer them in very deed? Certainly it is so horrible a matter to suffer pains and torments everlastingly, that although there were but one alone among all the children of Adam, that should suffer in hell in this wise, it were enough to make us all to tremble, and quake. There was but one among Christ's disciples, that should sell his master, and yet when Christ said: *One of you shall betray me:*[15] all began to be afraid, and wax sad, for that the matter was of so great importance. Now then why do not we much more tremble, and quake, knowing certainly: *That the number of fools is infinite:*[16] *and that the way unto life everlasting is very narrow, and strait:*[17] *and that hell hath enlarged her mouth without any limit,*[18] to receive the multitudes that go into it? If we believe not this, where is our faith? If we do believe and confess it, where is our judgement, and reason? And if we have both judgement, and reason, why do we not publish and preach this matter in the open streets, and market places? Why go we not into the deserts, (as many of the Saints have done) there to do penance for our sins, and to live an austere life among beasts, that we may escape these most horrible and everlasting torments? How is it, that we can sleep in the night? Yea, how happeneth it, that we be not quite out of our wits, when we do think attentively, and consider of so strange a peril as this is, seeing less dangers than these have been able not only to fright and bestraught men out of their wits, but also to bereave them of their lives.

This is the greatest pain that the miserable damned persons have in hell, to understand that almighty God and their most grievous torments shall be of one like continuance: and therefore their misery can have no comfort, because their pain hath no end. If the damned persons could be persuaded that after a hundred thousand millions

15 Matt. 26:21.
16 Eccles. 1:15.
17 See Matt. 7:14.
18 See Is. 5:14.

of years their pains should have an end, even that persuasion alone would be a great comfort unto them. For then all their torments (albeit it were very long) would yet at the length come to an end. But assured they are that their pains shall have no end at all. For as St. Gregory saith. *There the wicked have death without any death, an end without any end, and a defect without any defect.* For their death always liveth, their end always beginneth, and their defect never faileth. And for this cause the Prophet saith: *They are in hell as it were sheep, and death feedeth upon them.*[19] The herb that is there fed upon is not wholly plucked up, because the root is alive, which is the beginning of life: and this causeth the herb to spring again, that it may still be fed upon. And therefore the pasture of those fields is immortal, forsomuch as it is always eaten, and always reviveth again. Now after this sort shall death feed upon the damned persons: and as death cannot die, so shall it never be filled with this kind of food, nor ever be weary in doing this office, neither shall it ever make an end of devouring this morsel. For that death shall evermore have somewhat in them to devour, and they shall evermore minister somewhat unto death to be devoured: so as the damned in hell shall suffer their most horrible pains and torments for ever, and ever, without any end.

19 Ps. 48:15.

SATURDAY NIGHT

Of the Everlasting Glory and Felicity of the Kingdom of Heaven.

THIS day (when thou hast made the sign of the Cross, and prepared thyself hereunto,) thou hast to meditate upon the felicity of eternal glory in the kingdom of heaven.

This consideration is so profitable, that if it were holpen with the light of a lively faith, it were able to make all the bitter pains and labors which we should take for the obtaining thereof to become sweet, and pleasant. For if the love of lands and riches do cause the pains, and labors, that be taken for them to seem sweet, and pleasant: If the love of children also do cause women to wish for the pains of childbearing, what would the love of this most excellent and passing great felicity do, in comparison whereof all other felicities are of non accompt. If it be said of the patriarch Jacob, that his seven years service seemed but short unto him, in respect of the great love he bare to Rachel,[1] what would the love of that infinite beauty work in our hearts, what would that everlasting marriage cause us to do, if it were considered with the eyes of a lively faith?

Wherefore that thou mayest understand somewhat of this felicity thou hast to consider (among other things) these five points that are in it: to wit: The excellency and greatness of the place: The fruition of the company of those blessed inhabitants: The vision of almighty

1 See Gen. 29:20.

God: The glory of the Saints bodies: And finally, the perfect fruition of all good things that are there.

First of all therefore consider the excellency of the place, and especially the greatness thereof, which is surely very wonderful. For when a man readeth in certain grave authors, that every one of the stars of heaven is greater than all the whole earth, yea, and which is more marvelous, that there be some stars among them of such notable greatness, that they be ninety times greater than all the whole earth: when a man heareth these things, and lifteth up his eyes to heaven, and seeth in the same such a multitude of stars, and so many void spaces where many more stars might be set, how can he but wonder? How can he but be astonied, and in a manner besides himself considering the passing greatness of that place, and much more of that mighty Sovereign Lord, that created it of nothing?

Then as touching the goodly beauty of that place it is a thing that can not be expressed with words. For if almighty God hath created things so wonderful and so beautiful in this vale of tears, and place of banishment: what wonderful things hath he created (trow ye) in that place, which is the seat of his glory, the throne of his mighty Power, the palace of his majesty, the house of his elect, and the paradise of all delights?

After thou hast considered the excellency of the place, consider also the great worthiness of those blessed inhabitants that dwell in it: whose number, holiness, riches, and beauty, are greater than any man can imagine. St. John saith, that the number of the elect is so great, that no man is able to count them.[2] St. Dionysius saith, that the number of the Angels is so great, that they exceed without comparison all corporal and material things in the earth. St. Thomas agreeing with this opinion saith, that like as the greatness of the heavens exceedeth the greatness of the earth without any proportion: even so doth the multitude of those glorious spirits exceed the multitude of all corporal and material things that are in this world with the like advantage, and proportion. Now what thing can be imagined more

---

[2] See Apoc. 7:9.

wonderfully than this? Certainly, this is such a matter, that if it were well considered, it were able to astonish all men. Again, if every one of the Angels (yea though it be the very least Angel among them all) be more goodly and beautiful to behold than all this visible world, what a glorious sight shall it then be to behold such a number of beautiful Angels, and to see the perfections, and offices, that every one of them hath in that high and supreme city? There the Angels go as it were in ambassages: The Archangels are occupied in their ministry: The Principalities triumph: The Powers rejoice: The Dominations govern: The Virtues shine: The Thrones glitter: The Cherubins give light: The Seraphins burn with love: And all of that heavenly court do find lauds and praises unto almighty God. Now if the company and conversation of good and virtuous persons be so sweet, and amiable a thing, what a blessed thing shall it be, to converse, and keep company with so many good and blessed Saints as be there, to speak with the Apostles, to be conversant with the Prophets, to communicate with the Martyrs, and to dwell and have a perpetual familiarity with all the elect?

Now if it shall be so great a glory to enjoy the company of the good, what shall it be to enjoy the company and presence of him, whom the morning stars do praise, at whose excellent beauty the Sun and moon do wonder, before whose majesty the Angels bow down, and at whose presence men do marvelously rejoice? What a glory shall it be, to behold that universal goodness, in whom are all good things? That greater world, in whom all worlds are contained? What a joy shall it be to see him, who being one, is all things, and yet being one, and most simple in himself, comprehendeth the perfections of all things? If to hear and see king Salomon were thought so great a matter, that the Queen of Saba said of him: *Blessed are they that stand before thy presence, and enjoy thy wisdom*:[3] what a thing shall it be to behold that most high Salomon? That everlasting wisdom? That infinite greatness? That inestimable beauty? That exceeding goodness?

---

[3] 3 Kgs. 10:8.

This is the essential glory of the Saints. This is the last end and center of all our desires.

After this, consider the glory of the bodies, in which there shall be no part but shall be glorified. For there every one of the members and senses shall have his particular glory, and object, wherein to take delight. There the bodies of the Saints shall be indued with those four singular qualities, and dowries: to wit, with subtility, swiftness, impassibility, and clearness. And this clearness shall be so great, that every one of the Saints' bodies shall shine like the sun in the kingdom of their father. Now if this sun that standeth in the midst of the firmament being but one be sufficient to give light and comfort to all this world, what a light shall so many suns and lamps make, as shall shine so brightly in that place altogether?

To conclude, in this glory all good things shall be found wholly together, and all evil things shall be banished from thence. There shall be health without infirmity, liberty without bondage, beauty without deformity, immortality without corruption, abundance without necessity, quietness without vexation, security without fear, knowledge without error, fullness without loathsomeness, joy without heaviness, and honor without contradiction. There (as St. Augustine saith) shall be true glory. For there shall none be praised, either by error, or flattery. There shall be true honor. For there it shall neither be denied to such as deserve it, nor given to such as deserve it not. There shall be true peace. For there shall no man be molested neither by himself, nor by others. The reward of virtue shall be given he that gave the virtue, and hath promised himself for a reward of the same, who is the greatest and best of all things, (to with, almighty God.) He shall be the end of our desires, He shall there be seen without ceasing, loved without loathsomeness, and praised without weariness. There the place is large, beautiful, bright, and secure. The company very good, and delightful. The time always after one sort, not distincted into evening, and morning, but continued with a simple eternity. There shall be a perpetual spring, which through the freshness and sweet breathing of the holy Ghost shall flourish for evermore. There shall all rejoice, all shall sing, and give continual praise to the chief giver of all things, through whose bountiful goodness they live, and reign in glory. O heavenly city! O secure dwelling place! O blissful country, where all delightful things are to be found! O happy people, without any grudging! O quiet neighbors, where no one is subject to any want, or necessity! O that the strife, and contention of this present state were at an end! O that the days of my banishment might be finished! O how long is the time of my peregrination prolonged! When shall this day come? When shall I come and appear before the face of my sweet Lord, and Savior?

The Sixth Treatise: Of the Consideration of the Glory of Paradise: Wherein the Former Meditation is Declared More at Large.

One of the things whereupon it behooveth us most to have our eyes always fixed in this vale of tears is the blessed state of glory in the kingdom of heaven. For this consideration alone were able to encourage us to sustain willingly all labors and pains that are to be suffered for the obtaining of it. When almighty God promised to give to the Patriarch Abraham the land of promise he commanded him to walk and view it all round about: saying, *Arise, and walk all over this land both in length, and breadth, and consider it on every side. For I will give it unto thee.*[4] Arise up therefore (O my soul,) advance thyself on high, leave all earthly cares and affairs here beneath, and flee up with the wings of thy spirit unto that most excellent noble land of promise, and consider with good attention the length of the eternity, the largeness of the felicity, and the greatness of the riches, with all the rest that is therein.

It is written of the Queen of Saba, that when she heard of the great fame of Salomon, she went to Jerusalem to see the great and wonderful things that were reported of him.[5] Considering therefore

4 See Gen. 13:17.
5 See 3 Kgs. 10.

that the fame of that heavenly Jerusalem, and of that supreme king that governeth it, is no less than the renown of Salomon was, ascend thou now up on high with thy spirit unto this noble city, to contemplate the wisdom of this supreme king, the beauty of this temple, the service of this table, and orders of them that attend upon it, the liveries that the whole family wear, and withal the policy and glory of this noble city. For if thou be able to consider every one of these things, it may be that thy spirit shall be lifted up above itself, and thou shalt perceive that there hath not been declared unto thee so much as the very least part of this glory. But for this purpose it shall be requisite to have a special light of almighty God, as the Apostle signifieth, saying: I beseech the God of glory and the father of our Lord Jesus Christ to give you the spirit of wisdom, and to lighten the eyes of our hearts, that you may understand how great the hope of your vocation is, and the riches of that inheritance, and glory, which he hath prepared for the Saints.[6] And although in this glory there be many things to contemplate upon, yet mayest thou now especially consider these five principal things, that we touched before: to wit: The excellency and greatness of the place: The fruition of the company of those blessed inhabitants: The vision of almighty God: The glory of the Saints bodies: And the everlasting continuance and eternity of all these so great and wonderful benefits.

§. I. Of the Goodly Beauty and Excellence of the Place.

First of all consider the goodly beauty of the place which St. John describeth unto us in a figure in his Apocalypse in these words: One of the seven Angels spake unto me, saying: Come, and I will shew thee the spouse of the lamb: and he carried me away in spirit to a high and great mountain, and shewed me the holy city of Jerusalem, which descended from heaven, and shined with the clearness of almighty God, and the light thereof was like to the glistering brightness of precious stones. This city had one great and high wall,

---

6 See Eph. 1:17–18.

in which were twelve gates, and in the gates twelve Angels, according to the number of the gates. The foundations of the walls of this city were wholly wrought with precious stones, and the twelve gates thereof were twelve pearls, every gate made of one pearl, and the street of this city was of pure gold like unto a very clear glass: and I saw no temple therein, because our Lord God almighty and the lamb were the temple: and the city had no need of Sun or Moon to give light unto it, forsomuch as the clearness of almighty God doth lighten it, and the lamp that burneth there is the lamb. Moreover the Angel shewed me a flood of the water of life, as clear as the Christal, which issued out of the seat of almighty God, and of the lamb. In the midst of the street and both on the one side of the flood and on the other was planted the tree of life, which brought forth twelve fruits in the year, every month his fruit, and the leaves of this tree served for the health of nations. No manner of malediction shall ever be seen there, but there shall be the seat of almighty God, and of the lamb. And his servants shall serve him, and they shall see his face, and have the name of him written in their foreheads, and they shall reign for ever, and ever, world without end.[7]

Behold here (dear brother) the beauty of this city described unto thee: not that thou mayest think that these things are there in such a material sort as the words do sound, but that by means of these thou mayest conceive other more spiritual and more excellent things, which are figured unto us by these material things.

The situation of this city is above all the heavens, and the greatness and largeness thereof exceedeth all measure. For if every one of the stars of heaven be so great as we have before declared, how great then must that heaven be, that containeth in it all the stars, and all the heavens? Surely there is no greatness in the world that may be compared unto this. For (as a holy father saith) from the west part of spain unto the uttermost boarders of the Indians a ship may sail (if it have a prosperous wind) in few days: but that region of heaven is so

[7] See Apoc. 21–22.

great, that the stars (which are more swift than the sun beams) can not finish their course in it in many years.

Now if thou demand of the workmanship of that building, there is no tongue able to express it. For if that work that appeareth outwardly to our mortal eyes be so goodly, and beautiful, what is to be supposed of all the rest that is there reserved for the sight only of immortal eyes? And if we see that by the handywork of men certain works are made here so sightly, and so beautiful, that they astonish the eyes of them that do behold them, what a work must that be, which is wrought by the hand of almighty God himself in that royal house, in that sacred palace, in that house of joy, and solace, which he hath built for the glory of his elect? O how amiable are thy tabernacles (saith the Prophet) O Lord God of virtues! My soul desireth and fainteth in beholding the palaces of our Lord.[8]

The thing that most principally commendeth a city is the state and condition of the citizens: to wit, if they be noble, if they be many, if they live in peace, and concord among themselves. Now who is able to declare the excellency of this city in this behalf? All the inhabitants therein be noble personages, there is no one among them of base linage, forsomuch as they be all the sons and children of God. They be so friendly and loving one towards an other, that they be all (as it were) one soul, and one heart. And they live in so great peace, and concord, that the very city itself is called Jerusalem, that is to say, the vision of peace. If thou desire to understand the number of the inhabitants in this city, unto this desire St. John maketh answer in his revelations, where he saith: That he saw in spirit such a great company of blessed Saints, that no man was able to reckon them, gathered together of all kinds of nations, people, and tongues, which stood before the throne of almighty God, and of his lamb, appareled in white garments, and with triumphant palms in their hands, singing unto almighty God songs of praise.[9] And unto this saying of St. John, doth that agree very well, which is signified by

---

8 See Ps. 83:2–3.
9 See Apoc. 7:9.

the Prophet Daniel concerning this holy number: where he saith: *Thousand thousands serve the Lord of majesty, and ten hundred thousand thousands stand before him.*[10]

And think not because the number is so great that they be therefore disordered. For there the multitude is no cause of confusion, but of greater order, and harmony. For almighty God that hath with such a wonderful consonance and agreement disposed the movings of the heavens, and the courses of the stars, calling them every one by his proper name, hath also ordained all that innumerable army of blessed Saints with a most wonderful goodly order and disposition, appointing to every one his place, and glory, according to his merit. And so there is one place for the virgins, an other for the Confessors, an other for the holy Martyrs, an other for the Patriarchs, and Prophets, an other for the Apostles, and Evangelists, and so forth in all the rest. And in like sort as men are there divided, and placed, even so after their manner are the Angels also, which be divided into three Hierarchies, and those three Hierarchies into nine orders. And above all the Saints and Angels is placed the throne of that most excellent Queen of Angels, the mother of almighty God, who alone is an order by herself: forsomuch as she hath no peer, nor any one that is like unto her. And above them all the holy humanity of our Savior Christ hath the chief place and preeminence, who sitteth at the right hand of the majesty of almighty God in the highest.

Now (thou Christian soul) take a view of all these orders: walk through these streets: and ways: consider the order of these citizens, the beauty of this city, and the nobleness and worthiness of these inhabitants. Salute them every one by their names, and desire them to help and succor thee with their prayers. Salute also this sweet and pleasant country, and as a pilgrim beholding it as yet a far off, direct thine eyes, and withal thy heart unto it, and say. All hail sweet country! The land of promise! The house of blessing! The kingdom of all worlds! The Paradise of delights! The garden of eternal flowers! The market place of all treasure! The crown of all just persons! And

[10] See Dan. 7:10.

the end of all our desires! All hail our mother, and our hope! After thee have we sighed a long time! For thee have we mourned, and do mourn even at this present! For the love of thee have we fought and do still fight a long battle in this our transitory life. For we know assuredly, that none shall be rewarded and crowned in thee, but only such as have here foughten faithfully.[11]

§. II. Of the Second Joy That the Soul Shall Have in the Kingdom of Heaven: Which Is the Enjoying of the Company of the Saints.

Who is able after this great joy to declare what a further joy the soul shall have by being in this most happy and blessed company? For there the virtue of charity is in her full perfection, the property of which virtue is to cause all things to be common. There shall that petition be perfectly fulfilled which our Savior made, saying: *I beseech thee O father, that they may be one* (by love,) *as we are one* (by nature.)[12] For there shall the elect be more straitly united together in one than the members of one same body, because all shall participate of one same spirit, which giveth unto all one same being, and withal one blessed life. If thou imagine it to be otherwise, tell me, what is the cause why the members of one body have so great a unity and love one towards an other? The reason is, because they all are partakers of one same form, that is, of one soul, which giveth one same being and one life to them all. Now if the spirit of a man have power to cause so great a unity between members that are so different in offices, and natures, is it any wonder if the spirit of almighty God by whom all the elect do live (which spirit is as it were the common soul to them all) should cause a far greater and more perfect unity among them: especially considering that the spirit of God is a more noble cause, and of a more excellent virtue, and power, yea, and giveth also a more noble being?

11 See 2 Tim. 2:5.

12 See John 17:11.

Well now, if this manner of unity and love do cause all things to be common, as well good, as evil, (as we see in the members of one body, and in the love of mothers towards their children, who rejoice as much at their felicity, as at their own,) what a wonderful joy shall one of the elect there have of the glory of all the rest, considering that he shall love every one of them as well as himself? For as St. Gregory saith. *That heavenly inheritance unto all is one, and unto every one is all: forsomuch as every one of the blessed Saints rejoiceth as much at the joys and felicities of all others, as if he were himself in possession of the same.* But what can we infer of all this? Marry thus much, that as the number of the blessed Saints is after a sort infinite, even so the joys of each one of them shall also after a sort be infinite, and that every one of the Saints shall have the excellencies of all, forsomuch as whatsoever any one of them shall not have in himself, he shall have it in others. These be spiritually those seven sons of Job, among whom there was such a great love and communicating one to an other, that every one of them in his order made a feast one day of the week unto all the rest: whereby it came to pass that every one of them was no less partaker of the goods of others, than of his own proper goods.[13] And so that which was proper to one was common to all: and that which was common to all was proper to every one. This effect wrought love and brotherly affection in those holy brethren. Now how much greater shall the brotherly love of the elect be in the kingdom of heaven? How much greater shall the number of brothers be there? How much more treasure and riches shall they have to enjoy?[14] Now by this accompt, what a feast shall that be, which the Seraphins shall there make unto us, who are in the highest degree of all blessed Spirits, and most near unto almighty God, when they shall discover unto our eyes the nobleness of their state, and condition, the clearness of their contemplation, and the most fervent burning heat of their love? What a feast also shall the Cherubins make, in whom the treasures of the wisdom of almighty God are enclosed? What a

13 See Job 1:4.

14 See Luke 18 and 19.

feast likewise shall that be of the Thrones, and Dominations, and of all the other blessed spirits? What a joy shall it be to see and have the fruition of that glorious army of Martyrs, clothed with white garments, with their palms in their hands, and with the glorious ensigns of their triumphs?[15] What a joy shall it be to behold there those eleven thousand virgins altogether, and those ten thousand Martyrs, which were the true followers of the glory, and Cross of Christ, with other innumerable multitudes of them? What a joy shall it be to see there that glorious Deacon (St. Laurence) with his gridiron in his hand, shining now much brighter than the flames wherewith he was burned, having defied the cruel tyrants, and wearied the tormentors with an invincible patience? What a joy shall it be to behold there the beautiful and glorious virgin St. Catherine crowned with roses, and lilies, who overcame the wheel of their rasers with the weapons of faith, and hope? What a joy shall it be to see those seven noble Machabees with their godly and valiant mother, having contemned all kind of deaths and torments for keeping the law of almighty God? What chain of gold and precious stones are so goodly to behold as the neck of the glorious forerunner of Christ. St. John Baptist, who chose rather to lose his head, than to dissemble the filthiness of the adulterous king? What purple shall shine so bright as the body of blessed St. Bartholomew, who had his skin flayed from his flesh for our Savior Christ his sake? What other thing shall it be to see the body of St. Stephen that was bruised with the strokes of the stones, than to behold a rich long robe trimly garnished and set all over with goodly precious rubies, and diamonds? What a joyful sight shall it be to see those two glorious princes of Christ's Church, St. Peter, and St. Paul, shining there very brightly, the one with his sword, and the other with the glorious standard of Christ (to wit, the Cross) wherewith they were crowned? Now what a joy shall it be to enjoy the glories of each one of all these blessed saints, as if they were properly our own? O glorious feast! O royal banquet! O table meet for almighty God, and his elect! Wherefore let these worldlings get

[15] See Apoc. 7.

them to their filthy and carnal banquets: let them burst their bellies with their gluttonous excess, and superfluities: Such a feast as this is where such excellent meats are served is convenient for almighty God, and his elect.

Ascend yet up higher above all the orders of Angels, and there shalt thou find an other singular glory that doth wonderfully rejoice all that supreme Court, and maketh the city of God as it were drunk with marvelous delight. Lift up thine eyes, and behold (the most blessed virgin Mary) that Queen of mercy full of clearness, and beauty, at whose glory the Angels do wonder, and in whose excellency men do glory. This is the Queen of heaven crowned with stars, clothed with the son, shod with the moon, and blessed above all women.

Consider now what a great joy it shall be to behold this our blessed Lady, and mother, not kneeling now upon her knees before the manger, not troubled and molested now with the frights and fears of such things as holy Simeon prophesied unto her, not lamenting and seeking now her lost child in all parts, but with inestimable peace and security placed at the right hand of her dear son, without all fear of ever leesing that her most precious treasure.[16] Now hath she no need to seek the dead time of the secret night, to deliver the child from the conspiracies of Herod by fleeing into Egypt.[17] Now doth she no more stand at the foot of the cross, receiving upon her head the drops of blood that fell from above, and carrying in her upper garment a perpetual remembrance of that her great grief. Now she feeleth no more the grief of that doleful exchange, when she had assigned unto her the disciple in steed of the master, and the servant in steed of the lord.[18] Now are those sorrowful words to be heard no more which she uttered with great weeping and lamentation under that bloody tree: saying: *O that I might die for thee Absolon: my son: my son Absolon.*[19] Now is all this sorrow at an end, and she that was more

16 See Luke 2.
17 See Matt. 2.
18 See John 19.
19 2 Kgs. 18:33.

afflicted in this world than any other mere creature, is now seen there exalted above all creatures, enjoying for ever that chiefest goodness, and saying: *I have found him whom my soul loveth: I will hold him, and will not let him go.*[20]

And if this be so great a joy, what a joy shall that be to behold the most sacred humanity of our Savior Christ, and the glory and beauty of that body, which was so foully disfigured for our sakes upon the cross? *It shall be undoubtedly* (as St. Bernard saith) *a thing full of all sweetness, and delight, when men shall there see and behold a man, the creator of men, and Lord of all things created.* We are wont to esteem it for a singular honor to our whole family, to see some one of our kindred to be made a Cardinal, or a Pope. Now how far greater honor shall this be unto us, to see that Lord who is of our flesh, and blood, sitting at the right hand of the father, and made king both of heaven, and earth? With what a passing great joy shall men stand among the Angels, when they shall see that the Lord of the whole house, and the universal creator of all things is not an Angel, but a man? For if the members do accompt that to be an honor unto them, that is done to their head, (by reason of the great union that is between them and it,) what shall it be there, where there is such a strait union between the members, and the head? What shall it be else, but that every one of the saints shall accompt the glory of their Lord as their own peculiar glory? This joy shall be so passing great, that no words are able to express it according to the worthiness thereof. Now who shall be so happy, as to be thought worthy to enjoy so great a bliss, and felicity? O that thou were as my brother sucking the breasts of my mother, that I might find thee without, and kiss thee with the lips of devotion, and embrace thee with the arms of love![21] O most sweet loving Lord! When shall this joyful day come? When shall I appear before they face? When shall I be filled with thy excellent beauty? When shall I see that countenance of thine, whereupon the Angels are desirous to behold?

---

20 Cant. 3:4.

21 See Cant. 8.

§. III. Of the Third Joy That the Soul Shall Have in the Kingdom of Heaven: Which Is, the Enjoying of the Clear Vision of Almighty God.

Now what a joy shall it be above all this to have a clear sight of that divine face, in the sight of whom consisteth the essential glory of the Saints? All the things we have hitherto spoken of are certainly great motives towards the accomplishment of glory: but they all are little in comparison of the clear vision of almighty God. Of Issachar it is written, *That he saw that rest was good, and that the land was best: and therefore he put his shoulders to labor, and made himself subject to tribute.*[22] The rest and glory of the Saints is good: but the land that bringeth forth this rest is best in the superlative degree. For this land is the face and beauty of almighty God, of the vision and beholding of whom proceedeth the rest and glory of the Saints. This clear vision of almighty God is the thing that of itself alone is able to give perfect rest unto our souls. For all the sweetness and pleasantness of creatures well may it give delight to the heart of man, but it can never wholly satisfy and fill it. Now if all these good things before rehearsed shall so much delight us, how much then shall that good thing delight us that containeth in itself the perfection and sum of all good things? And if the only sight and beholding of creatures be so glorious, what a glory shall it be to behold that divine face, that most bright light, and that most excellent beauty of almighty God, in whom all beauties do shine? What a glorious sight shall it be to behold that essence, so wonderful, so simple, and so communicable, and with one sight to behold in the same the mystery of the most blessed Trinity? The glory of the father, the wisdom of the son, and the goodness and love of the holy Ghost?

There shall we see God, and in God both ourselves, and all things. St. Fulgentius saith, that like as he that hath a glass before him, seeth the glass, and himself in the glass, and all other things that are before the glass, even so when we shall have that unspotted

---

22 Gen. 49:15.

glass of the majesty of almighty God present before us, we shall see him, and ourselves in him, and withal whatsoever is without him, according to the knowledge (greater, or less,) that we shall have of him. There shall the appetite of our understanding rest, and shall not desire to know any thing else, because it shall have before it all that can be known. There shall the appetite of our will rest, in loving that universal good thing in whom are all good things, and out of whom there be no more good things to be enjoyed. There shall our desire rest, and be fully satisfied with the morsel of that supreme joy, which shall in such wise fill the mouth of our heart, that there shall be nothing else for it to desire. There shall those three Theological virtues, to wit, Faith, Hope, and Charity, wherewith almighty God is here honored be perfectly rewarded: when unto faith shall be there given for a reward the clear vision of almighty God: unto hope the possession of him: and unto charity imperfect, charity in all her perfection. There shall the elect see, love, enjoy, and praise almighty God. There shall they be filled without glutting, and be hungry without necessity.

There is the place where that song is always sung, that St. John heard in his revelations, which song he termeth, *Quasi canticum novum: As it were a new song.*[23] For that although the song be always after one manner, (forsomuch as it is one common praise, answerable to one common glory, which all that blessed company enjoyeth,) yet is it always new, as concerning the taste and delight it hath. For look what taste it had at the beginning, the same very taste also shall it have for ever, and ever, without end. The joy of the Saints in heaven shall never diminish, nor decay, neither shall their bodies ever decay, or wax old. For he that causeth the heavens to be always fresh and new after so many thousand years as have passed since they were created, shall also cause the flower of the glory of the Saints always to be lively, and flourishing, and never to wither or decay in any one point.

---

23 Apoc. 14:3.

§. IV. Of the Fourth Joy That the Soul Shall Have in the Kingdom of Heaven: Which is the Enjoying of the Glory of the Body.

The clear vison of the divine majesty is (as hath been declared) the essential glory of the blessed souls in heaven. Howbeit our most just judge and bountiful father thinketh it not enough to glorify the souls only, but for the honor of them extendeth his magnificence and liberality yet further, even to glorify their bodies also: giving thus a room and place unto beasts in his royal and everlasting heavenly palace. O lover of men! O honorer of the good, and virtuous! What hath this rotten and stinking flesh of ours (which like a beast followeth always his appetites) to do with the sanctuary of heaven? What? Shall this flesh (which should rather be tied up in a stable among beasts) be placed among the Angels in heaven? Let dust (O Lord) continue with dust: for it is not seemly that earth should be placed above the heavens.

But he that said unto Abraham, I will honor and multiply Ismael, notwithstanding he is the son of a bondslave, because he appertaineth unto thee,[24] will also shew this favor to the bodies of the Saints, for the nigh kindred that is between the souls, and them. It is our Lord's pleasure also that he that hath holpen to bear the burthen, shall likewise be partaker in the division of the glory: and that like as the soul by conforming itself in this life unto the will of God, cometh afterwards to be made partaker of the glory of God: even so the body which (contrary to his nature) was conformable and obedient unto the will of the soul, shall also be made partaker of the glory of the same soul. And thus shall the just be glorious both in body, and soul. And (as the Prophet saith:) *They shall possess in their country double riches*:[25] Whereby is understood the glory of the souls, and the glory of the bodies.

Now what shall I say of the glory of the senses? Each one of them shall there have his own proper delight, and glory. The eyes

---

24 See Gen. 17:20.
25 Is. 61:7.

shall be renewed and made more clear than the light of the sun: They shall see those royal palaces, those glorious bodies, and those beautiful fields, with other infinite goodly things that are there to be seen. The ears shall always hear that wonderful music, which is so exceeding sweet, and pleasant, that one only sound of it were able to bring all the hearts of this world asleep. The sense of smelling shall also be recreated with most sweet and pleasant savours, not of such vaporous things as we have here, but of such as be proportionable to the glory that is there. In like manner the taste shall be satisfied with incredible sweetness, and delights, not for sustentation of life, but for accomplishment of all glory. Now what an exceeding joy shall the blessed soul conceive at that time, when for the mortification and diligent looking unto the senses (which continued so short a time) she seeth herself so wholly drowned in that most deep fountain of glory, without finding any bottom or end of so many and of such passing great joys? O labors and pains well employed! O services well rewarded! O treasure not so much to be spoken of, as to be wished, and desired, and to be purchased with a thousand lives, in case we had so many to give for the same!

§. V. Of the Fifth Joy in the Kingdom of Heaven: Which Is the Everlasting Continuance of the Glory and Felicity of the Saints.

But now let us see for how long time this great glory and felicity is to be enjoyed. This is a point that were able alone to cause us even to cry out, and desire that all manner of tribulations, afflictions, pains, and labors, might rain and pour down upon us as thick as hail, so that we might serve and please almighty God in this transitory life, who is to bestow so great and inestimable benefits upon us in the everlasting life to come. This reward of so great glory and felicity in the kingdom of heaven shall endure so many thousand years, as be stars in the firmament, yea, and a great deal longer: It shall endure so many hundred thousand millions of years, as have fallen drops of water upon the earth, yea and a great deal longer: yea to conclude, it shall endure so long as almighty God himself shall endure, which shall be everlastingly world without end. For it is written thus: Our Lord shall reign for ever, and ever.[26] And in an other place: Thy reign is the reign of all worlds, and thy dominion endureth from generation to generation.[27]

Wherefore (O father of mercies, and God of all consolation) I humbly beseech thee by the bowels of thy mercy, that I may not be deprived of this supreme glory, and felicity. O Lord my God, that hast vouchsafed to create me after thine own image, and likeness, and to make me capable of thyself, fill this heart of mine (which thou hast created,) with thyself, sith thou hast created it for thyself. *Let my portion* (O my almighty God) *be in the land of the living.*[28] O Lord I beseech thee give me not in this transitory life either rest, or riches: but reserve all in store for me for the everlasting life to come. I desire not to inherit with the children of Ruben in the land of Galaad, and to lose my right and title of the land of promise.[29] *One thing only* (O Lord) *have I demanded of thee, and this will I always require, that I may dwell in the house of our Lord all the days of my life.*[30]

---

26 Ps. 145:10.
27 Ps. 144:13.
28 See Ps. 141:6.
29 See Num. 32:1–5.
30 Ps. 26:4.

SUNDAY NIGHT

Of the Benefits of Almighty God.

THIS day (when thou hast made the sign of the Cross, and prepared thyself hereunto,) thou hast to meditate upon the benefits of almighty God: that in so doing thou mayest give him thanks for them, and enkindle in thyself a more fervent love of him, who hath shewed himself so bountiful towards thee, and withal procure thereby more grief and sorrow for the sins and offences that thou hast committed against such a loving benefactor.

And albeit the benefits of almighty God towards us be innumerable, yet they all may be reduced to five kinds: to wit, to the benefits of creation, conservation, redemption, vocation, and to the secret benefits, that every one hath received particularly in himself.

As concerning the first benefit, which is of creation, Consider first with great attention what thou wast before thou were created, and what almighty God hath done for thee, and bestowed upon thee, before thou didst merit or deserve any thing at all: to wit, he gave thee thy body with all thy members, and senses, and thy soul which is of so great excellency, created after his own image and likeness for so high and excellent an end, as to have the fruition of almighty God. And withal he gave thee those three noble powers also of thy soul, which be, Understanding, Memory, and Will. And consider well with thyself, that to give thee this soul was to give thee all things. For it is clear that there is no perfection nor hability in any of all the inferior creatures, but that man hath the same in him in a far more high and greater perfection, and by means of the virtue and hability of his soul he is able to attain unto it. Whereby it appeareth, that by giving unto us this thing alone, (to wit, our soul) he gave us therewith at once all things together.

As concerning the benefit of conservation, consider how all thy whole being dependeth of the providence of almighty God: How thou art not able to live one moment, nor to step so much as one step, were it not by means of him. Consider also, how he hath created all things in this world for thy use, and service: insomuch as he hath appointed even the very Angels of heaven for thy guard, and defense. Consider moreover, how he hath given thee health, strength, life, sustenance, with all other temporal helps, and succors. And above all this, consider well the manifold great miseries, and calamities, into which thou seest other men fall every day, and how thou thyself mightest also have fallen into the same, had it not been that almighty God of his great mercy preserved thee.

As concerning the benefit of redemption thou mayest consider therein two things. First, how many and how great benefits almighty God hath given us by means of the benefit of redemption. And secondly, how many and how great miseries he hath suffered in his most holy body and soul to purchase these benefits unto us.

As concerning the benefit of vocation, consider first of all, what a great benefit it was of almighty God to make thee a Christian, to call thee to the Catholic faith by means of the holy Sacrament of Baptism, and to make thee also partaker of the other Sacraments. And then if after this calling of thee thou hast fallen into deadly sin, and thereby lost thine innocency, in case now our Lord have raised thee up from sin, and received thee again into his grace, and favor, and set thee in the state of salvation, how canst thou be able to give him sufficient praises and thanks for this so inestimable a benefit? What a great mercy was it to expect thee so long time? To suffer thee to commit so many sins? And in the mean time to send thee so many divine inspirations? And not to shorten the days of thy life, as he hath done to diverse and sundry others, that were in the very same state? And last of all, to call thee with so mighty a grace, that thou mightest rise up again from death to life, and open thine eyes to behold the eternal light? What a great mercy was it also (after that thou wast converted) to give thee grace not to return unto deadly sin again, but to stand and vanquish thine enemy, and to persevere in good life? This is that morning and evening dew that almighty God promised by the Prophet Joel, saying: *And ye sons of Sion rejoice, and be glad in our Lord God: for he hath given you a teacher of justice, and he shall cause the morning and evening dew to rain and pour down upon you.*[1] Meaning hereby that almighty God giveth us first his preventing grace, wherewith we begin to sow the seed of virtues: and afterwards he giveth us his grace subsequent, and final, which bringeth this seed to his full ripeness, and happy end.

These are the public and known benefits. But besides these there be other secret benefits, which no man knoweth but he only that hath received them. Again, there be other benefits also so secret that even he himself that hath received them knoweth not of them: and he only knoweth them that is the giver of them. How many times hast thou deserved in this world either through thy pride, negligence, or unthankfulness, that almighty God should have withdrawn his grace from thee, and utterly forsaken thee, as he hath done to many others for some one of these causes, (for whosoever they be that do fall from God, they fall by some of these means,) and yet hath not almighty God dealt thus with thee? How many evils and occasions of evils hath our Lord prevented and turned away by his providence, in overthrowing the snares of the devil thine enemy, and stopping him of his passage, and not permitting him to execute his wily practices and deceits upon thee? How oftentimes hath he done for every one of us, as he said he did for St. Peter? Behold, (saith our Savior) how Satan goeth busily about to sift you as corn in the barn, but I have prayed for thee, that thy faith fail not.[2] Now who knoweth these secrets, but only almighty God. The positive benefits be such as a

---

1 Joel 2:23.
2 See Luke 22:31–32.

man may sometimes understand and know them: but those benefits that are called privative, which consist not in doing benefits unto us, but in delivering us from hidden and secret evils that were coming toward us, who is able to understand? Wherefore as well for these benefits, as for the others, it is reason we should always shew ourselves thankful to our Lord, and understand how far in arrearages we be in our reckoning with him, and how much more we be indebted unto him, than we are able to pay, considering we are not able so much as to understand what they are.

The Seventh Treatise: Of the Consideration of the Benefits of Almighty God: Wherein the Former Meditation is Declared More at Large.

One of the greatest complaints that almighty God maketh against men, and wherewith he will most charge them at the day of their accompt, is their unthankfulness and ingratitude for his manifold benefits. With this kind of complaint the Prophet Isaias beginneth the first words of his prophecy, calling heaven and earth to witness against the ingratitude and unthankfulness of the wicked. Hearken (saith he) O heaven, and thou earth give ear unto my words, for our Lord hath spoken it: I have nourished children, and exalted them, and they have despised me: The ox knoweth his owner, and the Ass his master's manger: but Israel hath not known me, neither would my people understand me.[3] Now what thing is more strange, than that men should not acknowledge that thing, which the very brute beasts do acknowledge. And as St. Jerome saith upon this place: The Prophet would not compare men with other living beasts that are more quick of sense, as with the dog, that for a little piece of bread defendeth his master's house, but even with the Ox, and Ass, which are more dull, and rude: giving us hereby to understand, that ingrateful and unthankful persons are not to be likened to every kind of beasts, but that they be much more brutish than the most brutish beasts that are.

3 Is. 1:3.

Now what punishment (trow ye) doth so great beastliness deserve? Almighty God hath prepared many punishments for ingrateful persons: but the most just and ordinary punishment is to spoil them of all those benefits they have received, because they would not give thanks to the giver of them as of duty they ought to have done. For as St. Bernard saith: *Ingratitude is as it were a burning wind, that drieth up the river of God's mercy, the fountain of his clemency, and the flowing stream of his grace.*

Now as unthankfulness is the cause of so great evils, even so contrariwise thankfulness is the beginning of very great graces, and especially of three. The first is the love of God. For (as Aristotle saith) goodness is amiable of itself, and every man is naturally most inclined to love his own proper weal. Seeing therefore that men be naturally such lovers of themselves, and of their own proper commodity, when they see plainly that all that they have cometh of the gracious goodness of that chiefest benefactor, forthwith they be moved to love, and wish well unto him, whom they perceive and acknowledge to have bestowed so great benefits upon them. And hereof it cometh, that among the considerations that do most help us to attain unto the love of God, one of the most principal is the consideration of the benefits of almighty God. For every one of these benefits is as it were a firebrand that quickeneth and enkindleth more and more the flame of this love: and so consequently, to consider many of these benefits, is to join many firebrands together, whereby the flame of this fire is enkindled more and more in us.

This consideration helpeth also to stir up a desire in a man to serve almighty God when he considereth the great bounden duty, that he oweth unto him, unto whom he is so much indebted. For if the very birds and brute beasts be moved herewith to answer unto the voice of him that calleth them and do obey (as though they were reasonable creatures) unto all such things as are commanded them: how much greater provocations have we to do the like unto almighty God, that have received far more than they, and be able to understand far better then they, what great and inestimable benefits we have received from God.

This consideration is also profitable to stir and provoke in our souls a sorrow and repentance for our sins. For when a man considereth and weigheth deeply on the one side the multitude of benefits he hath received of almighty God, and on the other side the great number of offences he hath committed against him, how can he choose but be ashamed of himself? How can it be but that he must needs be confounded, and discern much better the black by comparing it with the white? I mean hereby, he shall much better discern the greatness of his own wickedness, by comparing the same with the greatness of God's passing great goodness, who hath continued so long time in doing good unto him, that contrariwise hath continued evermore for his part in heaping sin upon sin against almighty God.

For these three ends therefore ought a man to consider the benefits of almighty God: and withal in the consideration of them to give him most humble thanks for the same. So that when he setteth himself to meditate upon the benefits of almighty God, he must then be careful to have his recourses unto these three points in their due places, applying his heart some times to love him, who hath been so greatly beneficial unto him: some times to desire to serve him: some times again to be sorrowful and repentant for his sins: yea and some times also to offer unto him sacrifice of praise, and thanks giving for his so manifold benefits. These sacrifices are signified by those calves of our lips, which the Prophet would have us to offer unto almighty God for the benefits that we have received of him.[4]

True it is, that the benefits of almighty God be innumerable, but we will treat here only of five kinds of benefits, which are of all others the most chief, and principal, and whereunto all the others may be reduced. These five are the benefits of creation, conservation, redemption, vocation, and finally the particular and secret benefits that every particular person may recognize and acknowledge in himself.

---

4 See Osee 14:3.

And it is not required of a man to think upon all these benefits at one time, but it shall suffice to think upon one, or two, or three of them, and to consider and ponder them well and diligently in his mind. For the exercises of meditation are not to be taken in lumps, as a task, that must be fully wrought and finished within a certain time, but as a daily food, and sustenance, which the more moderately and temperately it is taken, and the better it is digested, the more profitable and wholesome it is to a man.

§. I. Of the Benefit of Creation.

To begin now with the benefit of creation: that thou mayest the better understand somewhat of the greatness of this benefit, thou shalt do well to consider first very deeply with thyself, what thou wast before thou were created. This is one of the principal advices, that the masters of the spiritual life do use to give in this behalf, as well for the understanding of the greatness of this benefit, as also for the annihilation (as they term it,) which is, that a man may hereby clearly and palpably perceive how of himself he is no more than very nothing. Consider then how it is not many years sithence, not a thousand, nor an hundred years, but even as it were yesterday, that is, within a very small time, that thou wast nothing, (at least wise as concerning thy soul) and from the beginning thou wast nothing, and mightest for ever have been nothing, that is, less than a clod of earth, less than a puff of wind, yea less than a straw, and to be short even nothing.

Consider then how the same nothing could not make itself any thing, and as little could it deserve that an other should make it any thing, for that party that is not, can neither work, nor deserve. Now when thou wast in this darkness, and in this deep bottomless pit of the same nothing, it pleased the infinite goodness and mercy of almighty God, before any desert of thine, only of his mere grace, to shew upon thee his power, and omnipotency, and with his mighty hand to pluck thee out of this darkness, and out of this deep bottomless pit of no being, and to bring thee to a being, and to make thee somewhat: and (as St. Augustine saith) not every somewhat, not a stone, not a bird, not a toad, not a serpent, but even a man, which is one of the most noble creatures in the world. He gave thee this being that thou now hast. He compacted and framed this thy body, and beautified it in all parts, both with members and senses, and that with such a wonderful providence, and art, that every one of them (if they be well considered) is of itself a great wonder, and a very great benefit. This is that benefit which the holy man Job did most humbly acknowledge, when he said: *Thy hands (O Lord) have made me, they have given me a due proportion in every part. Remember O Lord that thou hast made me, as it were of a lump of clay, and that thou shalt reduce me again into dust. Thou hast clothed me with skin, and flesh: Thou hast compacted me with bones, and sinews: Thou hast given me life, and mercy, and hast preserved my spirit with thy visitation.*[5]

Now what shall I say of the nobleness of thy soul, and of the excellency of the end for which it was created, and of the image and capacity that it hath. The image thereof is the image of almighty God himself. For in very deed there is nothing in all the earth that more resembleth almighty God, there is nothing whereby we may come to a more evident knowledge of him than by the soul. And therefore the ancient Philosophers (and namely Anaxagoras) knew no meeter name to be given unto God, than Men's, (the Mind,) which is as much to say, as a reasonable soul, by reason of the great similitude and likeness that they perceived to be between God, and it. And this is the cause why the substance of our soul can not be perfectly understood. For being as it is very like unto the substance of God, (which can not be known in this life) it followeth that the substance of the soul is also a thing not able to be known here by us.

Now the end for which this noble creature was created, is answerable to this dignity. For it is manifest that the soul was created to be partaker of that blessed glory and felicity of almighty God, to dwell in his house, to eat at his table, to enjoy those things that almighty God himself enjoyeth, to be clothed with the same garment

5 Job 10:8–9, 11–12.

of immortality that he himself is clothed withal, and to reign everlastingly with him.

And hereof it cometh, that the soul hath such a wonderful capacity: which is so great, that all the creatures and riches of the world put together, are no more able to fill her capacity, than a barley corn is able to fill all the whole world.

Now therefore, what recompence shall we make unto our most gracious and bountiful Lord for this so passing great benefit? If we think ourselves to be so much bound to our carnal parents, for that they have been some part in the building of this our body, how much more are we indebted unto our heavenly father, who by means of our parents hath formed our bodies, and without them hath created our souls, which be without comparison more excellent than the body, and without which our body were no better than a stinking dunghill? What are our parents, but only an instrument whereby almighty God hath made a small portion of this work? Now if thou be so much bound to the instrument of the work, how much more art thou bound to the principal agent, that made the work? And if thou be so much bound unto him, who was only a mean in framing one part, how much more art thou bound unto almighty God that made the whole? If thou esteem a sword so much wherewith a city was conquered, how much more oughtest thou to esteem the king himself that conquered it.

§. II. Of the Benefit of Conservation.

And our Lord hath not only created thee in such great dignity, and glory, but it is he also that maintaineth and conserveth thee after thy creation in the same? As he himself witnesseth by the Prophet Isaias, saying: *I am thy Lord thy God, that do teach thee whatsoever is meet for thee to know, and do govern thee in the way that thou walkest.*[6] Many mothers there be, that think it sufficient to sustain only the travail of child bearing: they will not burthen themselves with nourishing

6 Is. 48:17.

their children, but will seek out some other nurse that may discharge them of that trouble. But almighty God dealeth not so with us: for he vouchsafeth to take upon himself the whole charge, and burthen: insomuch as he is both the mother that bare us, and the nurse that nourisheth us with the milk and cherishings of his providence: according as he himself witnesseth by one of his Prophets: saying: *I was as it were the nurse of Ephraem, and carried them in mine arms, and they understood not that I had care of them.*[7] So that our Lord himself is both the creator and conserver of all things that be created. And like as without him nothing is made, even so were it not for him, all things would go to utter ruin, and decay. The Prophet David confesseth plainly both the one and the other in these words: The eyes of all things do look upon thee O Lord, and thou givest them their food in due season. And whilst thou givest it, they receive it, and when thou stretchest forth the hand of thy bountiful goodness, they are replenished and satisfied with all such things as they stand in need of. But if thou (O Lord) turn thy face away from them, they shall forthwith be disappointed, and utterly fail, and return again to the same dust whereof they were made.[8] Whereby it appeareth that like as all the moving and order of a clock dependeth of the wheels that do draw it, and make it go, insomuch that if they should stay, immediately all the whole frame and moving of the clock would stay also: even so all the workmanship of this great frame of the world dependeth wholly of the providence of almighty God, in such sort that if his divine providence should fail, all the rest would fail out of hand withal.

But how many benefits (trowest thou) are contained in this one benefit. Truly every minute and moment of an hour that thou livest are parts of this benefit. For thou couldest not live, nor have any being so much as one minute if almighty God should withdraw his providence, and turn his eye away never so little from thee. All creatures in the world are part of this benefit. For we see that they all do serve to this end. Insomuch as the heaven is thine, the earth is thine,

7 Osee 11:3.

8 Ps. 144:15; see Ps. 103.

yea, the Sun, the Moon, the stars, the sea, the fishes, the birds, the trees, the living beasts, and to be short, all things in the world be thine: forsomuch as they all are appointed to do thee service. This is that benefit which the Prophet wondered so much at, when he said: *What is man O Lord, that thou shouldest be mindful of him: and what is the son of man, that thou dost so visit him? Thou hast crowned him with glory, and honor, and hast made him Lord over all the works of thy hands. Thou hast put all things under his feet, sheep, oxen, and all the beasts of the field, the birds of the air, and the fishes of the sea, that walk over the paths of the Sea. O Lord our God, how wonderful is thy name over all the earth.*[9]

And almighty God hath vouchsafed not only to appoint all visible creatures for the service and behoof of man, but hath also of his great mercy appointed the invisible creatures, to wit, those most noble and excellent understandings, that be always in his presence, and behold his divine face.[10] For as St. Paul saith: They be all officers in this great house and family of almighty God, unto whom is committed the defense and safeguard of men.[11] Finally, he hath employed all the whole world to do thee service, to the intent that thou shouldest in like manner employ thyself in his service. And his will is, that there should be no one creature either under the heaven or above exempted from serving and helping thee. And this hath he done, that there should be nothing within thee, that should not likewise be employed in serving of him.

And although peradventure thou runnest slightly over all these things, yet oughtest thou not so to pass over the benefits that almighty God hath done unto thee in delivering thee from infinite mishaps, and calamities, which we see do daily happen to other men. Thou seest how one is troubled with the palsy, an other is blind, an other lame, an other broken legged, an other sore vexed with the stone, and others with the strangury, gout, fistula, or with other like terrible diseases, and miseries. For to say the very truth, this world is nothing

9 Ps. 8:5–10.
10 See Matt. 18:10.
11 See Heb. 1:14.

else but a main sea of infinite troubles, calamities, and miseries, and scarcely canst thou find any one house in all this land of Egypt free from sighing, mourning, grief, and sorrow. And now tell me (pray thee) who hath granted unto thee this bull and patent of exemption, to be quit and free from these so grievous calamities, and miseries? Who hath given thee so great a privilege, that among such a number of diseased and wounded persons, thou shouldest be free, and sound: and among such a number that do daily fall, thou shouldest yet stand upright upon thy feet? Art not thou a man as all others? A sinner as all others? And the son of Adam as all others? If then all these evils and miseries do come either on the behalf of nature, or else of sin, and the very same causes are in thee, how is it, that the very same effects are not also in thee? Who hath suspended the effects from their causes? Who hath stayed the streams of the waters, that thou shouldest not perish with others in this common flood, but only the very grace of God? Wherefore if thou cast this accompt aright, thou shalt find that all the miseries of this world are benefits unto thee, and that for every one of them in particular thou owest a special thankfulness and love unto almighty God. So that by the benefit before alleged thou mayest perceive, that all the good things in the world are benefits bestowed upon thee, (forsomuch as they all do serve for thy conservation:) and now also by this mayest thou understand, that all the miseries and evils in the world are likewise benefits unto thee, in that our Lord hath delivered thee from them all.

§. III. Of the Benefit of Redemption.

Let us come now unto the inestimable benefit of our redemption: although it should be much better to adore this mystery with an holy silence, than to speak of it in such gross and base wise as we must do with our mortal tongue. Thou didst lose through sin that first innocency and grace wherein thou wast created, and almighty God might with good equity and justice have left thee in that miserable state, (as he left the devil) and none should have been able to have reproved him therefore. And yet he would not so do, but rather contrariwise changing his anger into mercy, it pleased him of his infinite goodness to bestow greatest benefits at that time, when he was most provoked to wrath with greatest offences. And whereas he might have repaired this loss of innocency by sending some Angel, or Archangel, or by some other means, he would not so do, but vouchsafed to come even himself in person. And whereas he might have come with great majesty, and glory, he abased himself so far, as to come in great humility, and poverty. And this he did, to cause thee to be the more in love with him by reason of this benefit: and to make thee the more beholding unto him by this example: and to make thy redemption the more aboundant by reason of the great treasure, that he bestowed upon it: and to give thee more clearly to understand how much good will he beareth unto thee, that thou shouldest bear towards him the like again: and to shew plainly unto thee how much interest thou hast in him, that thou shouldest repose thy whole trust and affiance in him.[12] This is that benefit, which the Prophet Isaias extolleth (and that for great good cause) in these words: which after the translation of the Septuagintes sound thus, *In all the tribulations of men he never fainted, neither was he ever weary in suffering for them.*[13] Neither would he send any Ambassador or Angel to redeem them, but vouchsafed of his great mercy to come himself in person to redeem them, and to carry them upon his shoulders all the days of this world, notwithstanding that they did evil acknowledge this benefit, but did grieve and provoke the holy Ghost to anger.[14]

And if thou be so much bound to our Lord for that he vouchsafed to come himself in person to redeem thee, how much more art thou bound unto him for the manner of thy redemption, which was by suffering so great pains, and torments? It were certainly a great benefit, if a king would pardon a thief that had deserved to be whipped: But if the king would vouchsafe himself to receive the lashes upon his own shoulders for him, this were without comparison a far greater

12 See St. Thomas Aquinas, *Summa Theologica*, III, q. 1, a. 2; q. 46, aa. 1–2.

13 See Is. 43.

14 See Eph. 4:30.

benefit. Consider therefore how many benefits are comprehended in this benefit of thy redemption. Lift up thine eyes unto that holy rood, and consider all the wounds, and pains, that the Lord of majesty suffereth there for thy sake. For every one of them is a benefit of itself, yea, and a singular great benefit. Behold that most innocent body of thy sweet Savior and redeemer all of a gore blood, with so many wounds and bruises on all parts of him, and the blood gushing out on every side. Behold that most sacred head falling down for very faintness, and hanging upon his shoulders. Behold that divine face (which the Angels are desirous to behold)[15] how disfigured it is, and overflowed with streams of blood, in some parts fresh, and red colored, in other parts very foul, and black. Behold that most beautiful visage of all creatures, and that countenance that delighted the eyes of all such as beheld it, how it hath now lost all the flower of his former beauty. Behold that holy Nazareth, more pure than snow, more white than milk, better colored than old Juery, how he is now become blacker than coals, and so much disfigured, and berayed, that scarcely his own friends are able to know him.[16] Behold that holy mouth, how wane and deadly it looketh. Behold his lips, how black and blue they seem: Behold how they move, desiring pardon, and mercy, even for those that are his very tormentors.

Finally, wheresoever thou beholdest him, thou shalt find that there is no one part of him free from pain, and grief, but that he is covered all over with lashes, and wounds, even from the top of his head to the soles of his feet. That goodly clear forehead, and those eyes more beautiful than the Sun, are now dimmed and darkened with the blood and presence of death. Those ears that are wont to hear the songs of heaven, do now hear the horrible blasphemies of sinners. Those arms so well fashioned and so large that they embrace all the power of the world, are now disjointed, and stretched out upon the cross. Those hands that created the heavens, and were never injurious to any man, are now nailed and clenched fast with hard

[15] See 1 Ptr. 1:12.
[16] See Lam. 4.

and sharp nails. Those blessed feet that never walked in the ways of sinners, are now deadly wounded, and pierced through. But above all this, behold the bed where he lieth, and whereupon that heavenly bridegroom sleepeth at noon day, how narrow and hard it is, and how he hath nothing whereupon to rest his head. O precious head of my sweet savior! What meaneth this, that I see thee thus afflicted and tormented for my sake? O blessed body, conceived by the holy Ghost! How is it, that I see thee thus wounded and evil entreated for my sake? O sweet and loving side! What meaneth this great wound and open cleft in thee? What meaneth this so great abundance of blood? Alas wretch that I am, what a pitiful sight is this, to see thee thus furiously pierced with a spear for my sake? O rigorous cross, be not now I beseech thee so stiff, but mollify a little thy hardness, bow down unto me these high branches, let down to me this most precious fruit, that I may taste thereof. O cruel nails, leave I pray you those innocent hands and feet of my innocent Savior, and come and enter into my heart, and pierce it through: for it is I that have sinned, and not he. O good Jesus, what hast thou to do with so many cruel torments? What hast thou to do with death? With sharp nails? And with the cross? Undoubtedly the Prophet had good reason to say: That his works shall be very strange, and far unlike himself.[17] What is more strange and more contrary to life, than death? What is more disagreeable to glory, than pain? What is further of from the nature of most perfect holiness, and innocency, than the image and shape of a sinner? This title and shape O Lord, is certainly very strange for thee. O true Jacob, that with wearing the garments of others, and with disguising thyself in a strange habit, hast purchased for us the blessing of our heavenly father![18] For by taking upon thee the image of a sinner, thou hast purchased for us victory against sin. O goodness unspeakable! O mercy undeserved! O love exceeding all understanding! O charity incomprehensible! Tell me (O most merciful Lord) what sawest thou in us? What service have we done unto

[17] See Is. 28:21.
[18] See Gen. 27.

thee? With what works have we bound thee to suffer such grievous and cruel torments for our sakes? O wonderful bountifulness, that without any merit of our part, and without any necessity of thine own part, wouldst vouchsafe only of thy mere grace, and mercy, to purchase our redemption after this sort! *The benignity and clemency of our savior* (saith the Apostle) *hath appeared, not in respect of the works of justice that we have done, but according to his great mercy he hath saved us.*[19] O how wonderful desirous was our most gracious Lord, that we should understand his mercy, when by the Prophet Isaias he spake those so notable words: *Thou hast not called upon me O Jacob, and thou O Israel hast not travailed in my service. Thou hast not offered unto me thy rams in a whole burnt sacrifice, neither hast thou glorified me with thy sacrifices, etc. And yet for all this, thou hast made me to serve in thy sins, and hast put me to pains with thine iniquity. It is I, It is I, that do pardon thy sins for mine own sake, and that will never be mindful of them. Put me in mind, and let us enter into judgement: and shew if thou have any thing wherewith to justify thyself.*[20]

Wherefore O most merciful and sweet Lord, what thing is there in me, wherewith I may recompence thee for this so great benefit? If I should live all the lives of the children of Adam, and all the days and years of the world, If I were able to sustain all the travails and pains of all the men that either be, hath been, or shall be, all this were as nothing to recompence the very least grief and pain that thou hast suffered for me. Considering therefore that I can by no means possible discharge this inestimable great debt, let me pay thee O my almighty God if it be thy blessed will with the continual remembrance of the same. I beseech thee O Lord even by the bowels of thy infinite charity, that thou wilt wound my heart with thy wounds, and make my soul drunk with thy most precious blood, in such sort that whither so ever I shall turn myself, I may always see thee crucified, and wheresoever I shall cast mine eyes, all things may seem unto me to shine with thy precious blood. Let this be all my consolation to be

---

19 Titus 3:4–5.
20 Is. 43:22–26.

always crucified with thee: and let this be all my affliction to think upon any other thing besides thee. Consider O my almighty God the great price wherewith thou hast bought me, and suffer not so precious a treasure to be shed in vain for me. And grant me O most merciful Lord, that I be not as a child that is born before his time, whom his mother bringeth forth with exceeding great travail, and pain, and yet he enjoyeth not the commodity and fruit of life.

§. IV. Of the Fourth Benefit: to Wit, of Vocation.

After this, think upon the benefit of Vocation or calling of almighty God, without which all the other benefits tend to the greater damnation of a man. But here it is to be noted, that there be two kinds of callings of almighty God: one unto faith, by means of the Sacrament of Baptism: and an other unto grace, after that a man hath lost the first innocency which he had by baptism.

Consider now what a great benefit the first calling of thee was by means of the Sacrament of holy Baptism, whereby thou was cleansed from original sin, delivered from the power of the devil, made the son of almighty God, and an inheritor of his kingdom. There he took thy soul to be his spouse, and adorned it with such ornaments, as were convenient for such a state: to wit, with grace, and with the virtues, and gifts of the holy Ghost, and also with other jewels, and gifts, that are far more precious than those that were given to Rebecca, when she was taken to be the spouse of Isaac.[21] Now what hast thou done, whereby to deserve so great a benefit as this is? How many thousands not only of men, but also of nations and whole countries are there, that by the just judgement of almighty God do not obtain this inestimable great benefit? What had become of thee, if thou hadst been born among those infidels, and wanted this knowledge of the true living God, and worshipped stocks, and stones for God, as the infidels do? How much art thou bound to almighty God, that among such an infinite number of lost and damned souls, it pleased him that

21 See Gen. 24.

thou shouldest be saved, yea and be born in the lap of the Catholic Church, and be nourished there with the milk of the Apostles, and with the precious blood of our sweet Savior Jesus Christ.

Now if after the grace of this first calling thou hast through thine own default and sinful life lost the innocency which thou receivedst in the Sacrament of Baptism, in case it hath pleased our Lord all that notwithstanding to call thee a second time, yea and very many and often times, how much art thou then bound unto him for this so passing great benefit? How many benefits are contained in this benefit? One benefit it was to expect and tarry for thy conversion so long time, to give thee space to do penance, and to suffer thee so long to continue in that state of sin, and wickedness, and not to cut down the unfruitful and unprofitable tree, that occupied such a room in the earth and received the influences of heaven altogether in vain. An other benefit it was to suffer thee to commit so many and so heinous enormous sins, and not to cast thee down therefore into the most horrible bottomless pit of hell fire, where perhaps many others are now there tormented even for less offences than thine. An other benefit it was to send thee so many good inspirations, and holy purposes, even in the midst of thy very sins, and wicked life, and to persist in calling thee so long a time, whereas thou in the mean season didst nothing else but offend him very grievously that called thee. An other benefit it was also to bring thy great stubborns and long obstinate resistance at the length to an end, and to call thee with such a mighty and loud voice, that thereby thou mightest rise from death to life, and come forth as it were an other Lazarus out of the dark and obscure grave of thy wicked and sinful life, and not with thy hands and feet bound, but loosed and set at free liberty out of the stinking prison and thralldom of the enemy of mankind.[22] But above all this, what a benefit was it, to grant thee then not only pardon for thy sins past, but also grace from that time forwards not to return unto them again: giving thee moreover all such other ornaments as were given to the penitent prodigal son, when he was received into grace and

22 See John 11.

favor again:[23] by means of which ornaments and graces thou mightest live as the child of God, and contemn and laugh at the malice of the devil, and triumph over the world, and take a sweet taste of the things appertaining unto almighty God, which before seemed very unsavory unto thee, and withal conceive a certain loathsomeness and misliking of the things of the world, which before seemed very savoury and delightful unto thee.

But now besides this, what if thou do consider unto how many others almighty God hath denied this benefit, which he hath so freely granted unto thee. And whereas thou being a sinner as well as they, and as unworthy of this calling as they, yet it hath pleased almighty God to suffer them to continue in their wicked state, and to call thee unto the state of salvation, and grace? What an exceeding joy will it be unto thee, when by the virtue of this vocation thou shalt see thyself to have the fruition of almighty God for ever and ever in the kingdom of heaven, and shalt see other of thy companions and acquaintance for want of the like grace of God to remain everlastingly tormented in the horrible raging fire of hell? O good Lord, what a number of things are there included in this grace to be well weighed, and earnestly considered upon! Tell me I pray thee, when the blessed thief (who with one word purchased life everlasting)[24] seeth himself in that so great glory which he now possesseth in the kingdom of heaven, and seeth his companion also in those great horrible torments of hell fire, and calleth to mind withal, that he himself was a thief also as well as the other, and suffered for his robberies as the other did, and that a little before he blasphemed our Savior Jesus Christ in like manner as his companion did, and that yet for all this it pleased almighty God to cast his merciful eyes upon him, and to give him so great a light, leaving the other thief in his darkness, now in considering hereupon, what thanks thinkest thou doth he render to almighty God for this special grace? How wonderfully doth he rejoice at so great a benefit? How doth he marvel at so great

23 See Luke 15.
24 See Luke 23.

a judgement? With what a passing great love doth he love him, that would vouchsafe to prevent him with such a singular and wonderful grace? Now if this seem so great a benefit unto thee, remember thyself, that our savior Christ hath bestowed the like inestimable benefit upon thee, when the same loving Lord vouchsafed to cast his merciful eyes so specially upon thee, and did not with the like manner of calling call thy neighbor, companion, or friend, who peradventure had less offended his divine majesty than thou. Consider then how much thou art bound to our Lord for this his great benefit, and what a great occasion is here offered unto thee, to desire even to suffer death for the love of him.

Besides all this, consider how costly and chargeable this benefit of our redemption was to our Savior Christ, which was so freely given unto thee. Unto thee it was given frankly, and of mere grace, and it cost him even his own most precious blood, and life also: for it is manifest that without the same our sins could not be pardoned, nor our wounds cured.[25] It is said of the Pelican that she bringeth forth her young ones dead, and seeing them in that case, she striketh herself upon the breast with her beak, until she cause blood to issue out, and therewith she batheth her young ones, and so they receive heat, and life. Now if thou wilt understand how great this benefit is, make accompt with thyself, that when thou wast dead in sin, that most loving and merciful Pelican (our Savior Christ) moved with most tender pity and compassion stroke his sacred breast with a spear, and washed the deadly wounds of thy soul with the precious blood of his wounds, and so with his own death he gave thee life, and with his own wounds healed thy wounds. Be not thou therefore unthankful unto him for this so great and costly benefit, but as our Lord admonisheth thee, be mindful of the day in which thou camest out of Egypt.[26] This day was the day of thy Passover: this was the day of thy Resurrection: forsomuch as upon this day thou hast passed

25 See St. Thomas, III, q. 1, aa. 2–3; q. 46, aa. 1–2.

26 See Ex. 13.

through the red sea of the blood of Christ unto the land of promise, and upon this day thou hast risen again from death to life.

§. V. Of the Particular Benefits That Almighty God Bestoweth upon Us.

These benefits aforesaid are general. Other benefits there are more particular, that be given to particular persons, the which benefits none other knoweth but only he that hath received them.[27] In this accompt are reckoned many kinds of benefits, either of fortune, or of nature, or of grace, which almighty God hath given to each one in particular: and also divers and sundry miseries, and dangers, both of body, and soul, from which he of his mere mercy hath delivered us. For which particular benefits we are as well bound to give him thanks, as for the former general benefits: forsomuch as they are more certain signs and tokens of the special and particular love, and providence, that our Lord beareth towards us. Such benefits as these are can not be written in books, but every one ought to write them in his heart, and so to join them with the other general benefits, and to give most humble thanks unto our Lord for them.

There be also other benefits yet more secret and hidden than these, which are unknown even to the very party himself that hath received them. These are certain privy dangers, and secret snares, which our Lord is wont to prevent and disappoint by his divine providence, for that he understandeth what great damage and prejudice they might do unto us, in case he should not cut them off, and disappoint their course. What man is able to tell from how many temptations almighty God hath preserved him? And from how many occasions of sins he hath delivered him? And how often times he hath stopped the passages, and removed away the deceitful snares of the devil our enemy, that we should not fall into them. The devil himself saith of the holy man Job: That almighty God had environed

[27] See Apoc. 2.

him on every side, that nothing might do him hurt.[28] And even so is our Lord wont to keep, and preserve such as be his, (as it were a glass preserved in his case,) that nothing may hurt them.

It may also be that a man hath received of almighty God some secret gifts, although he himself knoweth not of them: as also a man may, and is wont to have many secret sins, which he himself that commiteth them knoweth not. Wherefore like as for these kind of sins we ought daily to pray with the Prophet, and say: *Ab occultis meis munda me Domine. Deliver me O Lord from my secret sins:*[29] Even so ought we also every day to yield him most humble and hearty thanks for these kind of benefits, that by this mean no sin may remain without penance, nor benefit without rendering of thanks for the same.

The end of the other seven Meditations for the seven days of the week at night.

[28] See Job 1:10.
[29] Ps. 18:13.